SIGNING ENGLISH

for **Parents, Teachers,** and **Clinicians**

Edgar H. Shroyer, Ph.D.

Sugar Sign Press
1407 Fairmont Street
Greensboro, NC 27403

Cover design by **Joan G. Kimmel**

To Susan
with love

Printed in the United States of America

Library of Congress Catalog Card Number: 88-90949

ISBN: 0-939849-04-6

TABLE OF CONTENTS

contents

Categories (con't)

OTHER MATERIALS AVAILABLE FROM SUGAR SIGN PRESS

BOOKS

The **Sign with Me Series** is the ideal way of introducing sign language to young children and their parents. The series consists of four books which use bold, colorful illustrations of familiar objects to teach vocabulary. This special series is the perfect addition to any child's library.

ABC Sign With Me
1 2 3 Sign With Me
Sign With Me Colors
Sign With Me Weather

Secret Signing Pre-K -1 and **Secret Signing Grds 1-3 -** These delightful fun activity books use signs to teach and reinforce many pre-reading and pre-math skills. Dot-to-dot, mazes, and matching games are some of the many activities found in these 64 page books.

POSTERS

Humpty Dumpty - This delightful full-color laminated poster is perfect for any nursery / child's room / classroom. The nursery rhyme is in Manual English.

Number Poster - This colorful poster represents the signs and numbers 1-10. Children love the bright, bold colors. A perfect compliment to any child's room.

SPECIALTY ITEMS

ABC Come Sign With Me Alphabet Teaching Frieze - This unique teaching frieze presents the lower case letters of the alphabet, the corresponding manual alphabet handshapes, and a large bold picture of a familiar object beginning with that letter. The bright colors stimulate infants, the illustrations promote vocabulary development in toddlers, and the letters expose older children to letter recognition.

Reinforcement pads - Recognizes child's good behavior, achievements, good work, birthdays and other special times. Excellent way to motivate your child.

Kid's Work - Develop good work habits and responsibility that will last a lifetime. Responsibilities for self care and activities around the house. For the non-reader.

Book Marks - A variety of colorful bookmarks showing signs, familiar sayings, and/or the manual alphabet.

ACKNOWLEDGEMENTS

A Summer Excellence Foundation Grant from the University of North Carolina at Greensboro allowed me to concentrate on the initial phases of this book during the summer of 1986. I am very grateful for this Grant and feel that through this award the University has indicated its support of the Education of the Deaf major in the Department of Communication and Theatre, and hearing-impaired people in general.

I am deeply indebted to several people whose help was invaluable. I want to thank my wife, Susan, for her encouragement, constructive criticism, and support, without which this book might never have come to fruition. Two graduate assistants, Laura Oleen and Marianne Rooks spent many hours helping me throughout the development of the book for which I am thankful. Two colleagues and friends, Edward Dry and Cindy King provided assistance as well as words of encouragement and support. Several deaf individuals and educational interpreters provided me not only with signs but with critiques of the signs that I eventually included. They also have my gratitude. Finally, all the students who have participated in my sign classes over the years, especially the majors in Education of the Deaf at UNCG in Com 555, the Advanced Sign Language/Interpreting class have my sincere thanks. It was through class discussions based on the students' observations and volunteer work at programs for hearing-impaired children that many signs included in this book were verified. I hope that everyone who assisted in the development of this book now feels not only a sense of accomplishment, but a sense of pride, knowing that they have contributed in some way to enhance the communication of hearing-impaired children.

INTRODUCTION

WHY THIS BOOK?

Signing English fills a need that has existed in the Manual English systems since their inception. That is, the need for a book that provides an interactive approach to communication among adults and children. Parents, teachers of hearing-impaired children, and other professionals can now see how Manual English is signed and have opportunities to use it in a practical, educational, and fun way.

One of the unique features of *Signing English* is that it provides model sentences in Manual English. The research findings of Peters (1983), Clark (1973), and Snow (1981) tend to show that children learning a first or second language rely heavily on whole "model" sentences and sentence "chunks" in order to "learn" a grammar. This is far different from the traditional view which focused more on children linking parts together; first one word, then two words and so forth. The new view centers more on the way that children may derive sentences by rearranging and substituting parts from and within memorized forms. The model sentences and carrier phrases, such as those in this book, can help children build a treasury of overlearned or routinized forms useful in deriving new related sentences and questions. Just how children acquire the rules of English from their reliance on routinized sentences and chunks is still a very unclear area in the study of language acquisition.

WHICH SIGNS ARE IN THIS BOOK?

The signs in this book were selected from several different sources, American Sign Language, the Manual English systems, professionals in the education of hearing-impaired children, students in sign classes, and educational interpreters. A majority of the signs were taken from American Sign Language (ASL) and will be recognized by most deaf adults who use ASL. I selected non-ASL signs from the other sources whenever I thought some confusion may arise regarding the selection of an English word for that ASL sign. In other words, ASL is a conceptual language without any written form; therefore, an English word or words (gloss) is/are used to represent a sign concept. As a result, there might be several different English words (glosses) to "represent" one ASL sign concept; e.g., in ASL, pointing your index finger upward with your palm in and moving the hand in a small circle can be glossed as: someone, something or somebody.

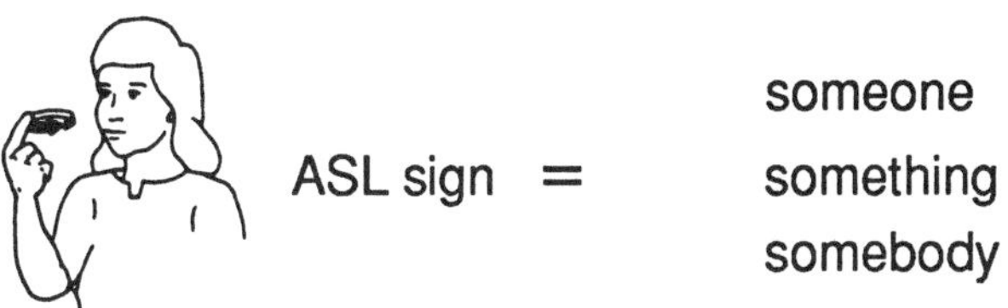

This may tend to confuse young children in their vocabulary and reading development because they are not seeing a one-to-one relationship between a sign and the written word. I tried, therefore, to adhere to the general one-word one-sign rule of the Manual English systems whenever possible and logical. Therefore, in *Signing English* you will see three separate signs for the three words in the above example. On the other hand, since ASL is a conceptual language, I have deferred to the conceptual meanings of ASL as much as possible. The word fly has three different conceptual meanings in ASL, thus three different signs are shown in *Signing English*, a different one for each conceptual meaning for the word fly, e.g., Fly like a bird. Fly an airplane. A fly in the soup. Some other examples of words which are conceptual and have two or more different signs are: dress, miss, run, mind, and long.

To summarize, what *Signing English* presents is one sign for one word unless the English word has multiple meanings for which there are comparable conceptual signs in ASL. I realize that what I have done runs counter to the philosophy of some of the Manual English systems which use one sign for a word regardless of the concepts involved. But to my knowledge, there is no research that indicates the one-word one-sign approach results in greater language acquisition in hearing-impaired children.

WHO WILL BENEFIT FROM THIS BOOK?

I sincerely believe that the vast majority of hearing-impaired children, their parents, teachers of hearing-impaired children, and other professionals will benefit from this book. The vocabulary, carrier phrases and activities will establish and enhance communication, thus benefit everyone involved in using Manual English in a simultaneous communication mode (signing and talking at the same time). One should not, however, overlook the large number of children with other handicapping conditions who can and have benefitted from the use of signs (Derr, 1983; Musselwhite, 1986; and Keogh, 1987). More and more teachers of non-handicapped children are also beginning to use signs with their children in public school settings for both remedial purposes and for the mere fun of learning a different and "secret" way of communicating (Isaacson, et.al., 1987; Ellison, et. al., 1982; and Carney, et. al., 1985). It is hoped that *Signing English* will serve as an excellent resource book for all of these populations.

WHEN SHOULD YOU SIGN WITH YOUR CHILD?

The answer to that is easy. You should sign all of the time. Every situation serves as a learning experience for your child. You should sign not only what you have to say but what people say to you, and the sounds that you hear around you, e.g., bells, crashes, thunder, messages over public address systems, etc. These are all parts of your child's everyday learning experiences. Language reactions to his environment, etiquette and the like are taught and reinforced through these daily interactions. I do not think that telling your child when someone sneezes or coughs, random horns honking, etc. are always necessary to share. You need to use good judgement on this; but remember, communication is the key to your child's language growth and development. Zwiebal (1987) studied three groups of deaf children ages 6 to 14 in Israel and found that those deaf children who were exposed to signing at home were cognitively superior to deaf children not exposed to signing. Kampfe (1984) found that signing skill levels of hearing mothers were positively related to reading comprehension skills of their deaf children. That is, mothers who possessed greater skill levels of signing had children who showed greater reading comprehension skills.

WHICH SIGNING SYSTEM SHOULD I USE WITH MY HEARING-IMPAIRED CHILD?

If we were to rely on the research in the field regarding using signs with children, I think the answer would be fairly evident. However, before that question is answered, familiarize yourself with the differences among the three signing systems which are used in the United States. See "Sign Language Systems" on page four.

Now that you have had a chance to look over the Sign Language Systems' chart, you should have some understanding of the differences between the three systems. The important point, however, is that all of the systems will benefit your child, but the Manual English systems appear to be most beneficial (Basel and Quigley , 1975; Bornstein, Saulinier and Hamilton, 1980; Champie, 1981; Garner and Zorfoso, 1983; and Babb, 1980). All of these studies have provided evidence that early exposure and

SIGN LANGUAGE SYSTEMS

American Sign Language (ASL)	Pidgin Sign English (PSE)	Manual English (ME)*
(Also called: Ameslan, Native sign language)	(Also called: Sign English, Signed English)	(Also called: English) Seeing Essential English (SEE1) Signing Exact English (SEE2) Local Sign Systems
--- A language separate from English, capable of great subtlety in a visual mode. --- Uses different syntax than English. --- Cannot be used simultaneously with voiced English. --- Many signs are more conceptual than those in English systems. --- Used by deaf adults, hearing children of deaf adults, and deaf children.	--- A combination of ASL and Manual English. --- Usually signed in English word order. Endings and grammatical markers are often not used. --- Can be used simultaneously with voiced English. --- Borrows a great many signs from ASL. Uses occasional fingerspelling of words. --- Used by deaf people and hearing people in social and formal situations. Often said to bridge the gap between deaf and hearing people. --- Widely used by sign language interpreters.	--- A visual code for the English language that assists deaf children in learning English. --- Follows English exactly, using word order and grammatical markers such as endings, suffixes, and prefixes. --- Can be used simultaneously with voiced English. --- Borrows a great many signs from ASL. Includes invented signs for grammar and vocabulary. Uses occasional fingerspelling of words. --- Widely used in public schools. --- Used by deaf children in formal situations. --- Rarely used by deaf adults or in social situations.

*Manual English is sometimes called Manually Coded English (MCE). Use of the terms English,Manual English, Manually Coded English, Signed English, and Pidgin Sign English varies.

use of Manual English may have a positive relationship to early language skills and later reading achievement (Kampfe and Turecheck, 1987).

On the other hand, Eagney (1987) tested three equal groups of hearing-impaired children on their ability to comprehend signing in American Sign Language, simplified English, which was grammatically correct and complete, and standard English. She found no significant difference among the groups; each group could read each of the three treatments with equal levels of comprehension. I include this study to emphasize the importance of communicating with your child using any and all the different modes or systems available to you.

I think an excellent article for all parents and professionals to read is, "Introducing Sign Language Systems to Parents of Young Deaf Children," by Barbara Walsh Moser in *Perspectives for Teachers of the Hearing Impaired,* Nov. Dec., 1987. Moser provides the parents of newly diagnosed deaf children with many practical and important suggestions. One of the sections in her article, "Beginning to Communicate," has several suggestions about how to make parents feel comfortable about signing with their deaf child. I have included Moser's suggestions here and have elaborated on them somewhat as they represent my philosophy regarding the teaching and use of signs.

1. Be flexible. Familiarize yourself with all of the systems by talking to people, taking classes, and meeting deaf adults.

2. Seek out classes that emphasize flexibility and that may teach primarily one language (sic) but supplement with another.

3. Use whatever signs you feel comfortable with. Ask people who know about signs which signs are most important to learn and which signs are commonly used in your area.

4. Use signs in English word order, but try to switch systems if you see that your child does not understand. Use expressions and mime along with your signs with whatever system you are using.

5. Try not to worry about "right" and "wrong" signs. Remember that there are often several signs for a word or idea. If your are flexible, you will be able to begin to communicate with deaf children and adults. (Moser, 1987 p 14)

Be flexible! Your approach to learning signs should be fun, relaxing, and most of all, enjoyable. Analyze signs as to why you think they are made that way. Try to think of mnemonic devices (see Shroyer, 1982, *Signs of the Times*) to help you remember signs, e.g., the sign "boy" looks like the bill of a hat. Attaching some clue or rationale to the sign will assist you in recalling it. Talking with others knowledgeable about deafness and, of course, with deaf adults, will give you the extra dimensions you are possibly looking for and need.

Seek out classes that emphasize flexibility. We all have our own biases, and finding a sign class where the instructor is flexible regarding the use of different systems may be easier said than done. The important thing is that you remain flexible. Keep your sense of humor and continue with the class with the attitude that you are definitely going to learn something that will be of value to you in the communication process.

Use signs that you feel comfortable with. If you are using a sign with your child that "works," and is different than what is shown in this book, or is different than what is shown in a class, for heaven's sake, don't change it for the sake of change. Again, be flexible and think how you might use the "new" sign in this book or from a class to introduce a new English word to your child. Remember, the name of the game is communication. Seize every opportunity to communicate and introduce new vocabulary.

Use signs in English word order. As cited above, signing in English word order has been shown to be more effective in most instances. Do not, however, sacrifice communication for the desire to have everything signed in straight English. Bornstein (1983) has said, "When communicating with older children, teachers tend to use only those elements that contain information necessary for understanding the message. Sometimes they substitute ASL constructions for English phrases." This is all part of being flexible and knowing your child and what works best for him in the communication process. When beginning with signing, I would suggest that you not incorporate Sign Markers with a young child, but would, however, suggest that you sign in straight English word order (Pidgin Sign English).

> " Instructing parents to focus on the meaning and the purpose of the message will undoubtedly prove more successful than attending to form alone." (Griffiths ,Johnson and Dastoli, 1985)

Most people use facial expressions, mime, intonation and gestures when talking with other hearing people because they aid the communication process. Do not be afraid or inhibited in this regard when you sign. These non-verbal cues in signing substitute for the verbal cues that send information in everyday, normal conversation. Use gestures, mime and facial expressions at all times with any system or combination of systems that you elect to use. At the same time, accept what children say without trying to get them to put it into straight English. Also pick up on the non-verbal clues that children use in communicating. Think of normal language development in children. Hearing children play with language, making up their own sentence patterns and words. Allow all children this same flexibility in signing.

"Right" and "wrong" signs? As far as I am concerned, there are no such things as "right" and "wrong" signs; and that is among the first things that I tell my students in sign classes. Someone may make a sign in the wrong position, or with the wrong handshape, or with the wrong movement , but who can honestly say that this sign is "wrong" or that sign is "wrong"? Signing is a living, constantly changing phenomenon.

You need only look at *Signs Across America,* 1984, by Shroyer and Shroyer to realize that it would be difficult to say that any one of the 14 different signs for tomato is wrong or any one of the 22 different signs for picnic is wrong. You use whatever means available to you to communicate with children. Children do it! At the far left hand side of the Sign Language Continuum in *Signs of the Times* (Shroyer, 1982) there is a group of signs labeled Childrenese. These are signs made up by very young hearing-impaired children to communicate with one another, and they are signs generally unknown to the adults in the children's environment.

IS SIGNING ENGLISH A SYSTEM?

Signing English is not a system like those shown in the chart on page four under Manual English, e.g., SEE 1, Signed English, and SEE 2. It was not my intention or purpose to come up with another system which parallels English. In my opinion, there are already enough Manual English systems for people to refer to for possible vocabulary and sign markers. It is interesting to note, however, that very few people follow one particular system to the exclusion of all others. There seems to be a mix and match, eclectic approach to the use of Manual English. A lot of exploring, searching and trial and error occurs until the "right mix" is found to be most effective with a particular child or group of children. I hardily recommend that approach and in *Signing English* have merely put together a contemporary sign vocabulary, carrier phrases, categories, levels of vocabulary acquisition, and activities to foster maximum communication. More than anything else, it is my hope that individuals who use this book will find it an easy and viable way to increase sign communication with all children.

WHAT ABOUT THE VOCABULARY IN THIS BOOK?

The vocabulary in this book is in large part a result of the categories that were selected as being representative of units of work that young children learn in school. They learn about community helpers - Occupation Category; names of clothing - the Clothing Category, and so forth. Therefore, almost all of the vocabulary associated with these categories was included. The Dolch List of most frequently used words by children was also consulted. Although I am sure that that the vocabulary represented in each category is not exhaustive, the vocabulary lists are sometimes extensive. At the same time, the question of "Why was this particular word represented and this one not?" will undoubtedly be raised. I can only say that I tried to be as pragmatic as possible in selection of the vocabulary for each category; and if I have omitted some signs that you feel should be included, I apologize. As to the selection of particular signs, several different sources were consulted before a sign was selected for inclusion. Sometimes as many as three different ways to sign the same conceptual word were found. Therefore, the final selection of the sign was based on: 1. does it following the basic grammatical principles of American Sign Language, and 2. how frequency is it used. The latter criterion was based on my informants and my own observations. This in no way implies that the other signs, those not included in this book, are wrong. As I stated before, there are, in my opinion, no wrong signs, only incorrect placement, handshapes, movements or body orientation for signs. My basic philosophy in using signs is that if it works, and if communication is taking place then by all means use it. Do not change for the sake of change.

WHY SIGN MARKERS?

Sign markers are prefixes and suffixes which you "add" to a basic sign to change its meaning in order to follow the grammatical rules of English. Most of the meanings you would want to change in most sentences, e.g., verbs, plurals, comparatives, adjectives and so forth, are done with the sign markers. The sign markers allow you to provide a complete model of English exactly as you would see it on the written page. All of the carrier phrases at the beginning of each category incorporate sign markers appropriately and serve as models while you are learning to communicate in Manual English. As mentioned previously, I would probably not use sign markers in the beginning stages of communication. Instead, slowly add one marker at a time when you see that the child is beginning to communicate in short sentences. When the child begins incorporating that marker in a consistent manner you should then add another marker using the procedure described in the Why Activities? section on how to teach concepts.

WHAT ABOUT THE CARRIER PHRASES?

The carrier phrases are included to provide you with easy access to some basic signs which may be used frequently in normal conversation, and to provide you with models of how to sign in Manual English. The models consist of open-ended statements and questions to use with children in establish communication and interaction. Newport, Gleitman and Gleitman (1977) found that question forms and expansions of children's utterances are positively correlated to language growth. Whereas McDonald and Pien (1982) found that the more negative aspects of communiction, such as imperatives, self repetitions, negation of the child's actions, monologing, and frequent topic changes were negatively correlated with language growth. (Griffith, Johnson and Dastoli, 1985). It appears, therefore, much more productive for an adult to interact in the following manner:

Child: Cookie, please. **Adult:** Oh, I understand, you want a cookie.

or

You want a cookie. I'm sorry, cookies are gone.

rather than

No.

Setting up open-ended situations or questions may result in an additional interaction.

Adult: I think I will get a cookie. **Child:** Me cookie, me cookie.

or

How many cookies do you want?

rather than:

Adult: Take a cookie. **Child:** (blank)

The carrier phrases are set up in a way that it is easy to draw vocabulary from two or more sentences on each page to generate a new sentence. Be creative; generate your own sentences and questions based on need, then write them in you book for future reference.

WHY ACTIVITIES?

Suggestions for an activity or activities are provided for almost all of the category sections either at the beginning or end of the section. They are included to encourage you to do "fun" types of learning activities to promote communication. The activities are designed to involve the child in the learning process in an interactive rather than passive way. It is, however, incumbent upon you to make sure the activity is at the child's level and that the child can be successful doing the activity. To achieve that end, you will have to think through and possibly change the activity to meet the child's communication and skill levels. This is very important because the level of communication and skill needed for each activity varies considerably. Be flexible and change the activity in any way necessary to insure success. I would like, however, to offer the following advice for all of the activities at any level.

Most psychologists and others involved with learning theory agree that with a majority of children it is more beneficial and productive to teach only one concept at a time. The following example, which incorporates that thinking, is presented as a model to be used with all the concepts that you will be teaching whether it is done through the activities in this book or another source.

The concept to be taught is "mouth".

1. With child sitting in front of adult, adult points to her mouth signing/saying mouth.

2. Adult takes child's finger pointing it to her mouth signing/saying mouth.

3. Adult takes child's finger pointing it to child's mouth signing/saying mouth. *It is very important that the child is actively involved in learning rather than being passive.*

4. Adult shows child a stuffed animal pointing to mouth then signing/saying mouth.

5. Adult gives child another stuffed animal (with mouth clearly visible) signing/saying, "Where mouth?"

6. Adult continues the activity pointing and asking,"Where mouth?" on a variety of objects and pictures. *Note that signing in straight English is not being done. Learning the concept is considered more important at this point..*

7. Adult points to something other than mouth signing/saying, "What is this?". Child signs/says, "Not mouth". *The adult is not to sign/say what is pointed at, e.g., "No, that is an eye, nose, or ear". The correct response is, "Not mouth". Remember, eye, nose and ear are other concepts to be learned in the same manner as mouth after the concept of mouth is mastered.*

8. After the child identifies mouth on a consistent basis, you can introduce another concept, e.g., nose in the same manner as mouth. But now, you need to occasionally point to mouth and accept, "That is mouth." All concepts other than the concept being introduced, and those already mastered, fall into the category of "Not mouth" and "Not nose".

Psychologists and learning theorists say that a child has learned a concept when he is able to generalize within a class and discriminate between classes. If a child calls a Great Dane a horse, the child obviously does not know all the attributes of a horse well enough to discriminate between classes (horses and dogs). Therefore, the attributes of a horse (mane, long tail, big, people can ride it, eats hay/grass, pulls wagons, etc.) need to be covered again one by one. On the other hand, if the child is able to recognize a Shetland pony, a pinto, a Clydesdale and a palomino all as horses, then he is able to generalize within a class (all horses). It is then safe to say that the child knows the concept of horse. It is necessary that the child not become confused by introducing many different concepts at the same time. To insure mastery, therefore, remember to teach just one concept at a time. Or, to put it another way, it is much more productive to teach a thimble full at a time than it is a bucket full. All of those little thimble fulls will eventually fill the bucket with relevant, interdependent, organized building blocks for future learning.

WHERE DO I START?

The average first grader who is hearing, enters school with an expressive vocabulary of approximately 2500 words. In *Word Express: the First 2,500 Words of Spoken English* by Stemach and Williams (1988), the words have been divided into ten levels (250 words at each level) with the vocabulary in levels one and two accounting for approximately 85 percent of all the words spoken by first grade children. Throughout this book, in each category, the vocabulary representative of level one is identified by the number 1 , e.g., eat 1 and the vocabulary found in level two is identified by the number two, e.g., dress 2 . It is important to know that the criteria which the authors used in the selection of a word or word form in *Word Express* is followed in *Signing English* with just a few exceptions (parentheses mine):

1. Root words are included. Word endings such as plural -s, tense markers, -ed, -ing were omitted (some ing endings are in *Signing English* and are considered part of the sign rather than an ending, e.g., morning). High frequency contractions e.g., I'll, they're, are included.

2. Each word appears in *The Random House Dictionary of the English Language, Second Unabridged Edition* (1987). A few trademark names e.g., Kool Aid, Scotch tape, also appear.

3. In general, slang ,e.g., "gee", neologisms, e.g., "pull ons", or invented words such as "falled", and expressions such as "uh-uh" were omitted.

4. Numbers 0 - 12 were included and written as words. (In *Signing English* these numbers are found in the Numbers category and are not marked with a one or two).

5. In general, letters of the alphabet, days of the week, except Saturday and Sunday, months of the year, except July, November, December, cities, states, and foreign countries were omitted. Days of the week and months of the year are typically taught as units rather than individual parts (the latter are in *Signing English*).

6. Other proper nouns, names of people and characters, e.g., Sarah, Popeye, were omitted. (p. 9)

An important note about multiple meaning words. The *Word Express* lists of words is shown by order of frequency and do not provide information about word meanings or context. The authors give an example of the word light.. Light can be used as a noun: "something bright and to help you see" or as a modifier with two meanings: "not heavy to lift; not dark" or as a verb: "to burn." Which of these meaning is most frequently used by children is not recorded although children probably use all four meanings. In *Signing English ,* words with multiple meanings often have different signs and the meaning can be determined by the category in which they are found. For example, the word dress , verb form, is found under the category Action Words and has one sign. While dress , noun form, is found under the category Clothing with a different sign. In both categories, dress is marked with a 2 indicating level two, the second group of 250 most frequently used words. Which one of the two meanings of the word dress is the most frequently used by children, in this case and others where a word can be used several different ways, is not determined.

You should begin working with the child on signs/vocabulary that are marked in the vocabulary lists with a one (1) or a two (2).

I hope that the Introduction to *Signing English* has been helpful and informative for you. I would strongly suggest that you look over the Bibliography for additional sources of information and readings. You now have before you a very challenging task which will result in some agonizing moments and many exciting, fun filled experiences. The amount of time and energy that you expend in communicating with your child will pay off proportionally in the quality and quantity of your child's communication. **I certainly wish you the very best of luck!**

BIBLIOGRAPHY

Benderly, B.L. (1980). *Dancing Without Music, Deafness in America.* Boston: Doubleday.

Carney, J. (1985). Using sign language for teaching sight words. *Teaching Exceptional Children,* 17:3, 214-217.

Clark, R. (1974). Performing without competence. *Journal of Child Language,* 1, 1-10.

Costello, E. (1986). *Religious Signing.* New York: Batam Books.

Eagney, P. (1987). ASL? English? Which? Comparing comprehension. *American Annals of the Deaf,* 132: 4, 272-275.

Ellison, G., Baker, S., and Baker, P. (1982). Hand to hand: The joy of signing among hearing children. *Young Children*, May, 53-57.

Forecki, M.C. (1985). *Speak to Me.* Washington, DC: Galluadet University Press.

Gannon, J. (1981). *Deaf Heritage: A Narrative History of Deaf America.* Silver Spring, MD: National Association of the Deaf.

Gardner, J., and Zorfass, J. (1983). From sign to speech: The language development of hearing-impaired children. *American Annals of the Deaf,* 128:3 120-124.

Griffith. P.L., Johnson, H.A., and Dastoli, S.L. (1985). If teaching is conversation, can conversation be taught?: Discourse abilities in hearing impaired impaired children. In D. Ripich and F. Spinelli (Eds.), *School Discourse Problems.* San Diego, CA: College Hill Press, 149-177.

Harris, G.A. (1983). *Broken Ears, Wounded Hearts.* Washington, DC: Gallaudet University Press.

Hooper, J. (1987). Blissymbols and manual signs: A multi-modal approach to intervention in a case of multiple disability. *Augmentative and Alternative Communication,* 3:2, 68-76.

Isaason, A., Rowland, T., and Kelley, P. (1987). A fingerspelling approach to spelling. *Academic Therapy,* 23:1, 89-95

Joyce, D. G. (1986). Sign language and the severely handicapped. *Journal of Special Education,* 20:2 , 183-192.

bibliography

Kelly-Jones, N., and Hamilton, H. (1981) *Signs Everywhere.* Los Alamitos, CA: Modern Signs Press Inc.

Keogh, D. (1987). Teaching interactive signing in a dialogue situation to mentally retarded individuals. *Research in Developmental Disabilities,* 8:1, 39-53.

Kmapfe, C.M., and Turechek, A.G. (1987). Reading achievement of prelingually deaf students and its relationship to parental methods of communication: A review of the literature. *American Annals of the Deaf,* 132:1, 11-15.

Lane, H. (1984). *When the Mind Hears: A History of the Deaf.* New York: Random House.

Lane, H. Ed. (1984). *The Deaf Experience: Classics in Language and Education.* Cambridge, MA: Harvard University Press.

Marion, I., and Bucher, B. (1986). Generalization of a sign language rehearsal strategy in mentally retarded and hearing deficient children. *Applied Research in Mental Retardation,* 7:2, 133-148.

McDonald, L., and Pien, (1982). Mother conversational behaviors as a function of interactional intent. *Journal of Child Language,* 9, 337-358.

Meadow, K. (1982). *Deafness and Child Development.* Berkeley: University of California Press.

Mendelsohn, J., and Fairchild, B. (1983). *Years of Challenge, A Guide for P Parents of Deaf Adolescents.* Silver Spring, MD: American Society for Deaf Children.

Moores, D. (1987). *Educating the Deaf: Psychology, Principles and Practices.* Boston: Houghton, Mifflin.

Moser, B.W. (1987). Introducing sign language systems to parents of young deaf children. *Perspectives for Teachers of the Hearing Impaired,* Nov., Dec.

Musselwhite, C. (1986). Using signs as gestural cues for children with communicative impairments. *Teaching Exceptional Children,* 9:1, 32-35.

Newport, E., Gleitman, H., and Glietman, L. (1977). Mother I'd rather do it myself: Some effects and non-effects of maternal speech styles. In C. Snow and C. Ferguson (Eds.), *Talking to Children: Language Input and Acquisition.* Cambridge, MA: Cambridge University Press.

Peters, A. (1983). *The Units of Language Acquisition.* Cambridge, MA: Cambridge University Press.

Pudlas, K.A. (1987). Sentence reception abilities of hearing-impaired students across five communication modes. *American Annals of the Deaf,* 132:3, 232-236.

Rittenhouse, R. (1985). Teaching functional sign language to severely disabled children. *Teaching Exceptional Children,* 18:1 62-67.

Schildroth, A., and Karchmer, M. , Eds. (1986). *Deaf Children in America.* San Diego: College Hill Press.

Schlesinger, H., and Meadow, K. (1972). *Sound and Sign.* Berkeley: University of California Press.

Schlinger, H., and Meadow, K. (1972). *Sound and Sign: Childhood Deafness and Mental Health.* Berkeley: University of California Press

Shroyer, E.H. (1982). *Signs of the Times.* Washington, DC: Gallaudet University Press.

Shroyer, E.H., and Shroyer, S.P. (1984). *Signs Across America.* Washington, DC: Gallaudet University Press.

Snow, C. E. (1981). The uses of imitation. *Journal of Child Language,* 8, 205-212.

Spradley, T., and Spradley, J. (1978). *Deaf Like Me.* New York: Random House.

Stemach, G., and Williams, W. (1988). *Word Express: the First 2500 Words of Spoken English, Illustrated.* Novato, CA.: Academic Thearapy Publications.

Walker, L.A. (1986). *A Loss For Words.* New York: Harper and Row.

Woodward, J. (1982). *How You Gonna Get To Heaven If You Can't Talk With Jesus: On Depathologizing Deafness.,* Silver Spring MD: T.J. Publishers.

Zweibel, A. (1987). More on the effects of early manual communication on the cognitive development of deaf children. *American Annals of the Deaf,* 132:1, 16-20.

MANUAL ALPHABET

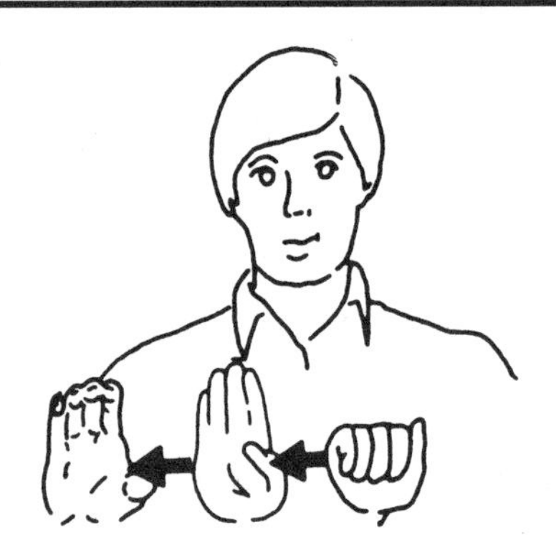

Aa

Bb

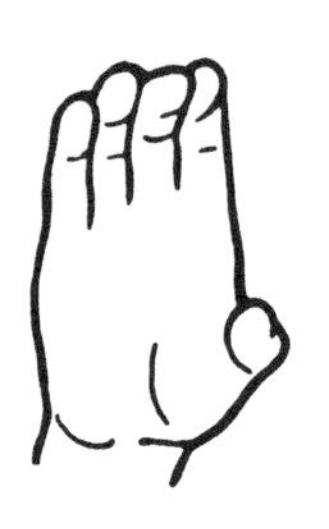

Cc

Dd

Ee

Ff

Gg

Hh

Ii

Jj

Kk

Ll

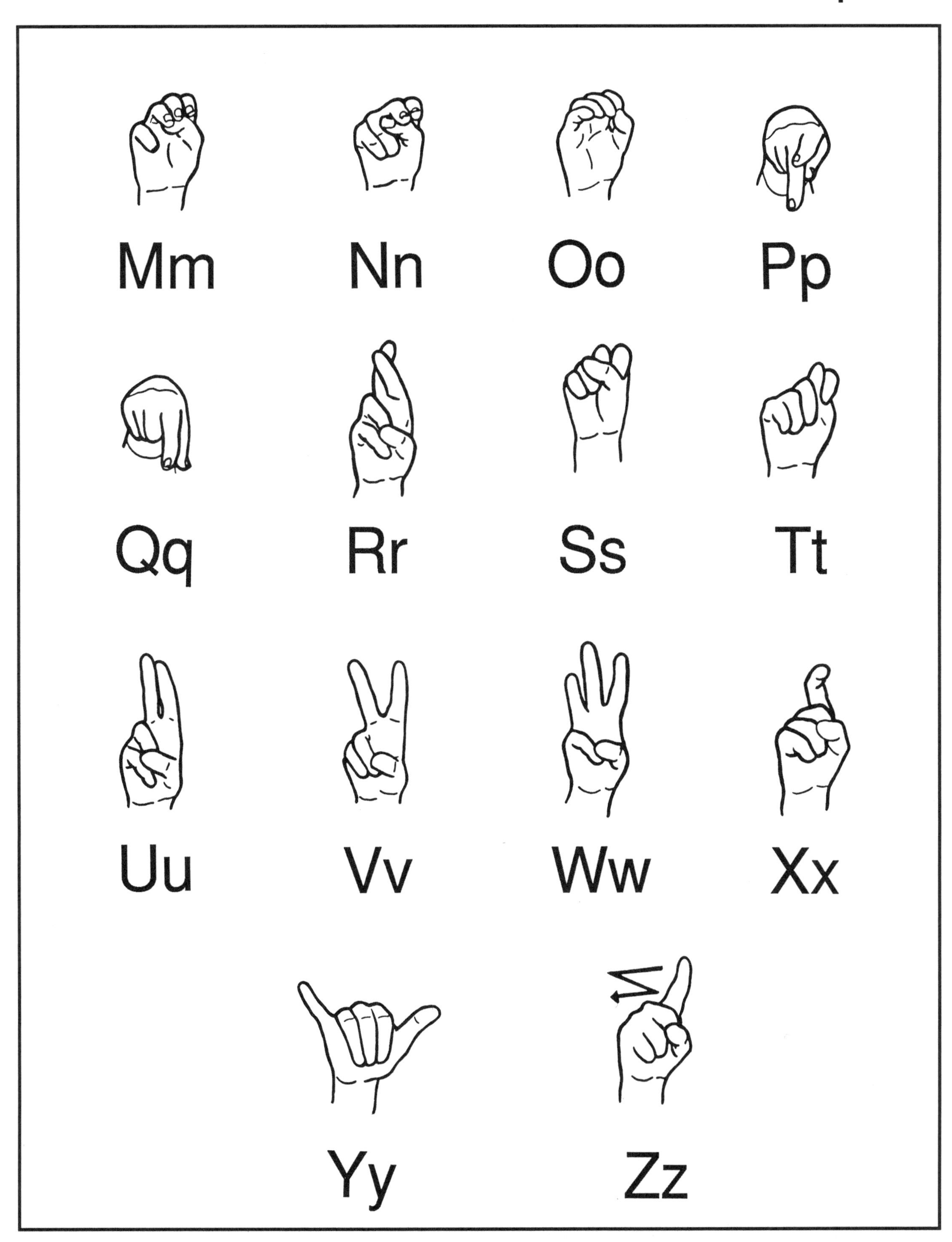
Mm
Nn
Oo
Pp
Qq
Rr
Ss
Tt
Uu
Vv
Ww
Xx
Yy
Zz

MOVEMENT OF ARROWS

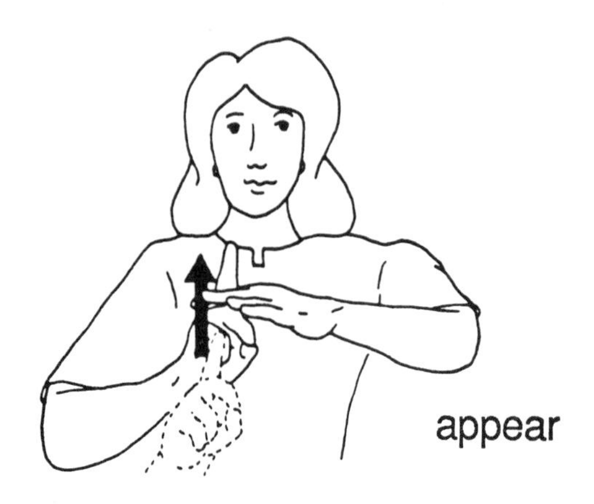

DOTTED LINES
represent the starting point of a sign.

ARCING LINES
represent a shaking or wiggling motion.

SINGLE POINTED ARROW
represents the direction in which the hand moves.

DOUBLE POINTED ARROWS
represent a double movement.

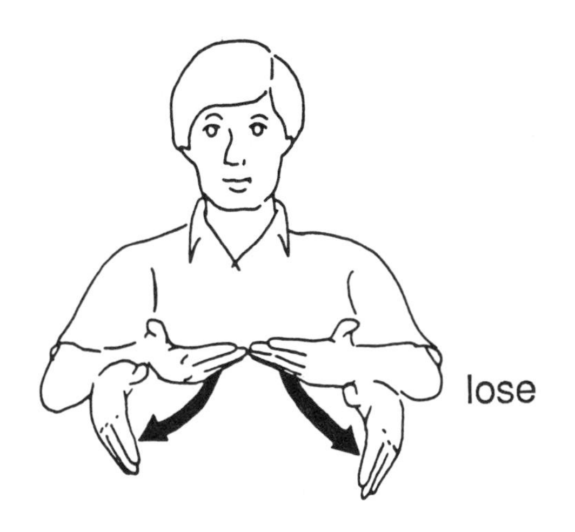

TWO BLACK ARROWS
represent both hands moving together.

ONE BLACK AND ONE WHITE ARROW
represent the hands moving in alternating directions

ARCING TWO POINTED ARROW
represents a twisting motion.

BLACK AND WHITE ARROWS
represent movement either forward or backward away from the body.

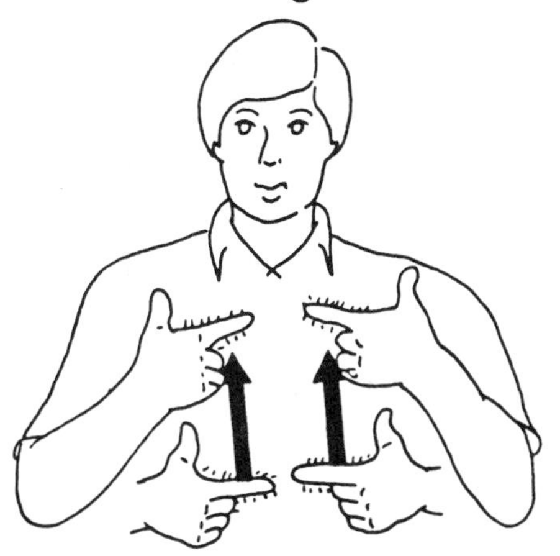

SHADED OR BLACKENED AREAS
represent contact or touching.

SIGN MARKERS
-d
(regular past verbs)
chase
chased
(irregular past verbs)
come
came

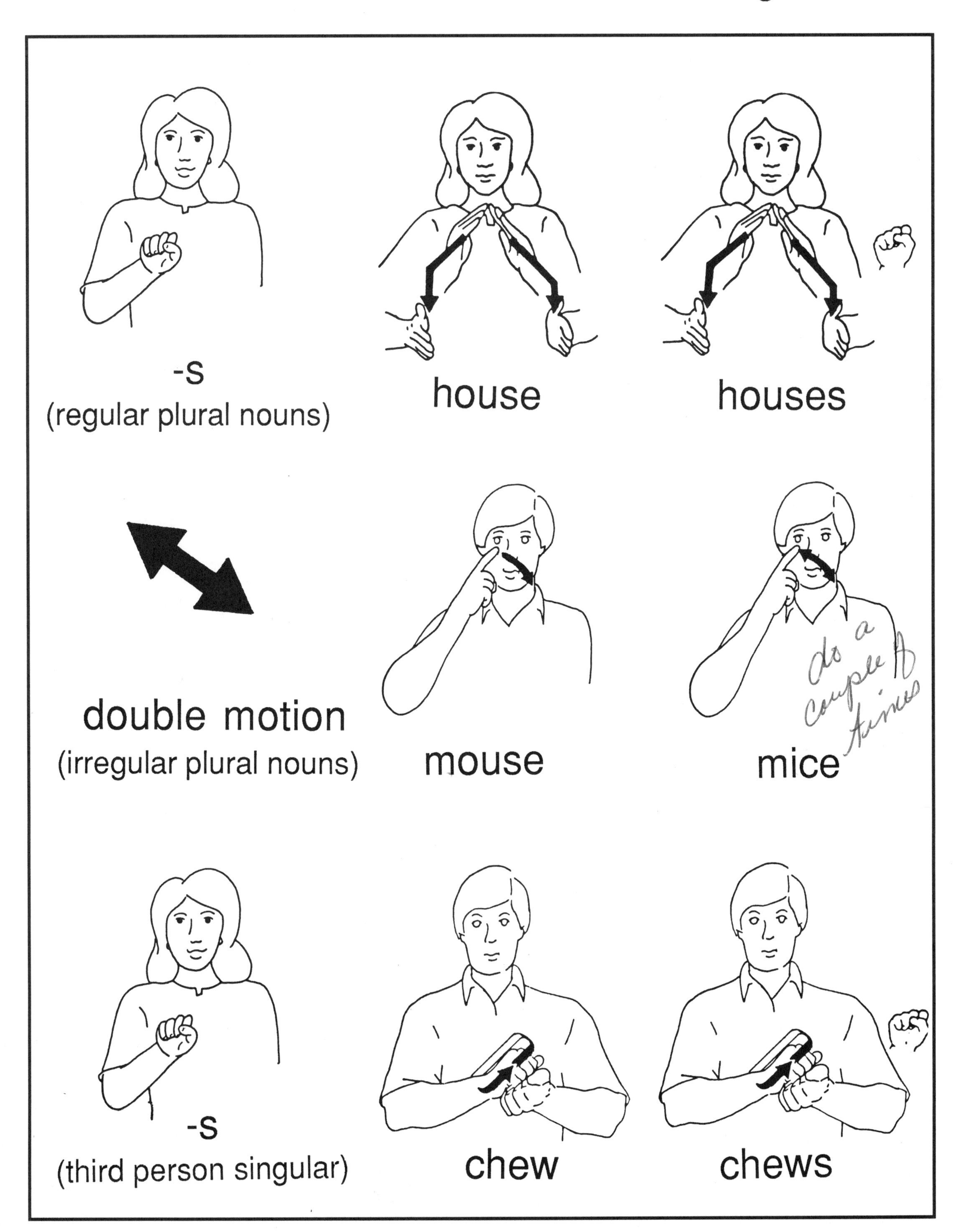
-s
(regular plural nouns)
house
houses
double motion
(irregular plural nouns)
mouse
mice
do a couple of times
-s
(third person singular)
chew
chews

sign markers

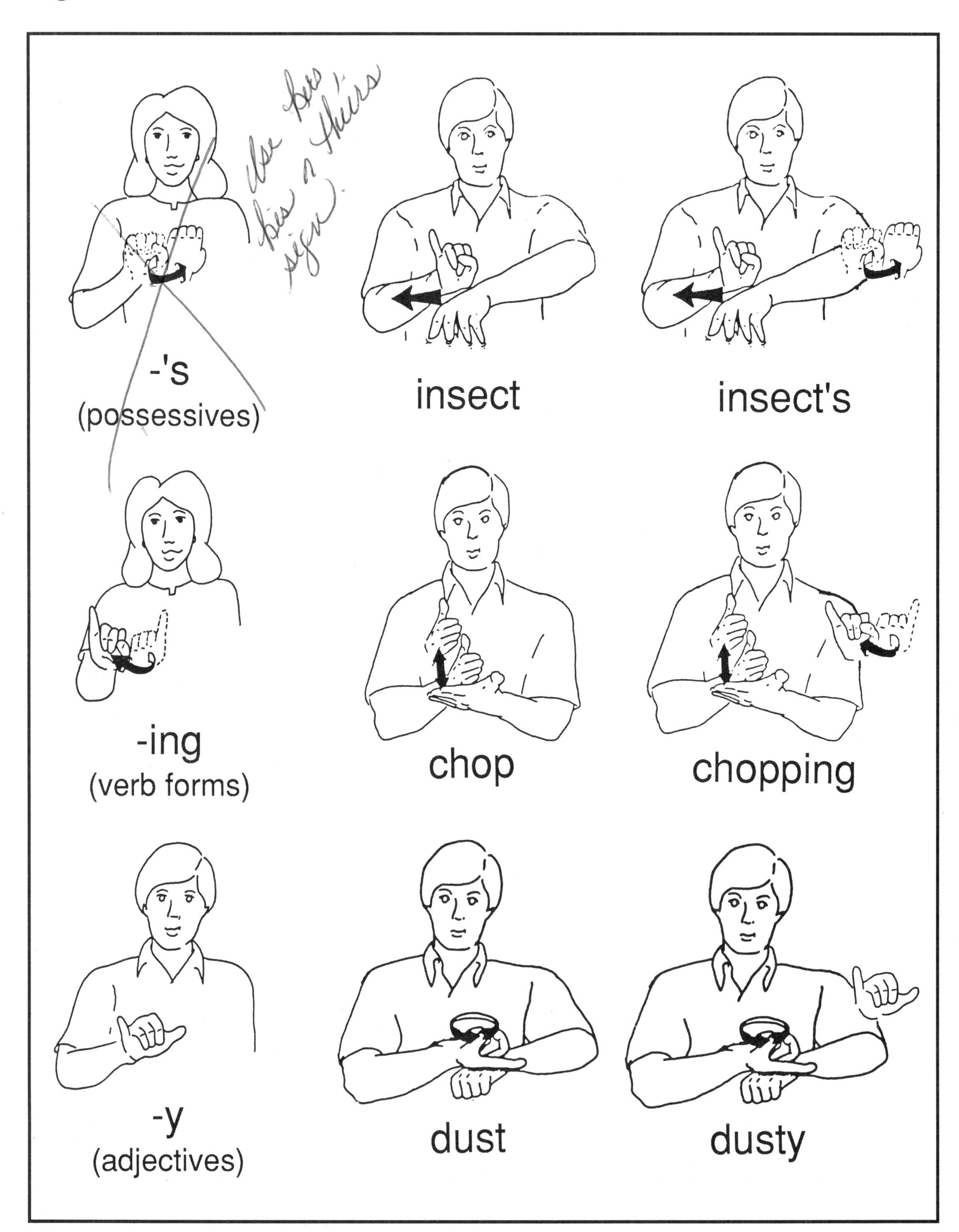

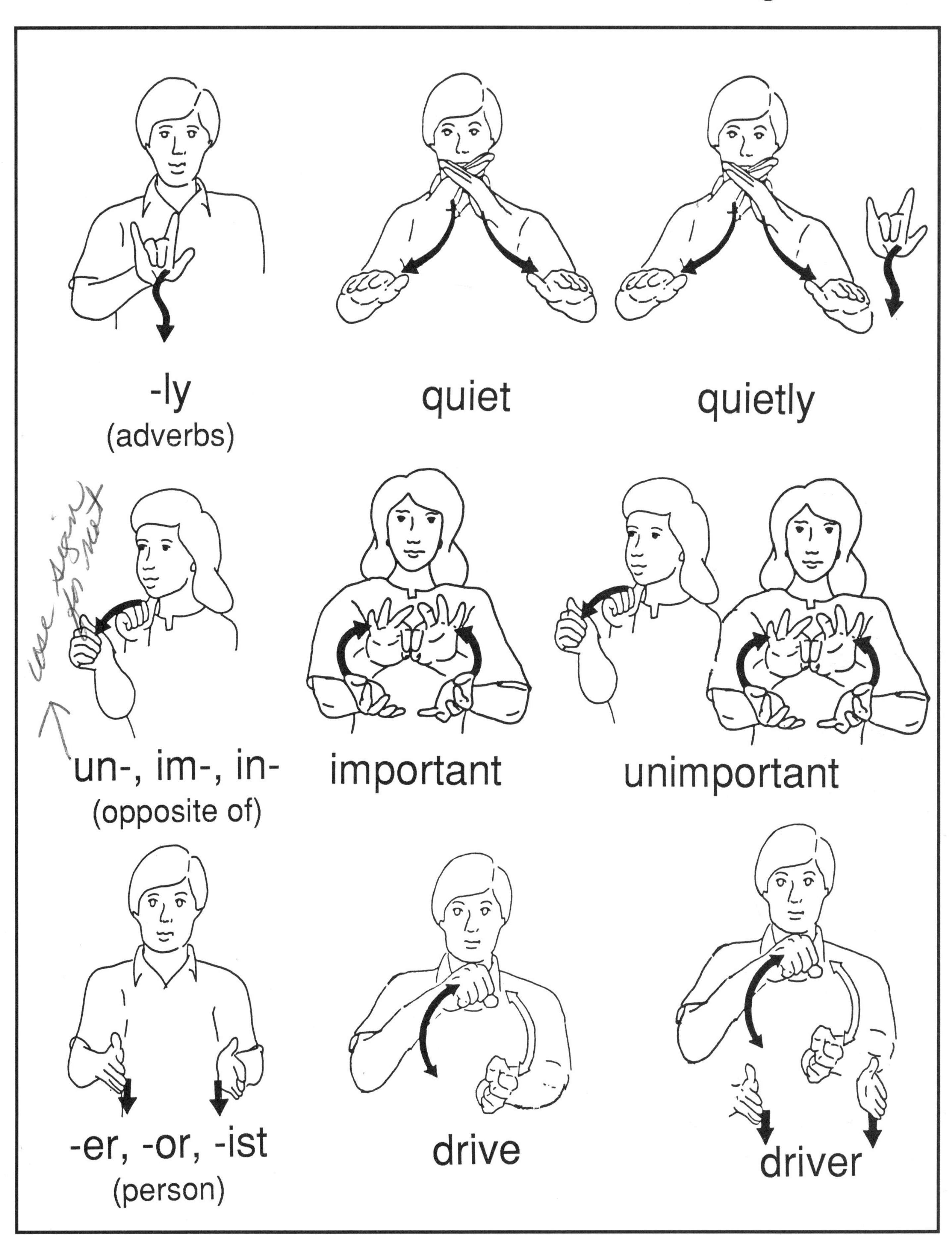
-ly
(adverbs)
quiet
quietly
use sign for not
un-, im-, in-
(opposite of)
important
unimportant
-er, -or, -ist
(person)
drive
driver

sign markers

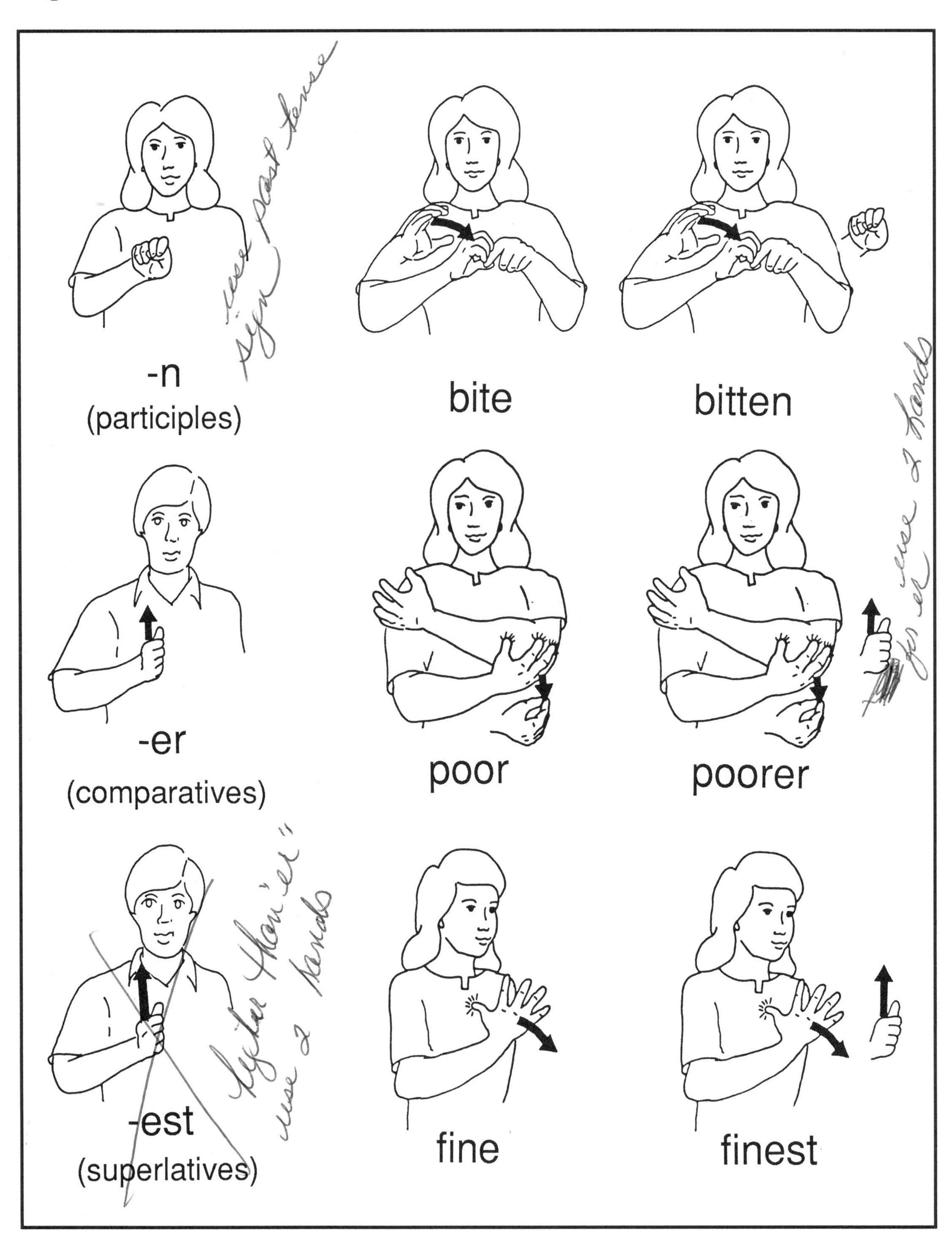

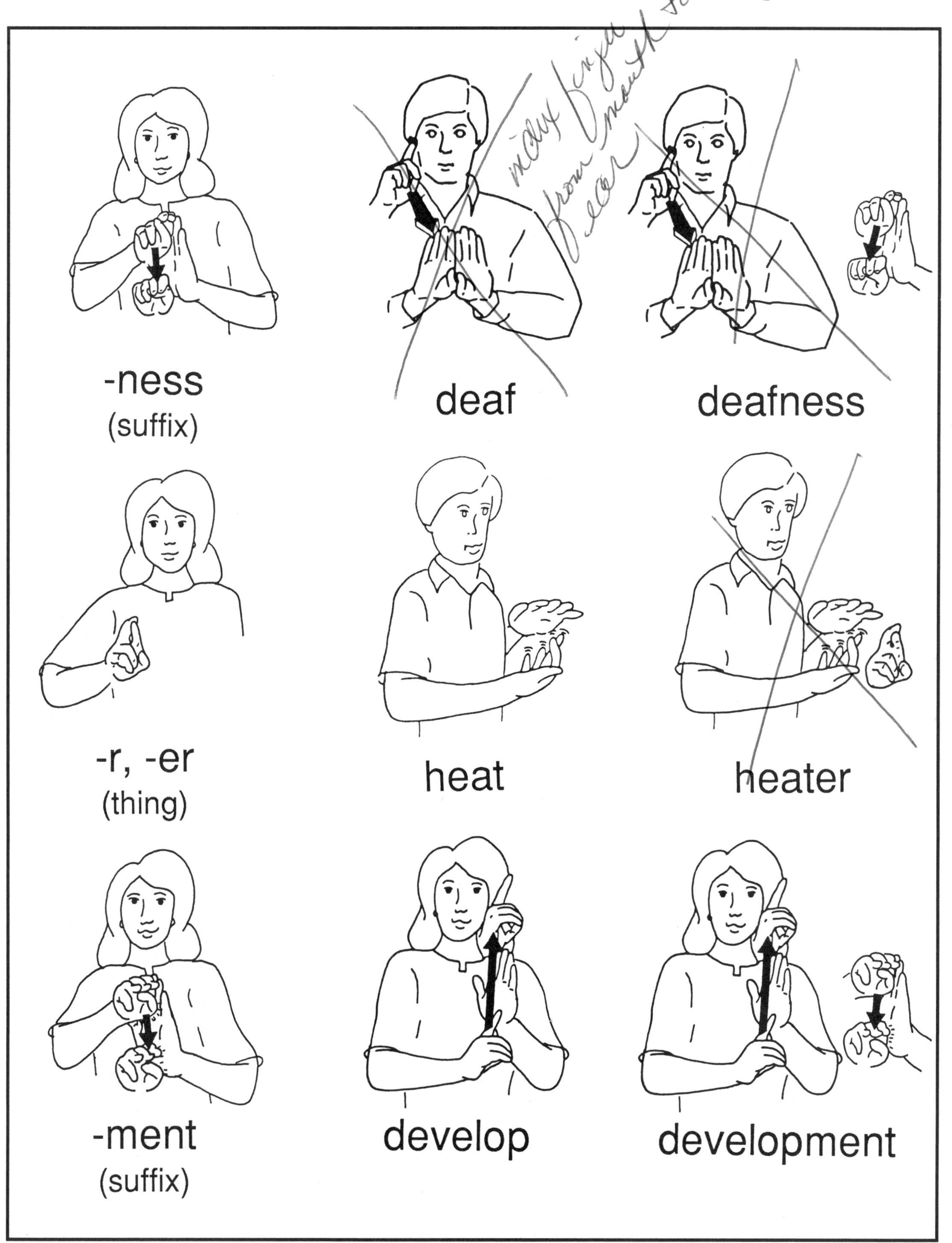
-ness
(suffix)
deaf
deafness
-r, -er
(thing)
heat
heater
-ment
(suffix)
develop
development

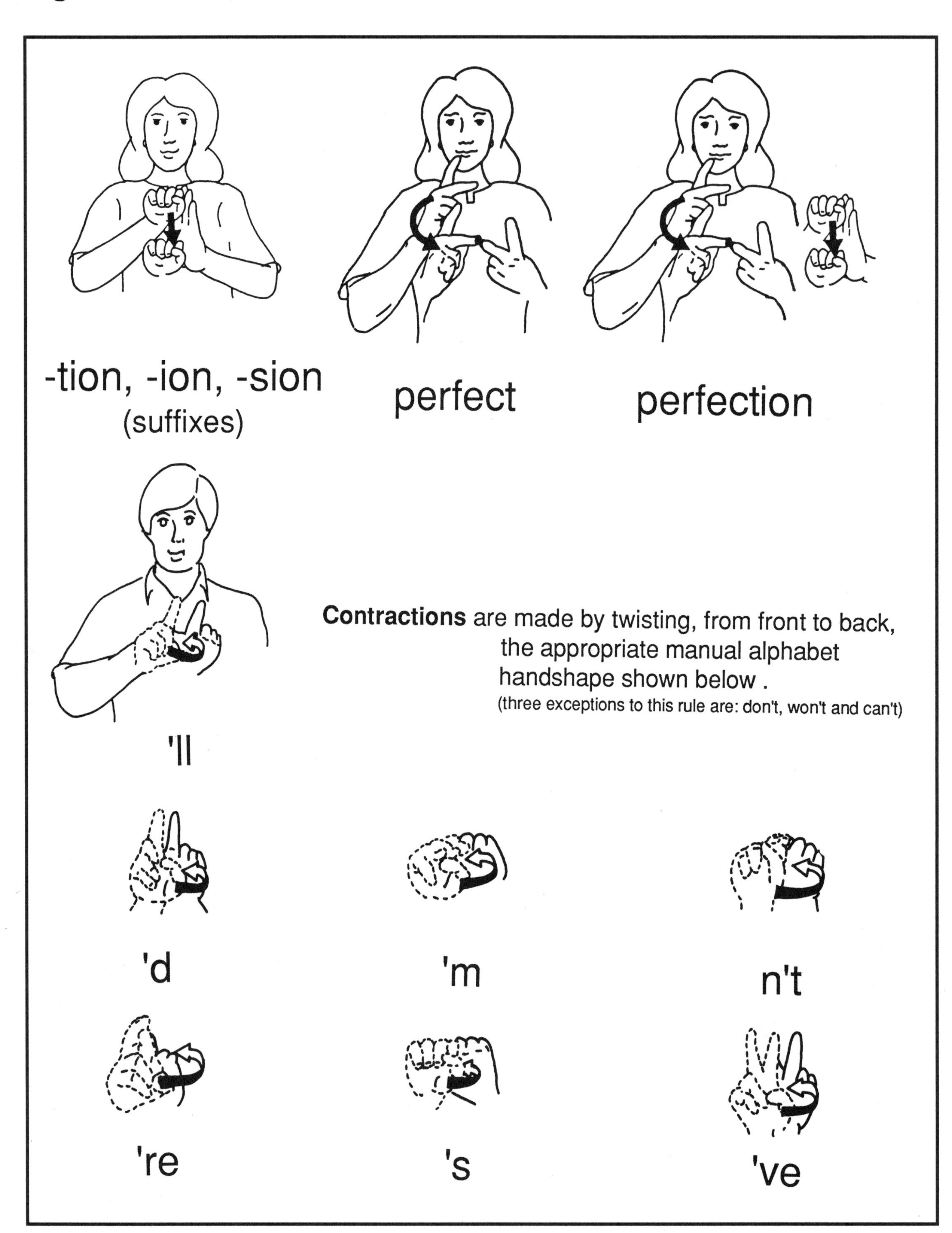
-tion, -ion, -sion
(suffixes)
perfect
perfection
'll
Contractions are made by twisting, from front to back, the appropriate manual alphabet handshape shown below .
(three exceptions to this rule are: don't, won't and can't)
'd
'm
n't
're
's
've

NUMBERS

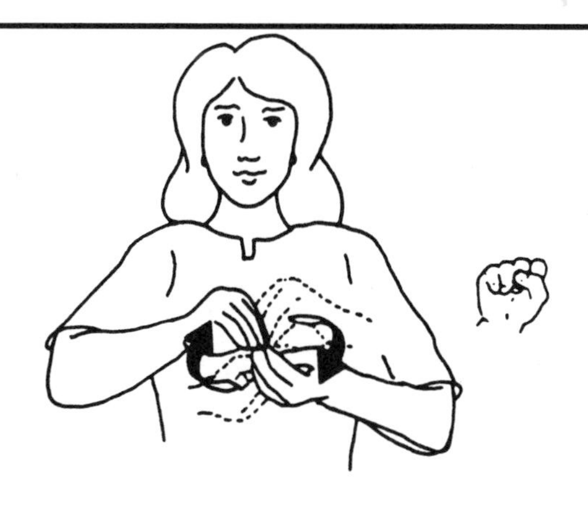

0

1

2

3

4

5

6

7

8

9

10

11

12

13

14

numbers

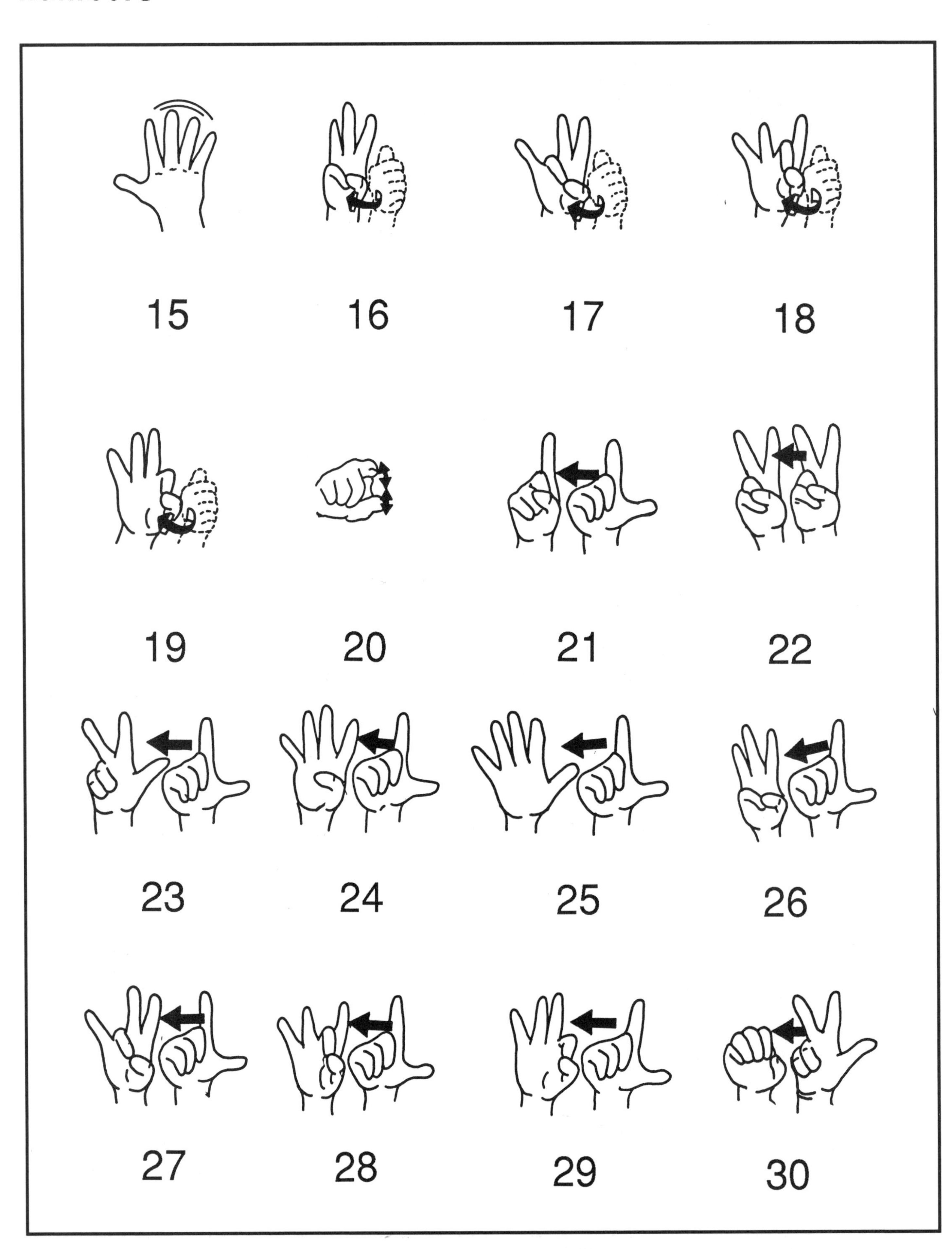

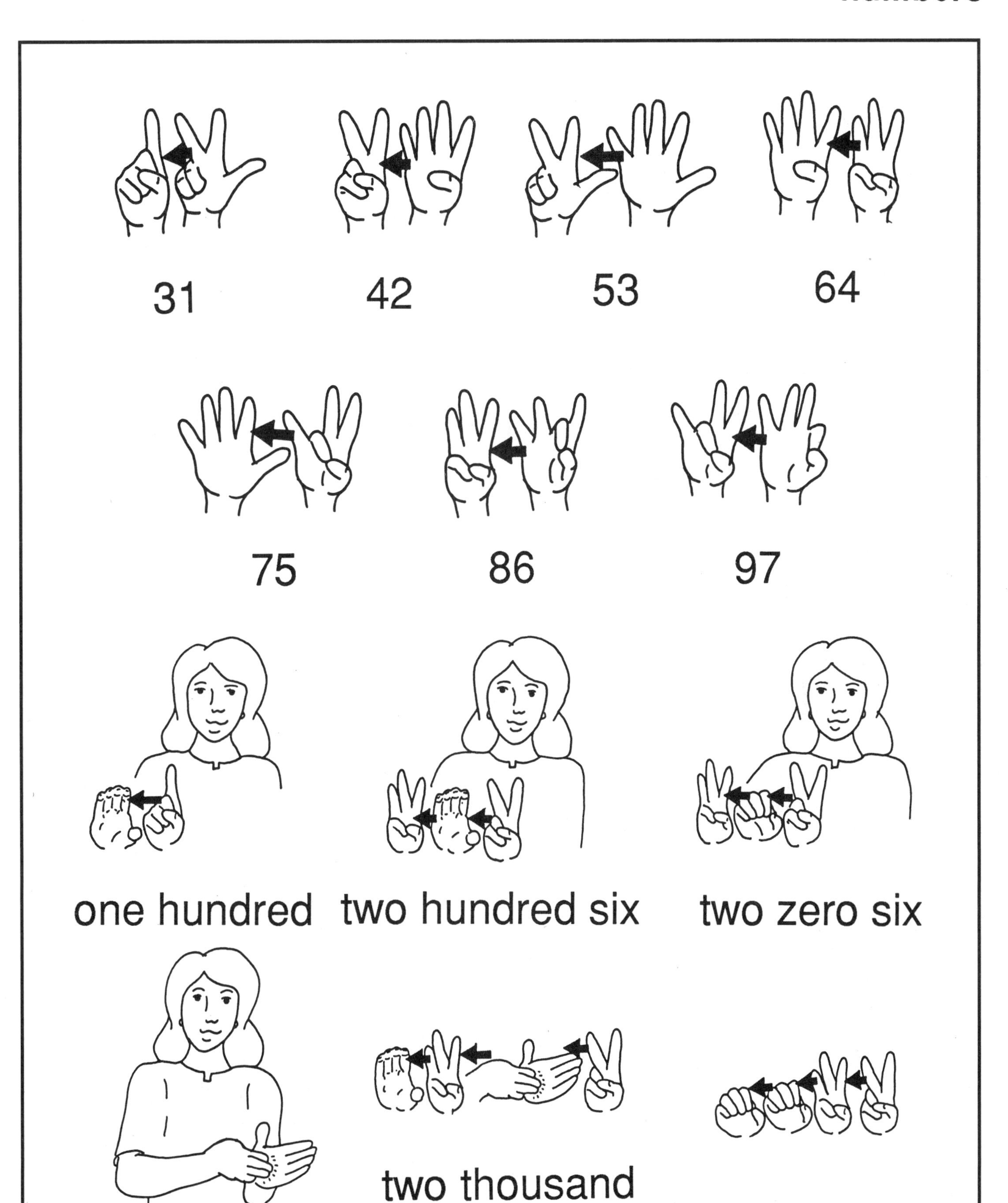
31
42
53
64
75
86
97
one hundred
two hundred six
two zero six
thousand
two thousand
six hundred
two six zero zero

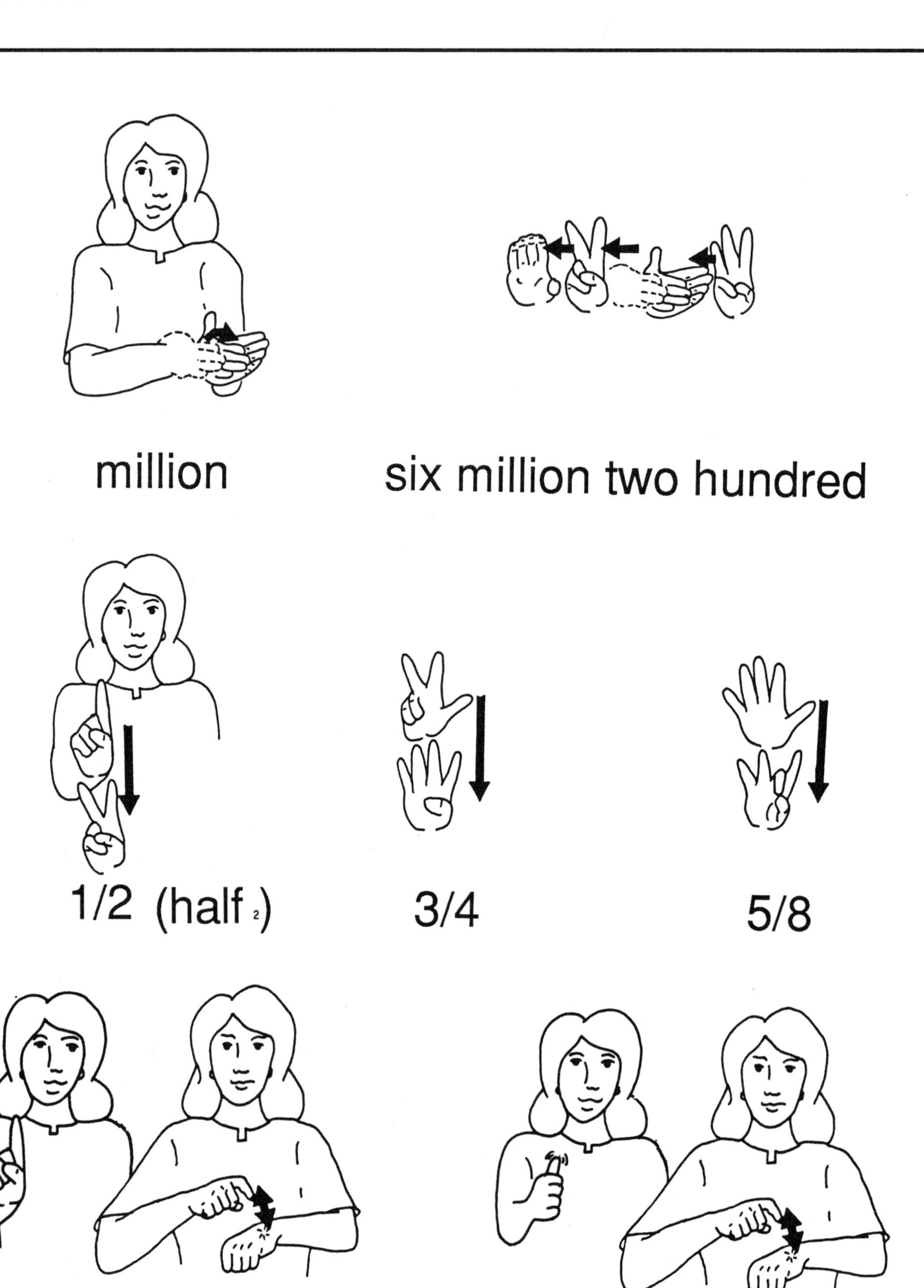
million
six million two hundred
1/2 (half 2)
3/4
5/8
1:00 (one o'clock)
10:00 (ten o'clock)

ACTION WORDS

accept
act
admit
advertise
advise
aid
aim
allow
am
announce
answer
apologize
appear
approach
are [1]
argue
arrange
arrive
associate
attempt
bake
bathe
be [1]
beat (defeat)
beat
become
been
begin
behave
believe
bike
bite [2]
blame
blow [2]
boil
borrow
bother
brag
bring [2]
brush (hair)
brush
brush (teeth)
build
call[1] (name)
call[1] (yell)
can [1]
cannot
catch[1] (arrest)
cause [2]
center
chase [2]
chew
choose
chop
climb [2]
combine
come [1*]
communicate
compete
complain
concentrate
connect
continue
cook
cooperate
cost
could [1]
cover
crack
damage
decide
decrease
demand
demonstrate
depend
describe
develop
didn't
die [2]
dig
direct
disagree
disappear
discover
disobey
divorce
do[1] (auxillary verb)
do [1]
doesn't [2]
don't [1]
don't want
doubt
dress [2]
drink
drive
drop
drop[2] (give up)
earn
eat [1]
educate
embarrass
emphasize
encourage
enter
equal
erase
escape
establish
evaluate
exaggerate
exchange
excuse
expect
experience
fall [1]
fault
feed

ACTION WORDS
(con't.)

fib
fight [2]
fill
find [2*]
finish
fire (expel)
fish
fit
fix [2]
float
fly[2] (airplane)
fly[2] (bird)
fold
follow
fool
force
forgive
free
freeze
gamble
get [1]
get even
get in
get out
give [1]
give up (surrender)
go [1]
grow
guard
guess
had
happen [2]
has[1]
hate
have [1]
have to
heat
hide [2]
hire
hit [1]
hold [2]
hold up
honor
hunt
hunt (look for)
hurry
ignore
imagine
improve
include
increase
inform
inspect
intend
introduce
invent
invite
iron
is [1]
isolate
jog
join (connect)
join (member)
judge
jump[1] (off)
jump[1] (up)
keep [1]
kick [2]
kill
kiss
kneel
knock [2]
know [1]
last (keep)
laugh
lay [2]
lead
leak
leave[2] (abandon)
leave [2]
lecture
lend
lie (falsehood)
lie down
lift
like [1]
limit
live [1]
lock
look [1]
look at (me)
lose [2]
make up
manage
march
mark
marry
mash
may[2*]
mind (care)
mind (obey)
miss[2] (to feel the absence of someone)
miss [2]
mix
move [1]
nap
need [2]
notice
obey
observe
offer
open [2]
operate
order
organize
owe

ACTION WORDS
(con't.)

pack
park [2]
pass
pass (give)
pass out
pay
pedal
peek
pet
pick[1] (select)
pick up
pinch
pity
plan
plant
poke
polish
postpone
pound
pray
preach
prefer
prepare
pretend
prevent
progress
pronounce
protect
prove
pull [2]
punish
push [2]
put [1]
put off
quarrel
question
quit
race [2]

raise
reach (touch)
reach (arrive)
realize
receive
recognize
reduce (slim down)
reduce
refuse
regret
reinforce
release
remind
remind (me)
repeat
report
represent
require
respect
return
reward
ride[1] (animal)
ride[1] (vehicle)
rob
rock
rub
ruin
sail
save
saw (cut)
say [1]
scare [2]
scold
scrape
scream
see [1]
seem
sell

send
separate
serve
settle
sew
shake
share
shave
shoot
shop
should
show [1]
show (me)
show off
sign
sign (signature)
sign
sit [1]
slap
sleep [1]
smell [2]
smile
smoke
spell
spoil
squeeze
stand [2]
stay [1]
steal
step [2]
stop [2]
stuck
summarize
supervise
suspect
swallow
swear
take [1]

ACTION WORDS
(con't.)

take (me)
talk [2]
talk[2] (conversation)
tame
tap
taste [2]
tease
telephone
tell [1]
tell me
thank [2]
throw [2]
throw out
tickle
tie
tiptoe
tolerate
toss
touch [2]
trap
travel
trick
trip
try [1]
turn [1]
turn off
turn on
twist
underline
understand
unlock
urge
use [2]
used to (habit)
used to (past)
untie
unzip
vote
wait [2]
wake
walk [1]
want [1]
warn
was [1]
wash
waste
watch [1]
wave
wear [2]
were [1]
weigh
welcome
whisper
will
win [1*]
wind (up)
wish
wonder
won't [2]
work [2]
worry
would [1]
wrap
wreck
yell
zip

NOTE:

An asterisk, 1* or 2*, indicates the word listed in *Word Express* was in the past tense.

ACTIVITY - ACTION WORDS

Purpose: To identify and act out actions words appropriately.

Materials: Flashcards with one action word written on each flashcard, e.g., run, walk, hop, jump, etc.

Procedure:

1. Adult shows child a flashcard containing an action word previously introduced.
2. Child performs action indicated on flashcard.
3. Child signs/says action word.
4. Repeat procedures 1 through 3.

Variations: Child and adult take turns performing actions; child signs/says action in a sentence, e.g., "I hopped to door.", flashcards can contain sentences for child to perform and then sign/say sentence, e.g., flashcard: Run to the table. Child signs/says, "I ran to the table."

ACTION WORDS

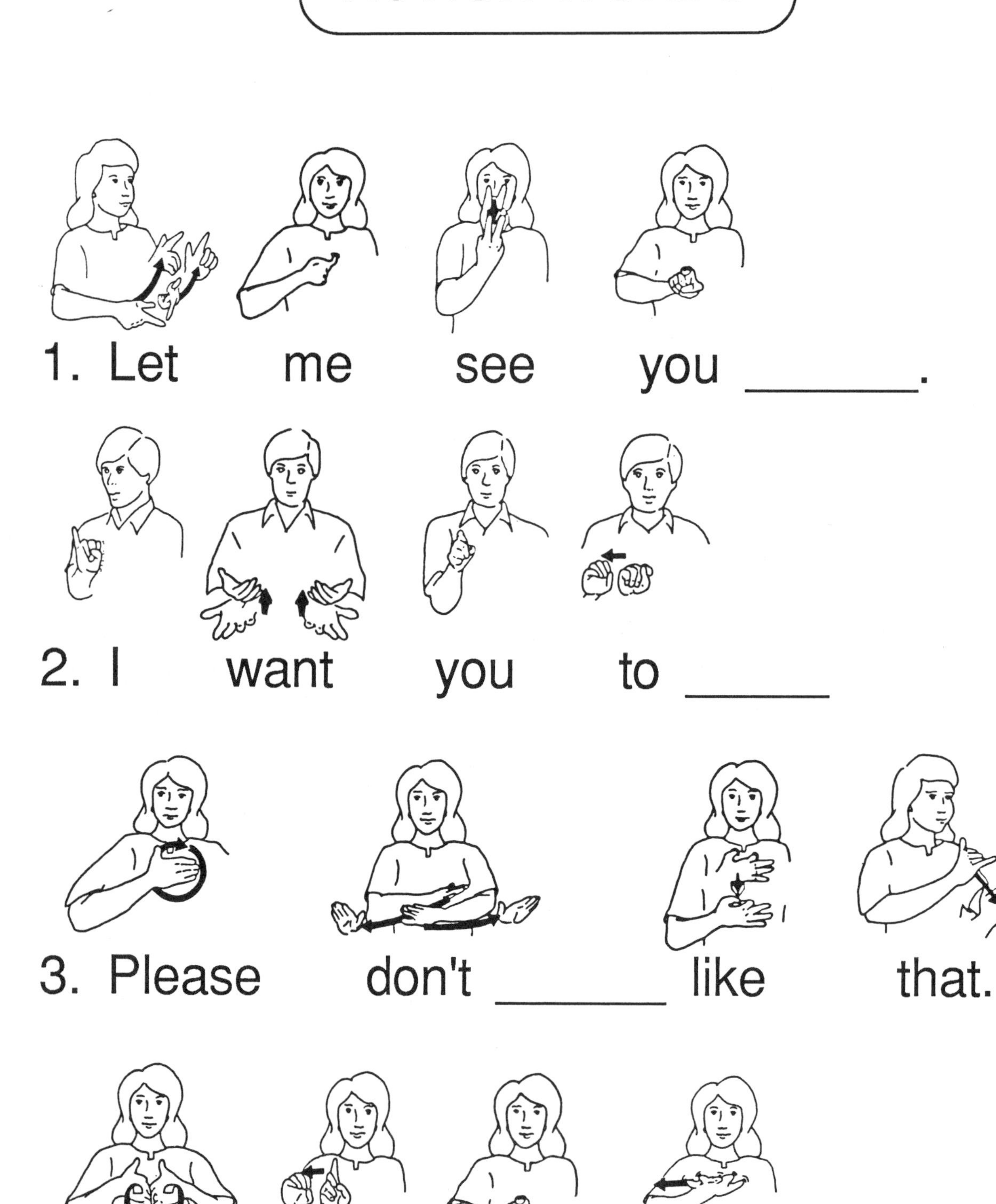

1. Let me see you ______.

2. I want you to _____

3. Please don't ______ like that.

4. How do you spell ______?

ACTION WORDS

accept

act

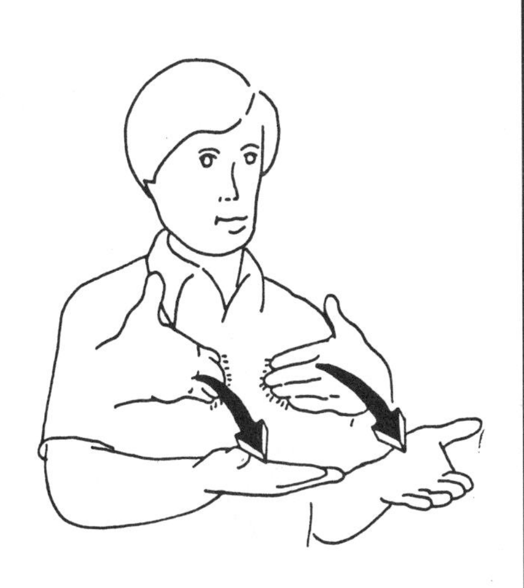

admit

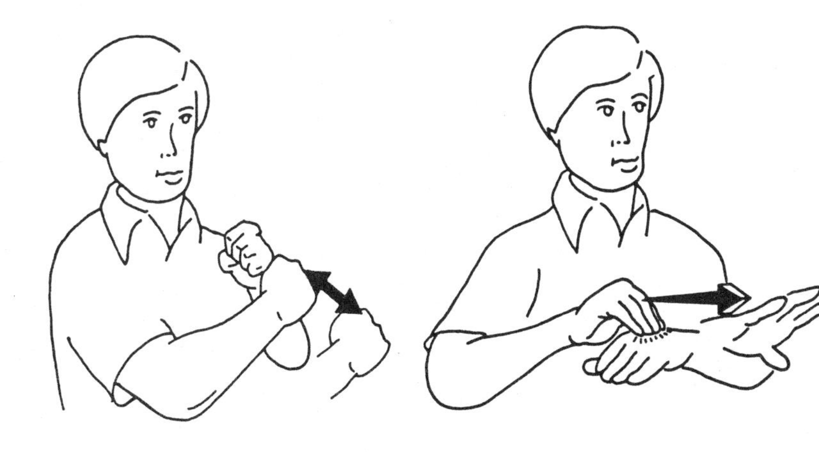

advertise

advise

aid

action words

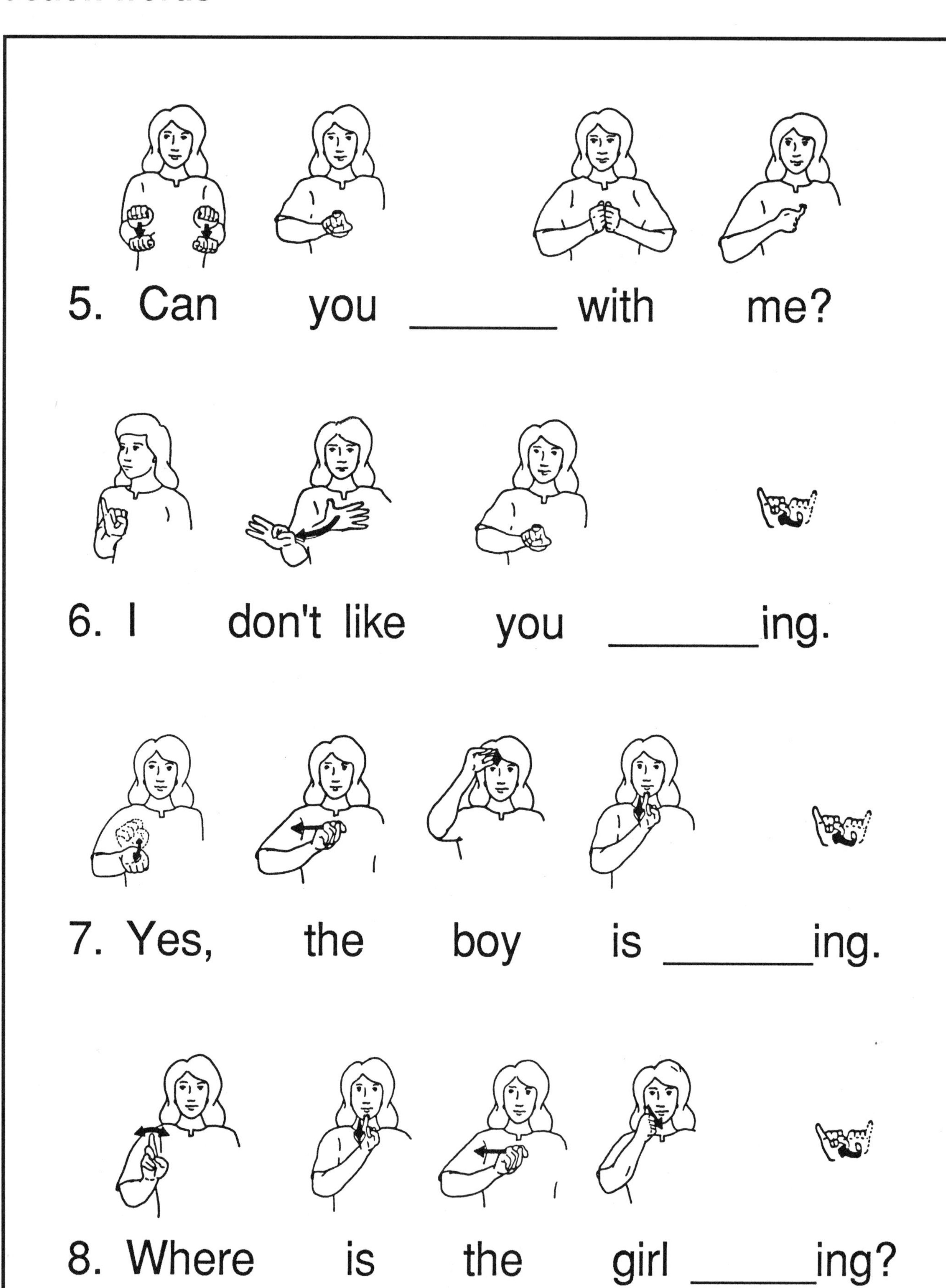
5. Can you ______ with me?
6. I don't like you ______ing.
7. Yes, the boy is ______ing.
8. Where is the girl ______ing?

aim
allow
am
announce
answer
apologize
appear
approach
are

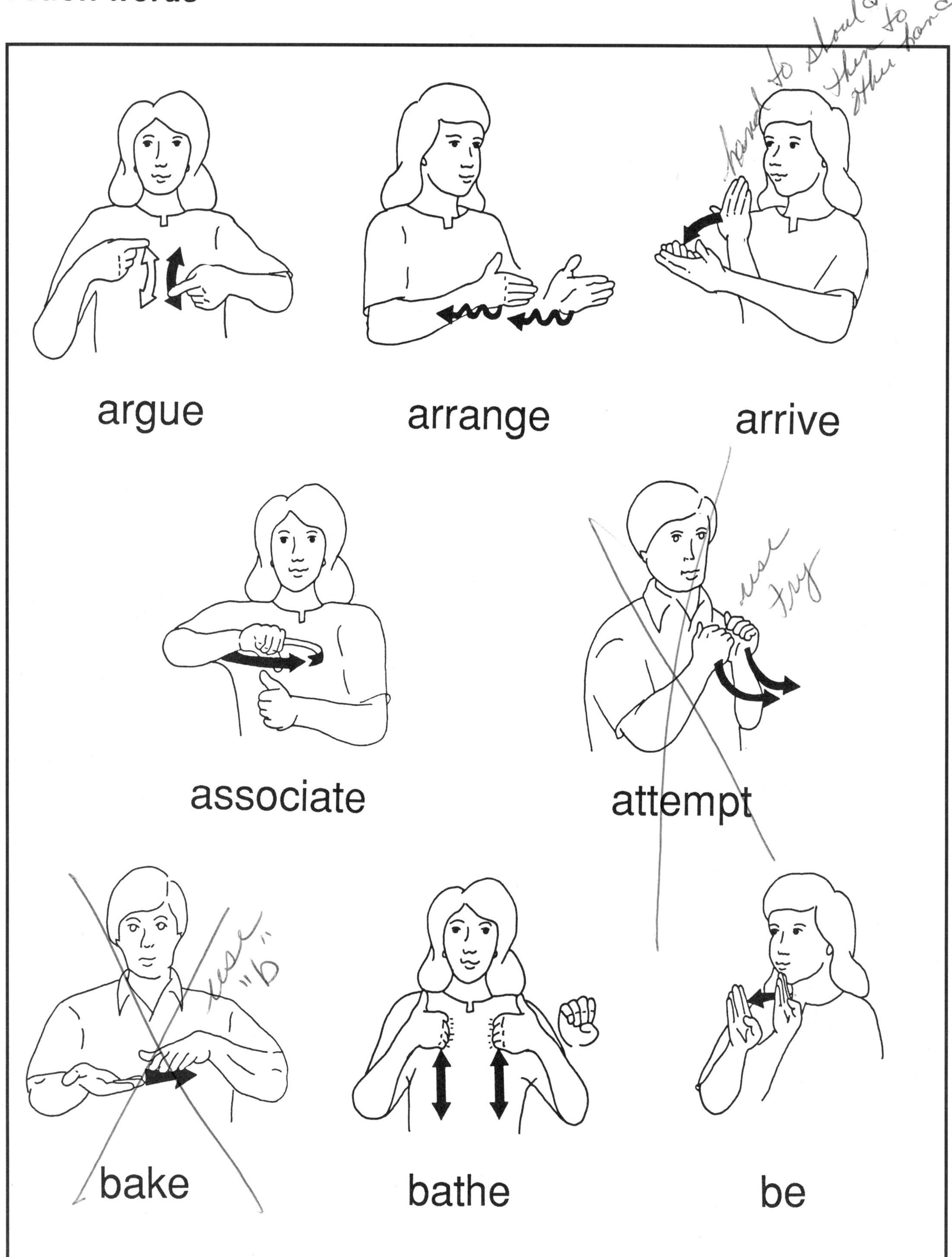
argue
arrange
arrive
hand to shoulder + then to other hand
associate
attempt
use try
bake
use "b"
bathe
be

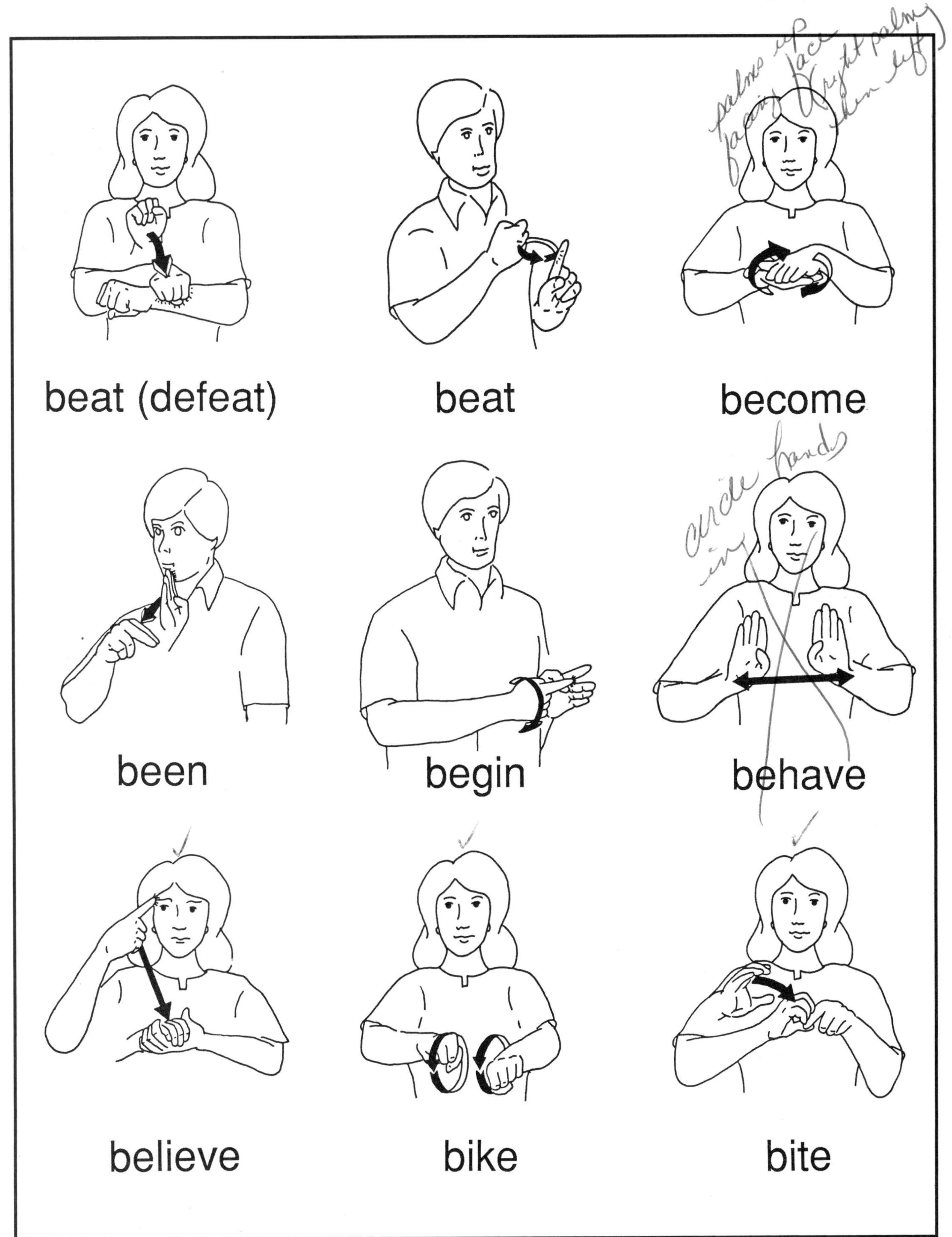
beat (defeat)
beat
become
been
begin
behave
believe
bike
bite

action words

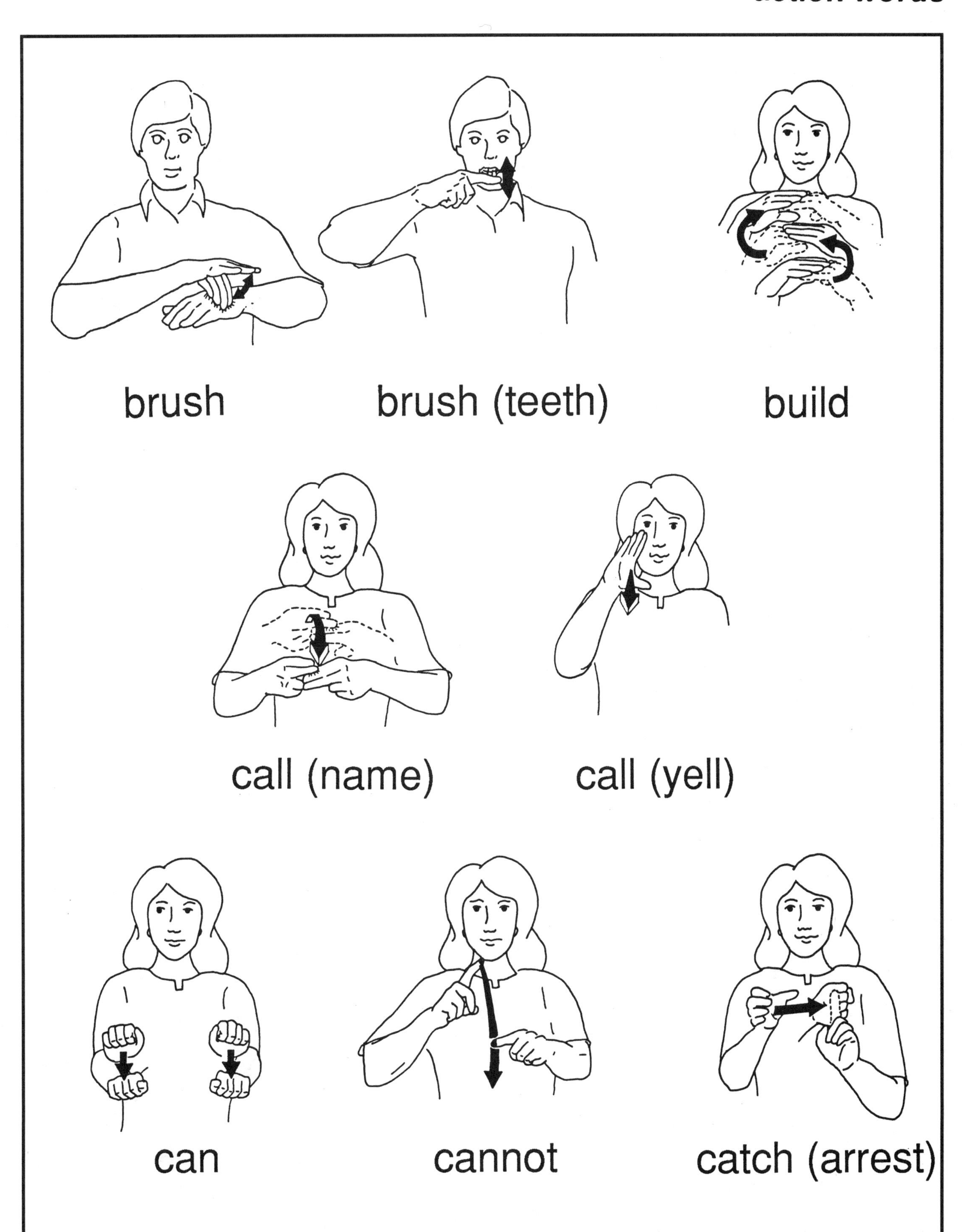
brush
brush (teeth)
build
call (name)
call (yell)
can
cannot
catch (arrest)

cause
center
chase
chew
choose
chop
climb
combine
come

communicate
compete
complain
concentrate
connect
continue
cook
cooperate

action words

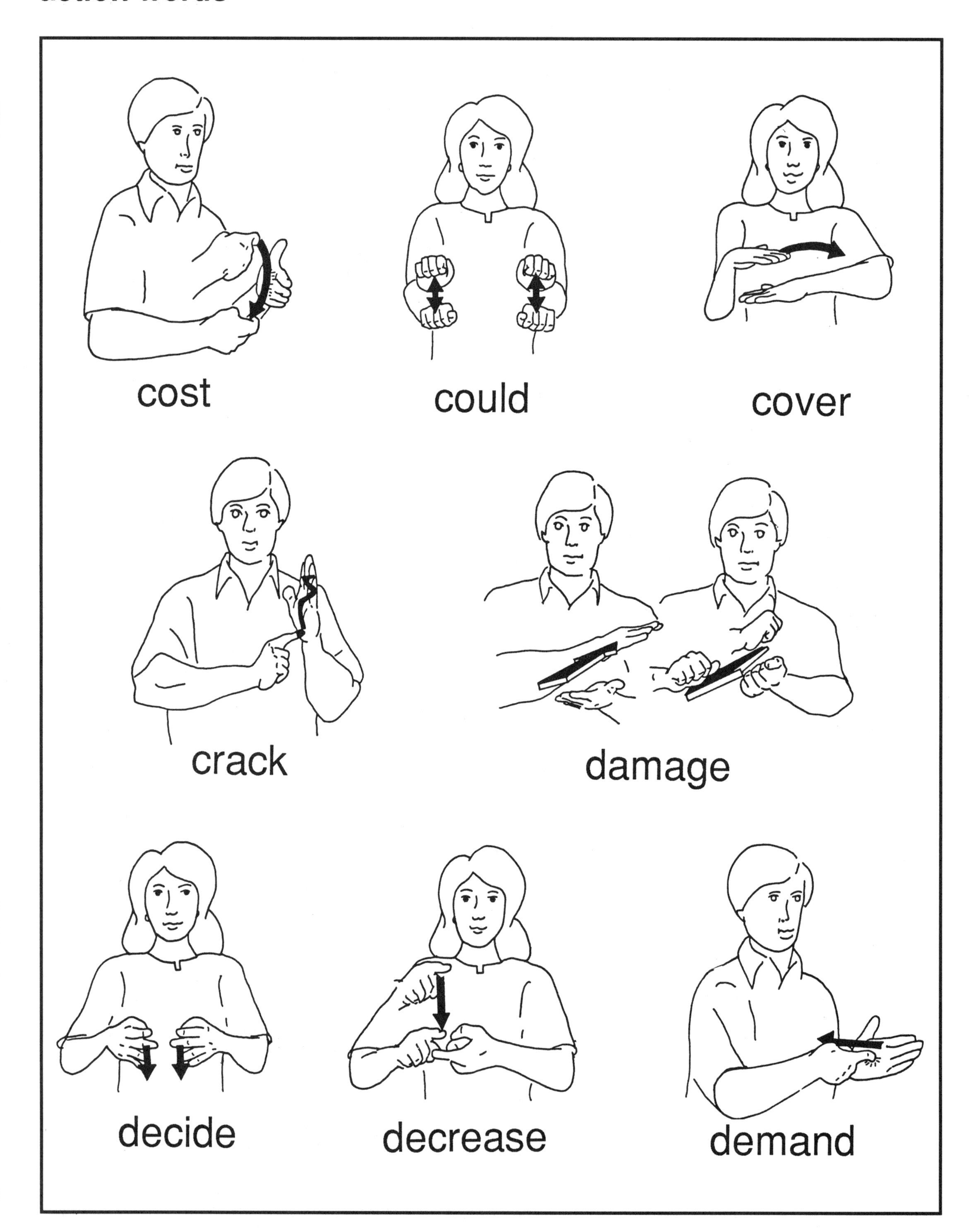

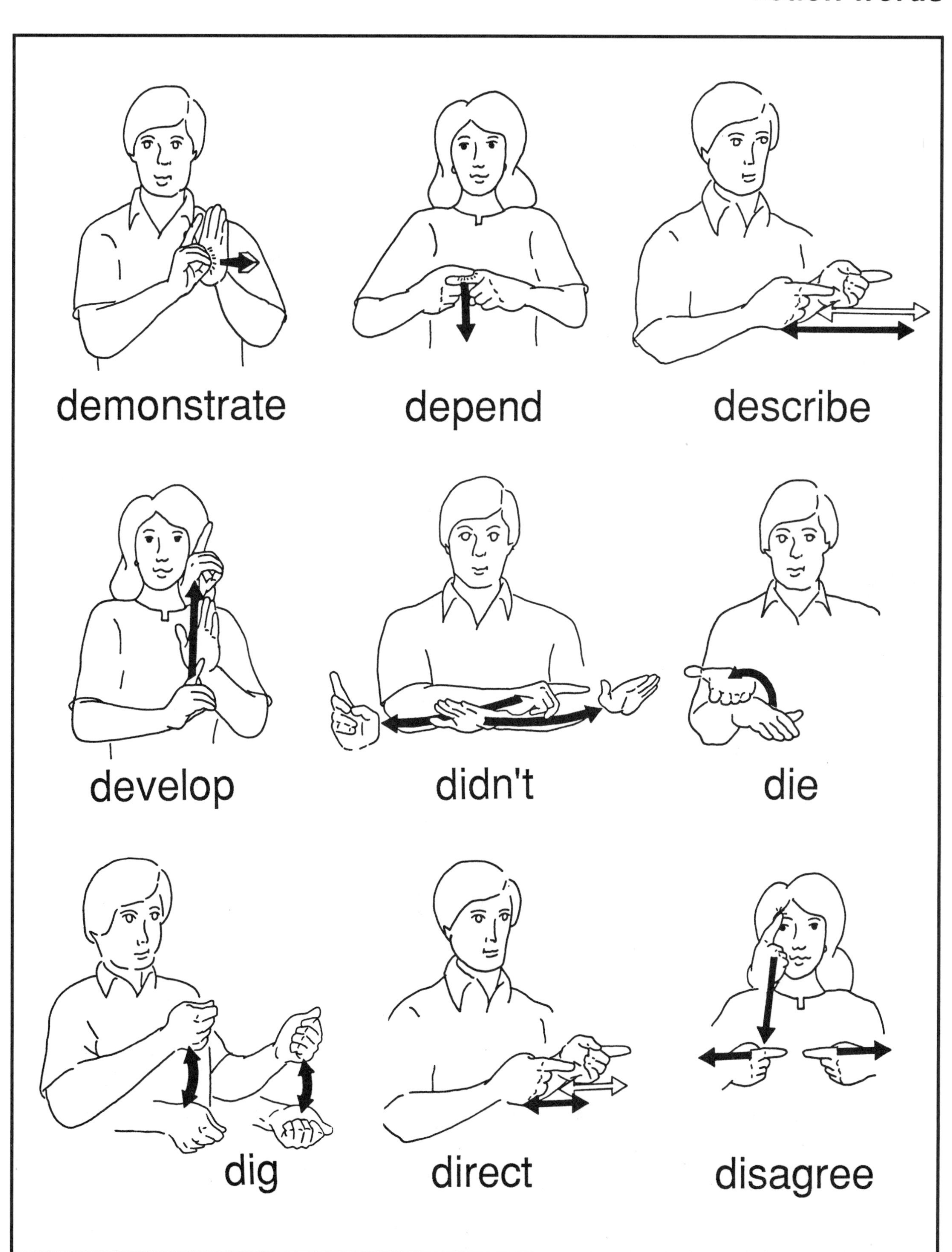
demonstrate
depend
describe
develop
didn't
die
dig
direct
disagree

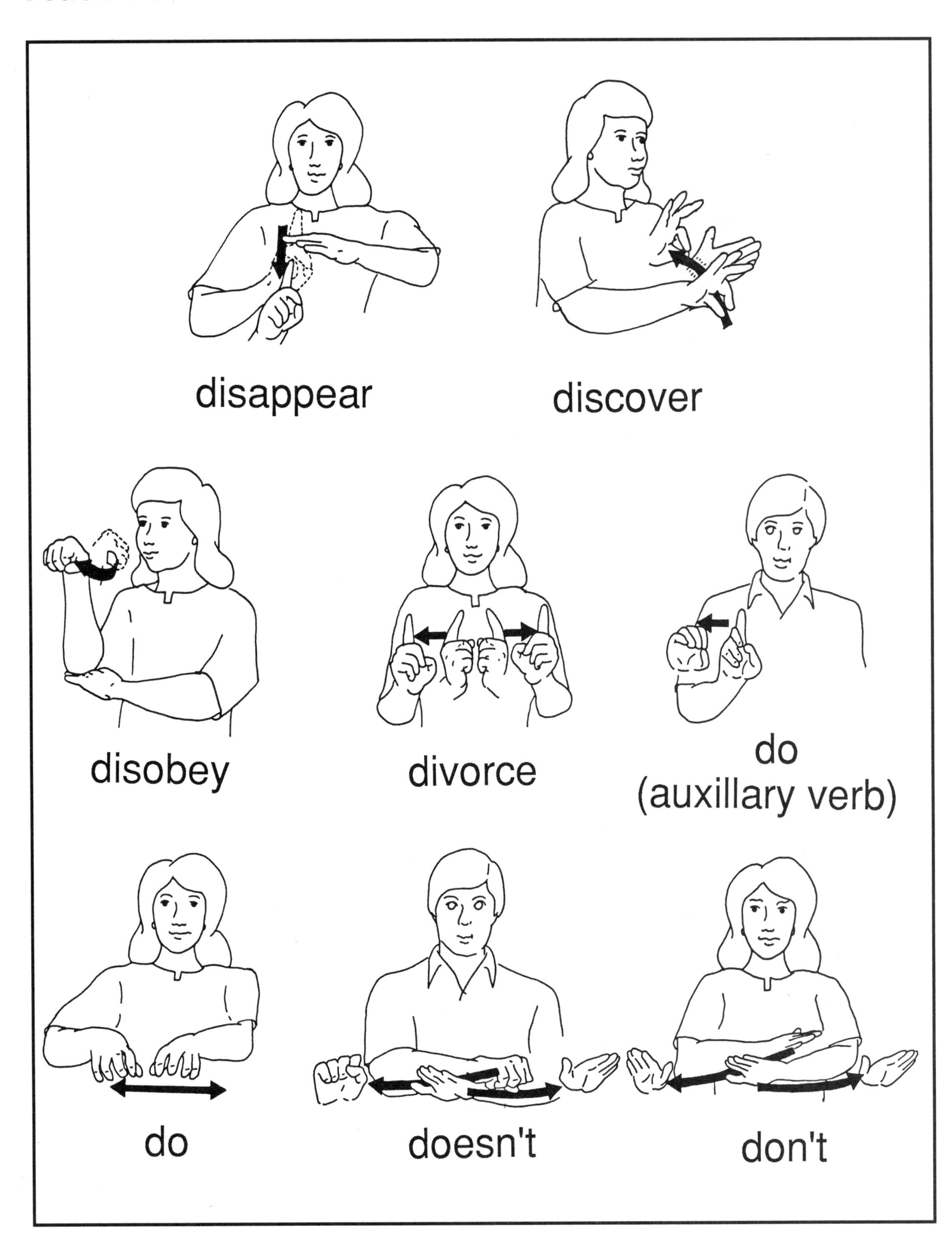
disappear
discover
disobey
divorce
do
(auxillary verb)
do
doesn't
don't

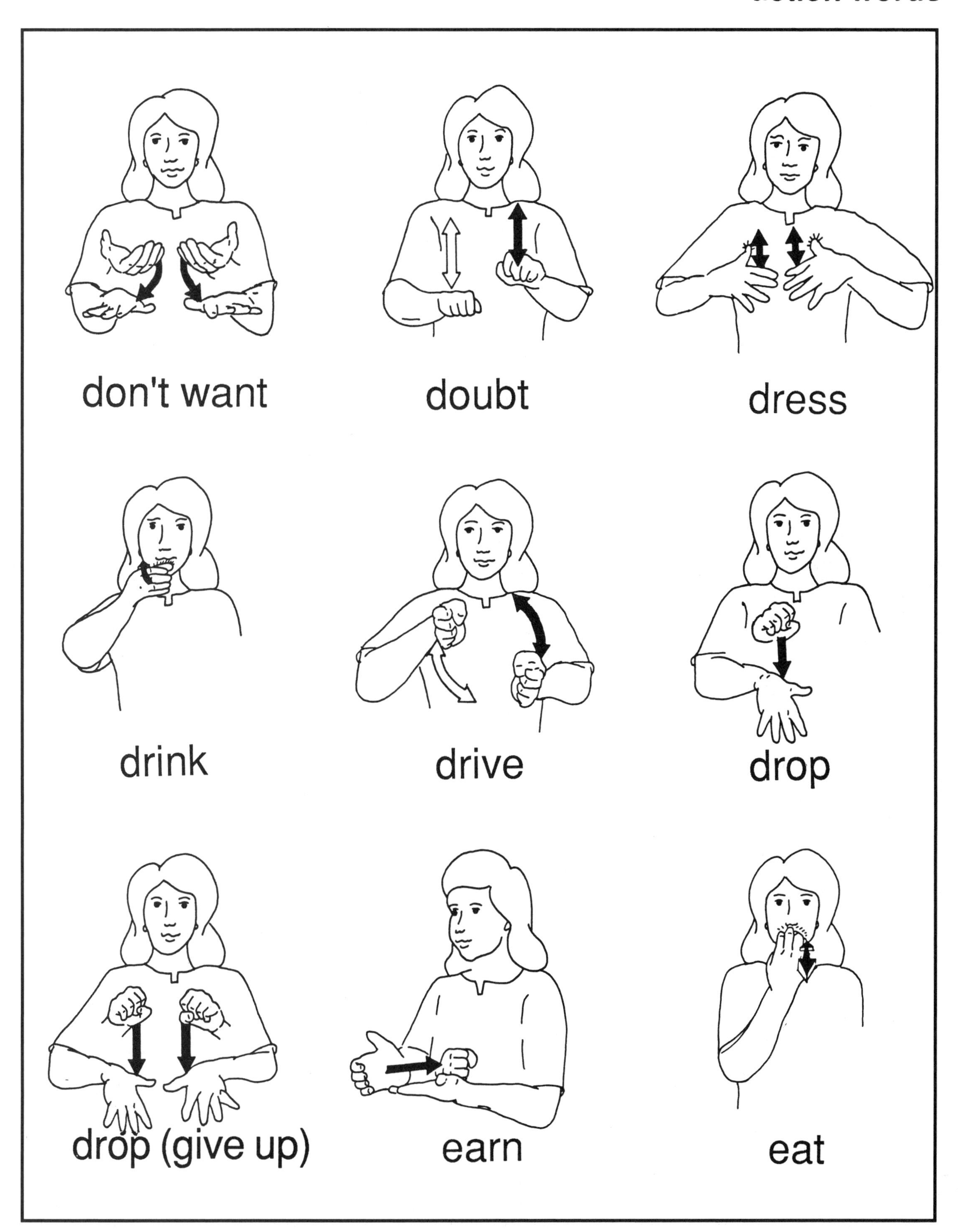
don't want
doubt
dress
drink
drive
drop
drop (give up)
earn
eat

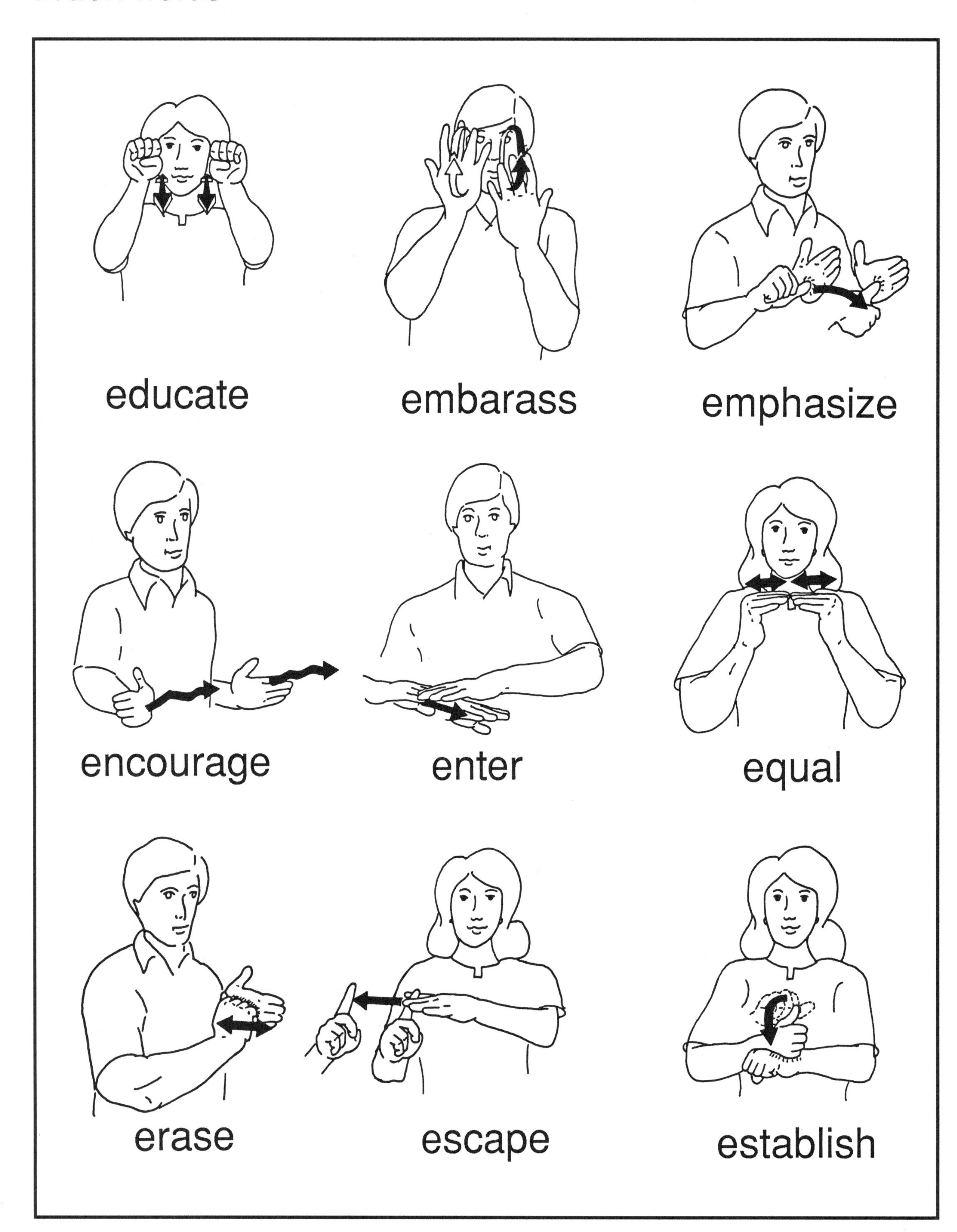
educate
embarass
emphasize
encourage
enter
equal
erase
escape
establish

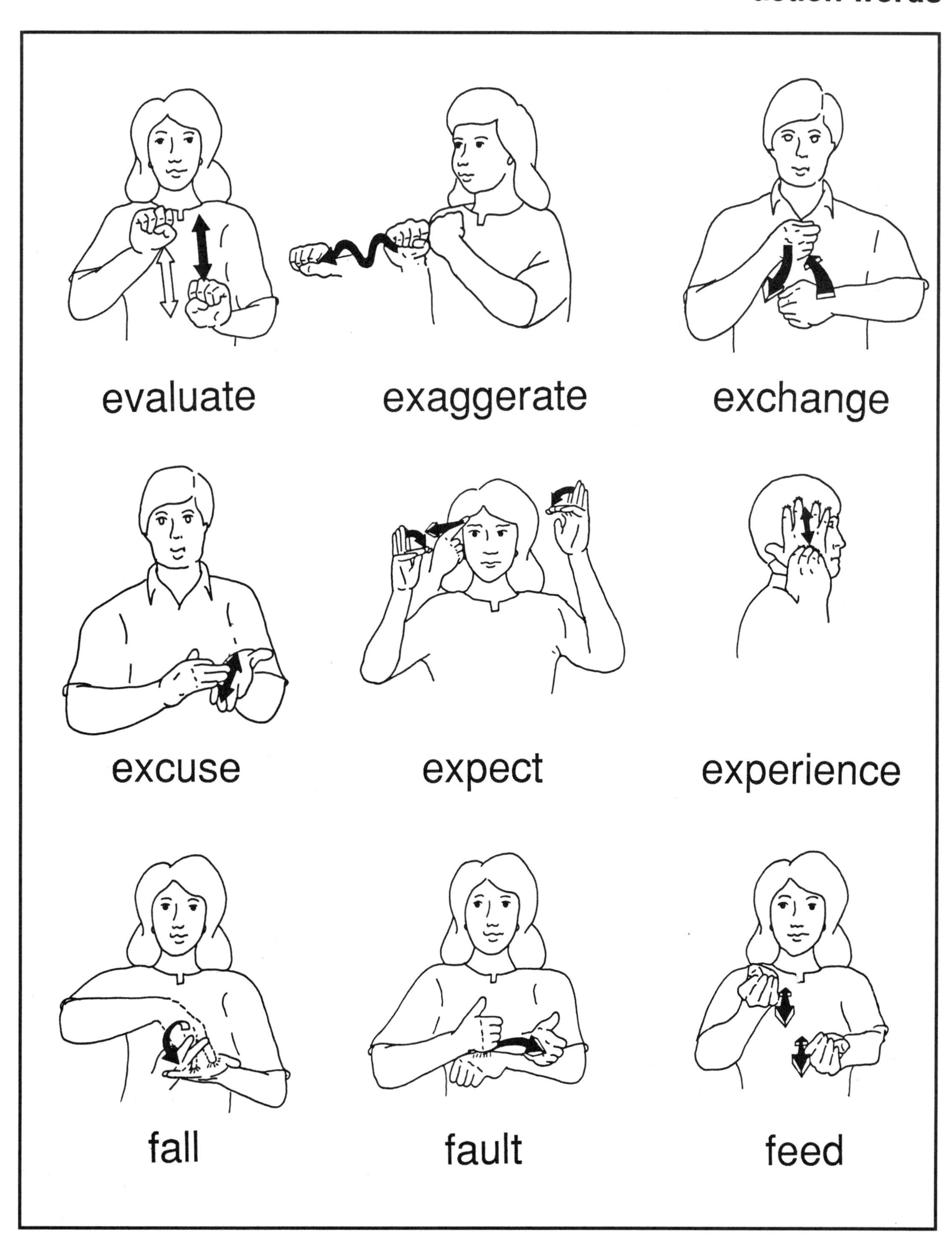
evaluate
exaggerate
exchange
excuse
expect
experience
fall
fault
feed

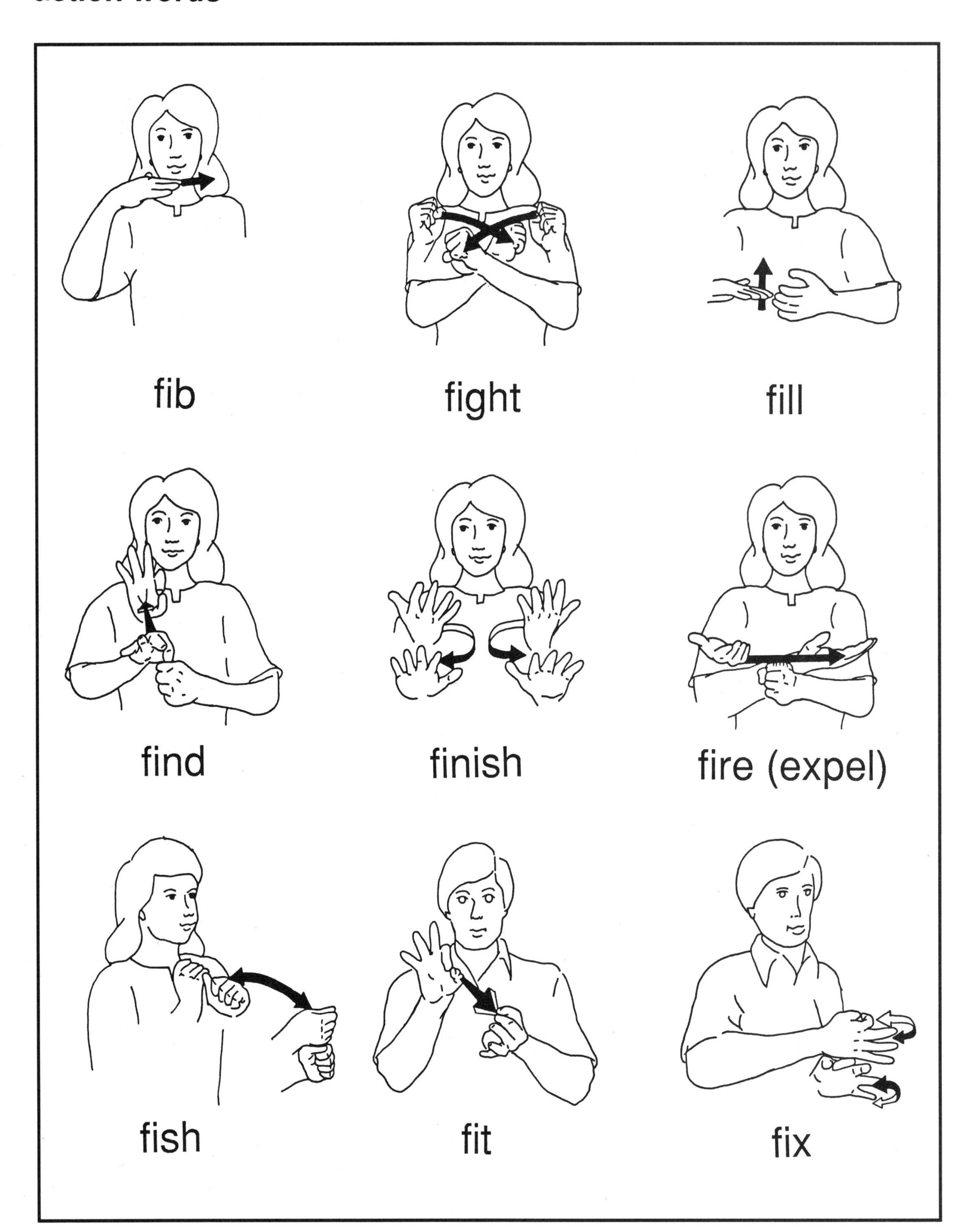
fib
fight
fill
find
finish
fire (expel)
fish
fit
fix

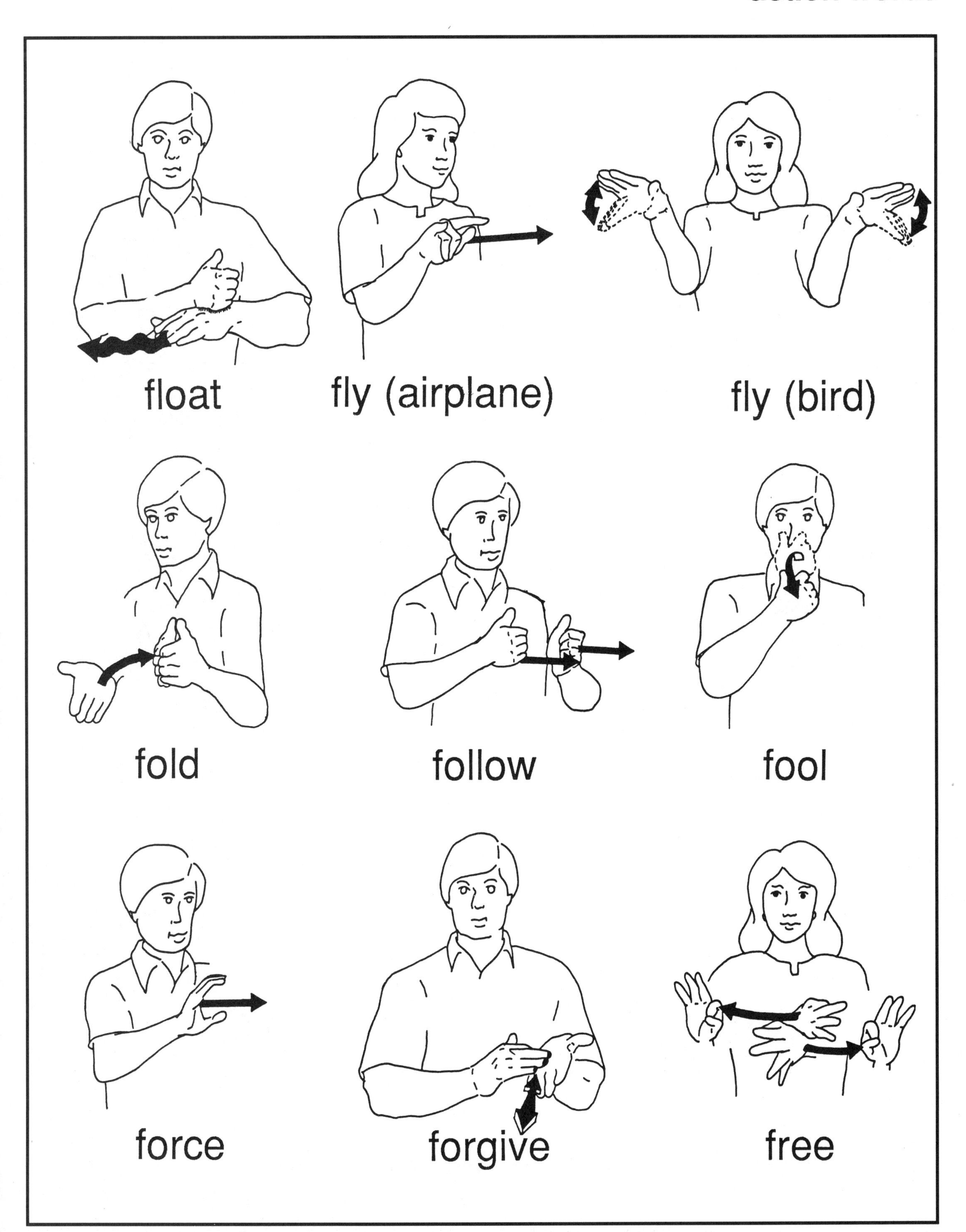
float
fly (airplane)
fly (bird)
fold
follow
fool
force
forgive
free

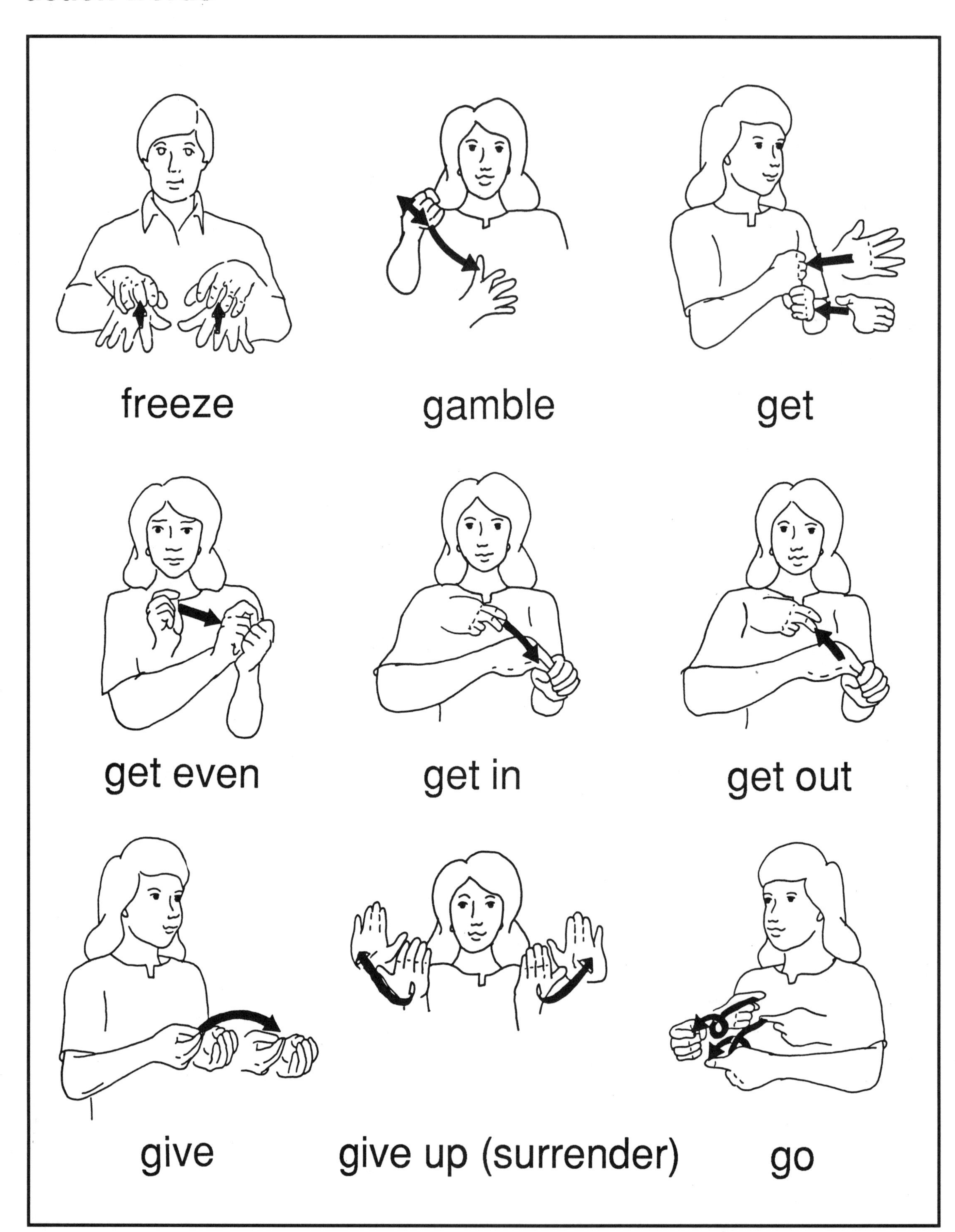
freeze
gamble
get
get even
get in
get out
give
give up (surrender)
go

grow
guard
guess
had
happen
has
hate
have

have to
heat
hide
hire
hit
hold
hold up
honor

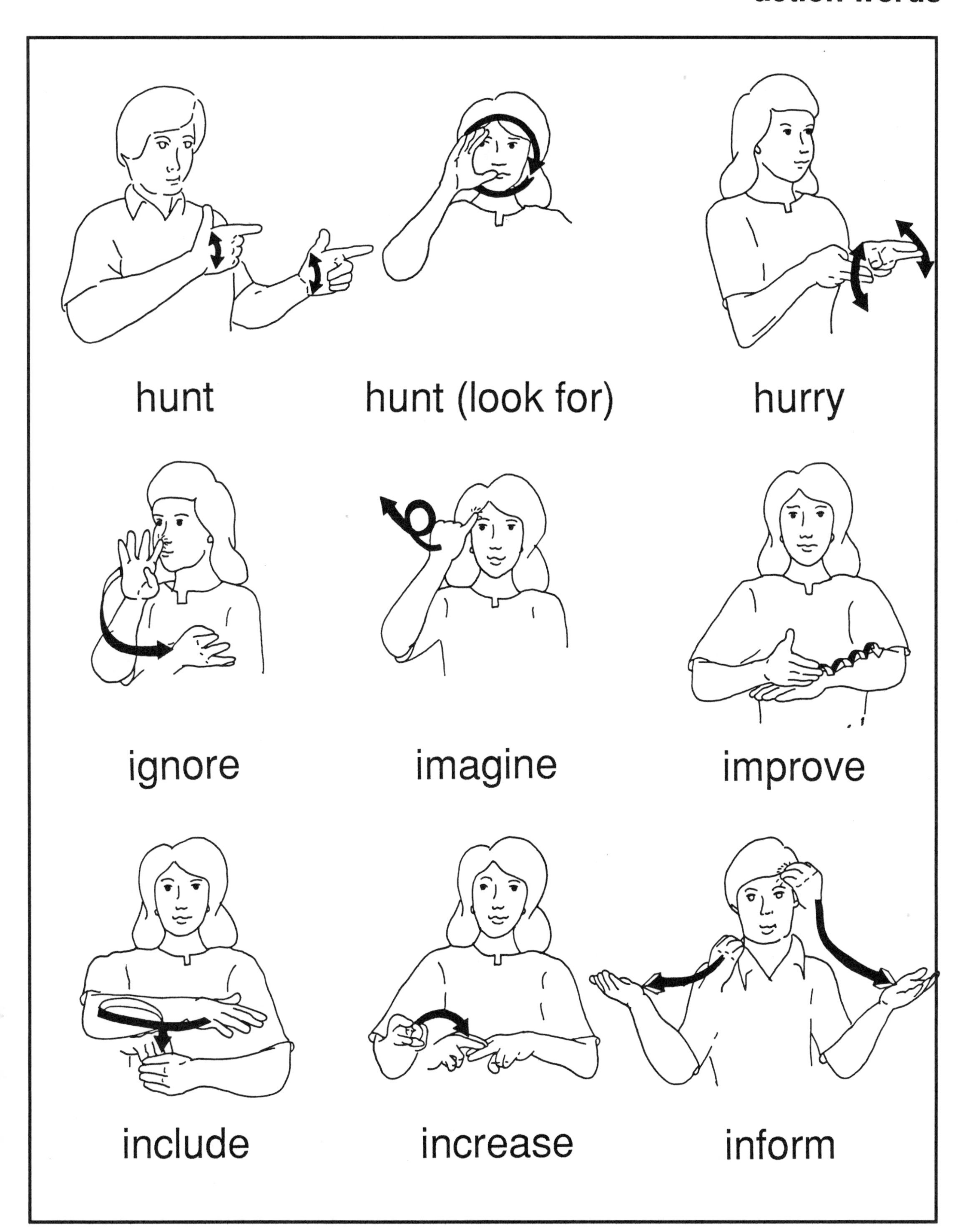
hunt
hunt (look for)
hurry
ignore
imagine
improve
include
increase
inform

inspect
intend
introduce
invent
invite
iron
is
isolate

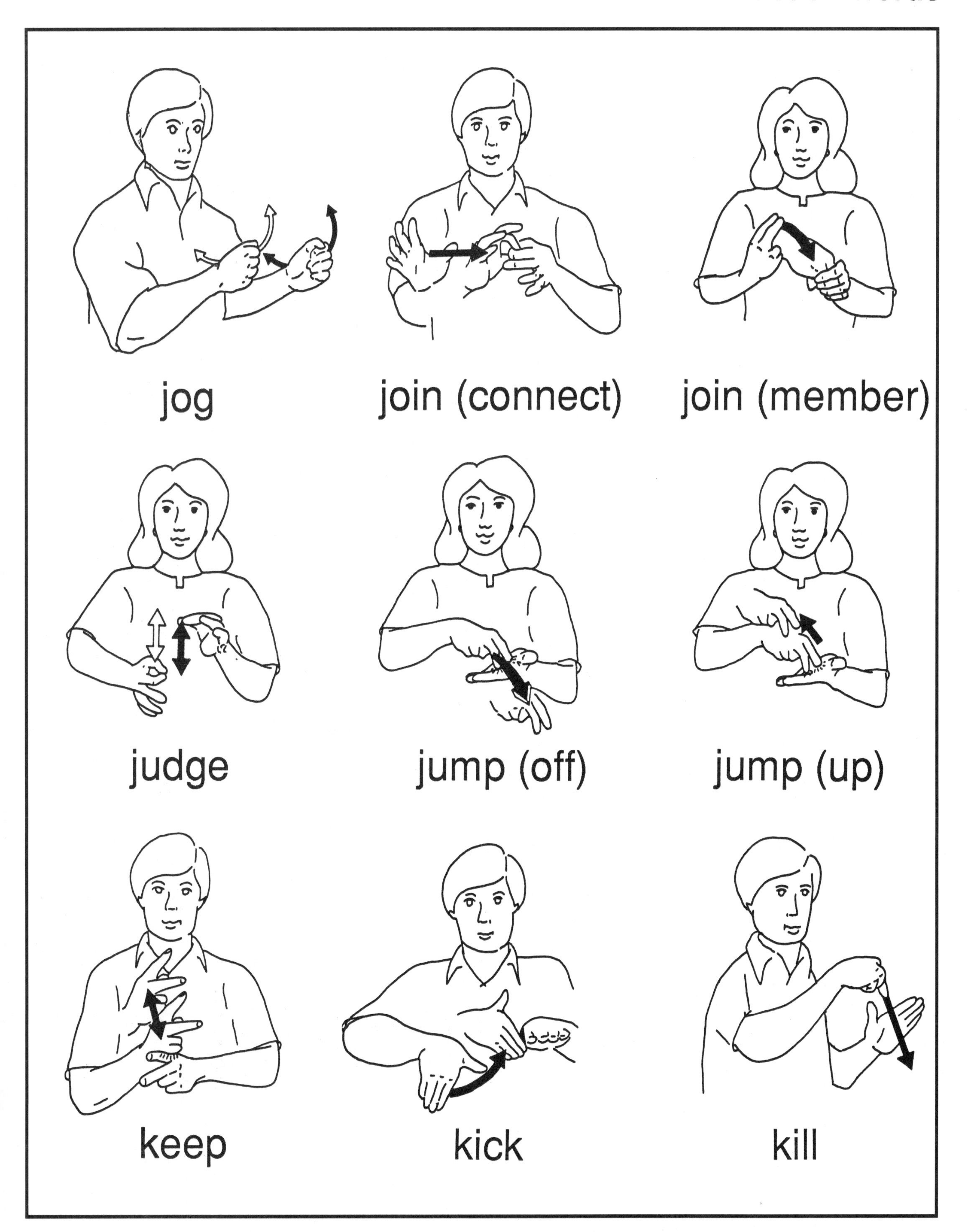
jog
join (connect)
join (member)
judge
jump (off)
jump (up)
keep
kick
kill

action words

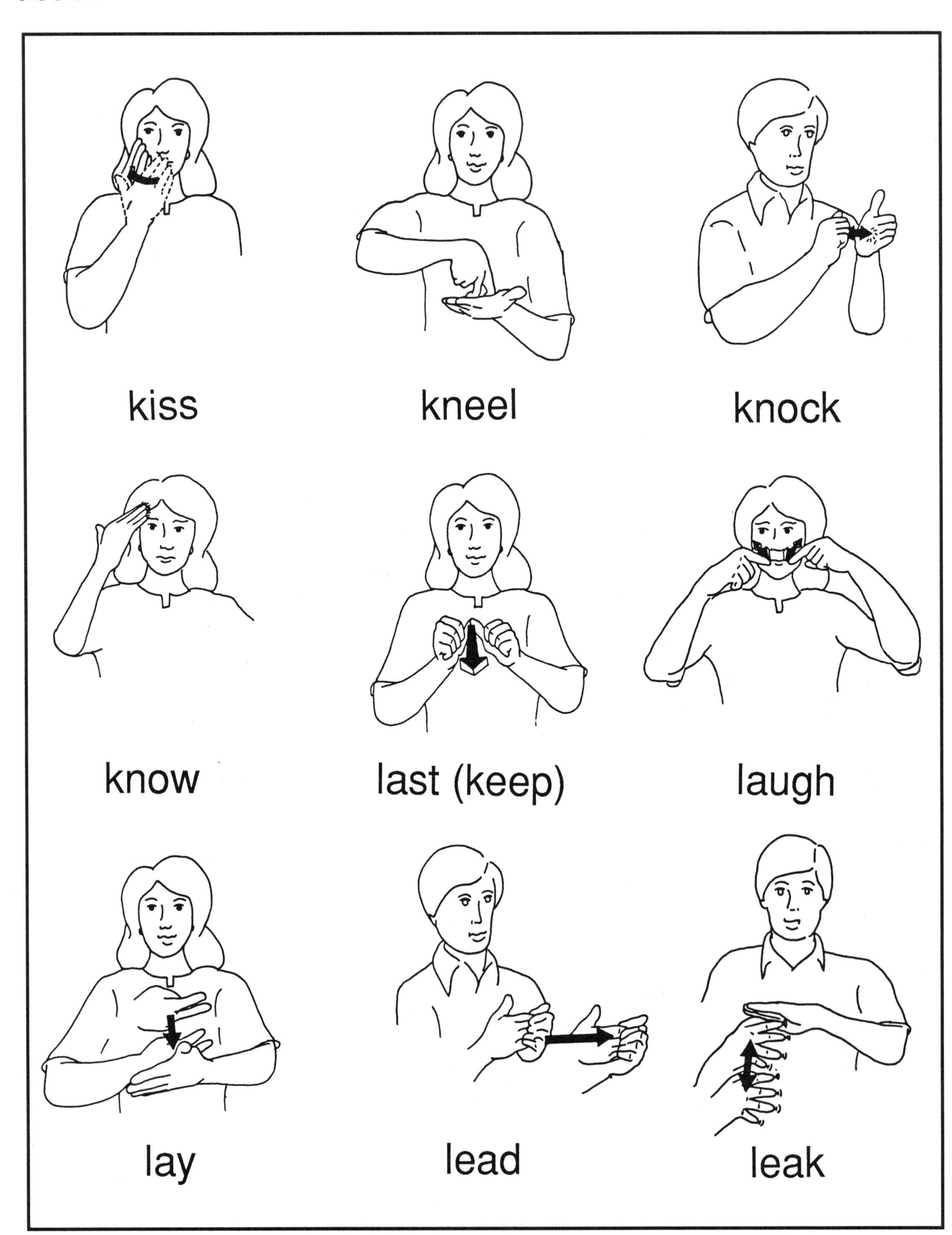

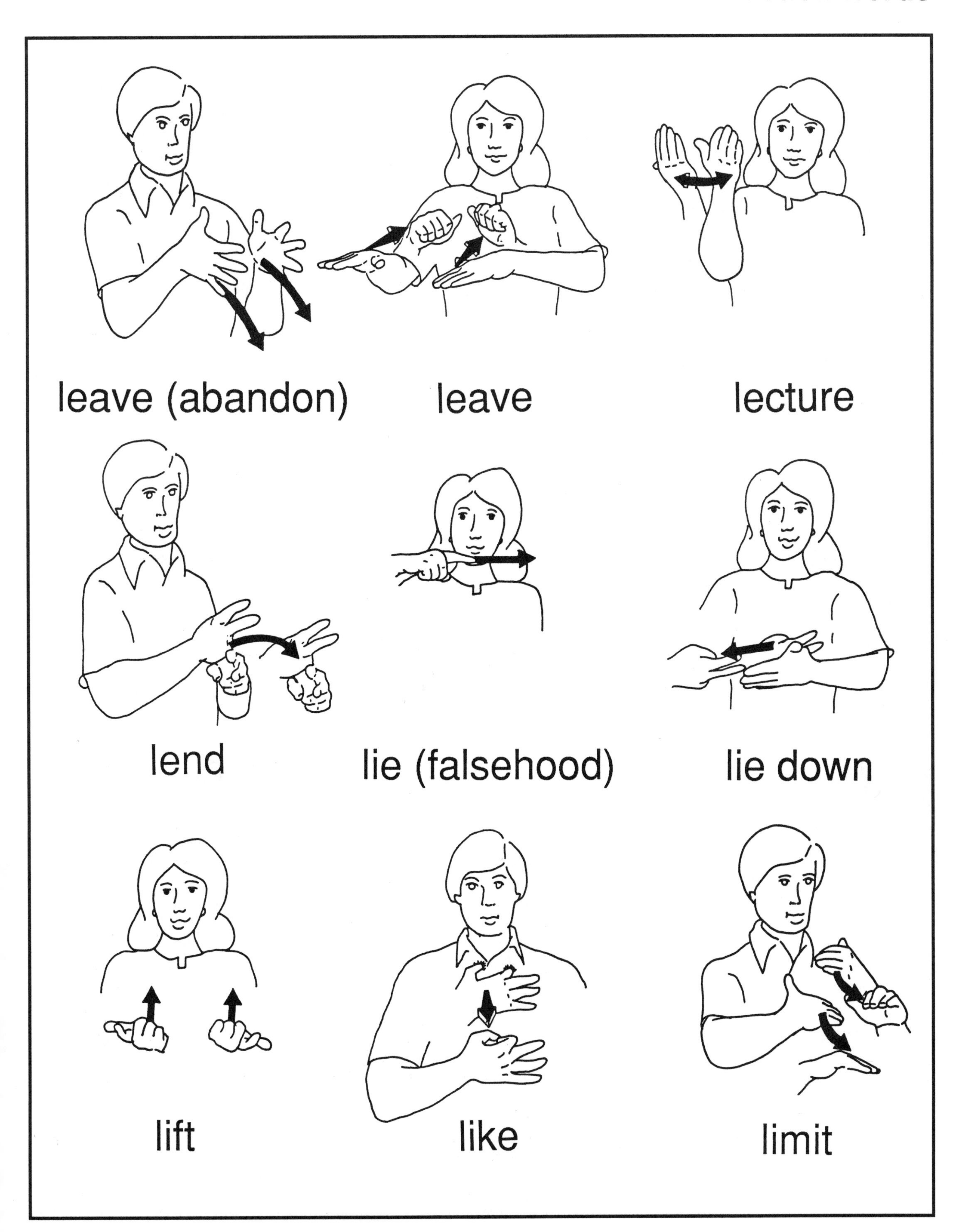
leave (abandon)
leave
lecture
lend
lie (falsehood)
lie down
lift
like
limit

action words

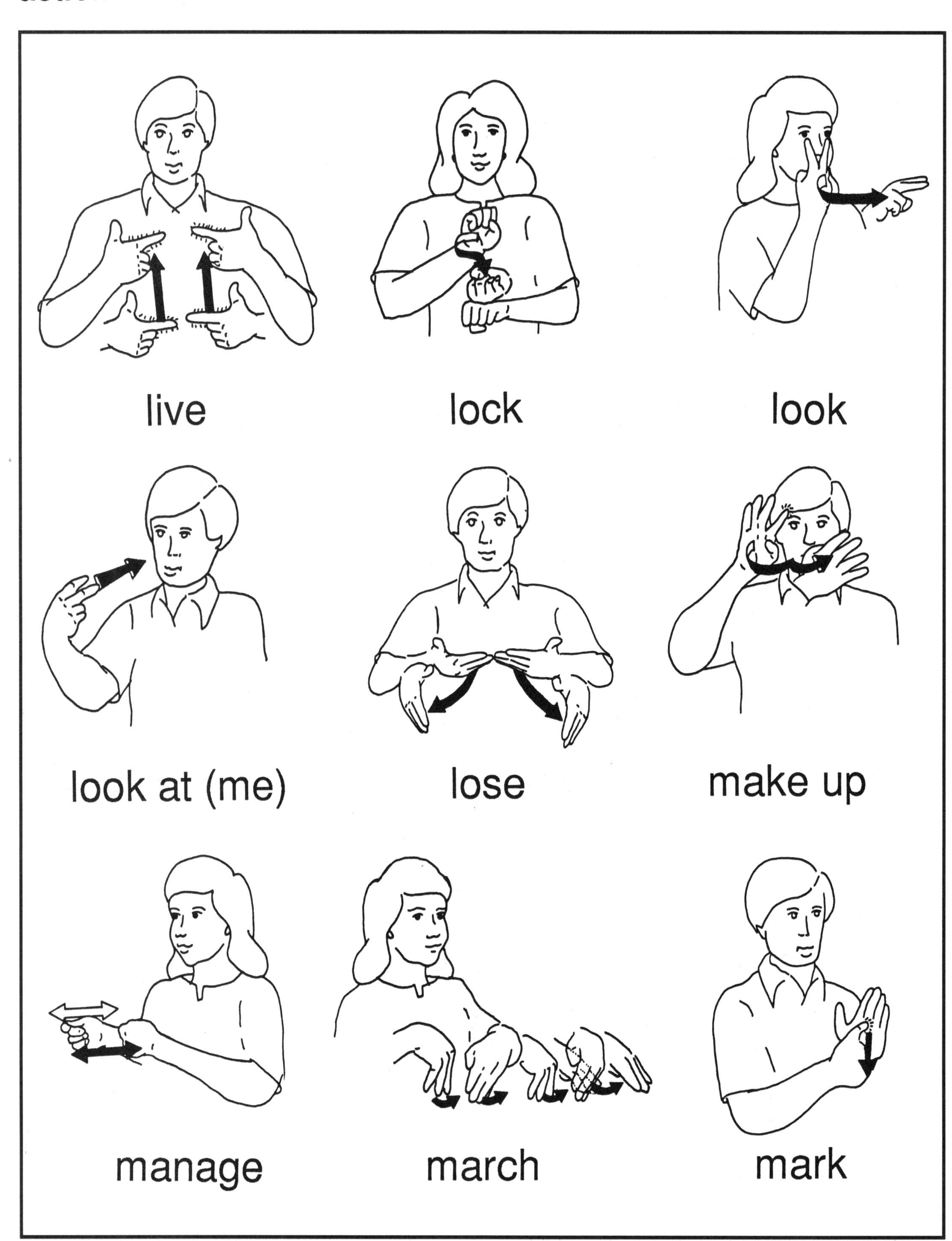

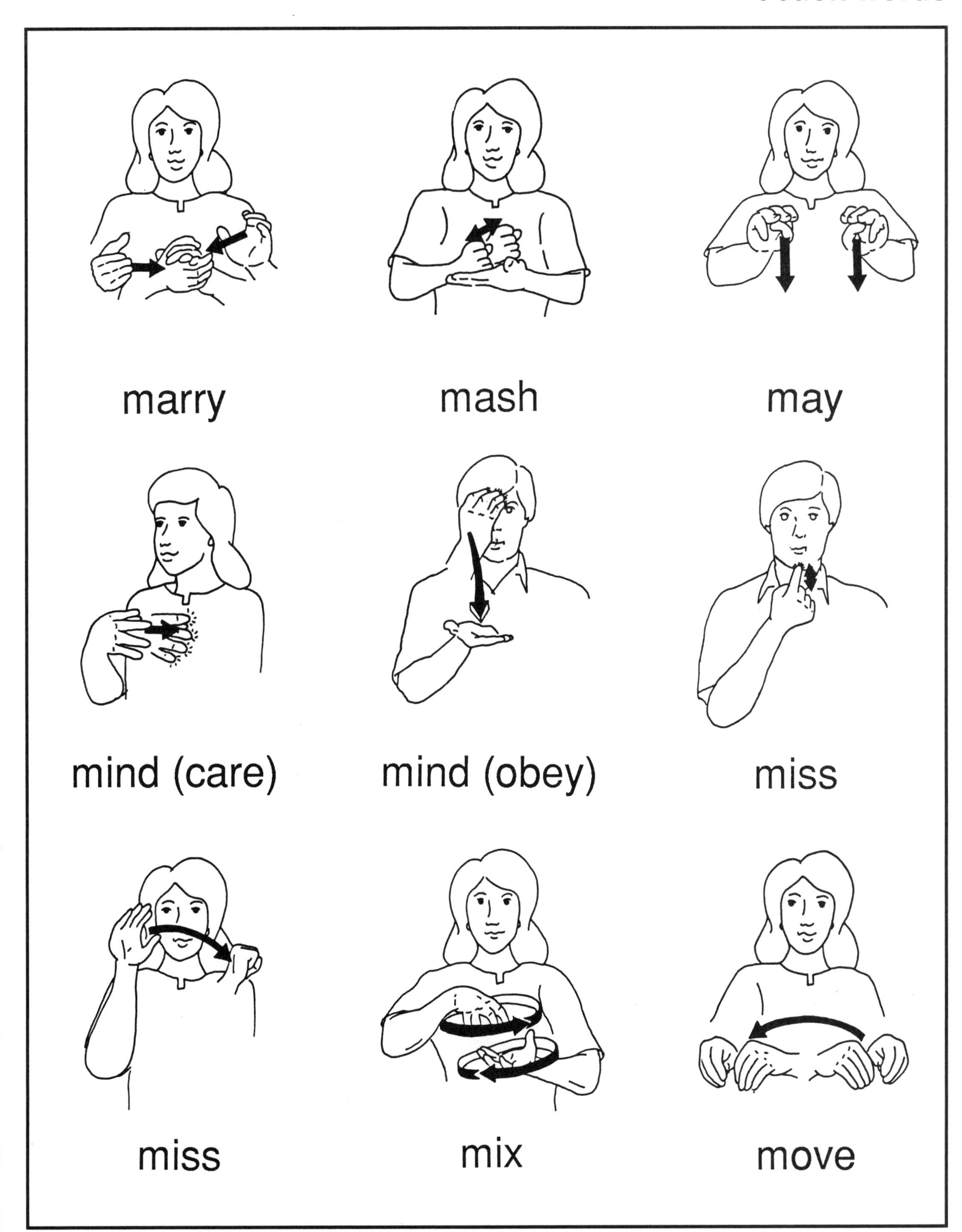
marry
mash
may
mind (care)
mind (obey)
miss
miss
mix
move

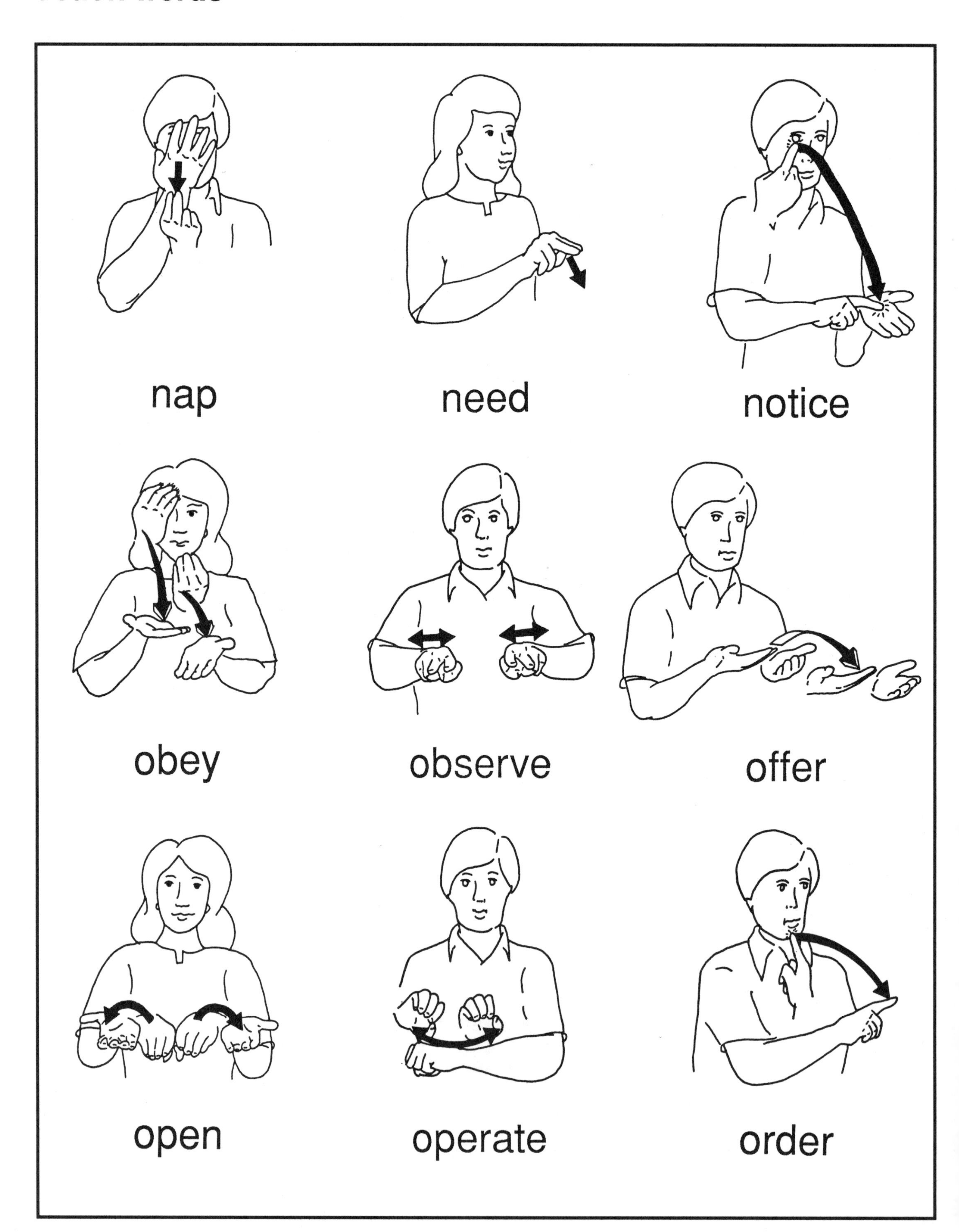
nap
need
notice
obey
observe
offer
open
operate
order

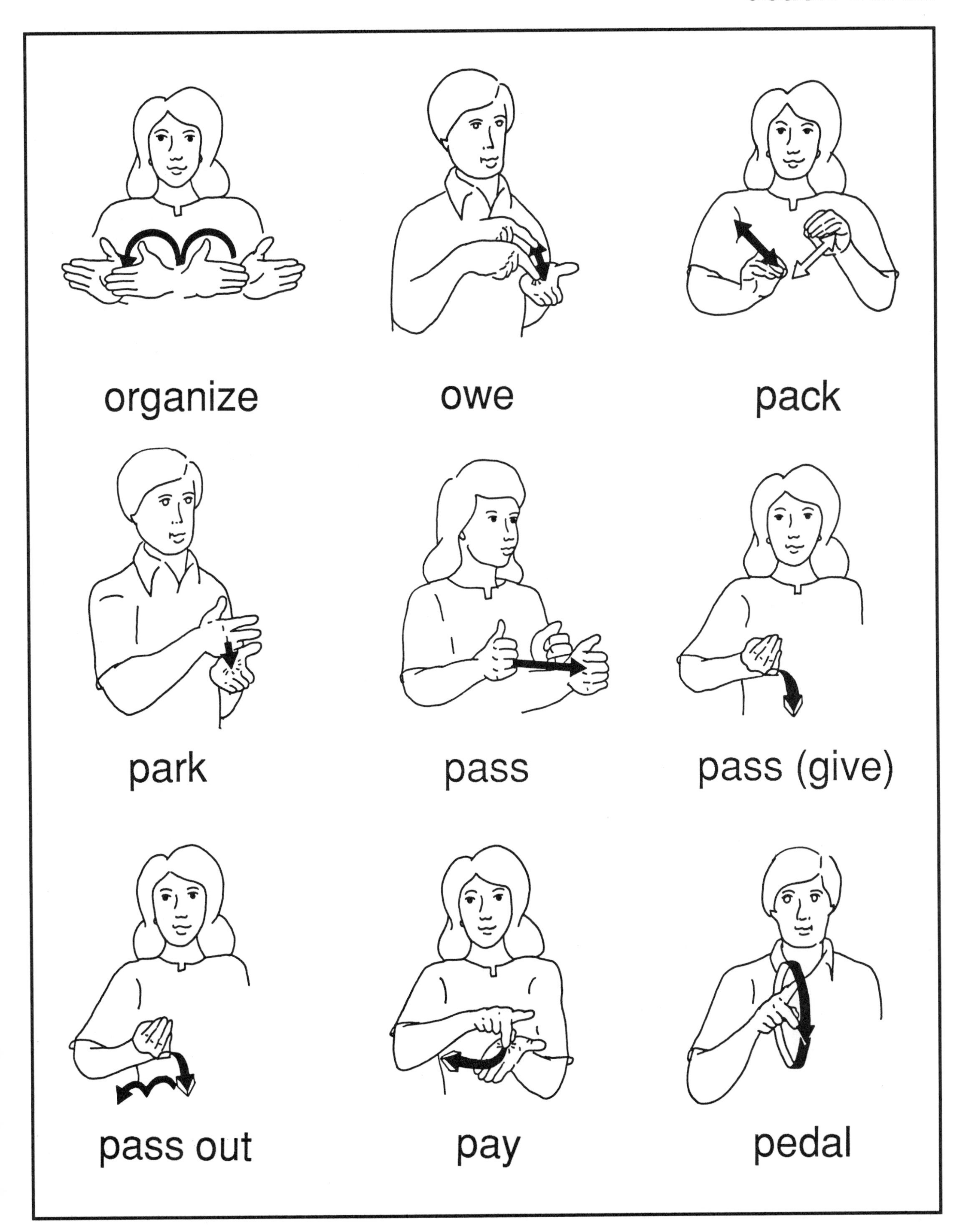
organize
owe
pack
park
pass
pass (give)
pass out
pay
pedal

peek
pet
pick (select)
pick up
pinch
pity
plan
plant
poke

polish
postpone
pound
pray
preach
prefer
prepare
pretend
prevent

progress
pronounce
protect
prove
pull
punish
push
put
put off

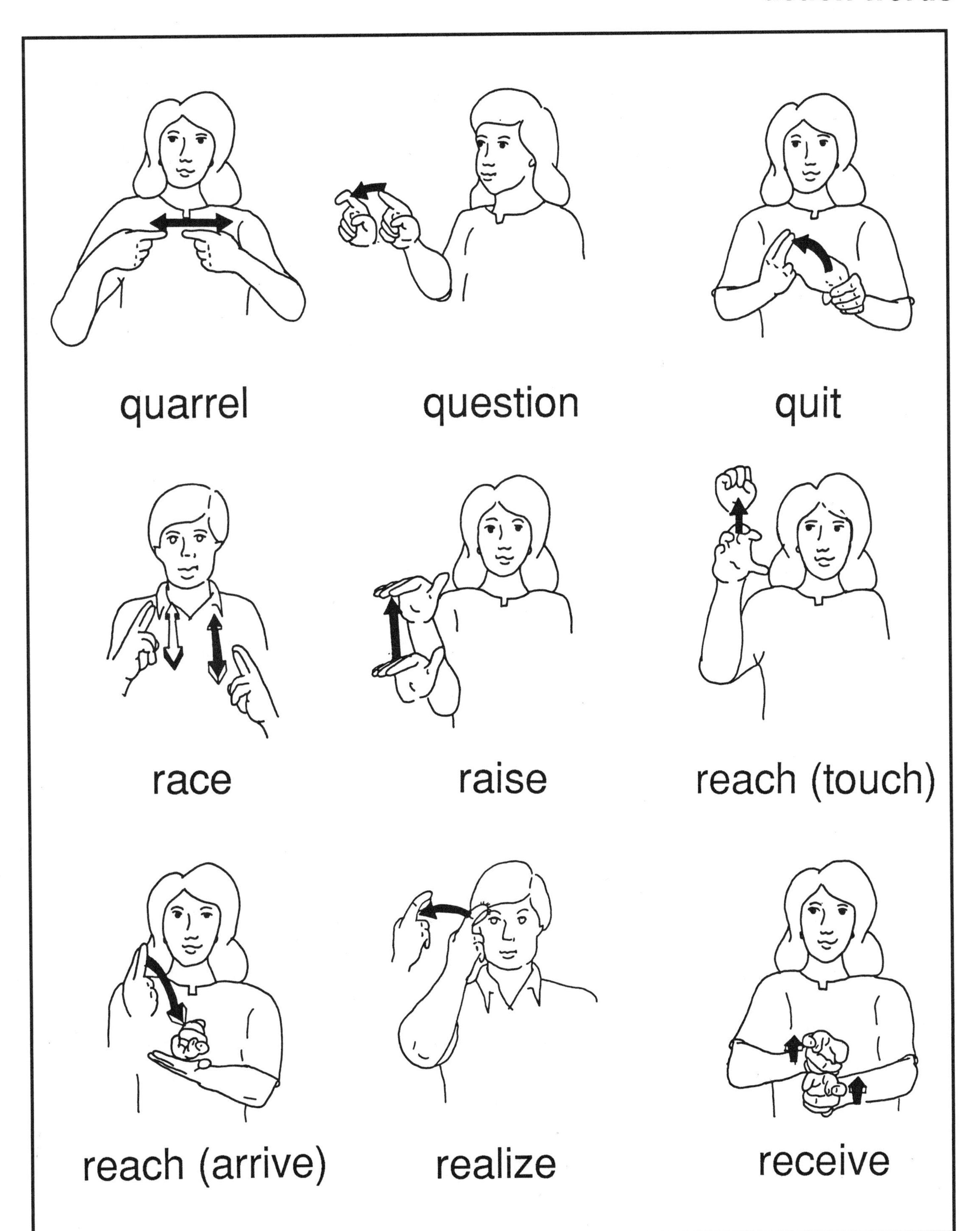
quarrel
question
quit
race
raise
reach (touch)
reach (arrive)
realize
receive

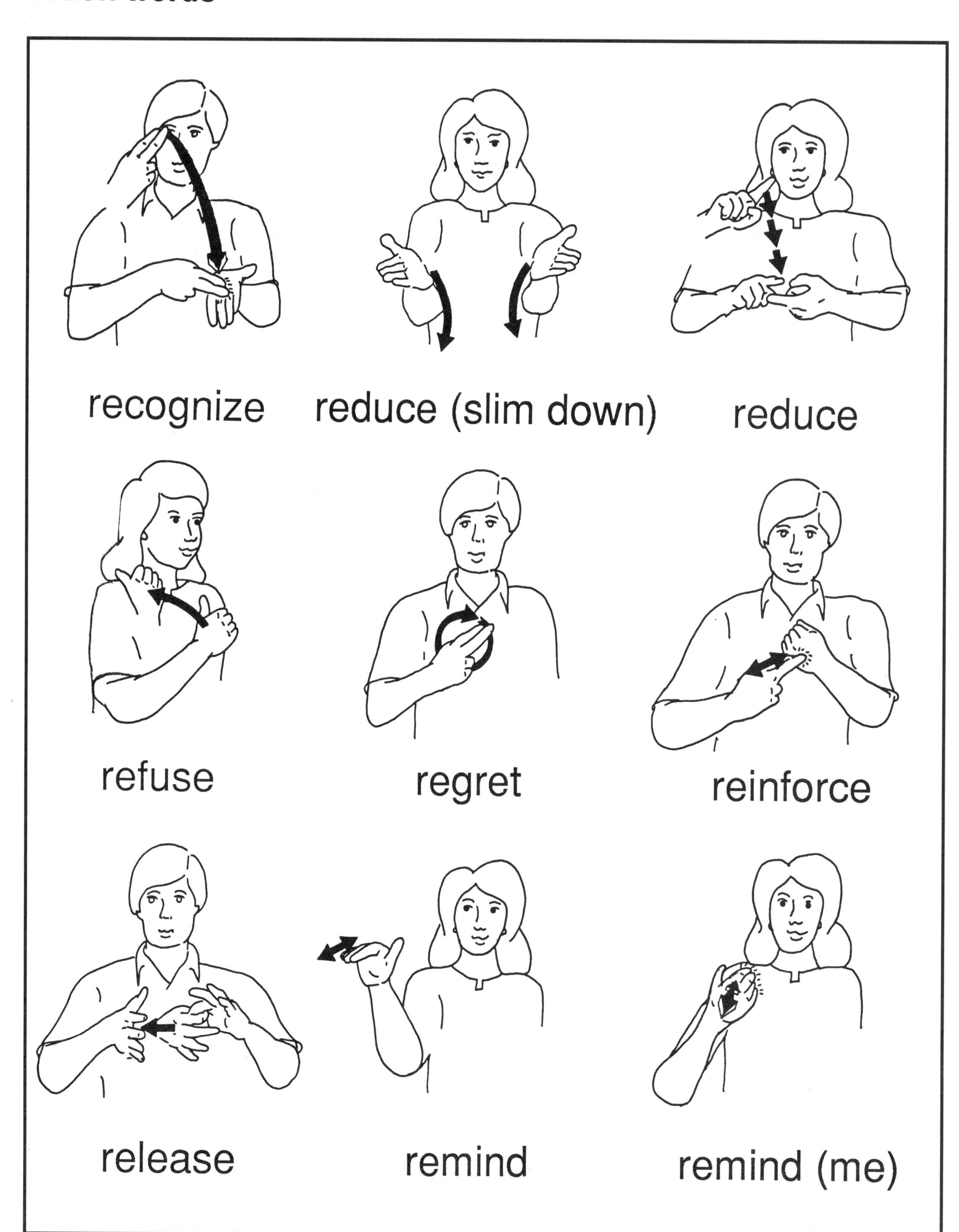
recognize
reduce (slim down)
reduce
refuse
regret
reinforce
release
remind
remind (me)

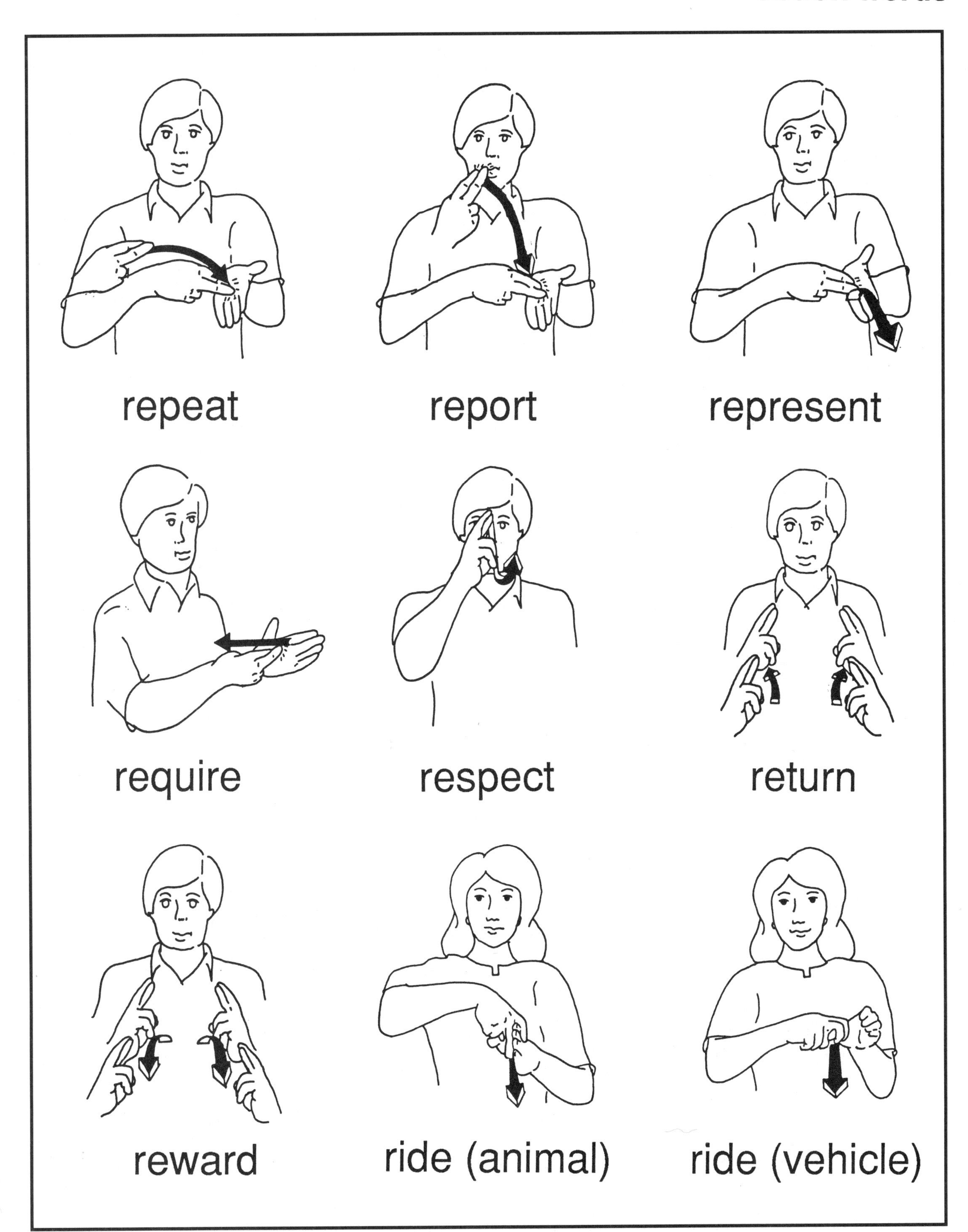
repeat
report
represent
require
respect
return
reward
ride (animal)
ride (vehicle)

rob
rock
rub
ruin
sail
save
saw (cut)
say
scare

scold
scrape
scream
see
seem
sell
send
separate
serve

settle
sew
shake
share
shave
shoot
shop
should
show

show (me)
show off
sign
sign (signature)
sing
sit
slap
sleep
smell

smile
smoke
spell
spoil
squeeze
stand
stay
steal

step
stop
stuck
summarize
supervise
suspect
swallow
swear
take

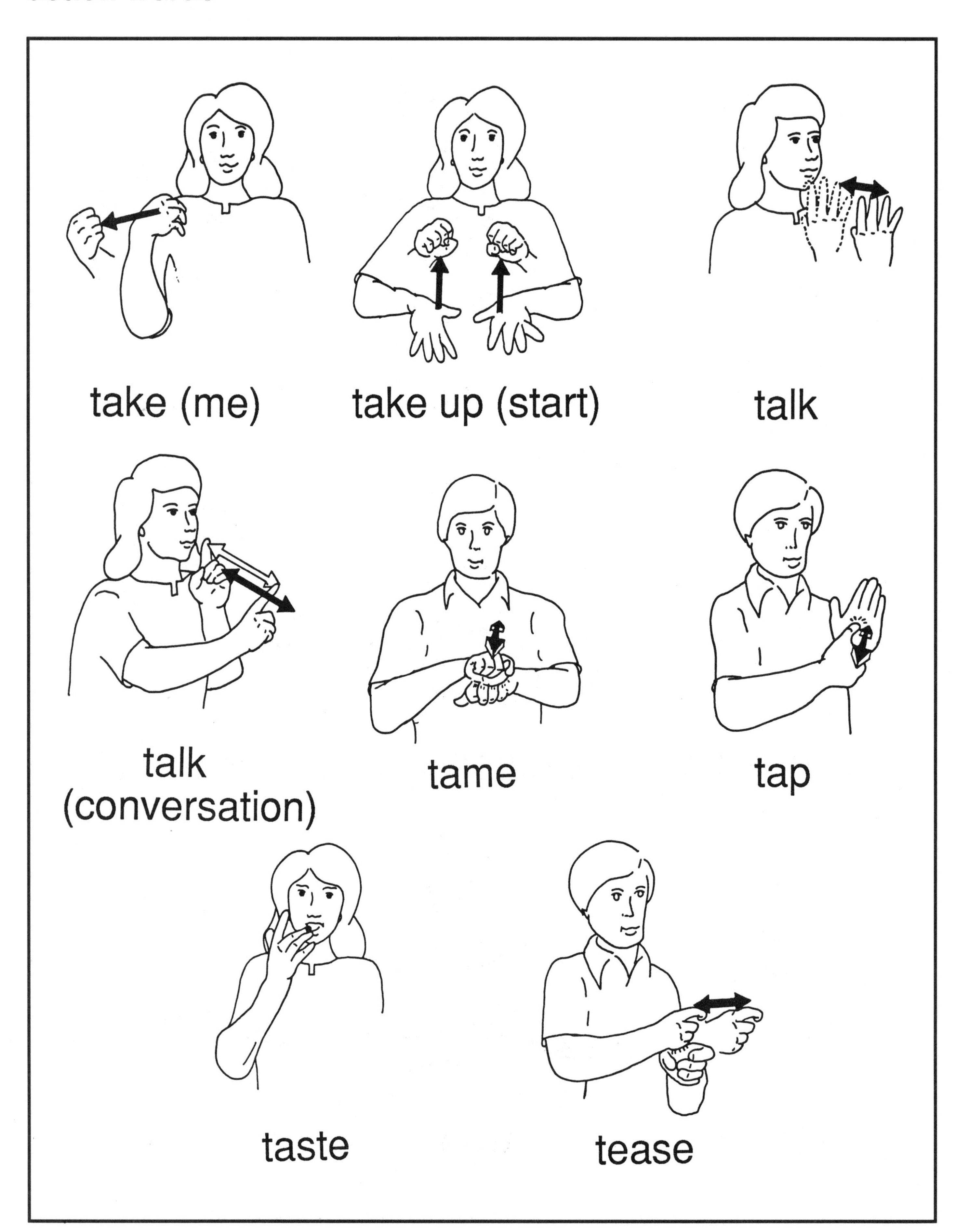
take (me)
take up (start)
talk
talk (conversation)
tame
tap
taste
tease

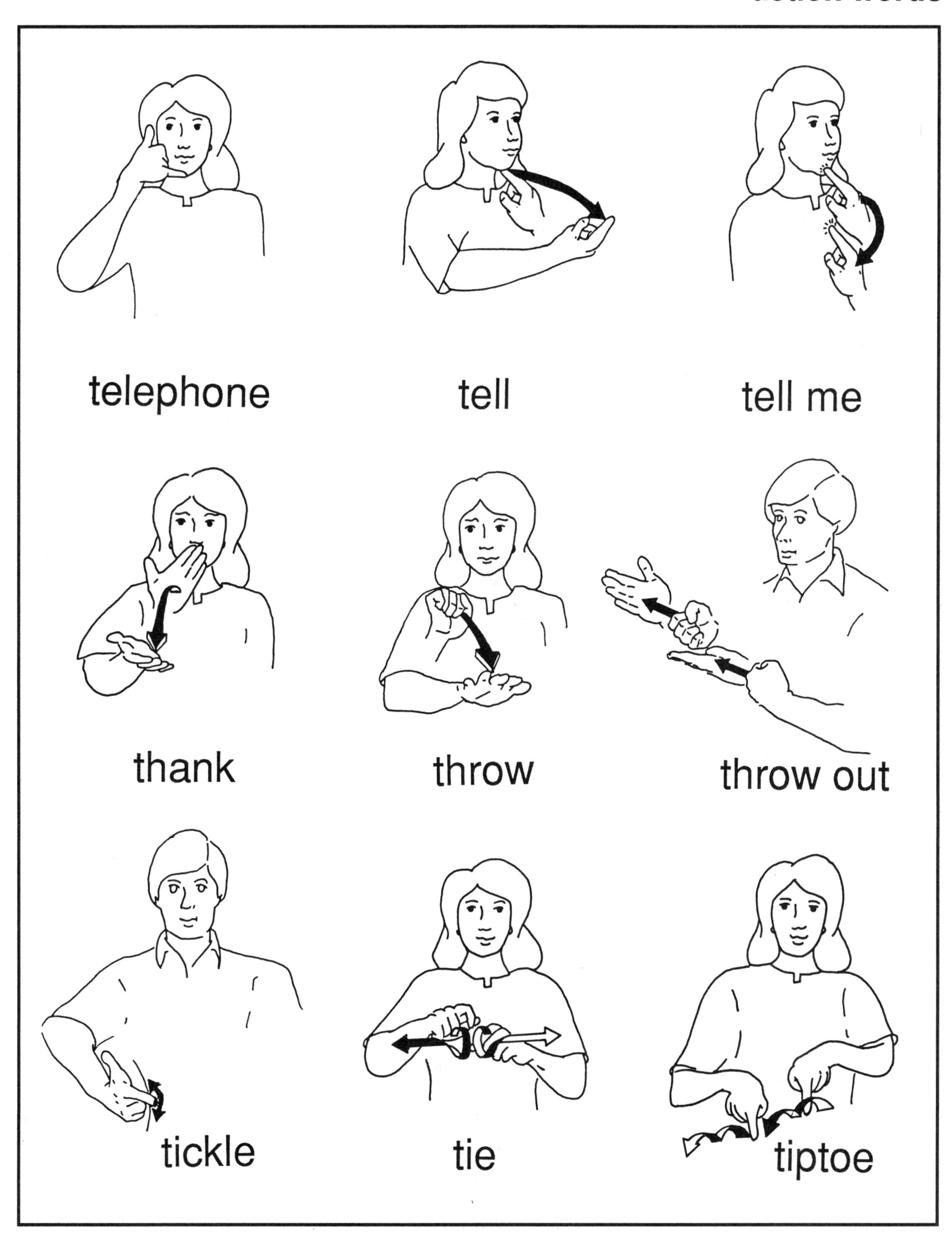
telephone
tell
tell me
thank
throw
throw out
tickle
tie
tiptoe

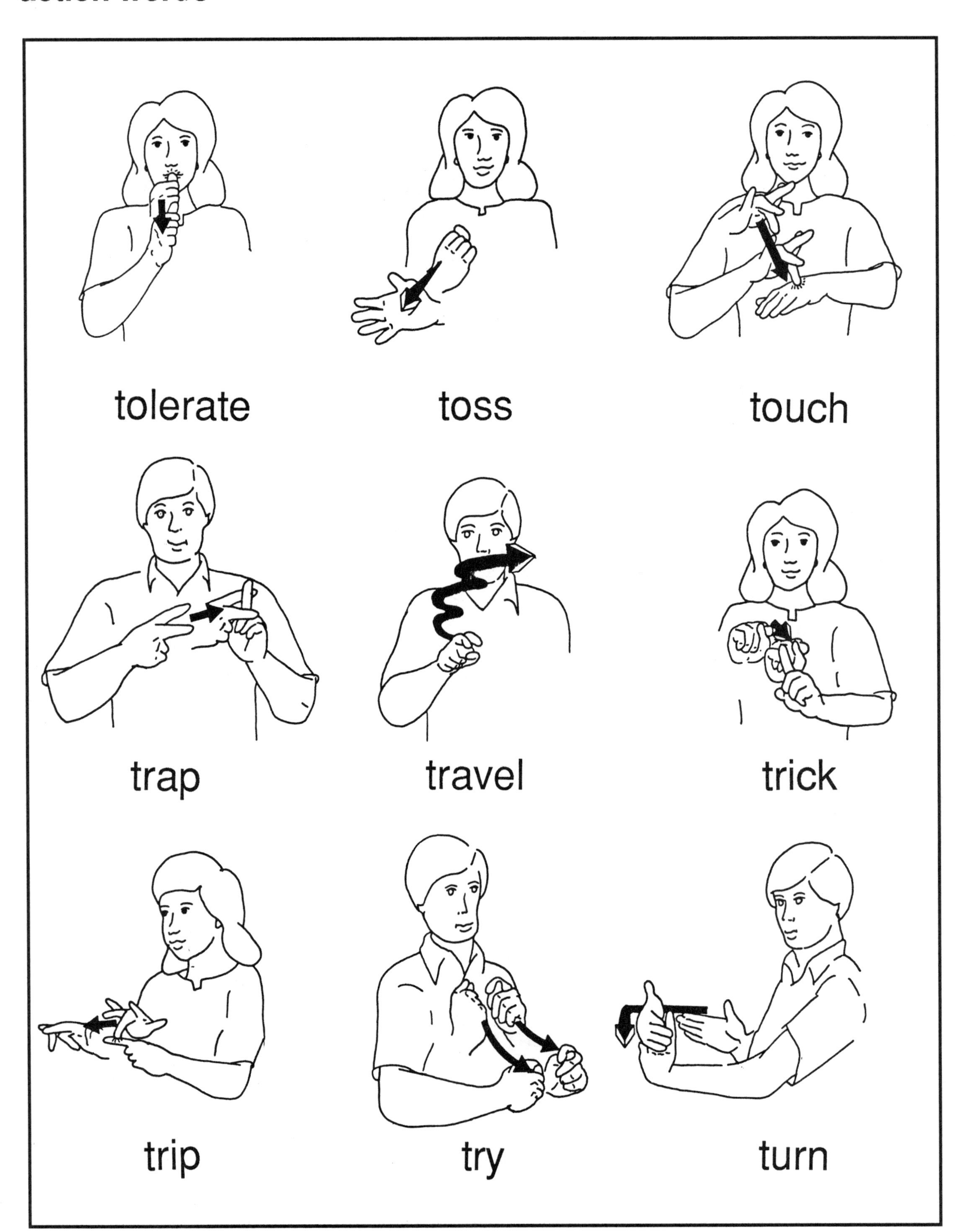
tolerate
toss
touch
trap
travel
trick
trip
try
turn

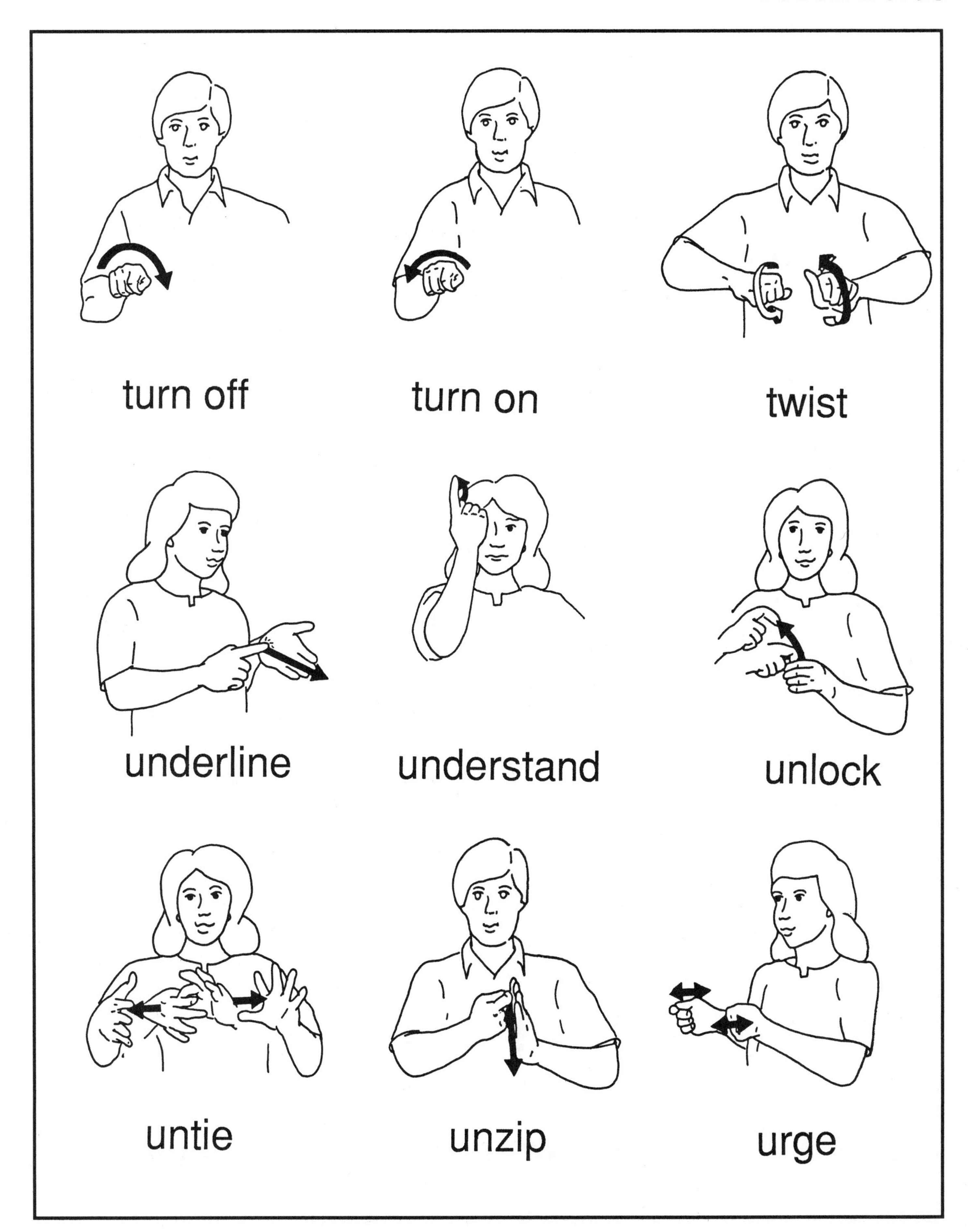
turn off
turn on
twist
underline
understand
unlock
untie
unzip
urge

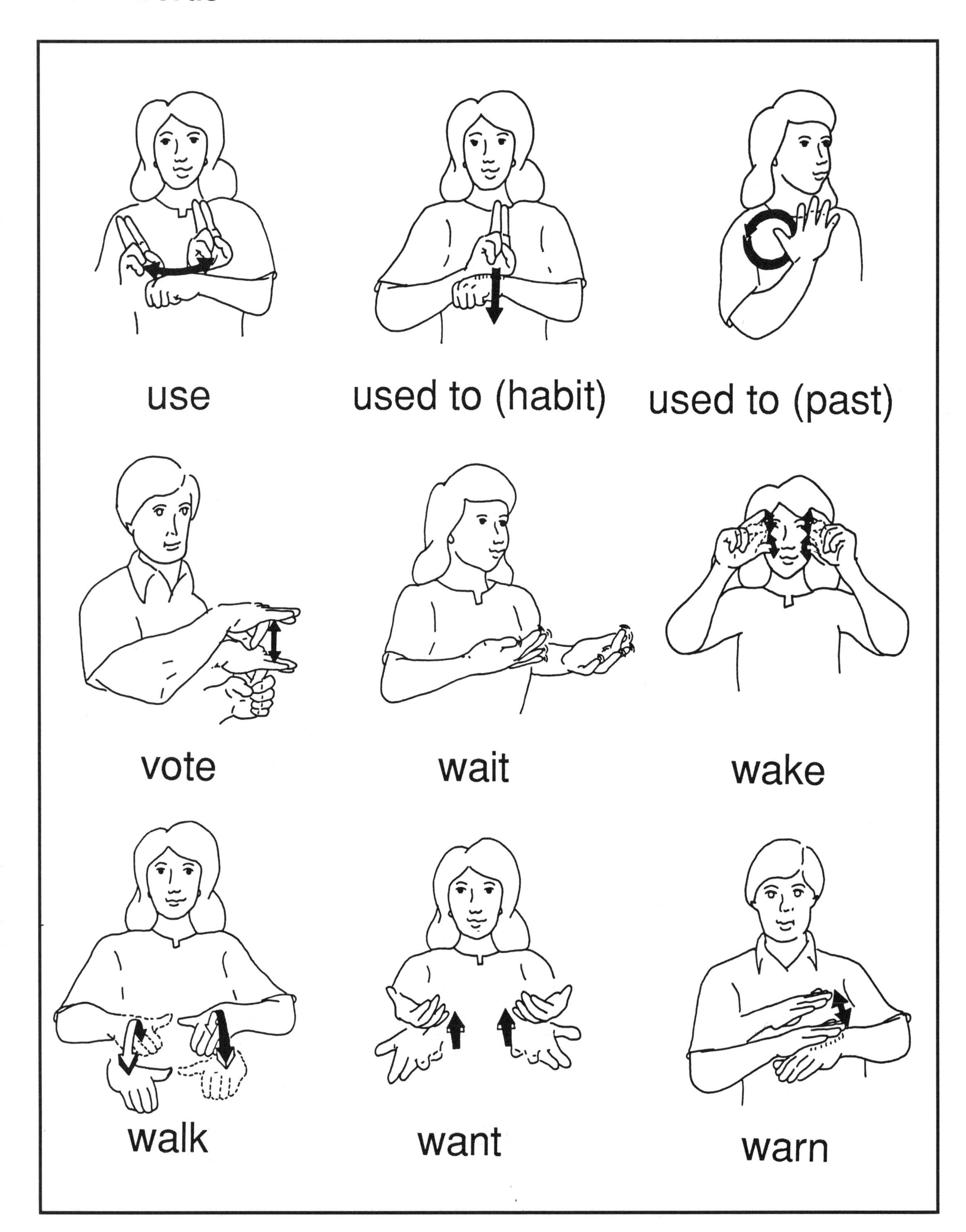
use
used to (habit)
used to (past)
vote
wait
wake
walk
want
warn

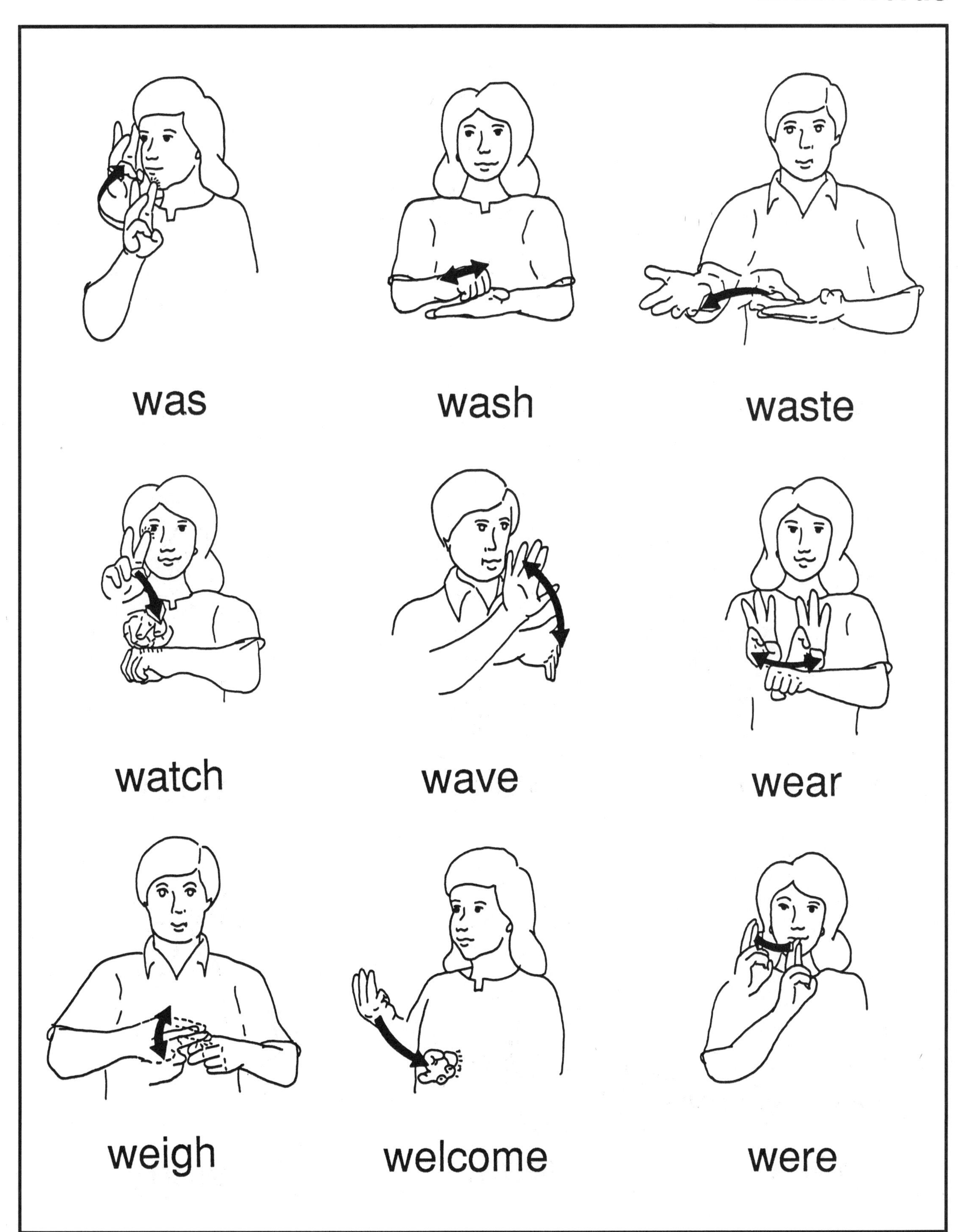
was
wash
waste
watch
wave
wear
weigh
welcome
were

whisper
will
win
wind (up)
wish
wonder
won't
work
worry

NOTE:

Directional verbs are signs that can vary their direction of movement according to the spatial location of the subject and /or object of the verb (Baker and Cokeley, 1980, p 229). Some examples of this are : remind, give, show, tell, and put.

ADJECTIVES

a lot
abstract
advance
afraid
alike
all [1]
all gone
alone
angry
around [1]
artificial
average
awful
bad [2]
bare
basic
beautiful
beauty
best [2]
big [1]
bitter
bore
both [2]
bottom
brave
bright
bright (intelligent)
broken
calm
careful
careless
clumsy
correct
cracked
cute
dangerous
dead
dear
deep
delicious
different [2]
difficult
each [2]
easy
empty
end [1]
enough
equal
even [2]
every [2]
evil
exact
except [2]
expensive
fair
fake
false
famous
fancy
fantastic
fast [1]
favorite [2]
few
final
fine
flexible
free
fresh
frighten
full
full (food)
funny [2]
general
great [2]
handsome
hard [2]
heavy
high [2]
honest
horrible
hot [2]
huge
important
independent
intelligent
international
large
last [1]
less than
level
light
little [1]
little bit
long [2] (length)
loose
loud
low
many [2]
marvelous
mean [1]
medium
more [2]
most
narrow
new [2]
nice [2]
none
normal
nude
perfect
plenty
polite
poor
pretty [2]

ADJECTIVES
(con't.)

quick
quiet
ready
really [1]
responsible
rich
right [1]
rough
safe
same [2]
selfish
several
shame
sharp
short
similar
simple
sloppy
slow
small
smart
smooth
soft [2]
some [1]
sour
special
sticky
stingy
strange
strong
sure
sweet
tall
terrible
that [1]
these [1]
thick
thin
thirsty
this [1]
those
top [2]
tough
true
ugly
unfair
upside down
vague
various
very [2]
whole [1]
wide
wild
wise
wonderful
worse
wrong
young

ACTIVITY - ADJECTIVES

Purpose: To use adjectives correctly in describing familar objects, and to develop language patterns.

Materials: Chalkboard and chalk; list of adjectives; pictures of different objects.

Procedure:

1. Adult writes three adjectives on chalkboard, e.g., ugly, beautiful, fat, signing/saying each.
2. Adult shows picture to child signing/saying, "Is the dog ugly?"
3. Child signs/says, "No, the dog is not ugly."
4. Adult signs/says the next adjective on the board, "Is the dog fat?"
5. Child signs/says appropriate response, "Yes, the dog is fat."
6. Adult repeats procedures 1 through 5 with three different adjectives and another picture.

Variations: Child can cut pictures out of magazines for a scrapbook and write appropriate adjectives to describe picture; child can identify objects in the environment and sign/say appropriate adjective for each object; child can identify and sign/say opposites, e.g., big - little; fat - skinny.

ADJECTIVES

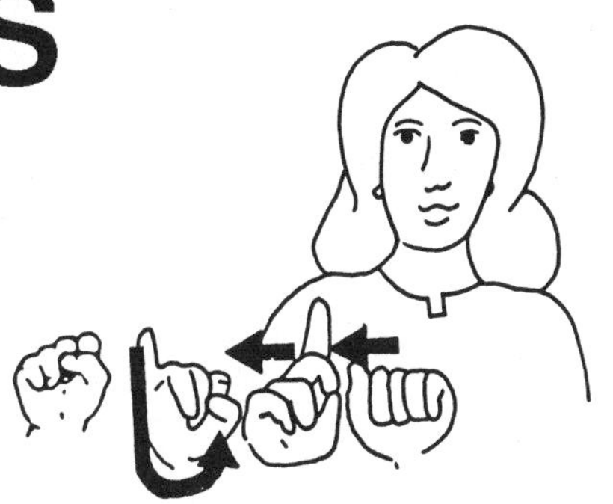

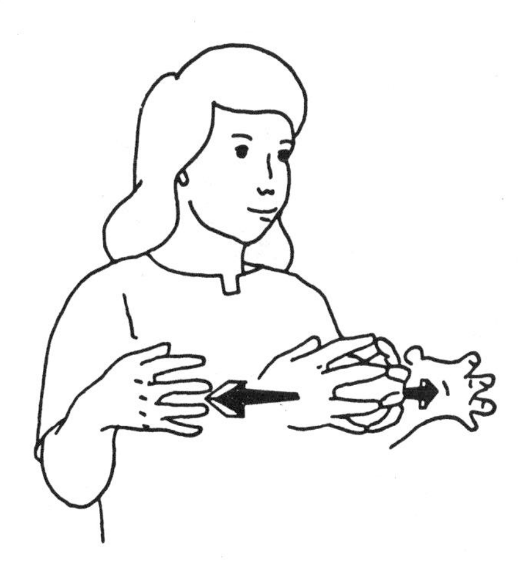

a lot

abstract

advance

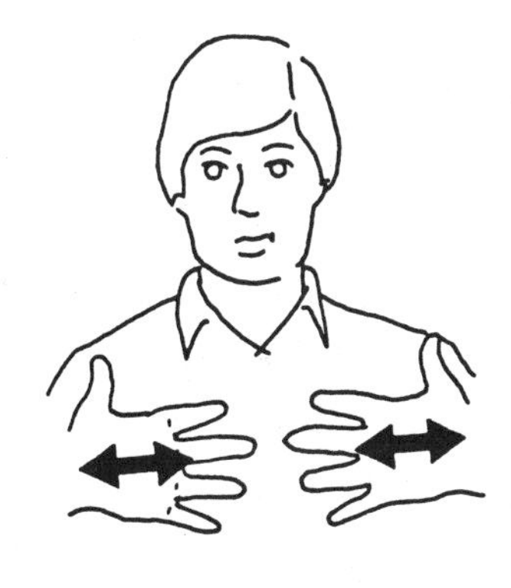

afraid

alike

ADJECTIVES

1. Yes, that looks ______.

2. I think you did ______.

3. Show me the _____ pictures.

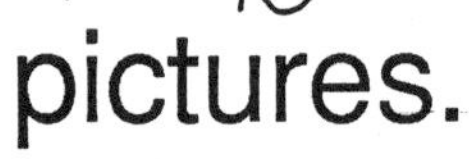

4. Where is the _____ man?

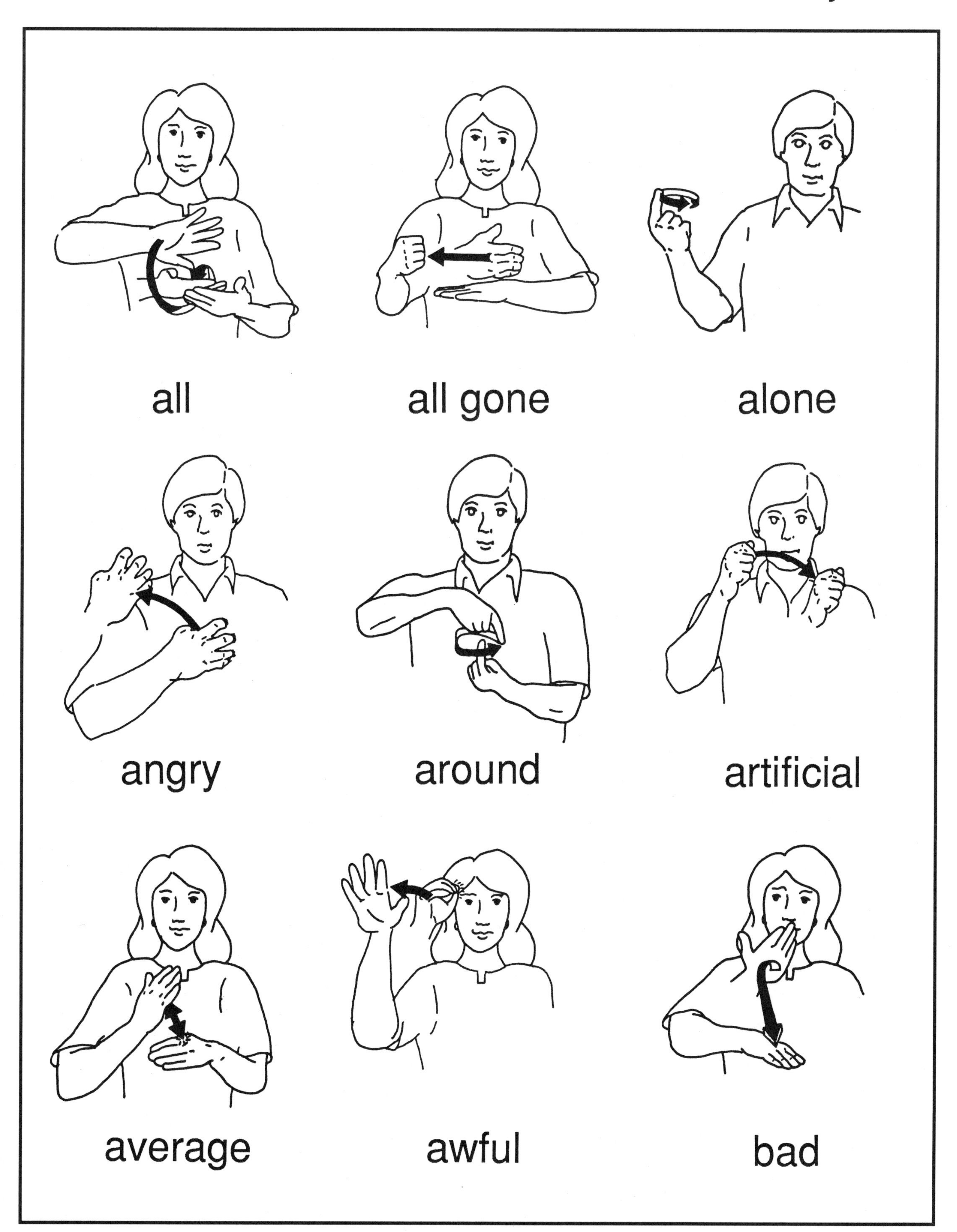
all
all gone
alone
angry
around
artificial
average
awful
bad

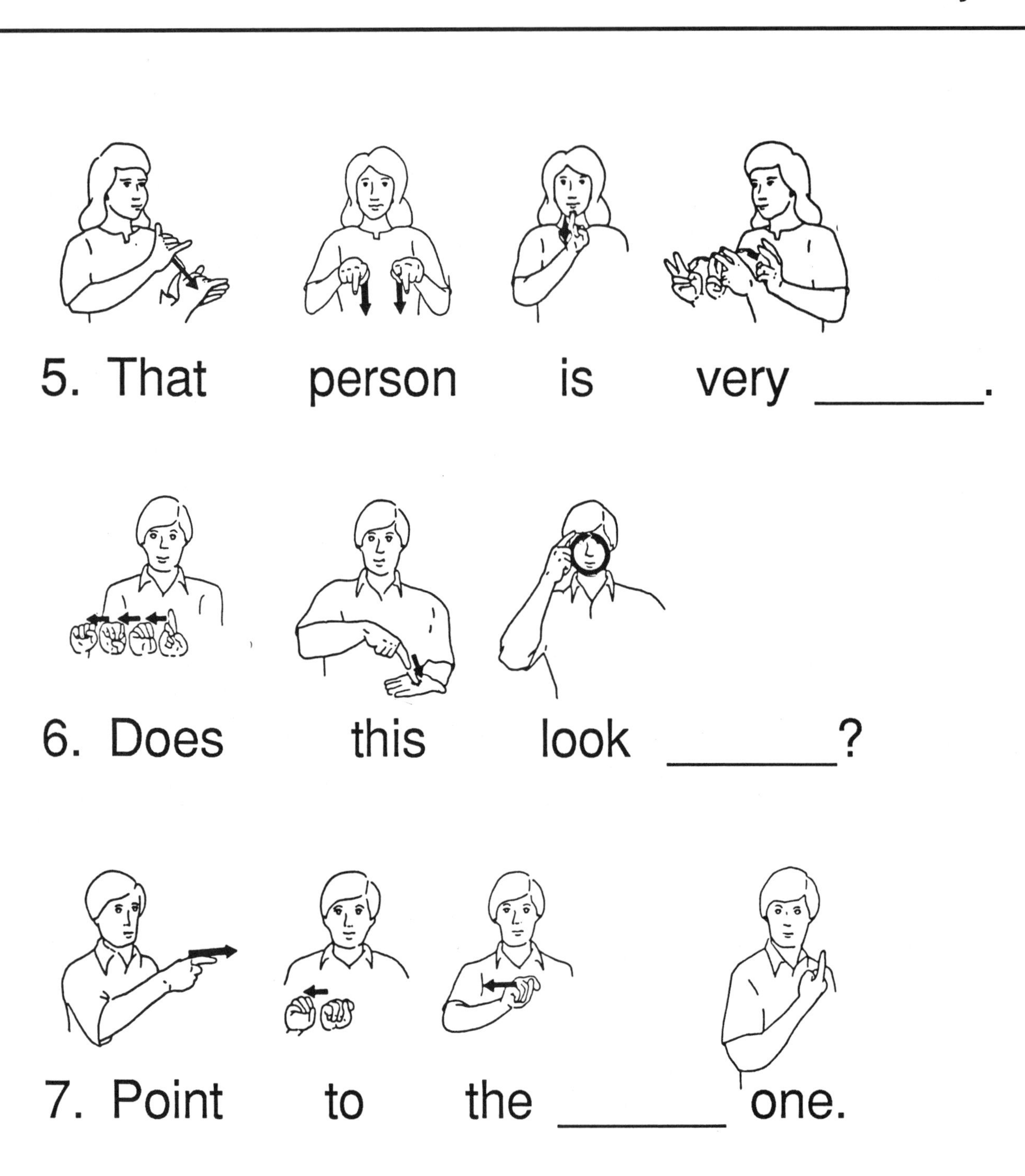

5. That person is very ______.

6. Does this look ______?

7. Point to the ______ one.

8. Please spell ______.

bare
basic
beautiful
beauty
best
big
bitter
bore
both

bottom
brave
bright
bright (intelligent)
broken
calm
careful
careless
clumsy

common
correct
cracked
cute
dangerous
dead
dear
deep
delicious

different
difficult
each
easy
empty
end
enough
equal

even
every
evil
exact
except
expensive
fair
fake
false

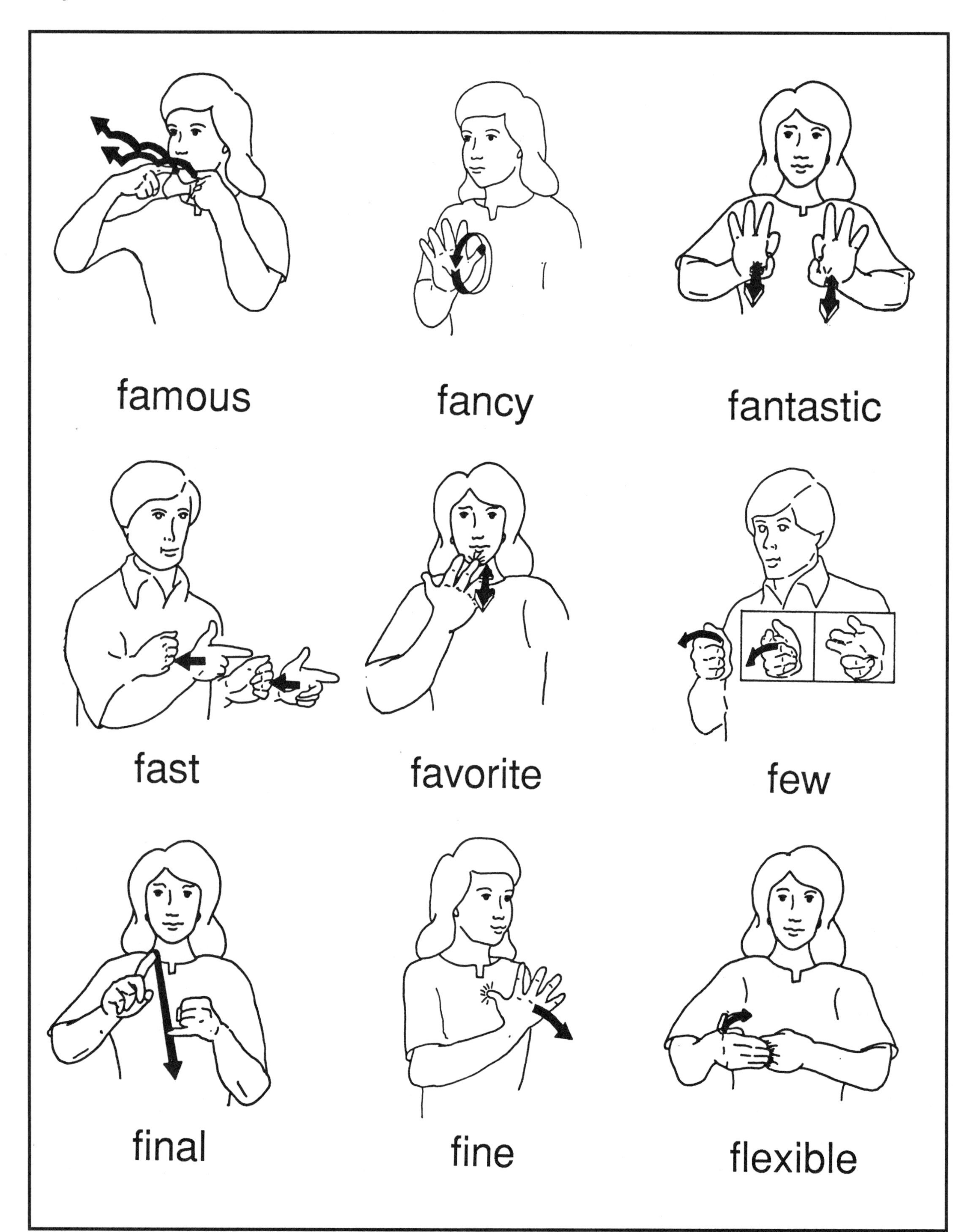
famous
fancy
fantastic
fast
favorite
few
final
fine
flexible

free
fresh
frighten
full
full (food)
funny
general
great

handsome
hard
heavy
high
honest
horrible
hot

huge
important
independent
intelligent
international
large
last
less than
level

light
little
little bit
long (length)
loose
loud
low
many
marvelous

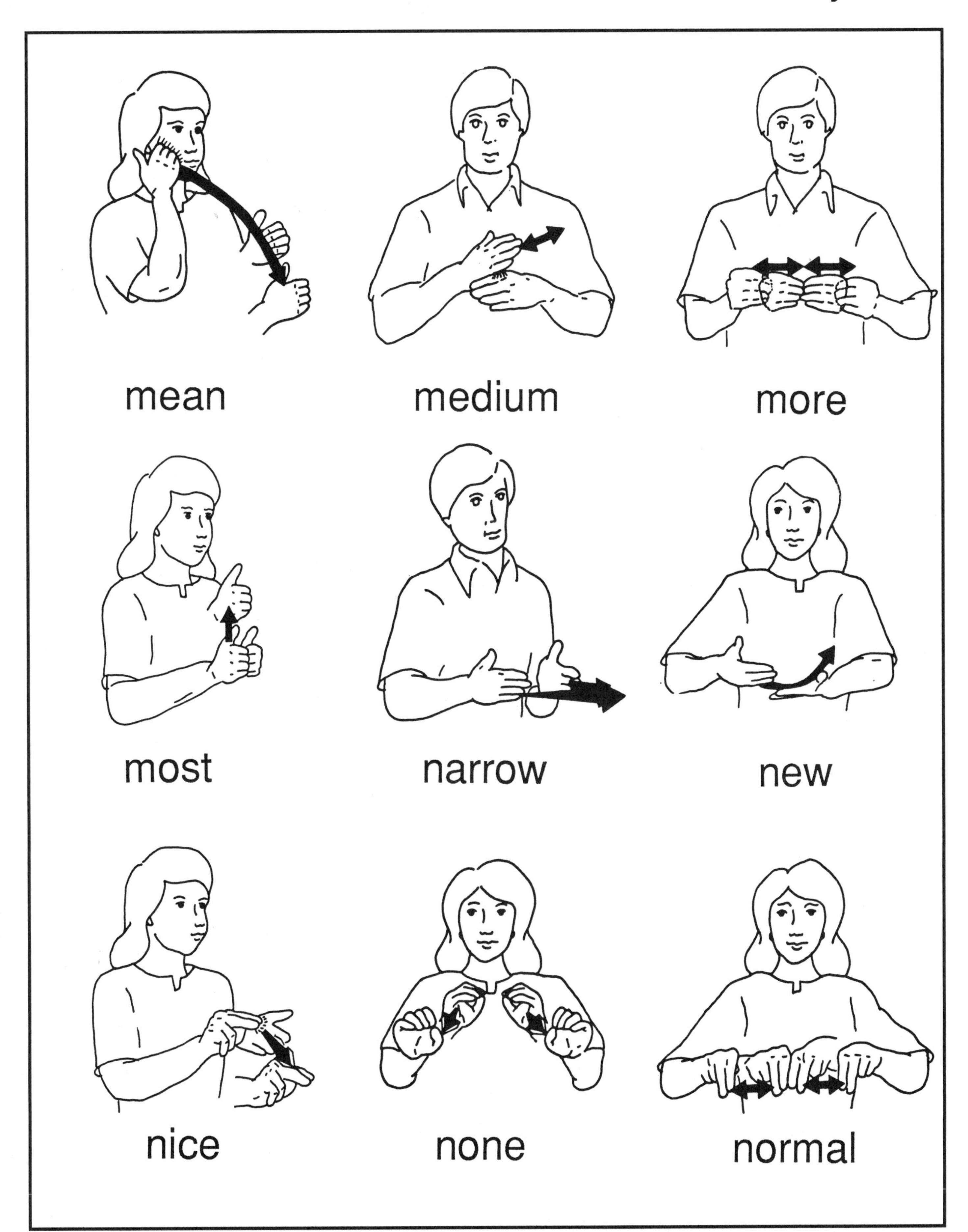
mean
medium
more
most
narrow
new
nice
none
normal

nude
perfect
plenty
polite
poor
pretty
quick
quiet
ready

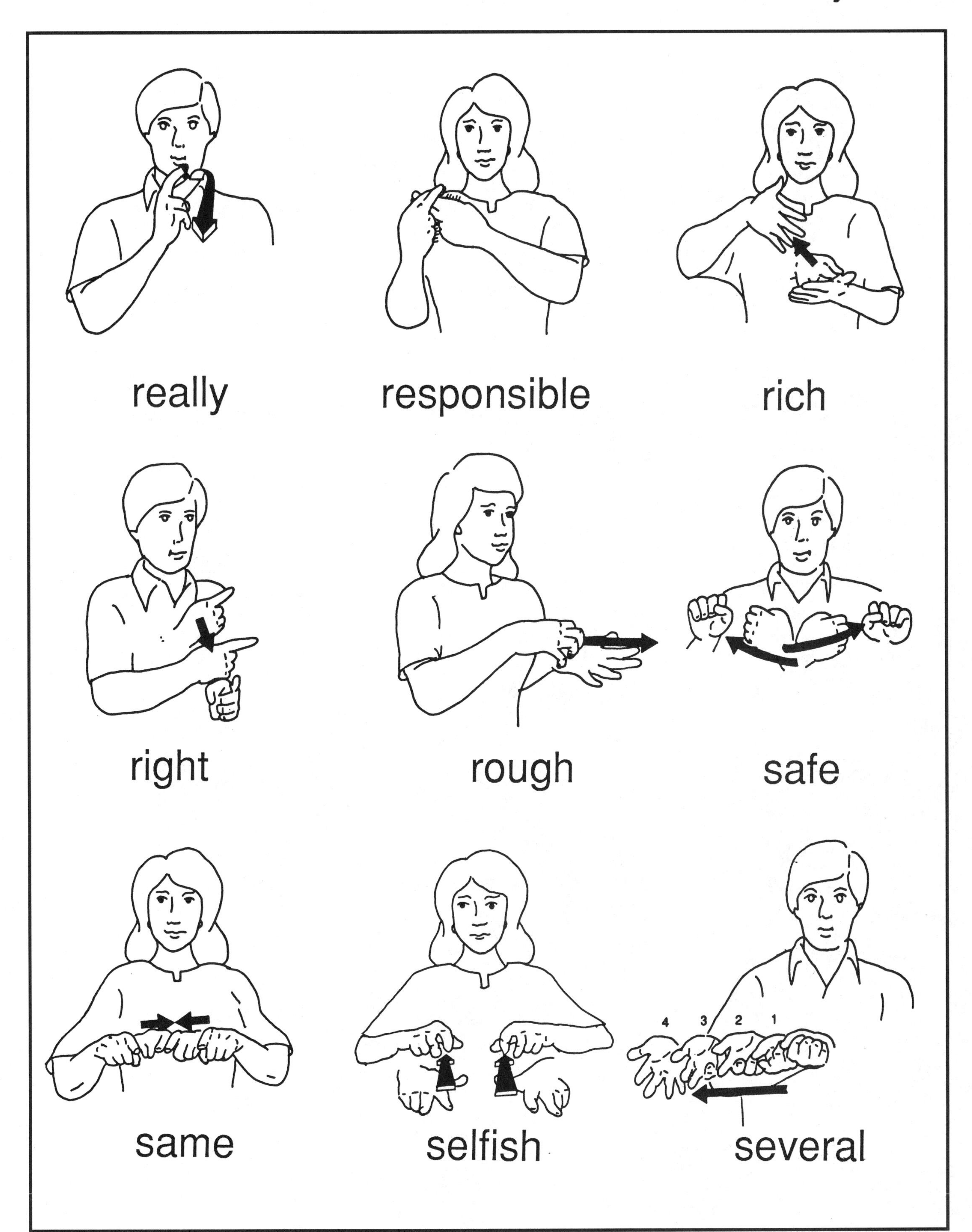

really

responsible

rich

right

rough

safe

same

selfish

several

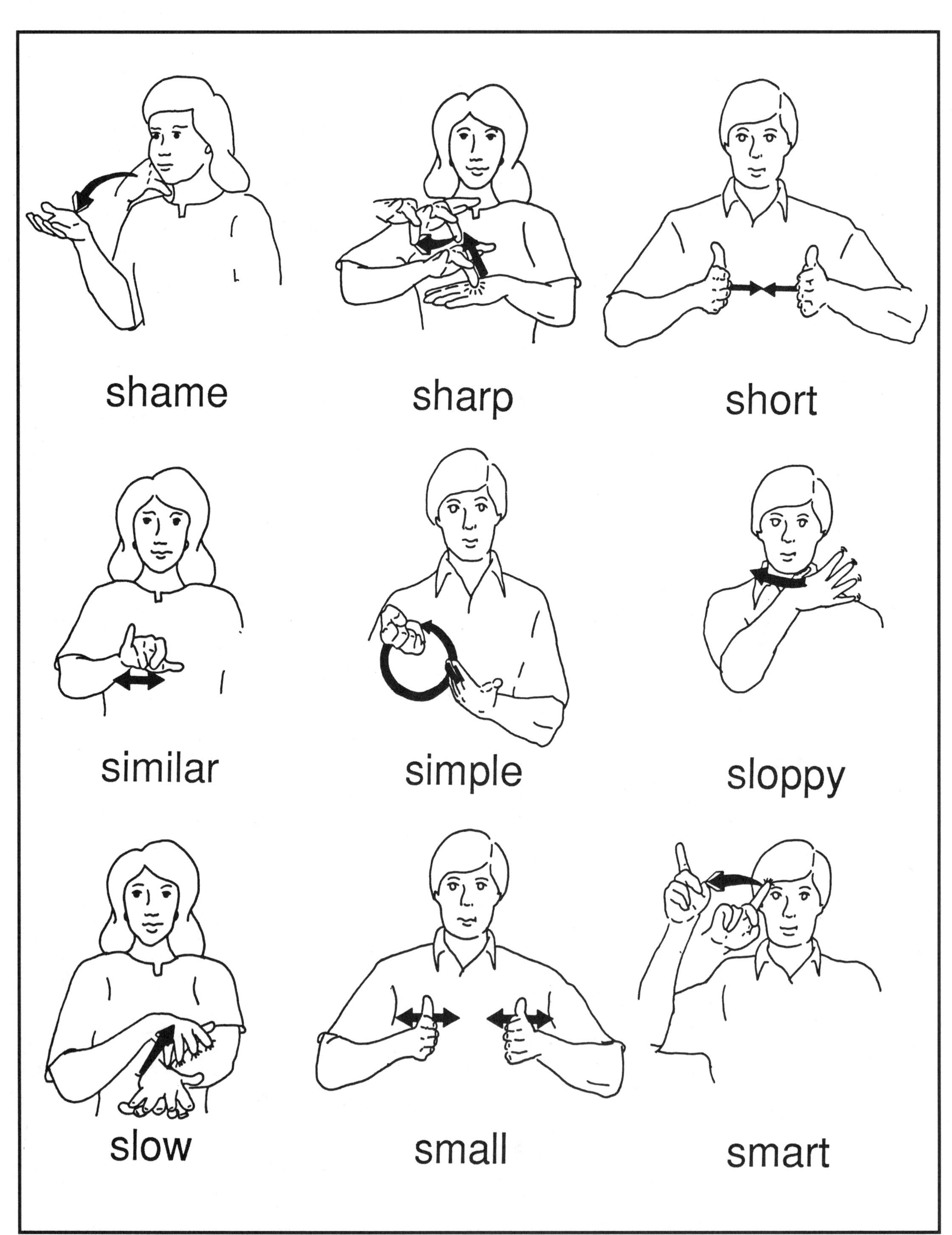
shame
sharp
short
similar
simple
sloppy
slow
small
smart

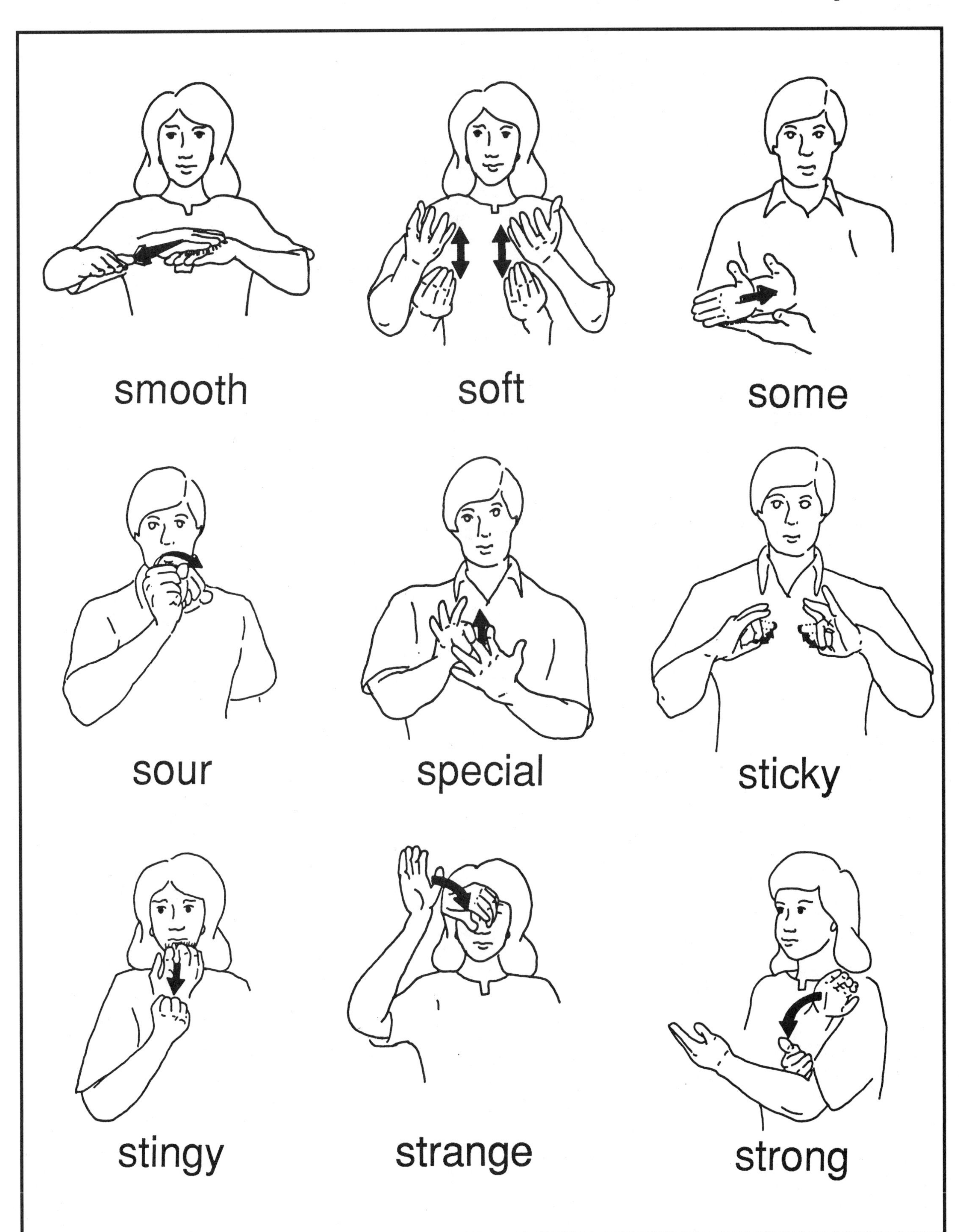
smooth
soft
some
sour
special
sticky
stingy
strange
strong

adjectives

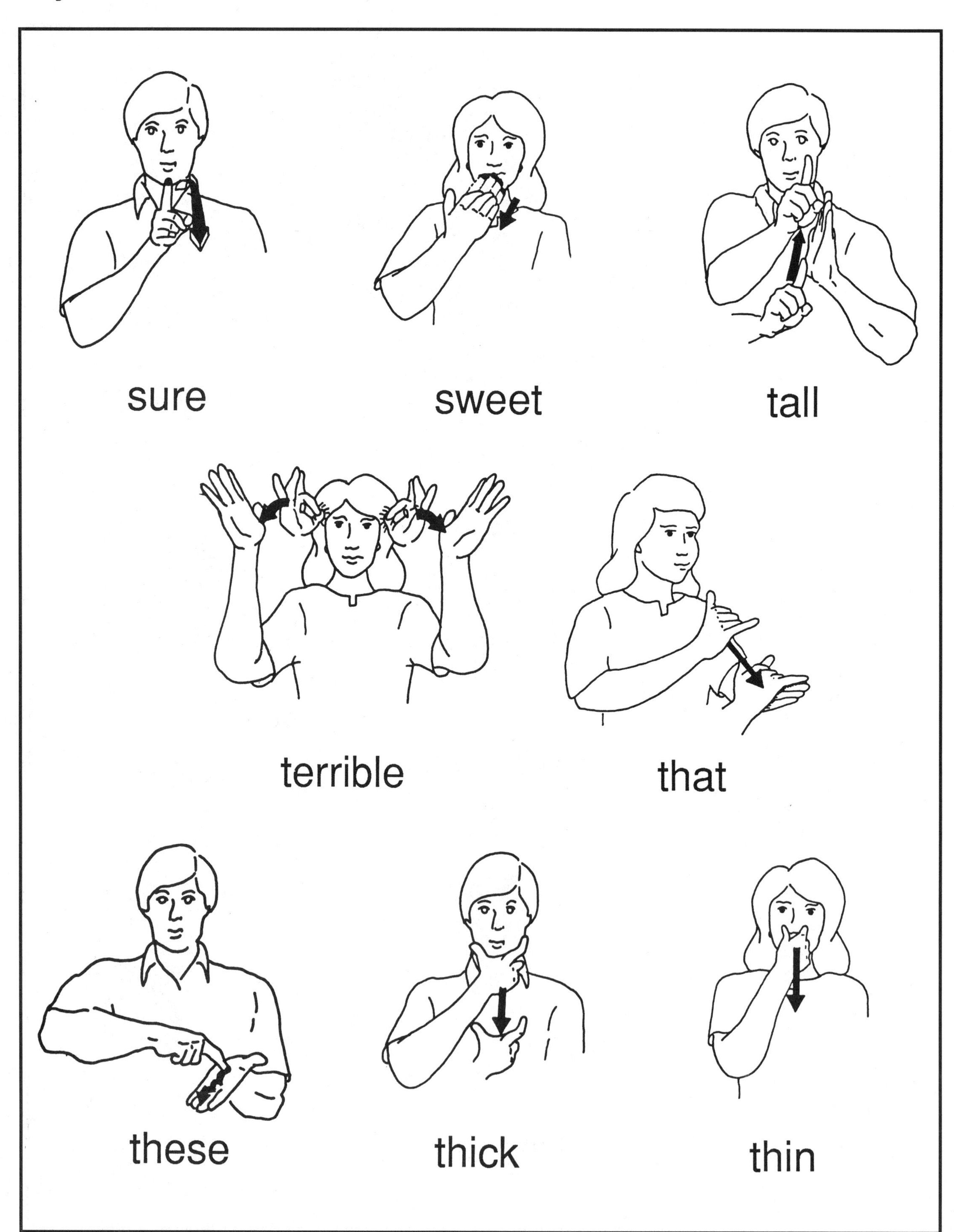

sure
sweet
tall
terrible
that
these
thick
thin

thirsty
this
those
top
tough
true
ugly
unfair

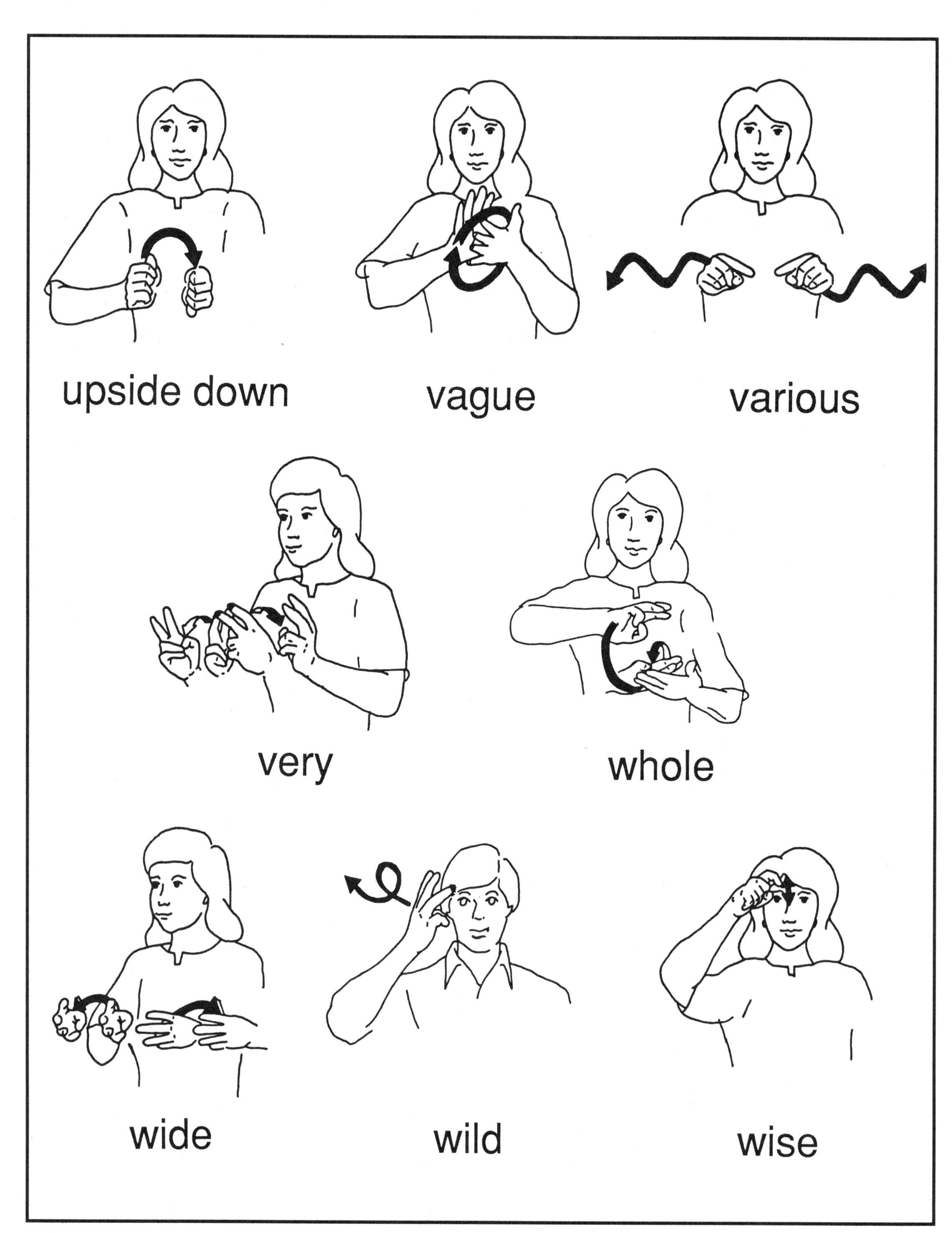
upside down
vague
various
very
whole
wide
wild
wise

wonderful

worse

wrong

young

ADVERBS

again[1]
alike
almost[2]
always[1]
anyway
away[2]
back[1]
else[1]
ever[2]
here[1]
just[1]
later

maybe
never[2]
no[1]
not[1]
now[1]
often
once[1]
only[1]
quickly
sometimes[1]
soon
still[2]

sure
then[1]
there[1]
together[2]
too (excess)[1]
too (also)[1]
usual
very
well[1]
yes[1]
yet[2]

ADVERBS

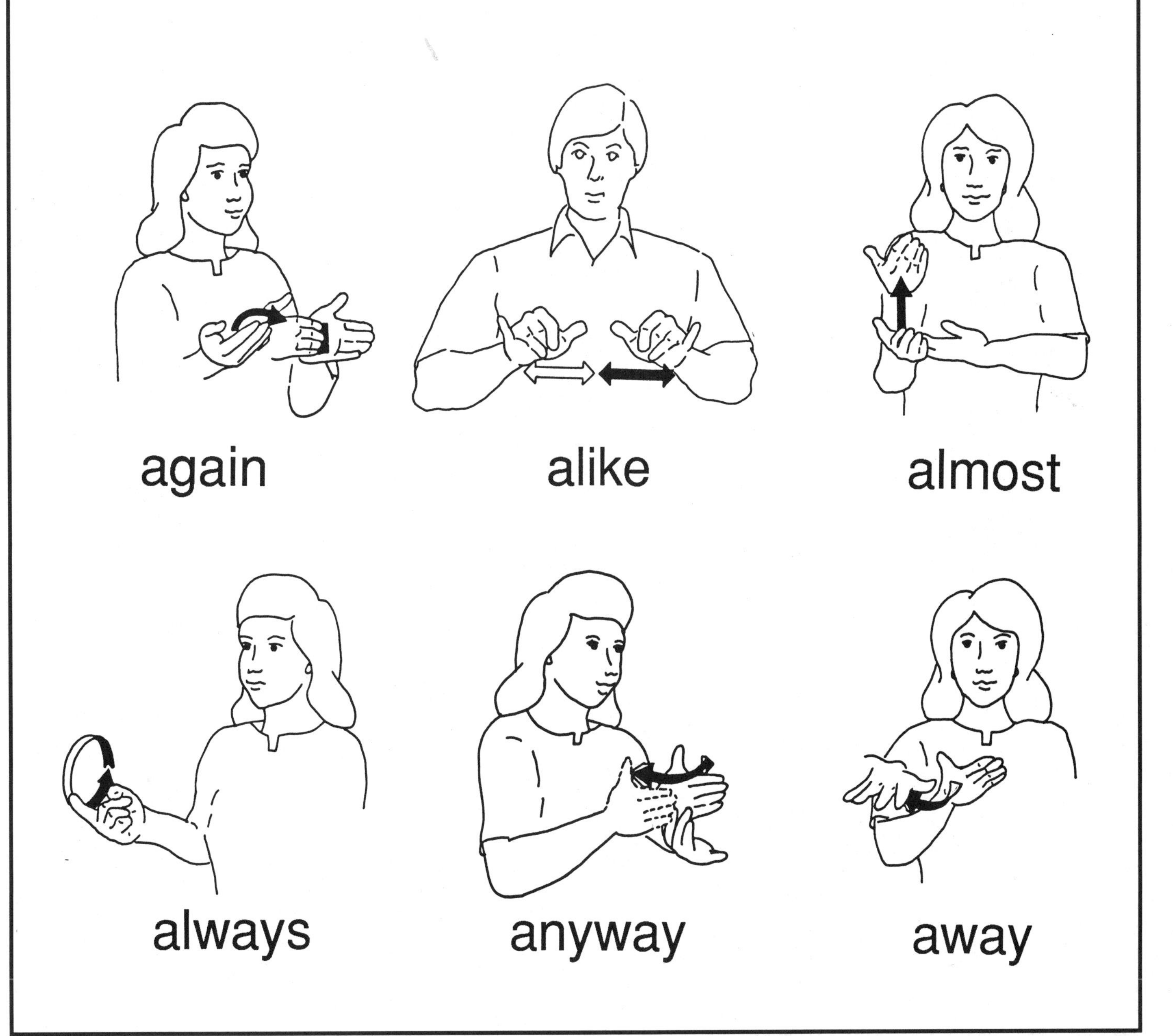
again
alike
almost
always
anyway
away

ADVERBS

1. I want you to come _____.

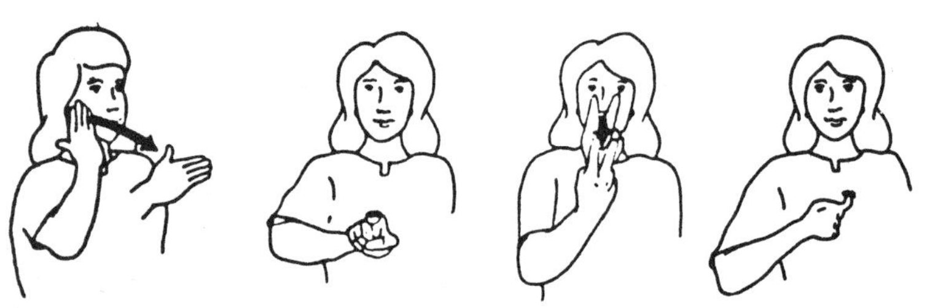

2. Will you see me _____?

3. We will do that _____.

4. I like that _____.

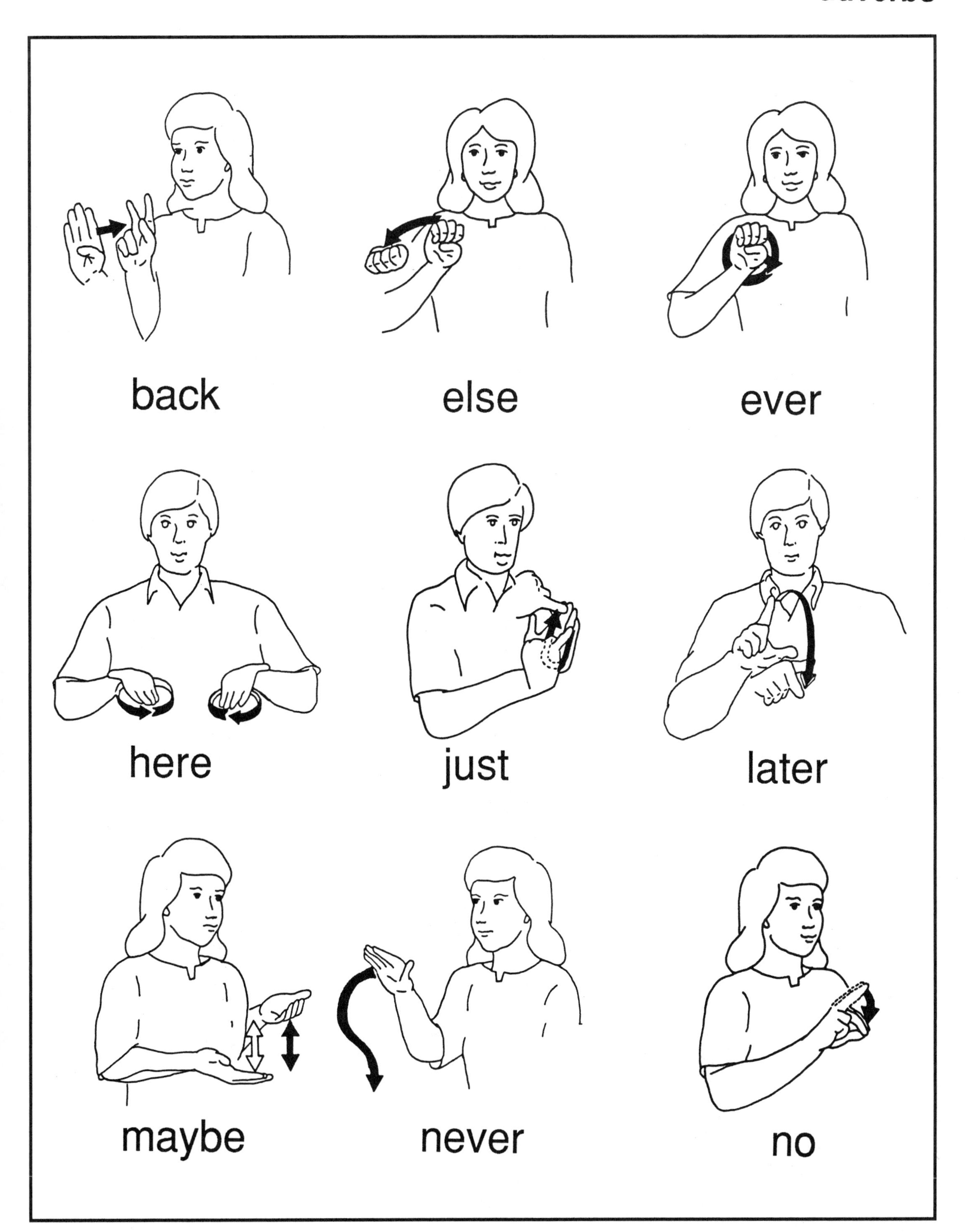
back
else
ever
here
just
later
maybe
never
no

not
now
often
once
only
quickly
sometimes
soon
still

sure
then
there
together
too (excess)
too (also)
usual
very
well

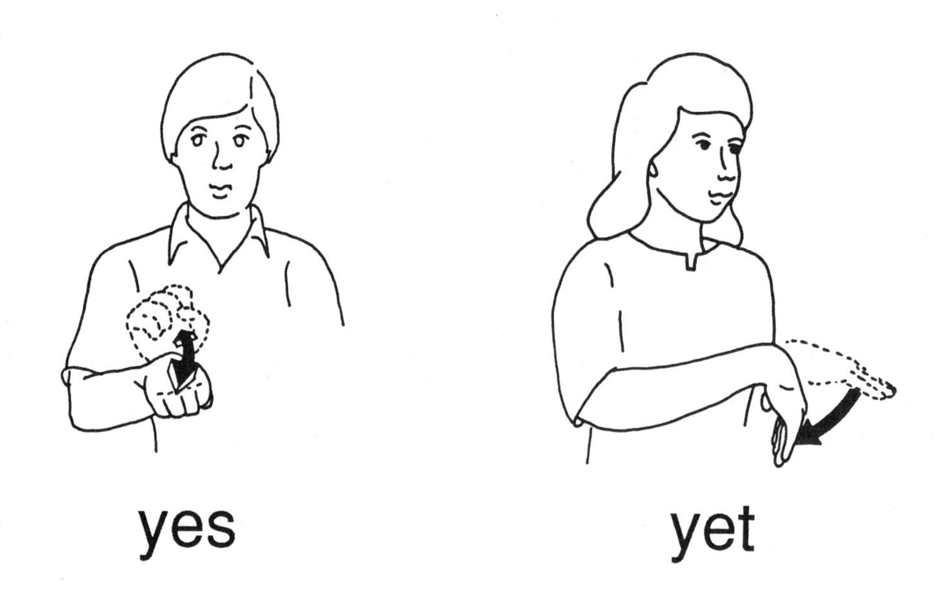

yes yet

ACTIVITY - ADVERBS

Purpose: To use adverbs correctly in sentences.

Materials: Chalkboard and chalk.

Procedure:

1. Child writes sentence number one under adverbs from book, Signing English, on chalkboard.
2. Adult writes two adverbs in blank space of sentence.
3. Child crosses out inappropriate adverb and then signs/says sentence.
4. Adult writes another sentence using the same adverb under the one on the chalkboard.
5. Child signs/says second sentence.
6. Repeat procedures 1 through five using the second sentence in the book.

Variations: Adult writes adverb on chalkboard and child writes her own sentence using that adverb; adult writes three or four adverbs from which child is to select appropriate one for correct usuage.

COUNTRY ANIMALS

antelope
bat
beaver
bird
chipmunk
deer
eagle
fox
gerbil
gopher
hamster
lizard
mole
moose
opossum
owl
pigeon
porcupine
rabbit
raccoon
rat
skunk
snake
squirrel
tortoise
vulture

COUNTRY ANIMALS

1. A _______ has pretty fur.

2. Do _______s live in trees?

3. Can a _____ run fast?

4. _______s have feathers.

COUNTRY
ANIMALS
antelope
bat
beaver
bird
chipmunk
deer

eagle
fox
gerbil
gopher
hamster
lizard
mole
moose
opossum

owl
pigeon
porcupine
rabbit
raccoon
rat
skunk
snake
squirrel

tortoise

vulture

ACTIVITY - COUNTRY ANIMALS

Purpose: To identify which country animals live on the ground.

Materials: Pictures of country animals.

Procedure:

1. Adult puts the pictures down in front of child and asks child to name the animals.
2. Child picks out the pictures of animals that she knows signing/saying each.
3. Adult signs/says each animal with child.
4. Adult puts the remaining pictures away.
5. Adult picks an animal and signs/says, "Rabbits live on the ground."
6. Child is to imitate signing/saying, "on ground." (all other animals are, "not on ground.")
7. Adult puts picture aside in front of child.
8. Adult picks another animal and repeats procedures 1 through 5.
9. After all "ground animals" are identified, adult goes back through the pile having child sign/say "________lives on ground."

Variations: Adult can assist child in identifying which country animals live "in trees", and "in water". Adult then mixes animals so child is able to identify where different country animals live.

FARM[2] ANIMALS[2]

bull
calf
cat [1]
cattle
chick
chicken [2]
colt
cow
dog [1]
donkey
duck
duckling
goat [2]
goose
hen
hog
horse [2]
kid [1]
kitten
lamb
mule
pig [1]
piglet
puppy
rooster
sheep
turkey

FARM ANIMALS

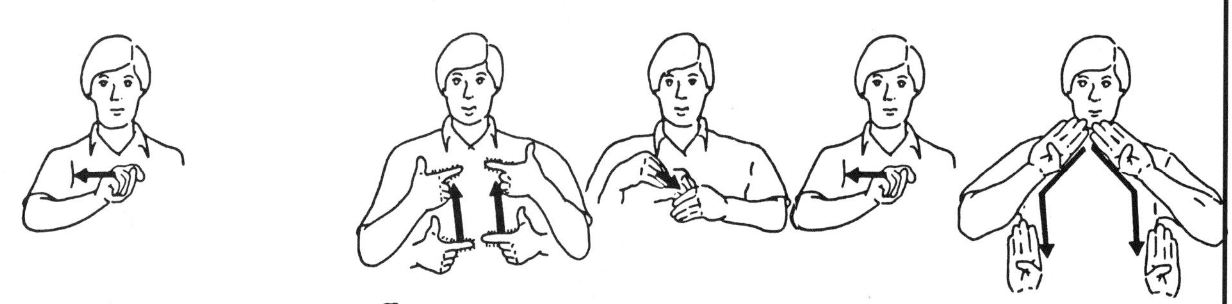

1. The ______ live in the barn.

2. Who feeds the ______?

3. Can we ride a ________?

4. What color is the ______?

FARM ANIMALS

bull

calf

cat

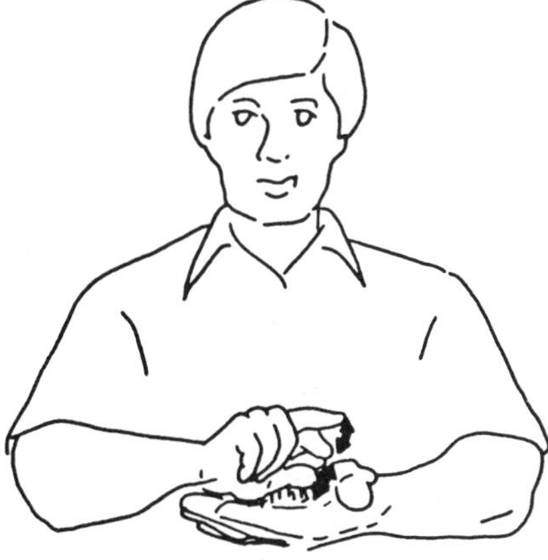

cattle

chick

chicken

colt
cow
dog
donkey
duck
duckling
2
1
goat
goose
hen

hog
horse
kid
kitten
lamb
mule
pig
piglet
2
puppy

rooster

sheep

turkey

ACTIVITY - FARM ANIMALS

Purpose: To identify and imitate different sounds that farm animals make.

Materials: Pictures of farm animals.

Procedure:

1. Adult shows picture of farm animal to child; adult signs/says name of animal in picture.
2. Adult signs/says, "A pig says oink, oink, oink."
3. Adult signs/says, "What does a pig say?"
4. Child signs/says, "A pig says oink, oink, oink."
5. Adult showns another picture to child while repeating procedures 2 through 5.

Variations: Adult writes several sounds that farm animals made on chalkboard, have child identify correct animal with sound; adult covers mouth with hand while making farm animal sounds for child to identify; write sentences with several choices for child to select, e.g.,

	chirps
A donkey	oinks
	hee haws

WATER[2] ANIMALS[2]

alligator
catfish
crab
crocodile
duck [2]
fish [1]
frog
gull
hippopotamus
lobster
octopus
penguin
polar bear
porpoise
sea star
seal
shark
shrimp
squid
swan
toad
tuna
turtle
walrus
whale

ACTIVITY - WATER ANIMALS

Purpose: To identify attributes / characteristics of water animals.

Materials: Pictures of various water animals.

Procedure:

1. Adult signs/says that she is going to describe an animal that lives in the water. Three clues will be given, child is to guess which animal was described.
2. Adult puts two pictures of water animals face down in front of child.
3. Adult signs/says characteristics of water animal, e.g.,
   a. It is a very big animal.
   b. It has white fur.
   c. It lives in the water and on the snow.
4. Adult turns over two pictures on table for child to see.
5. Child points to appropriate picture.
6. Adult signs/says name of water animal, child imitates.
7. Repeat procedures 2 through 6.

Variations: Child can explain characteristics to adult or another child. Put several pictures face up so child can look over pictures after each clue, but doesn't indicate which picture until after three clues are given. Based on the clues given (number of clues can vary), child draws picture of animal described.

WATER ANIMALS

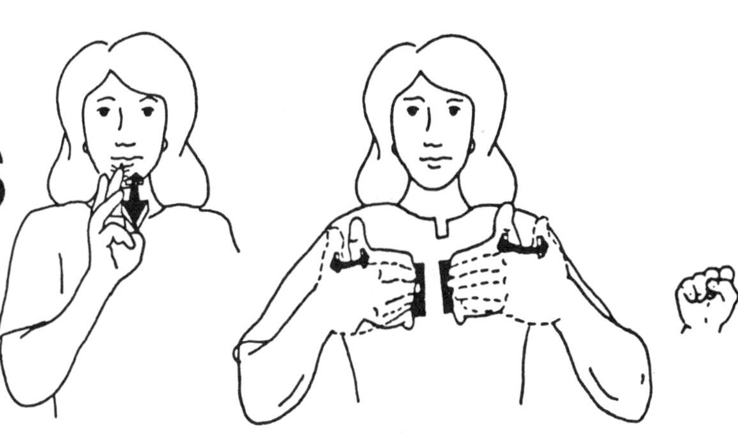

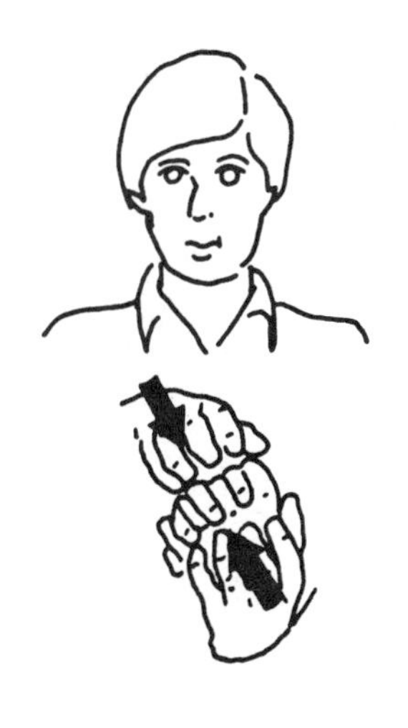

alligator

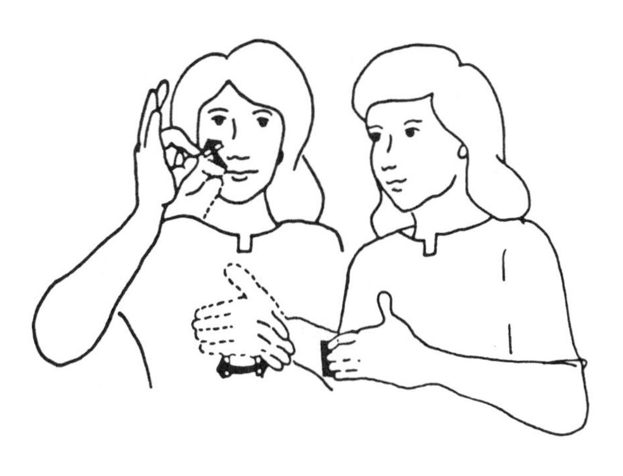

catfish

crab

crocodile

duck

WATER ANIMALS

1. ______ are not good to eat.

2. _______ are in the zoo.

3. Be careful, _____ will bite you.

4. A _______ is not a fish.

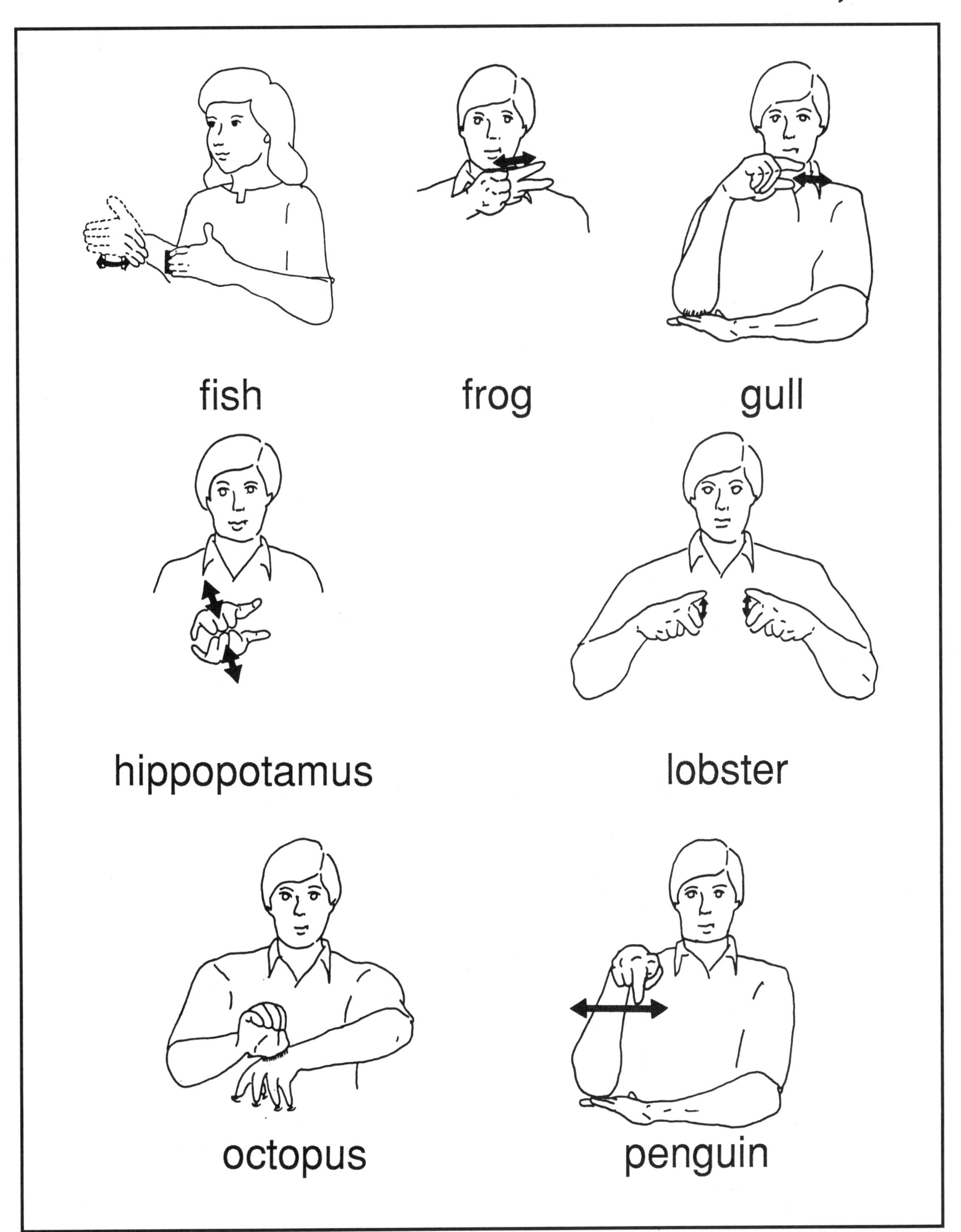
fish
frog
gull
hippopotamus
lobster
octopus
penguin

polar bear
porpoise
sea star
seal
shark
shrimp
squid

swan
toad
tuna
turtle
walrus
whale

ZOO ANIMALS

alligator
ape
baboon
bear
buffalo
camel
crocodile
elephant
giraffe
gorilla
hippopotamus
kangaroo
leopard
lion
monkey
ostrich
panda
panther
peacock
reindeer
rhinoceros
tiger
wolf
zebra

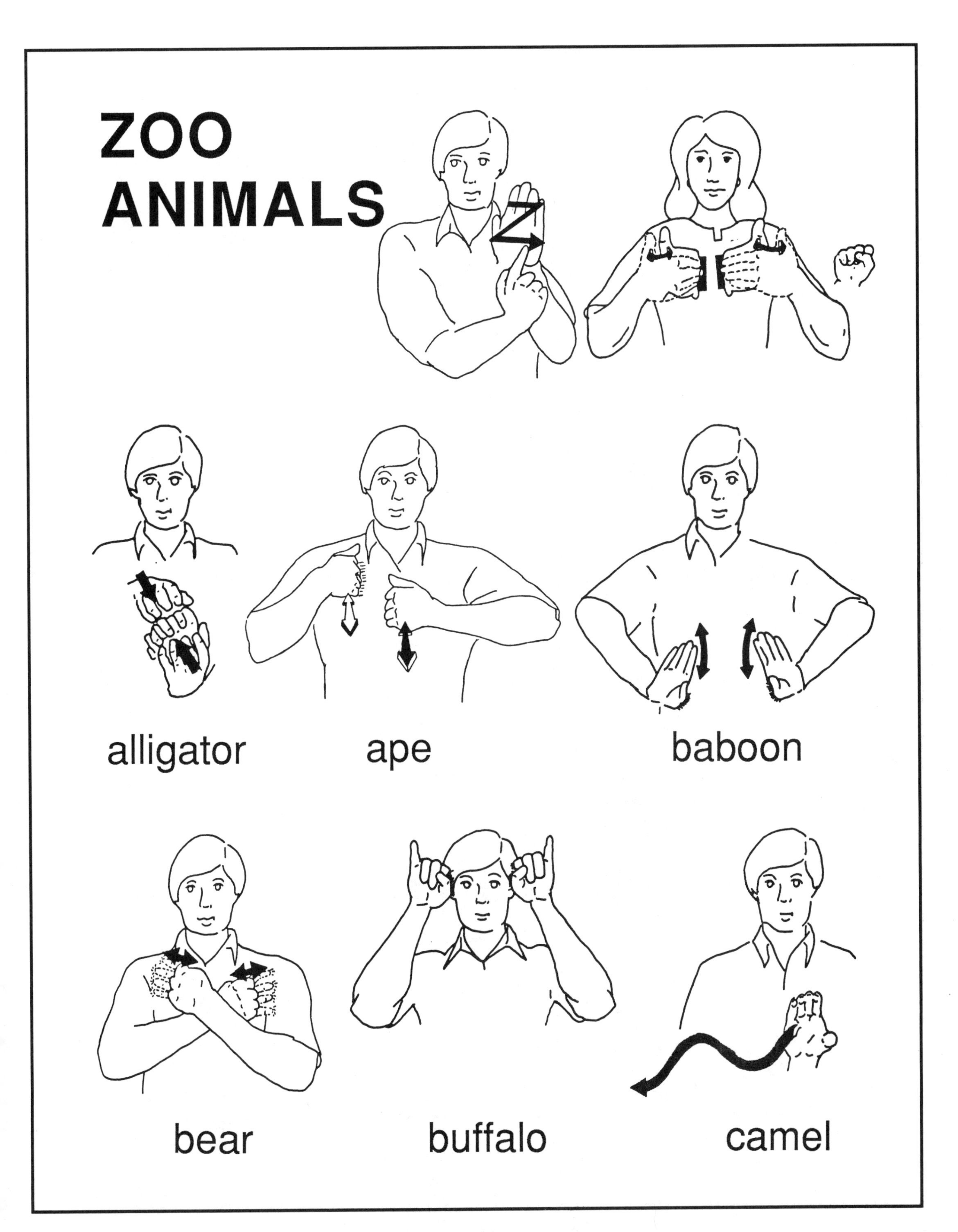
ZOO
ANIMALS
alligator
ape
baboon
bear
buffalo
camel

ZOO ANIMALS

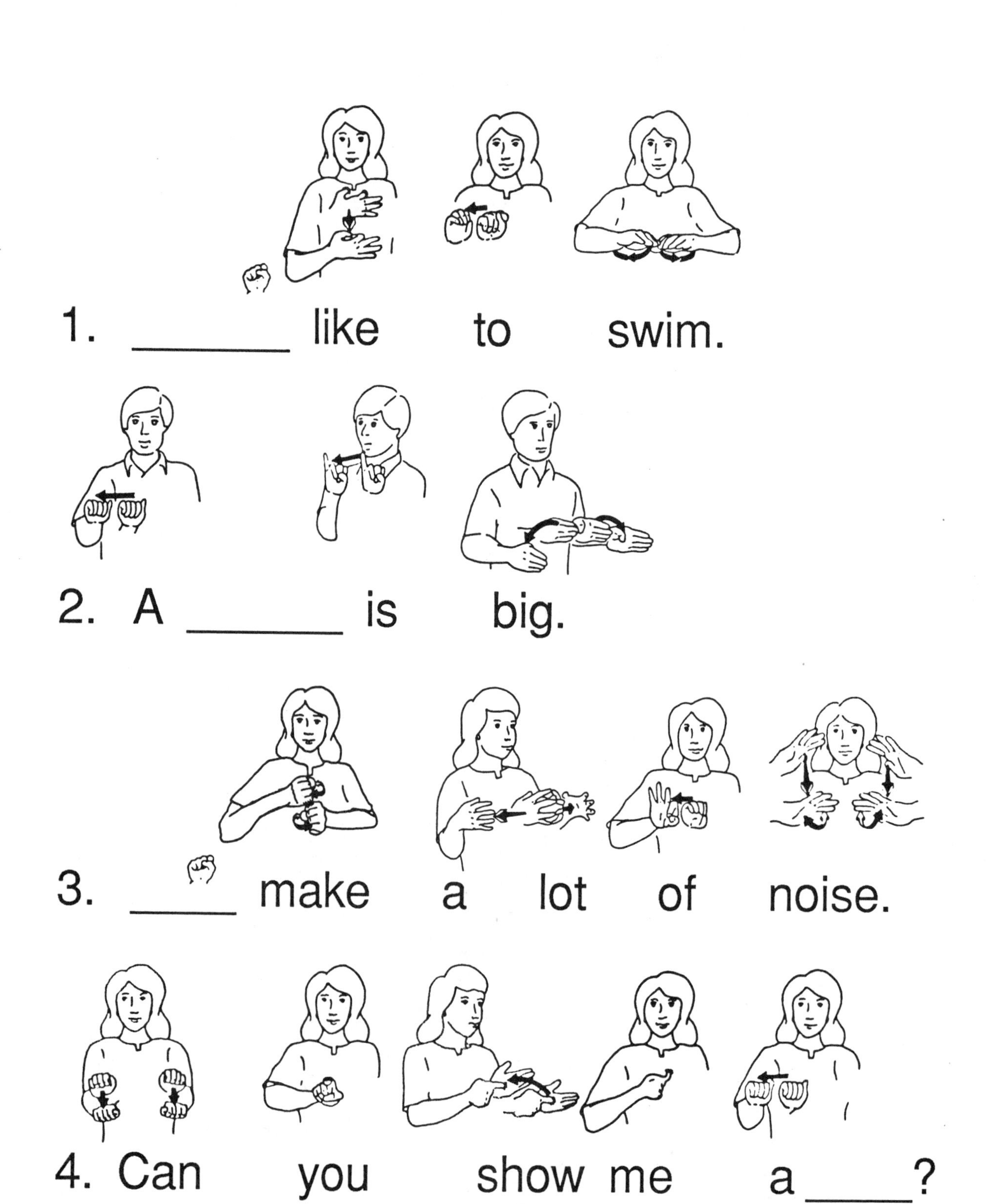
1. _______ like to swim.
2. A _______ is big.
3. _____ make a lot of noise.
4. Can you show me a _____?

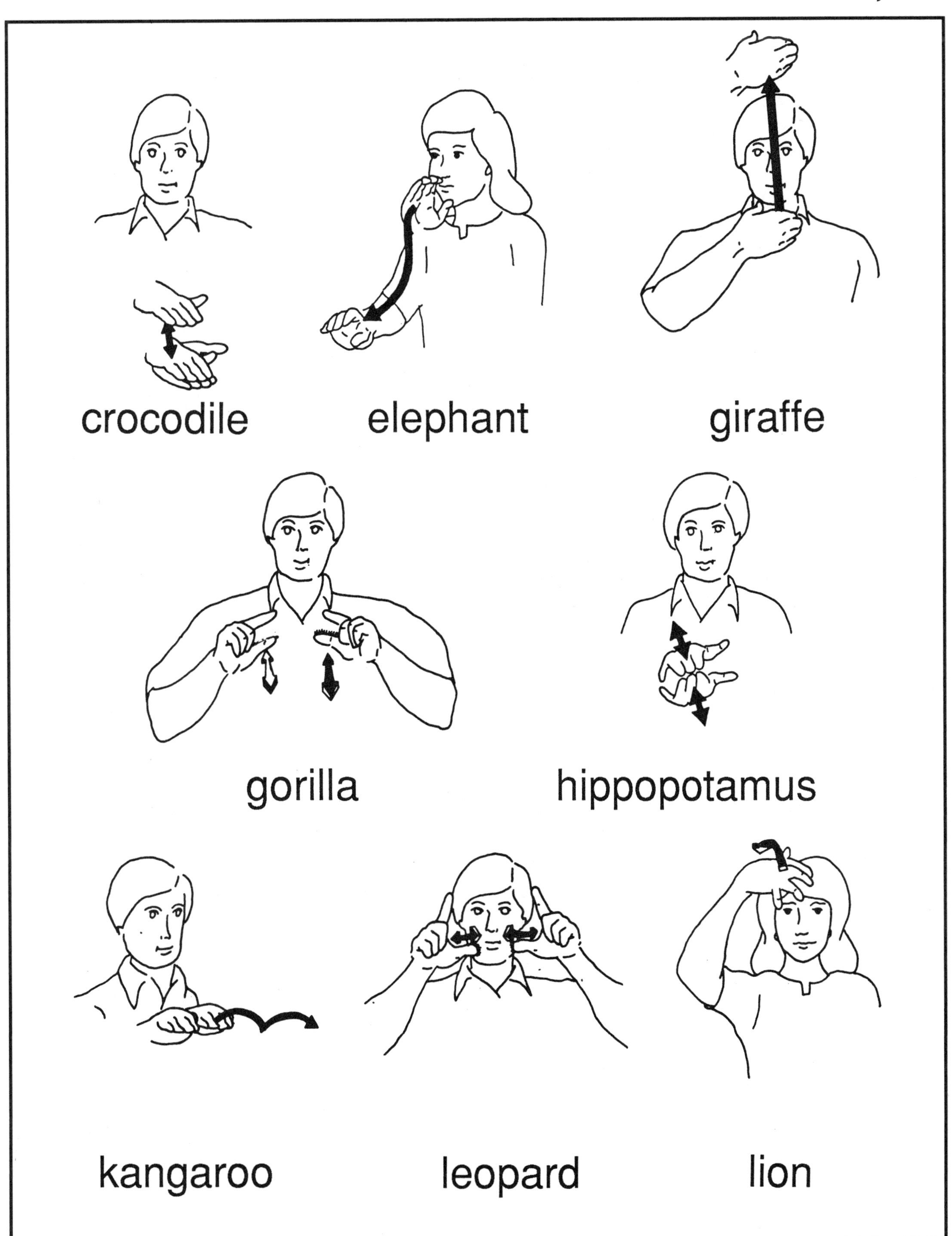
crocodile
elephant
giraffe
gorilla
hippopotamus
kangaroo
leopard
lion

monkey
ostrich
panda
panther
peacock
reindeer
rhinoceros
tiger
wolf

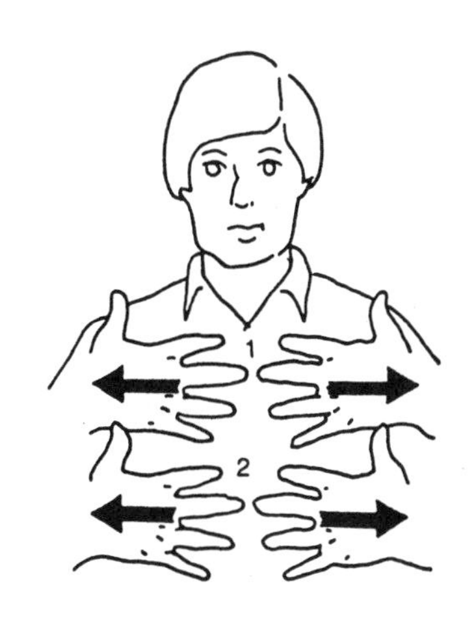

zebra

ACTIVITY - ZOO ANIMALS

Purpose: To develop the ability to concentrate and identify different zoo animals.

Materials: Pictures of zoo animals.

Procedure:

1. Adult shows child three pictures of zoo animals, one at a time, signing/saying each. Turn each picture face down on the table after showing it.
2. Adult signs/says one of the animal pictures face down on the table.
3. Child picks up correct picture signing/saying the animal's name. Child puts picture back on the table face down.
4. Adult signs/says the name of a fourth animal picture while showing it to child then puts it face down on table.
5. Adult signs/says one of the four animal pictures.
6. Child picks up correct picture signing/saying it. Child puts picture back on table face down.
7. Adult continues adding pictures of animals while quizing child, procedures 4 through 6.

Variations: Adult can fingerspell/say each of the animals rather than sign/say each; child can pick up and hold each picture identified correctly, which means that there will only be four pictures on the table at a time.

BIG THINGS

air
airport
area
battle
beach
bridge
castle
circus
city
community
convention
country
county
dinosaur
earth
environment

ferris wheel
giant [2]
ground [2]
heaven
hill [2]
house [1]
island
jail [2]
lake
monster [2]
moon
mountain
nation
planet
prison
region

river
rocket
sea
ship
sky
star
sun
sunshine
town
tree [1]
universe
valley
village
war
world

BIG
THINGS
air
airport
area
battle
beach

BIG THINGS

1. Tell me about something big.

2. Is a ______ big or small?

3. Is a ______ a big animal?

    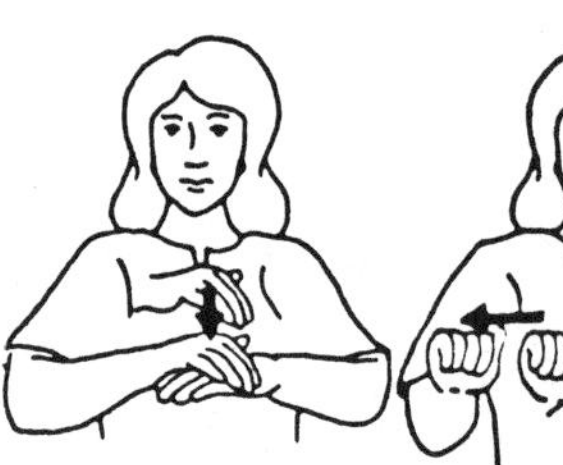

4. Can you sit on a ______?

bridge
castle
circus
city
community
convention
country
county
dinosaur

5. Where is the big ______?
6. Can you walk around ___?
7. Can you carry a ______?
8. Can you ride on a ____?

earth
environment
ferris wheel
giant
ground
heaven
hill
house

island
jail
lake
monster
moon
mountain

nation
planet
prison
region
river
rocket
sea
ship

big things

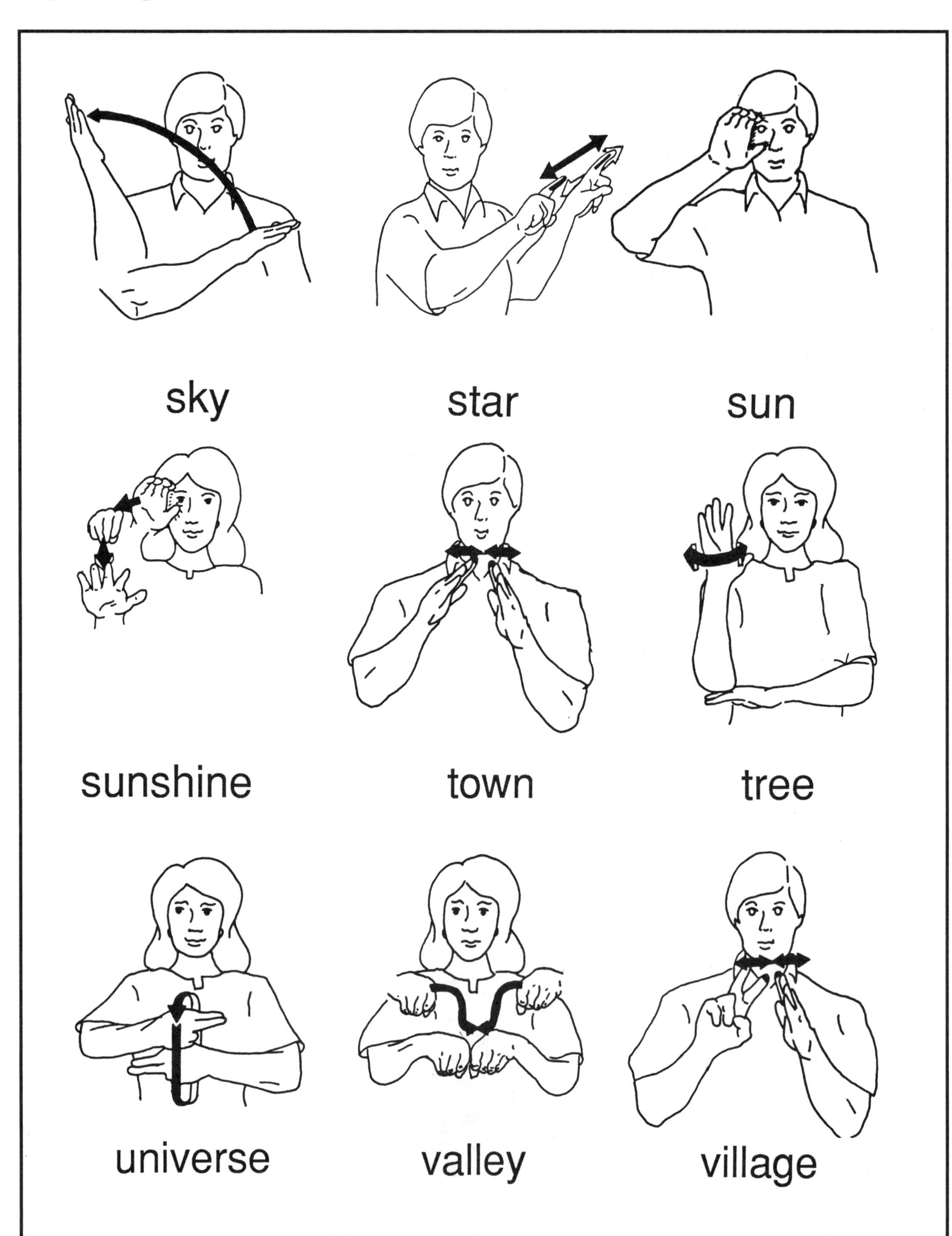

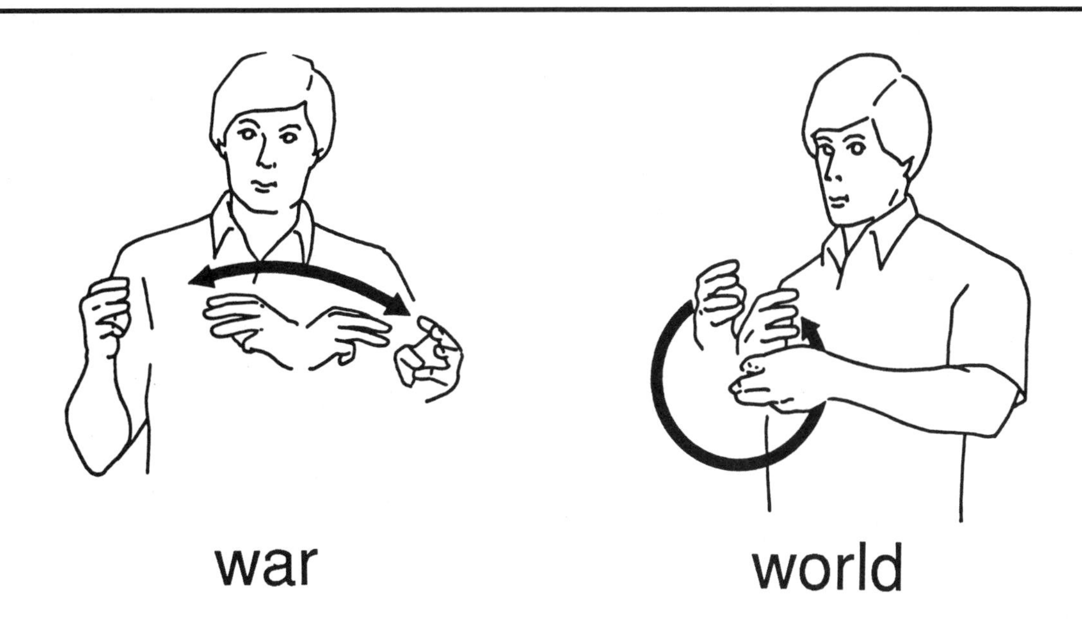

ACTIVITY - BIG THINGS

Purpose: To develop the concept of bigger.

Materials: Variety of objects varying in size, e.g., marble, pin, book, eraser, notebook, paperclip, etc., and a paper bag.

Procedure:

1. Adult puts all objects in bag without child seeing them.
2. Child takes something from bag and puts it on table.
3. Adult takes a bigger object from the bag and puts it next to the small object and signs/says, "bigger."
4. Child imitates by pointing and signing/saying, "bigger."
5. Adult removes one object. Child takes another object from the bag and puts it next to remaining object.
6. Adult points to the bigger object and signs/says, "bigger."
7. Child imitates by pointing and signing/saying, "bigger".
8. Adult continues procedures 5 through 7 until child demonstrates understanding of concept bigger.

Variations: After the concept of bigger is mastered, begin on concept of biggest by adding a third object while signing/saying biggest. Walk throught the house or outside pointing to two different objects while child points to and signs/says, "bigger."

BODY PARTS

abdomen
ankle
arm
back
beard
bone
breast
cheek
chest
chin
ear
elbow
eye 2
eyebrow
face 2
feet 2
finger
fingernail 2
foot 2
hair 2
hand 1
head 2
heart
jaw
lip
lung
mouth 2
muscle
mustache
navel
neck
nose
pupil
shoulder
skeleton
skin
teeth
throat
toe
tongue
tooth
waist

Note:

Other body parts are signed by pointing to them:

shin heel calf thigh arch knee hip knuckles forearm leg 2

ACTIVITY - BODY PARTS

Purpose: To have children follow directions and identify different body parts.

Materials: None

Procedure:

1. Adult stand in front of child touching some part of his body with both hands while saying the name of the body part, e.g., knees, nose, etc.
2. Child imitates adult by touching the same body part with both hands.
3. After child imitates accurately, adult shows child the name sign for Simon (an S handshape on the shoulder).
4. Adult goes through procedure of explaining that child is to touch only the body part touched by adult if Simon says. Provide many examples.
5. Adult begins game with child signing/saying , "Simon says". Then touch body part with both hands.
6. Child resonds appropriately.

Variations: Allow the child to be leader.

BODY PARTS

1. Can you touch your _____?

2. Show me your ______.

3. Where is your ______?

4. Yes, I see your ______.

BODY PARTS

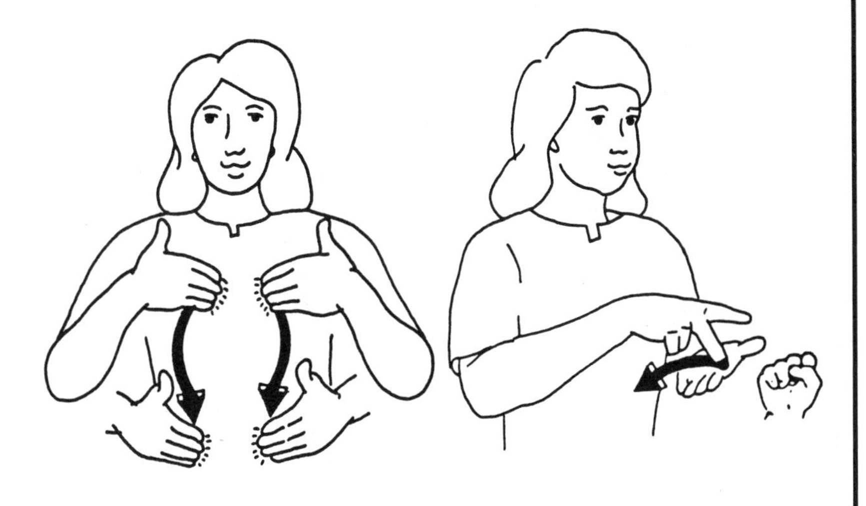

abdomen

ankle

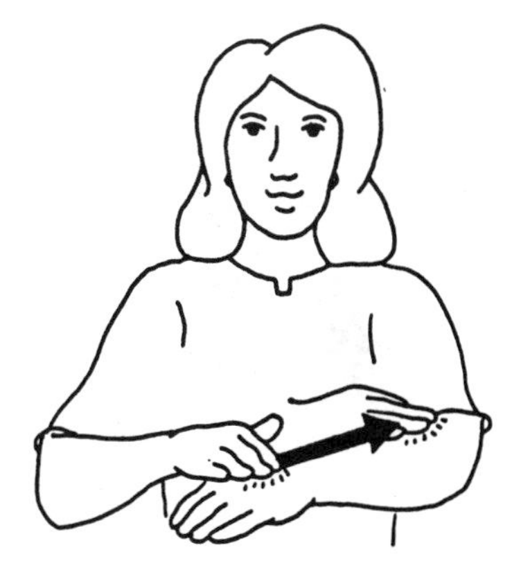

arm

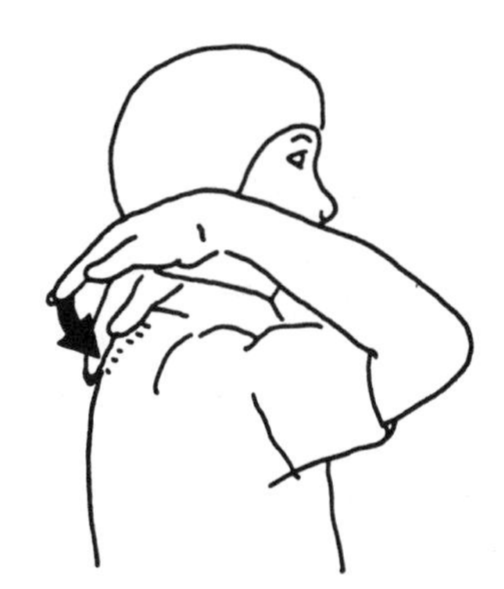

back

beard

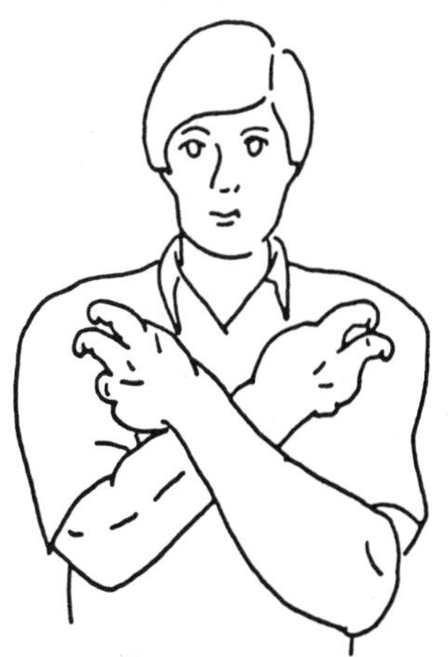

bone

body parts

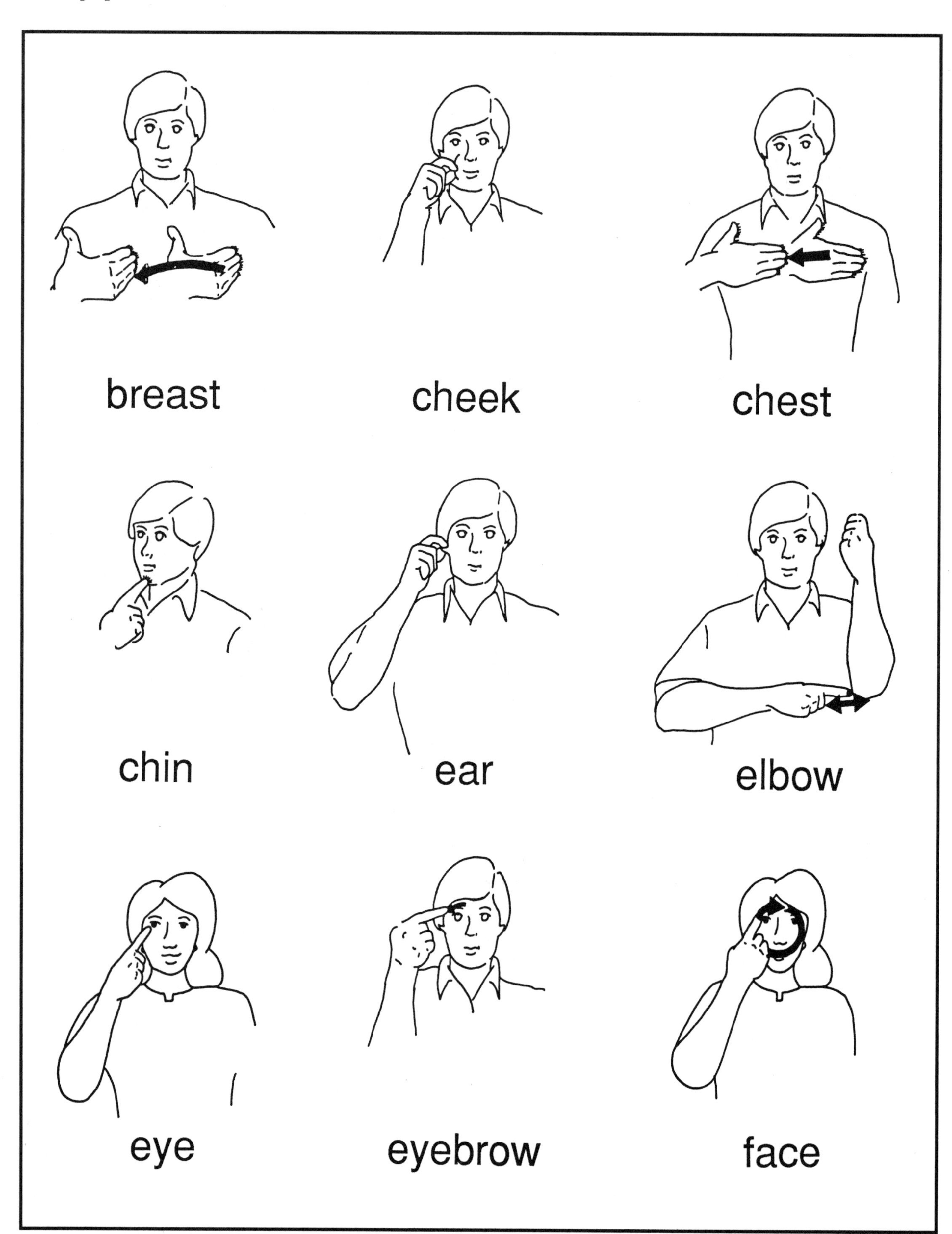

feet
finger
fingernail
foot
hair
hand
head
heart
jaw

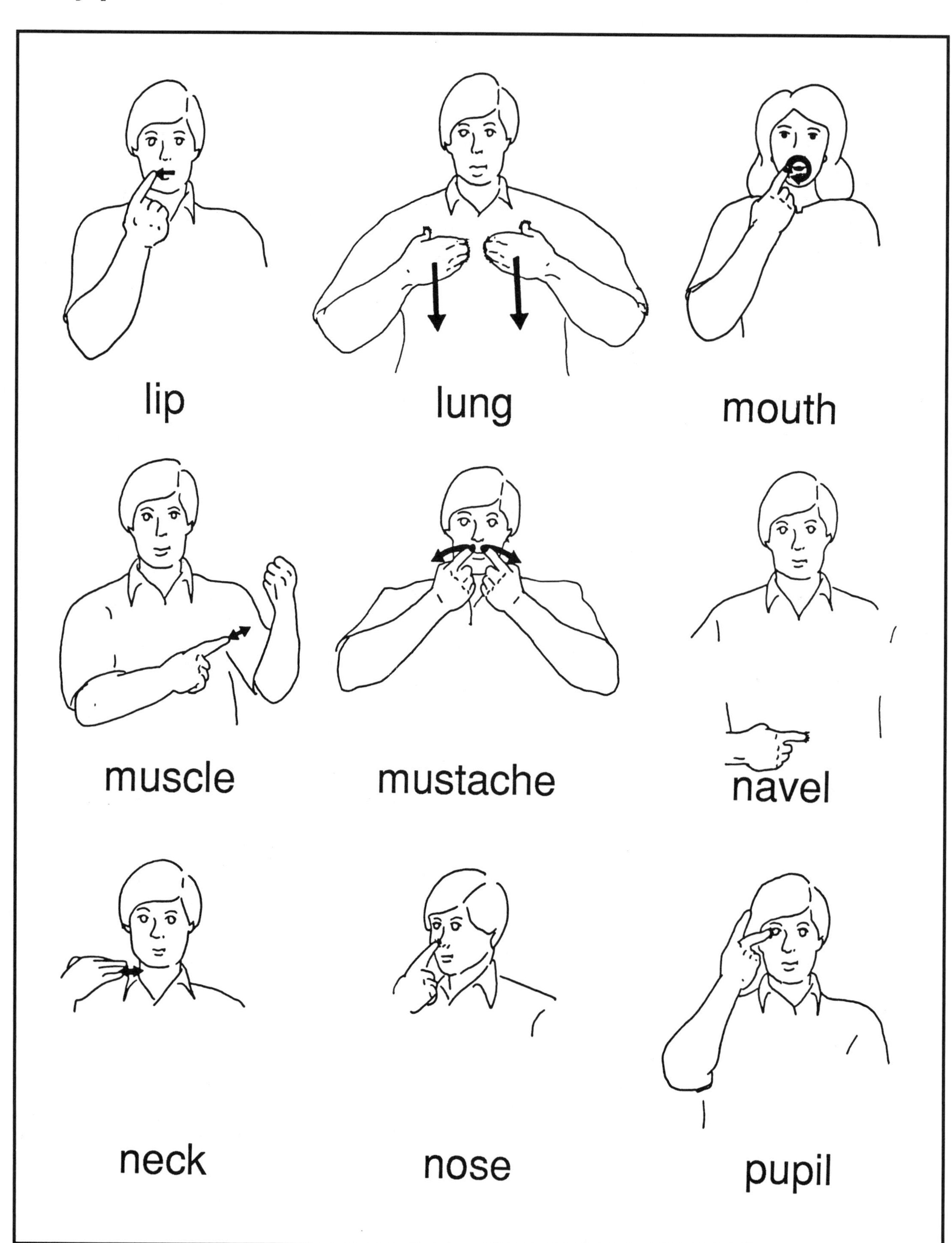
lip
lung
mouth
muscle
mustache
navel
neck
nose
pupil

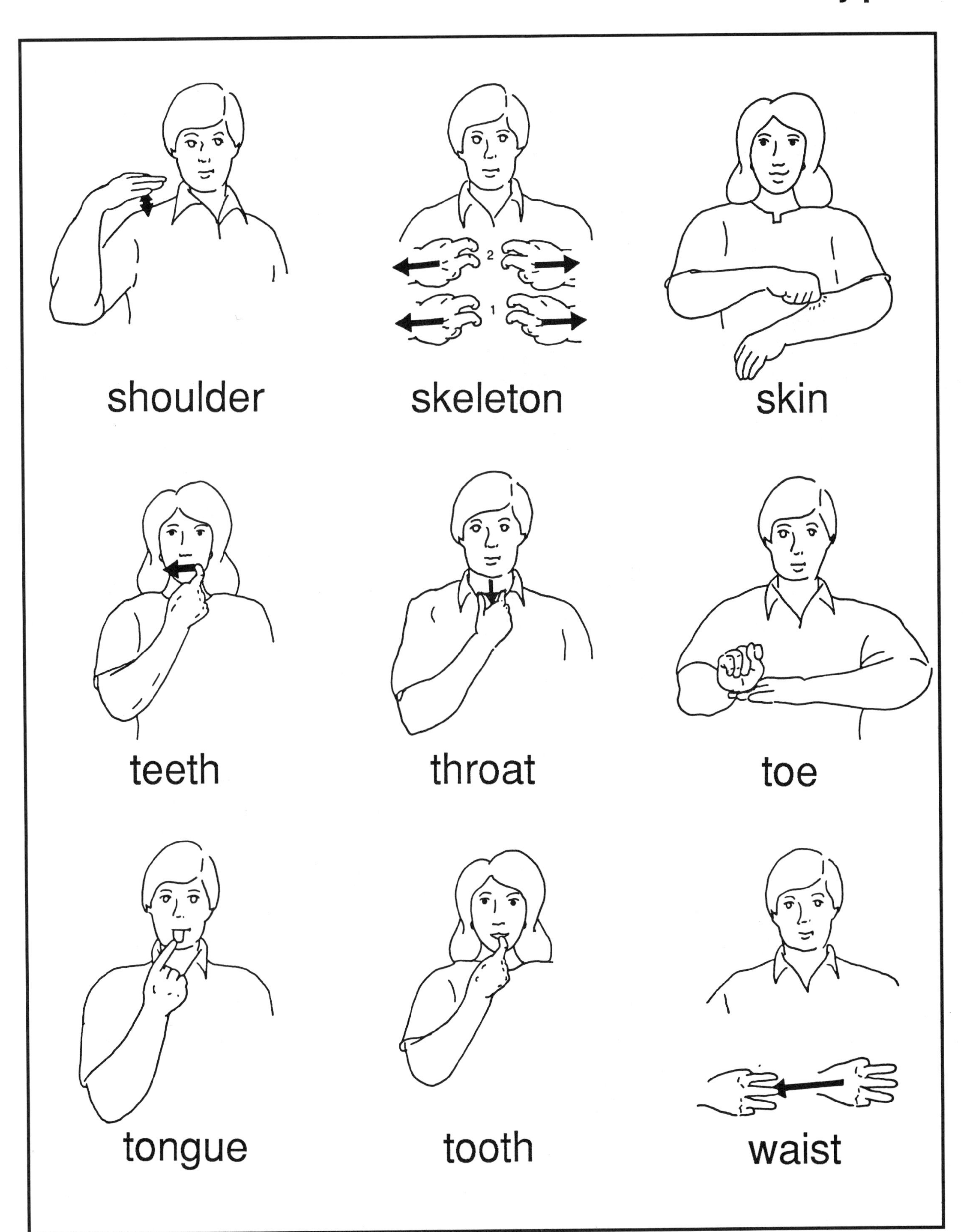
2
1
shoulder
skeleton
skin
teeth
throat
toe
tongue
tooth
waist

CALENDAR

MONTHS

January
February
March
April
May
June
July
August
September
October
November
December

DAYS[1]

Monday
Tuesday
Wednesday
Thursday
Friday
Saturday
Sunday

SPECIAL DAYS[1]

April Fool's Day
birthday[2]
Chinese New Year
Christmas[2]
Columbus Day
Easter
Election Day
Father's Day
Flag DayGood Friday
Halloween
Hanukkah
holiday
Independence Day
M.L.K. Jr's Birthday
(Martin Luther King Jr.'s Birthday)
Labor Day
Lincoln's Birthday
Mardi Gras
May Day
Mother's Day
New Year's Day
Passover
President's Day
St. Patrick's Day
Thanksgiving
vacation
Valentine's Day
Veteran's Day
Washington's Birthday

ACTIVITY - CALENDAR

Purpose: To identify different holidays through objects common to those holidays.

Materials: Paper bag; colorful , mounted pictures depicting objects for specific holidays, e.g., Santa Claus and Christmas trees for Christmas; Easter bunny and colored eggs for Easter, etc.

Procedure:

1. Adult puts pictures into bag and shakes it.
2. Child takes out one of the pictures
3. Adult signs/says, "Which holiday do you have?"
4. Child signs/says holiday and puts picture on the floor or table.
5. Repeat procedures 2 through 4 until all pictures are taken from bag and identified.

Variations: Child names objects in picture after identifying holiday. Put all pictures face up on table. Adult signs/says either object and/or holiday and child points to appropriate picture.

CALENDAR

1. When is your ______?

 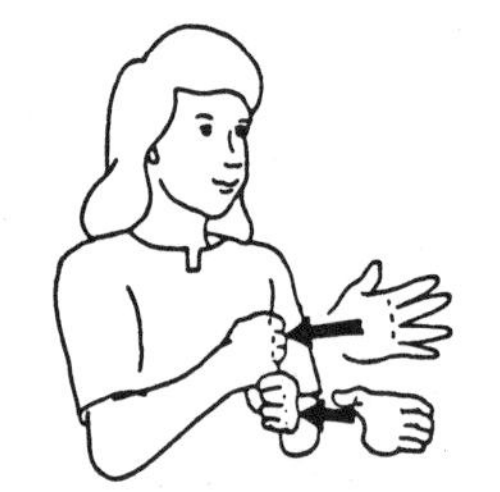 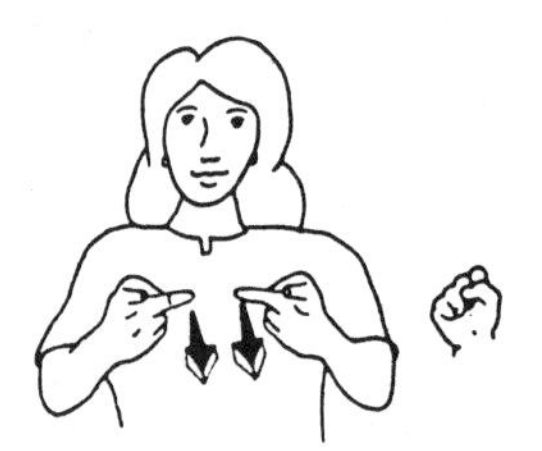 

2. You get presents on______.

3. School is closed for ______.

4. We go to church on____.

CALENDAR

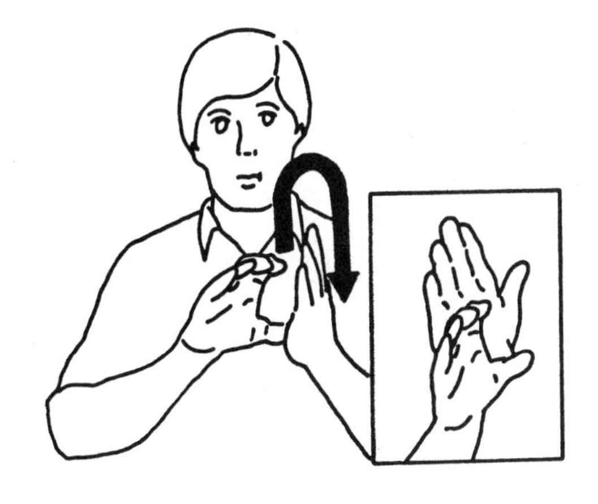

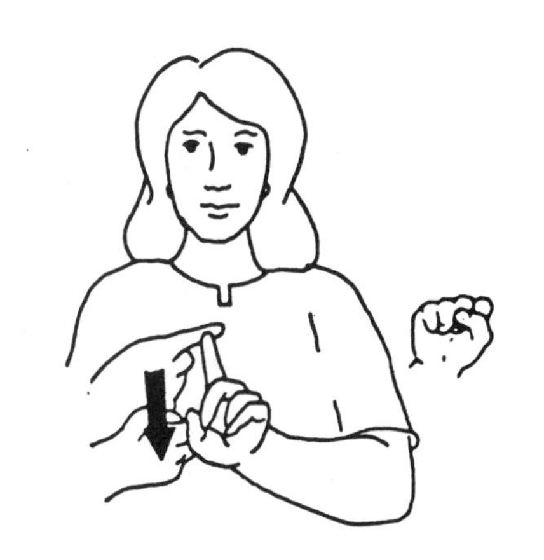

MONTHS

January

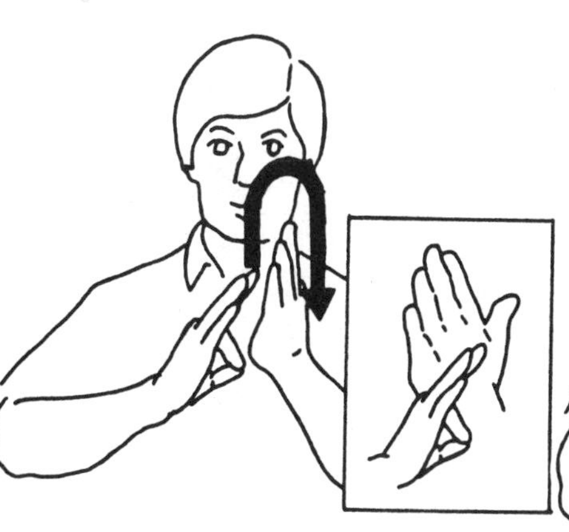

February

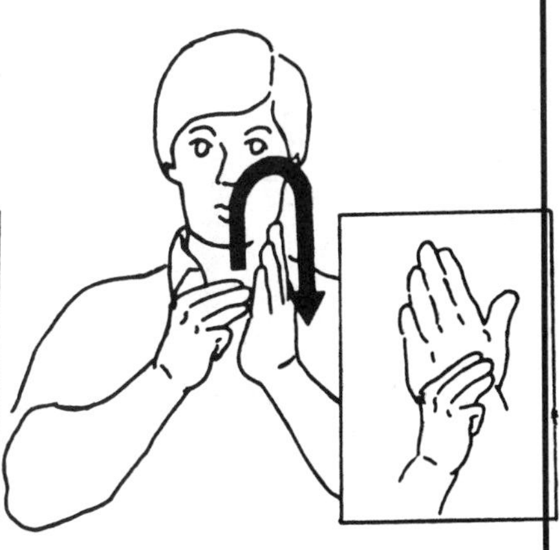

March

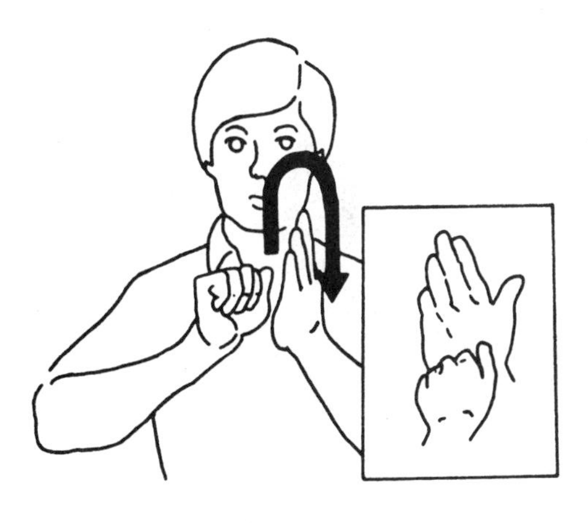

April

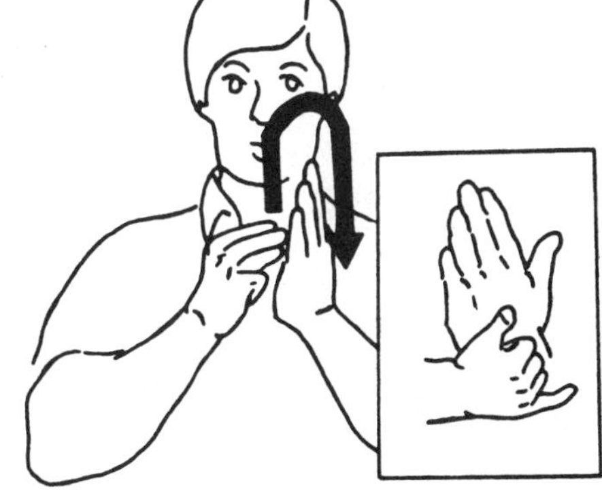

May

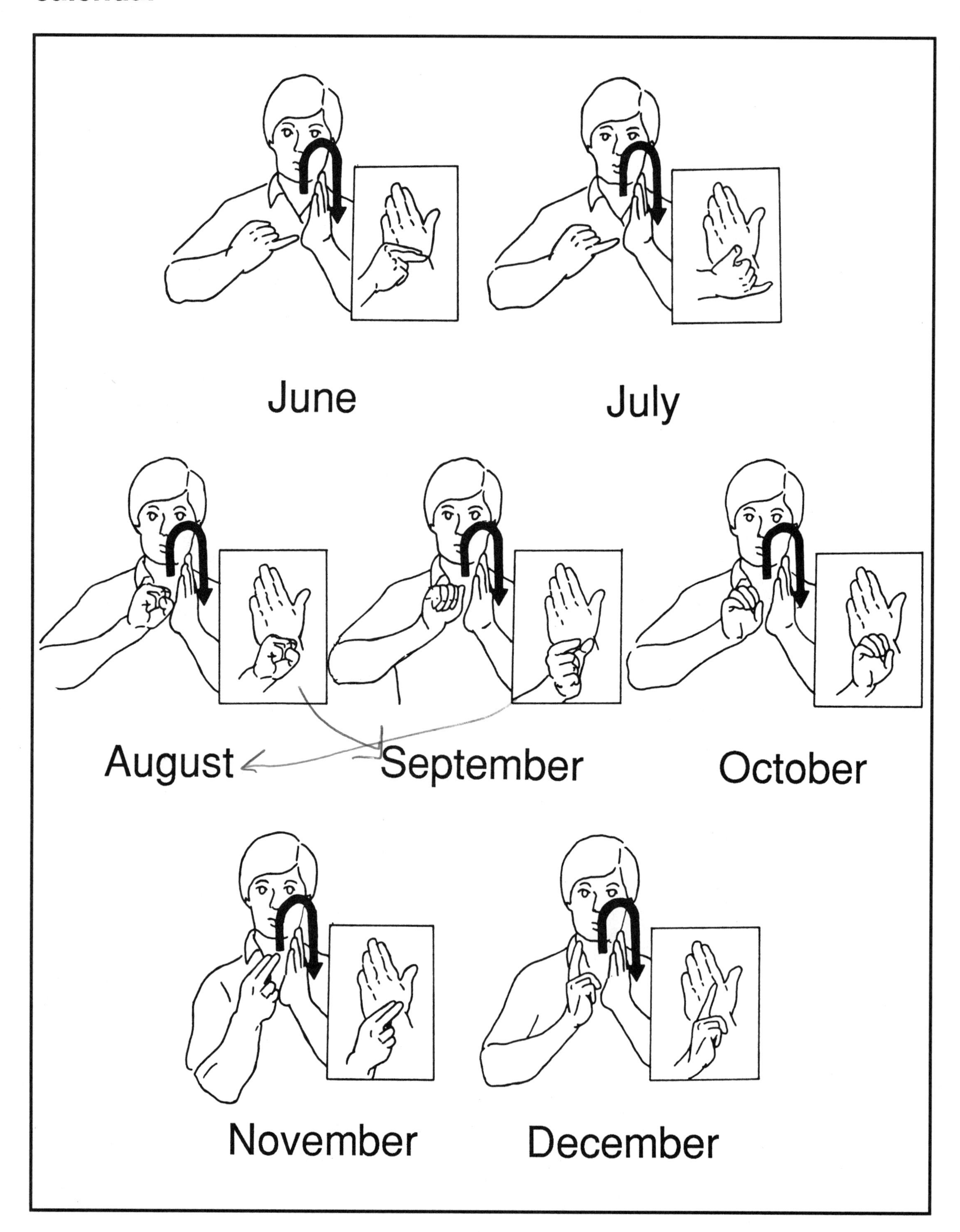
June
July
August
September
October
November
December

DAYS

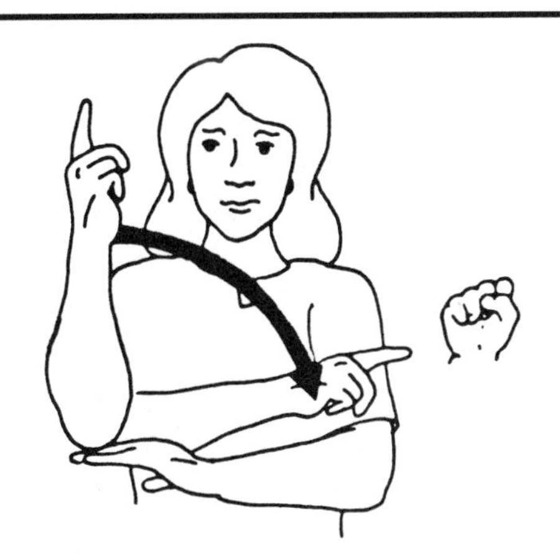

Monday

Tuesday

Wednesday

Thursday

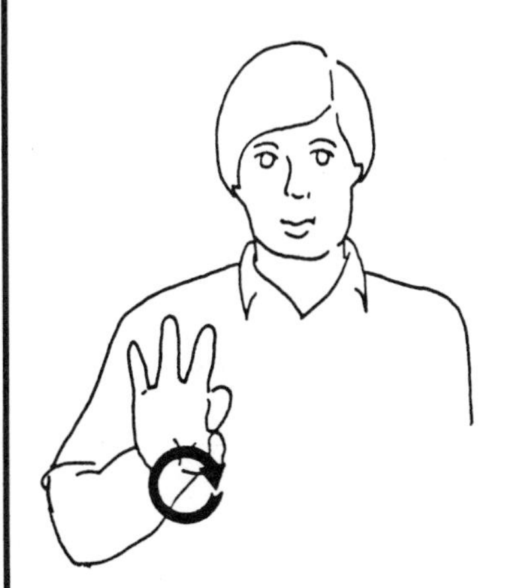

Friday

Saturday

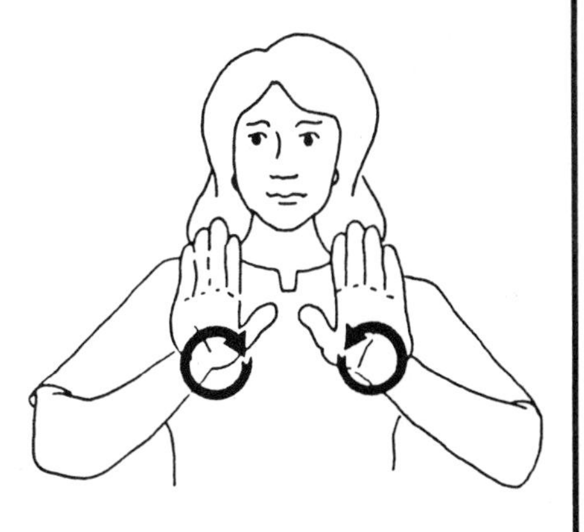

Sunday

SPECIAL DAYS

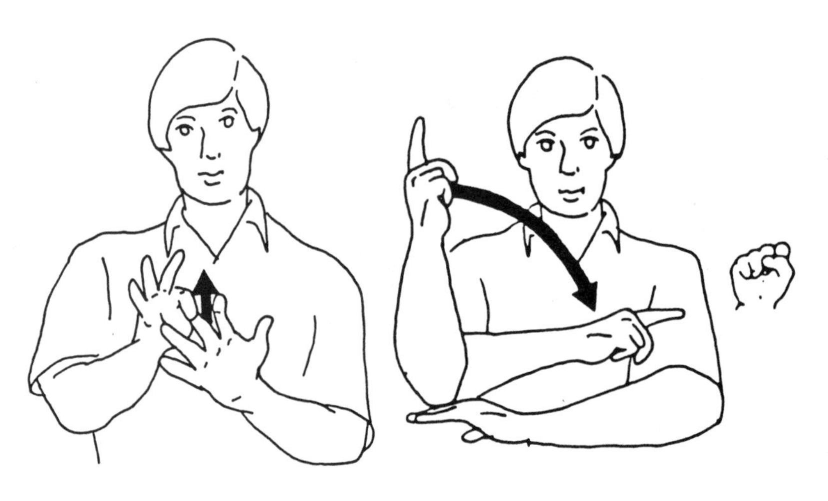

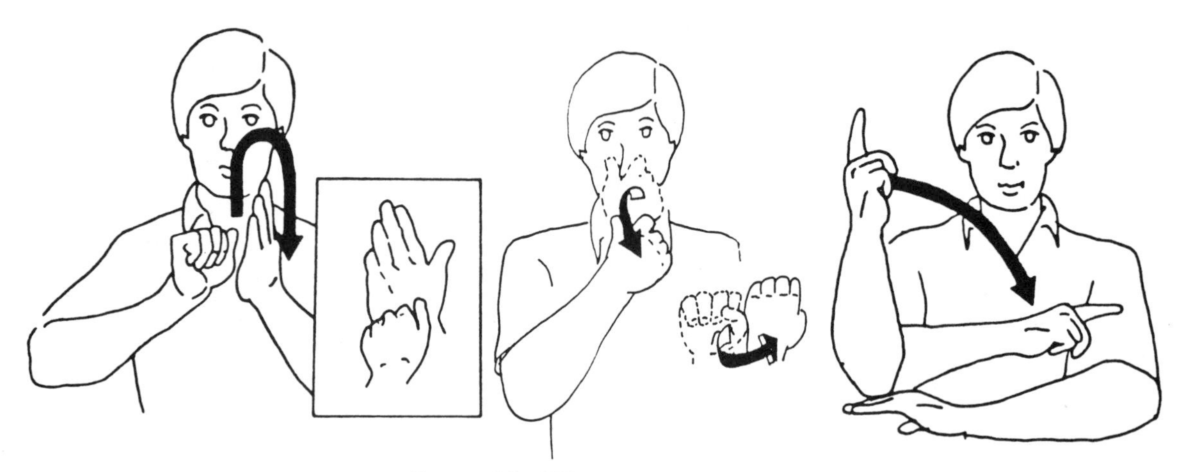

April Fool's Day

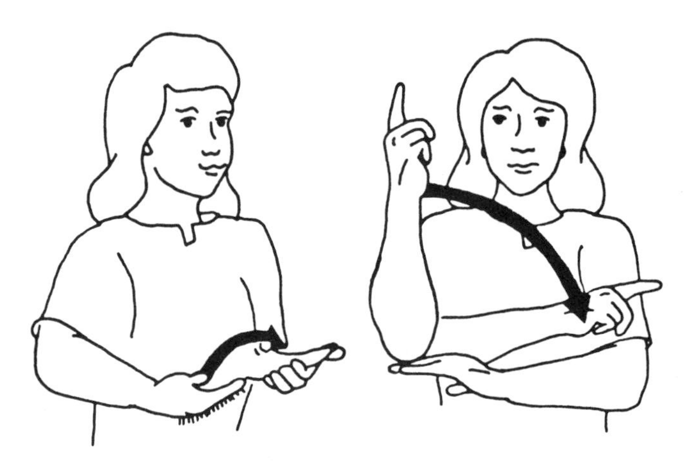

birthday

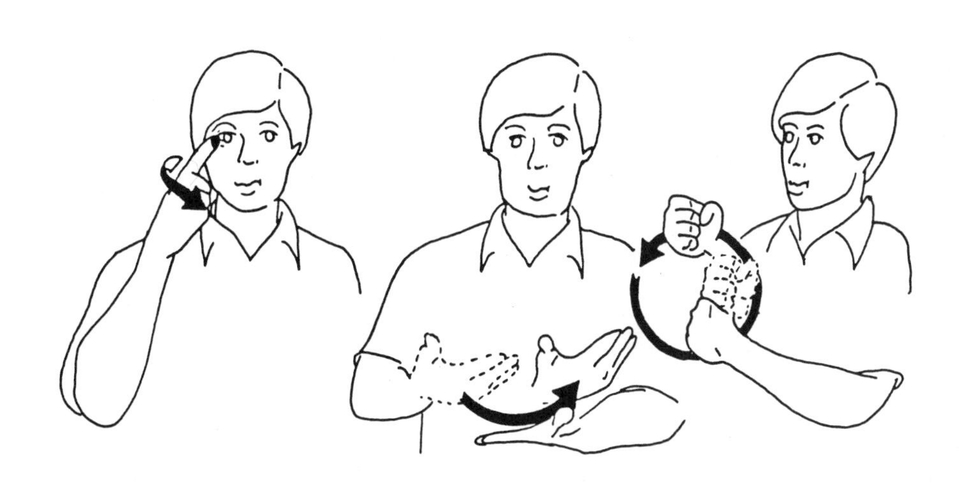

Chinese New Year

Christmas

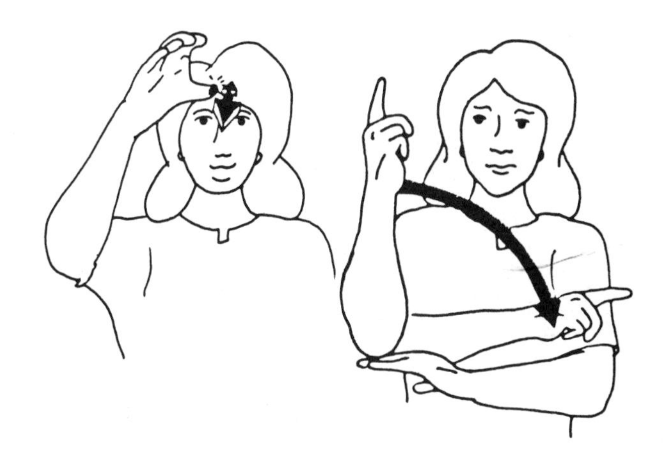

Columbus Day

Easter

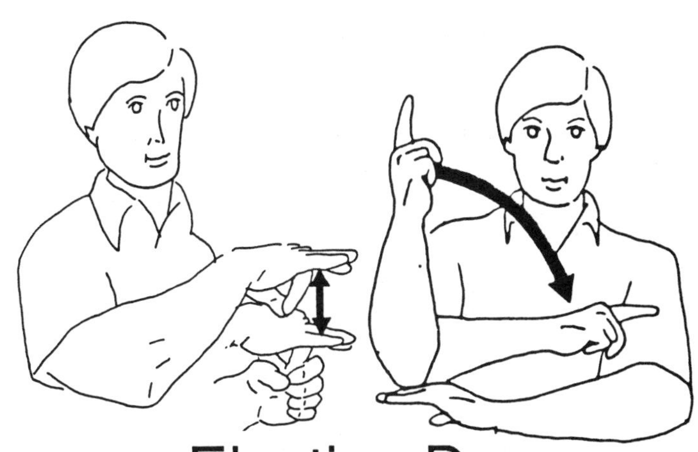

Election Day

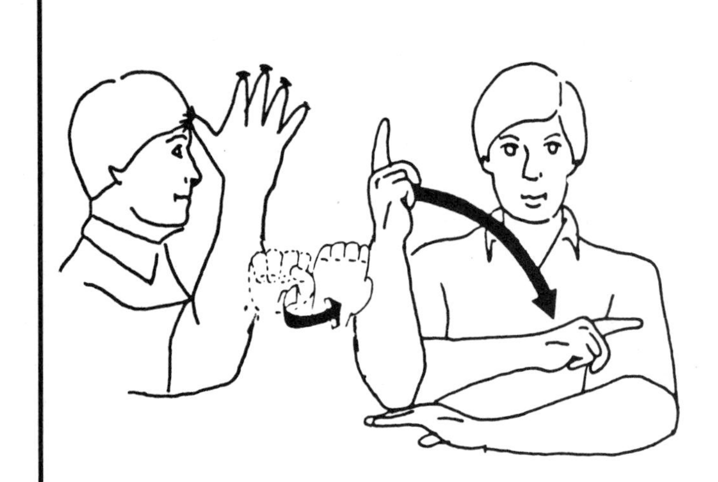

Father's Day

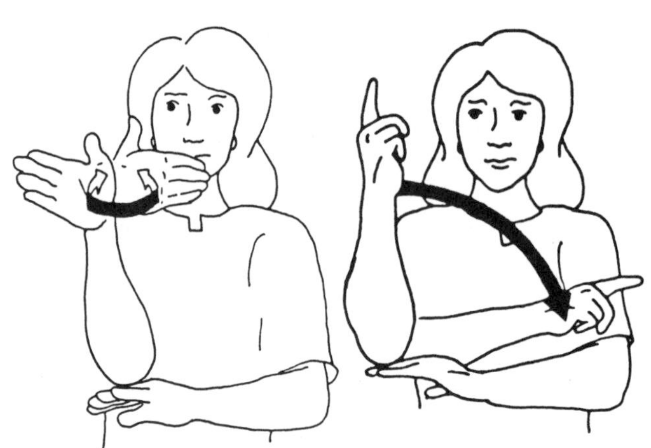

Flag Day

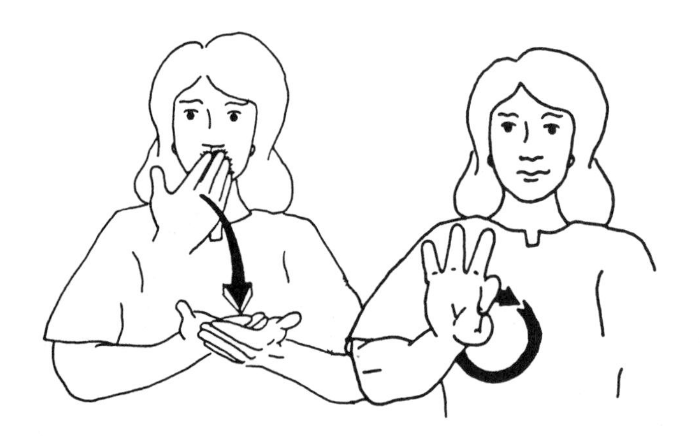

Good Friday

Halloween

Hanukkah

holiday

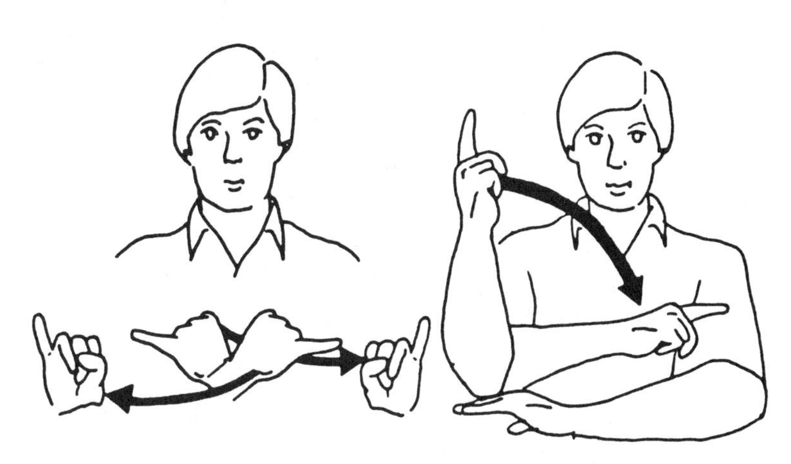

Independence Day

M.L.K. Jr.'s Birthday
(Martin Luther King Jr.)

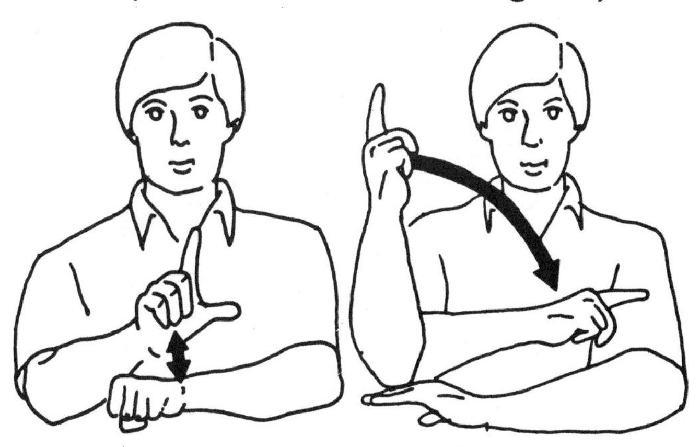

Labor Day

Lincoln's Birthday
Mardi Gras
May Day
Mother's Day

New Year's Day

Passover

President's Day

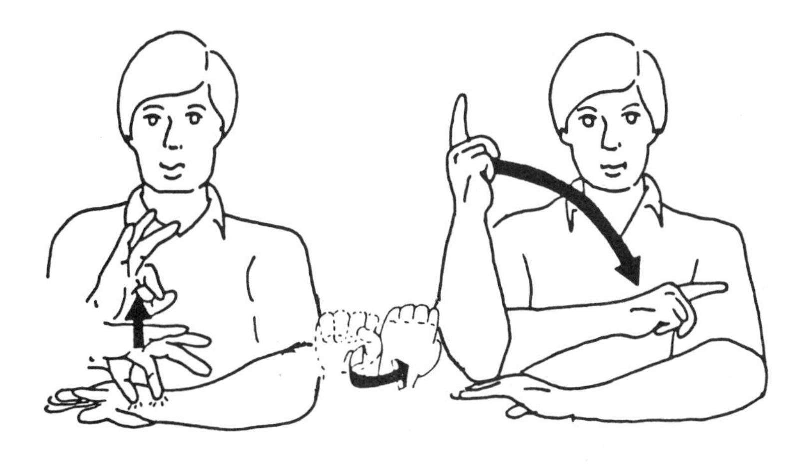

St. Patrick's Day

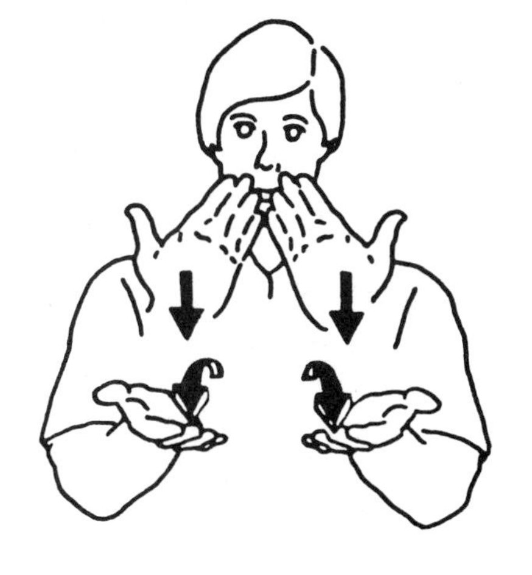

Thanksgiving

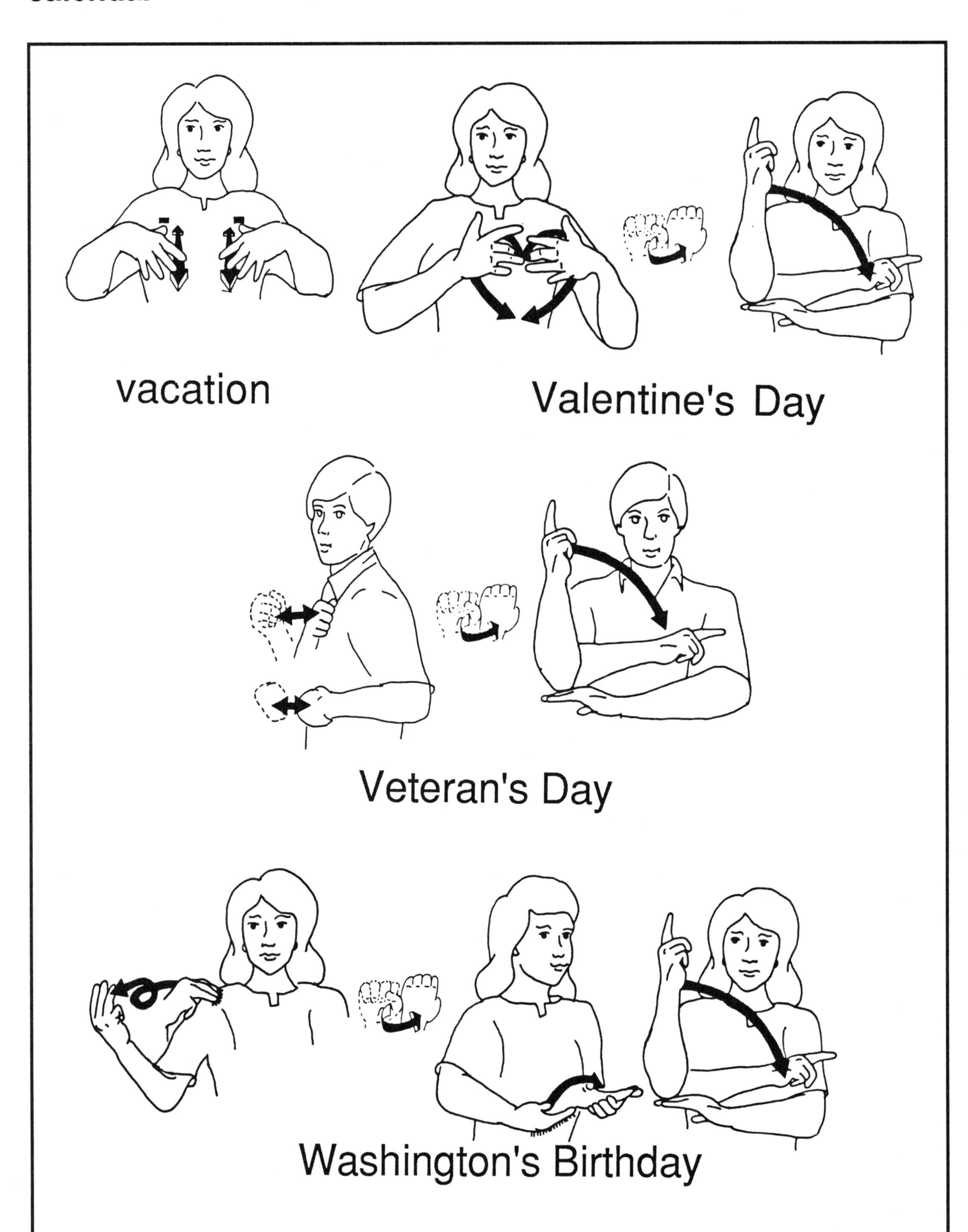
vacation
Valentine's Day
Veteran's Day
Washington's Birthday

CITY THINGS

accident
address
alley
apartment
art
auditorium
bank
building
business
campus
church
college
convention
department store
drugstore
elevator
escalator
factory
film
funeral
garbage
government
grocery
hospital
industry
iron
job
library
machine
market
money [2]
movie [2]
office
park
parade
pavement
post office
restaurant
show
sidewalk
sign
steel
store
street
temple
theatre
traffic
trash
warehouse
way
wedding

ACTIVITY - CITY THINGS

Purpose: To identify and know the purpose of things found in a city.

Materials: Pictures of various things found in a city; chalkboard and chalk.

Procedure:

1. Adult signs/says she is looking at a picture of something found in the city and will write four descriptive sentences about it on the chalkboard.
2. Child waits until all four descriptive sentences are written on the board, then tries to guess what the thing is.
3. Child may or may not guess what the thing is, in any case, adult shows the picture to child and explains the descriptive sentences.
4. Adult continues with procedures 1, 2, and 3 until a total of four different things in the city are described, four pictures are face up in front of child, and all descriptions are written on the board.
5. Child sits with back to writing on board while adult signs/says two descriptive sentences for one of the pictures.
6. Child tries to identify which picture in front of her is being described.
7. Repeat procedures 1 through 6 with new pictures of things found in the city and new descriptions.

Examples:

Manhole

1. It is in the street.
2. It is round.
3. Men go into it to fix things.
4. It has a cover on it.

Building

1. It is very big.
2. It has many windows.
3. People work in it.
4. It may have an elevator.

CITY THINGS

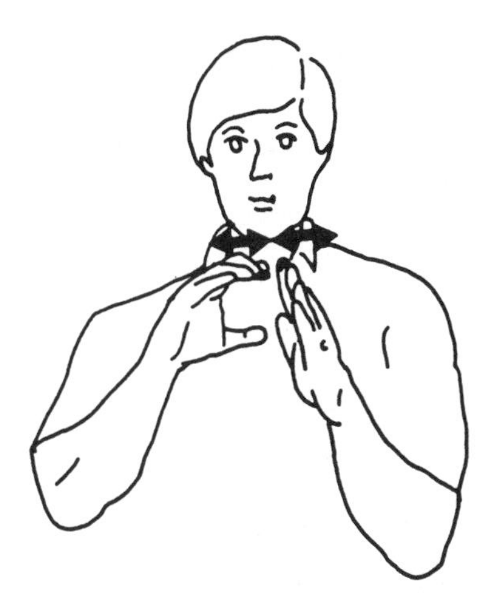

accident

address

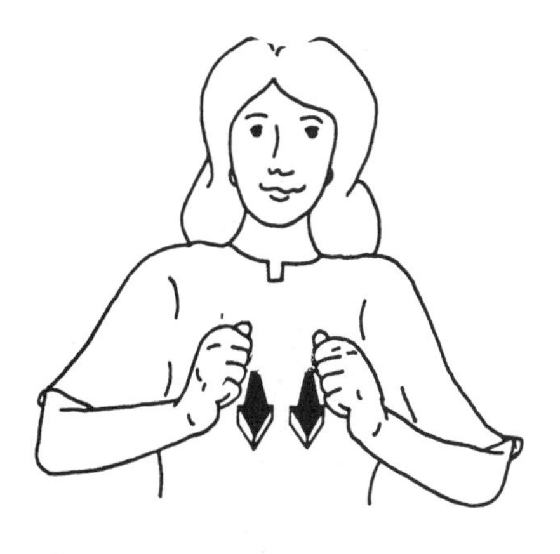

alley

apartment

CITY THINGS

1. Where can you find ____?

  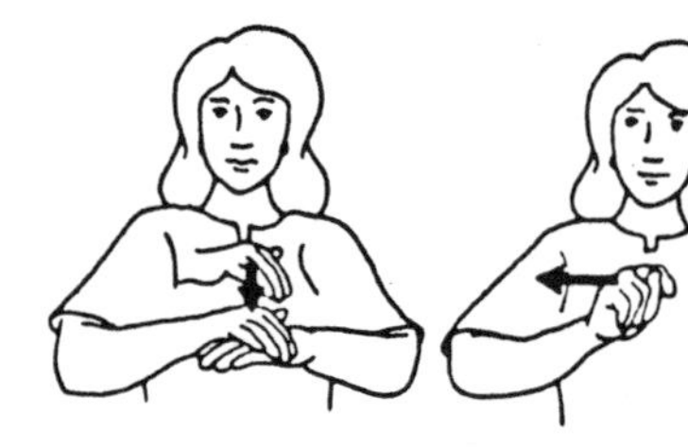

2. Don't throw_____ on the_____.

3. Show me the ______.

   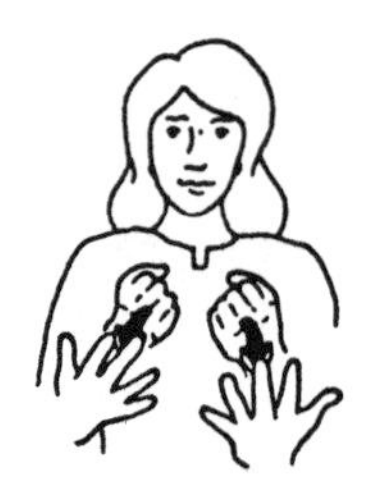 

4. The city has many ______.

art
auditorium
bank
building
business
campus
church
college

5. Is the ______ closed today?
6. Tell me what you saw.
7. In the______ you can get_____.
8. Why don't you like ______?

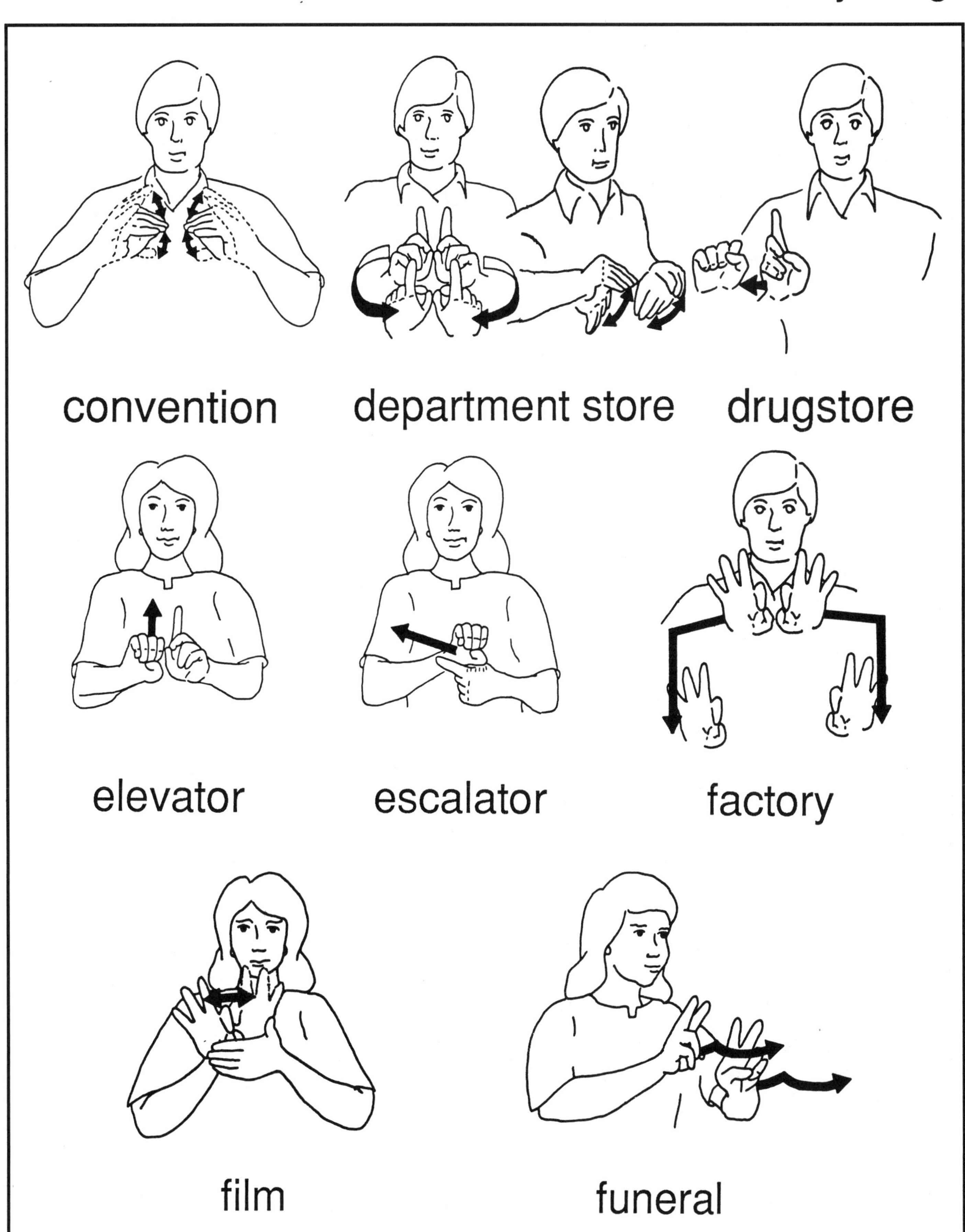
convention
department store
drugstore
elevator
escalator
factory
film
funeral

city things

garbage
government
grocery
hospital
industry
iron
job
library
machine

market
money
movie
office
parade
park
pavement
post office

restaurant
show
sidewalk
sign
steel
store
street

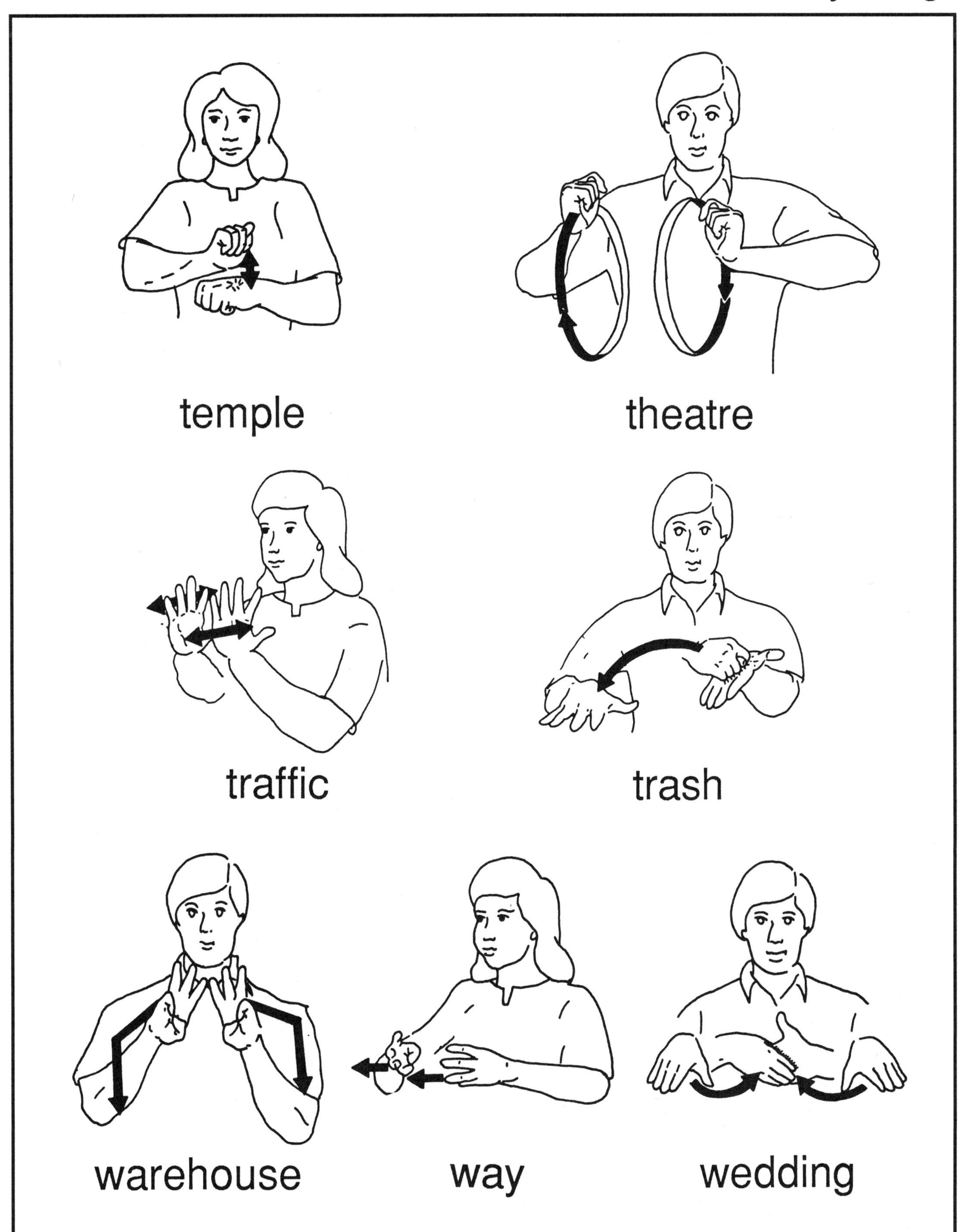
temple
theatre
traffic
trash
warehouse
way
wedding

CLOTHING

bathrobe
belt
bib
blouse
bonnet
boot
bra
bracelet
button [2]
cap
coat
costume
dress [2]
earring
glasses
glove
gown
hankerchief
hat
jacket
mitten
necklace
nightgown
pajamas
pants
pin
pocket
purse
raincoat
ring
sandal
scarf
shirt
shoe [2]
shorts
skirt
sock
stocking
suit
suitcase
sweater
swimsuit [2]
t - shirt
tie
umbrella
underwear
uniform
vest
watch
zipper

ACTIVITY - CLOTHING

Purpose: To name different parts of clothing and work on fine motor skills.

Materials: Paper doll and paper clothing.

Procedure:

1. Adult shows child fully dressed paper doll.
2. Adult gives doll to child, signs/says, "Give me a shoe."
3. Child responds appropriately.
4. Adult puts the clothing on table in front of child.
5. Adult continues asking child for different parts of clothing until doll is undressed.
6. Adult signs/says to child, to put clothing back on doll, one piece at a time, e.g., "Put on the shoe," until doll is fully dressed.

Variations: Have a variety of paper clothing scattered on table in front of child. Adult signs/says to child, "Put on the red hat," "Put on the blue shoe," etc. Child dresses doll appropriately.

CLOTHING

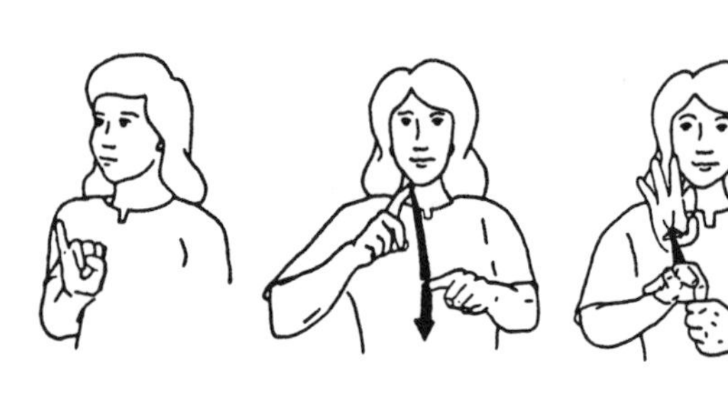 

1. I can't find your ______.

2. Is that my ______?

3. Which ______ are mine?

  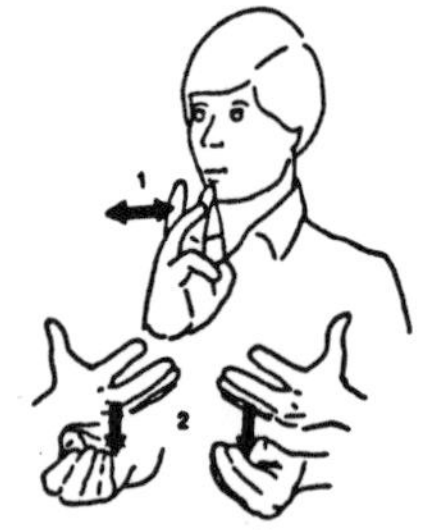

4. Those ______ are wet.

CLOTHING

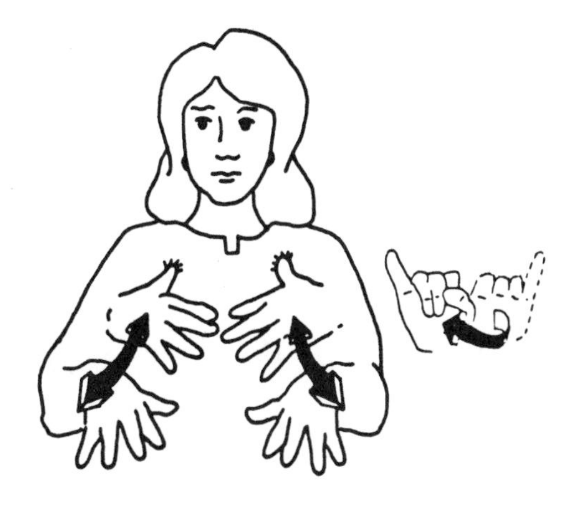

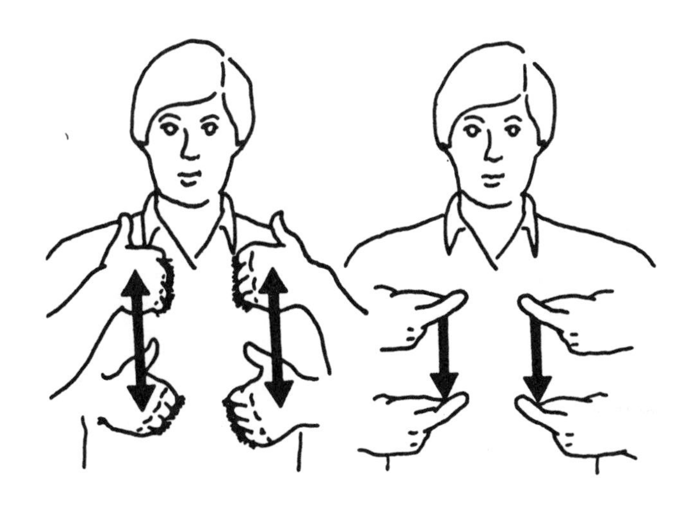

bathrobe

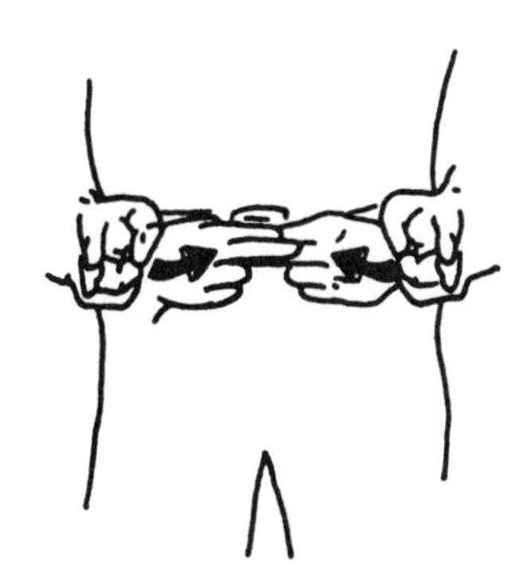

belt

bib

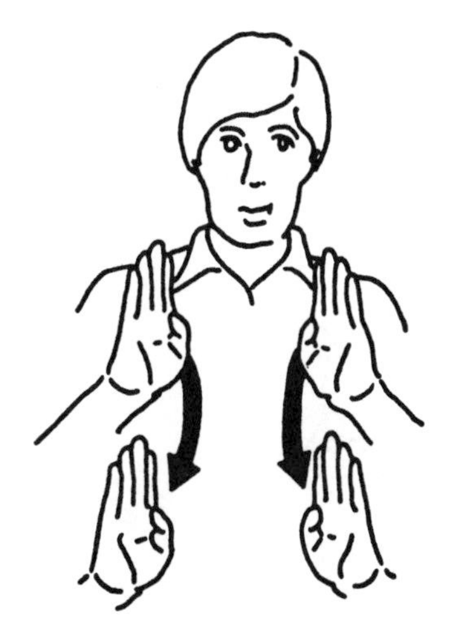

blouse

bonnet

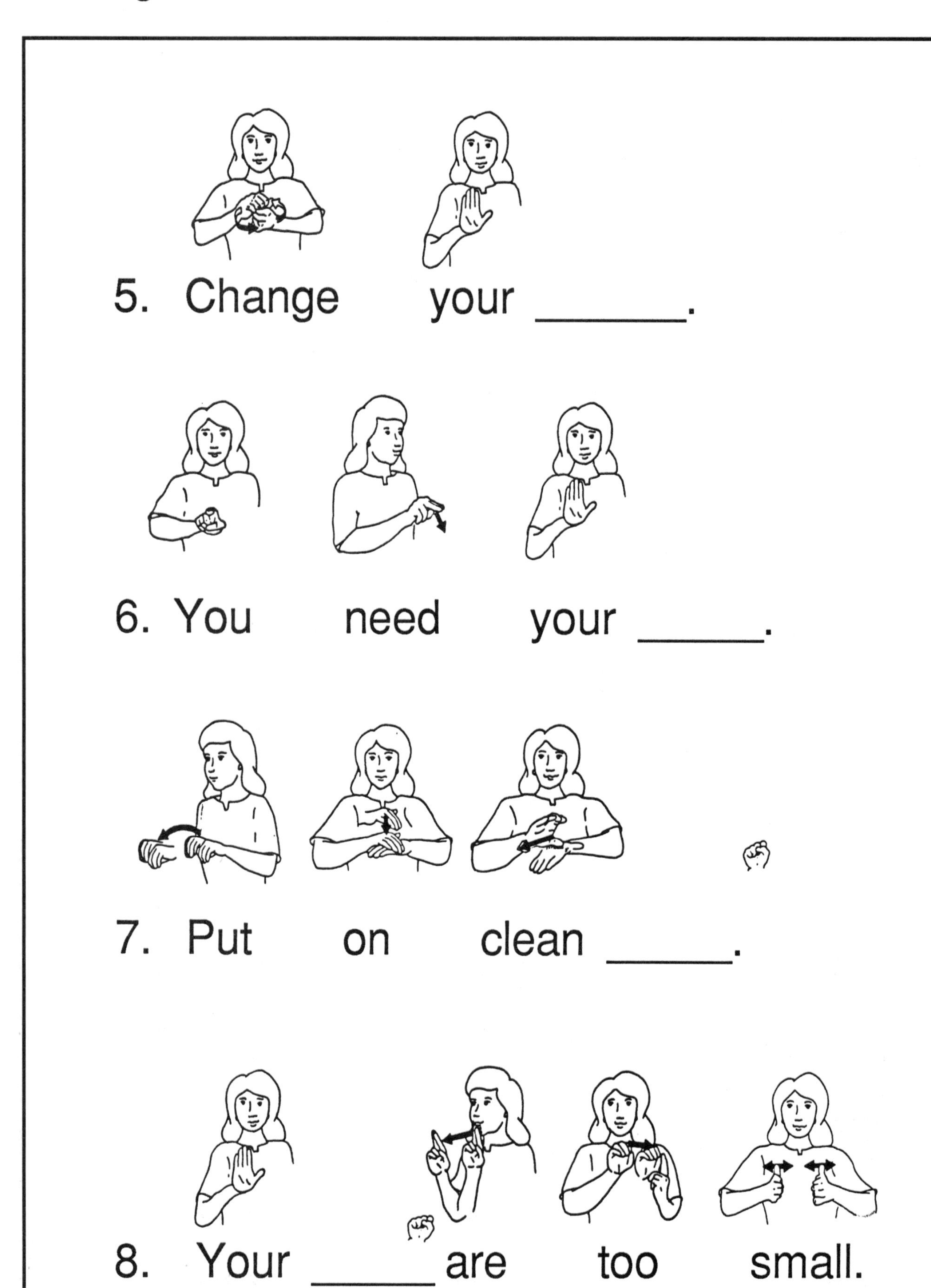
5. Change your ______.
6. You need your _____.
7. Put on clean _____.
8. Your _____ are too small.

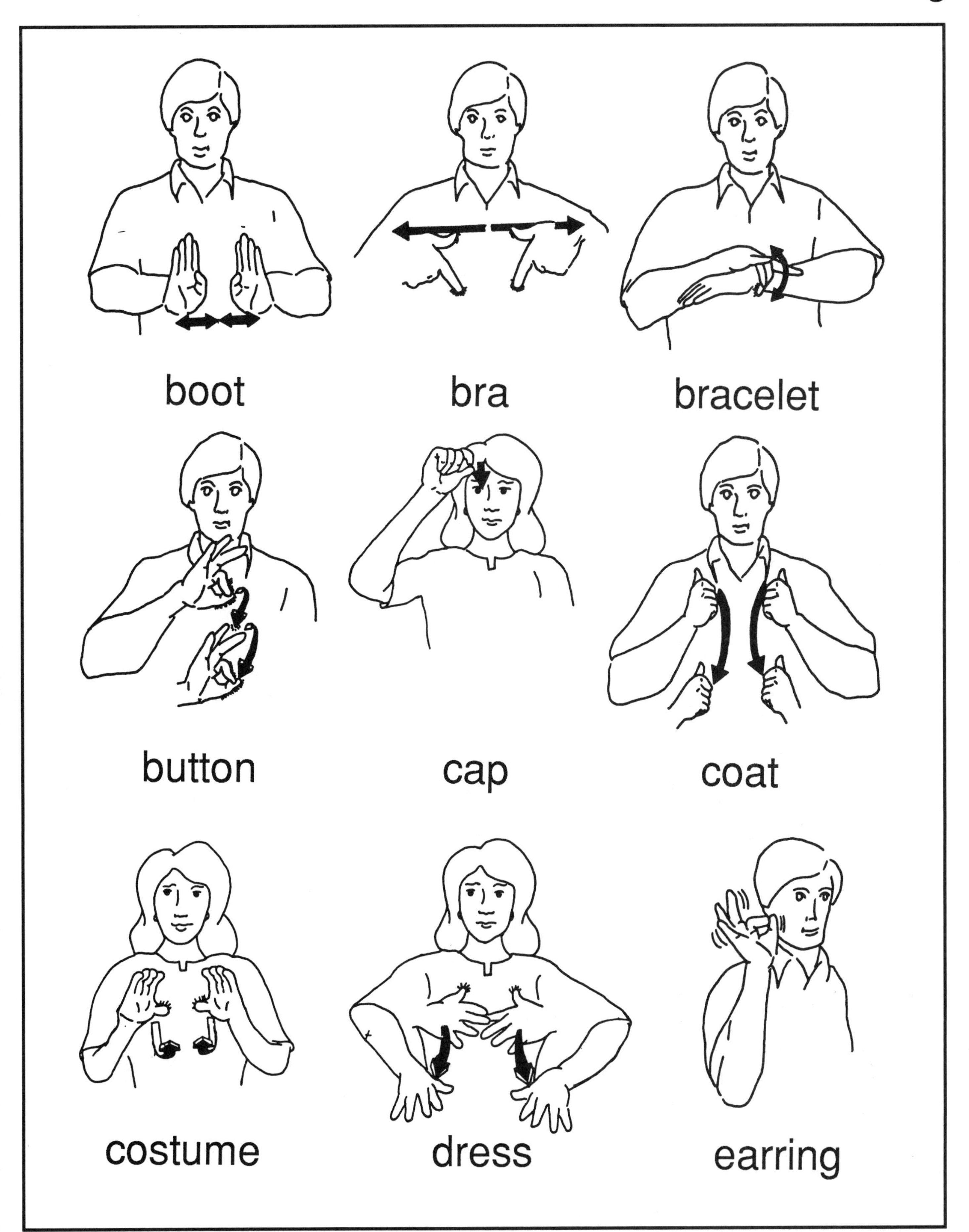
boot
bra
bracelet
button
cap
coat
costume
dress
earring

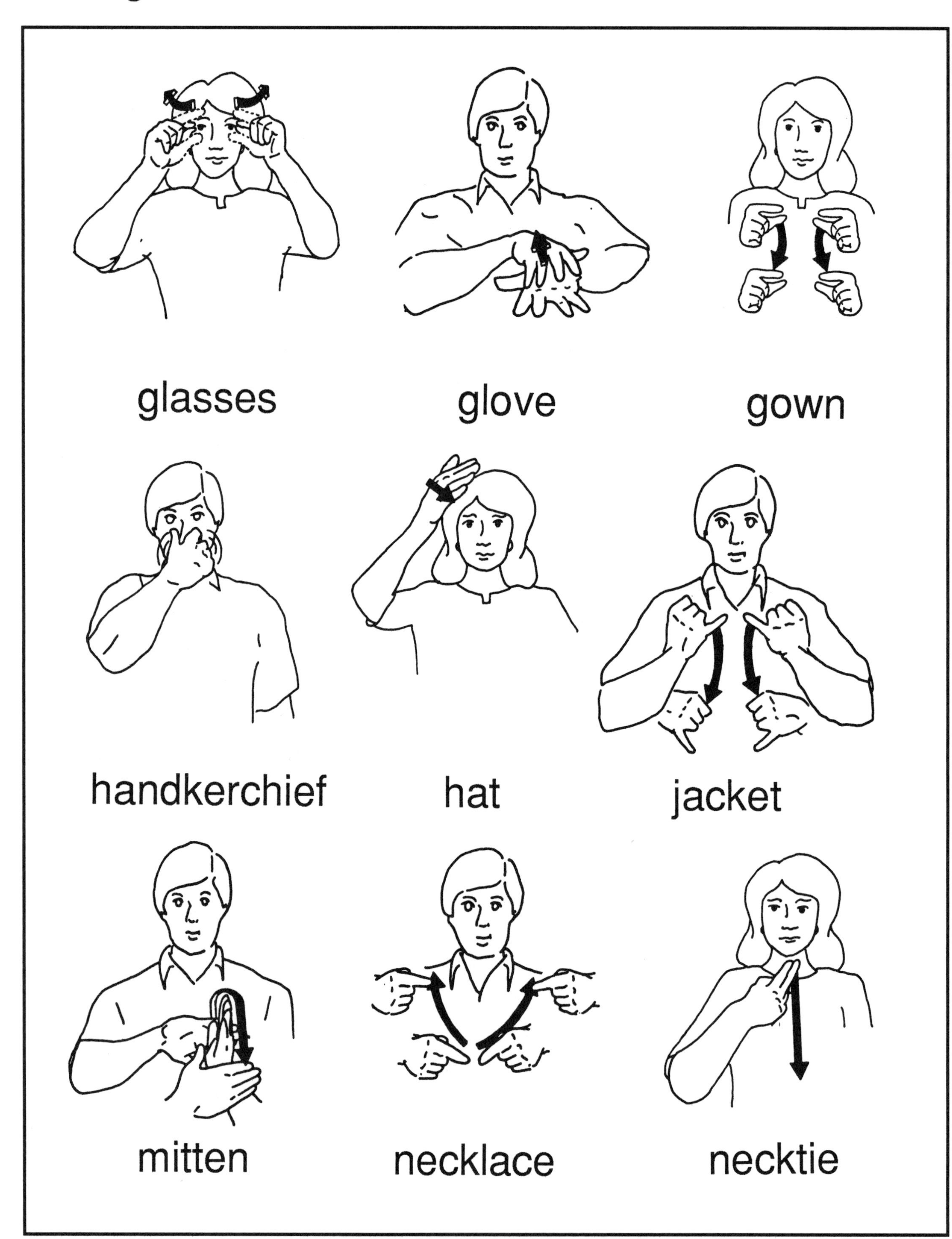
glasses
glove
gown
handkerchief
hat
jacket
mitten
necklace
necktie

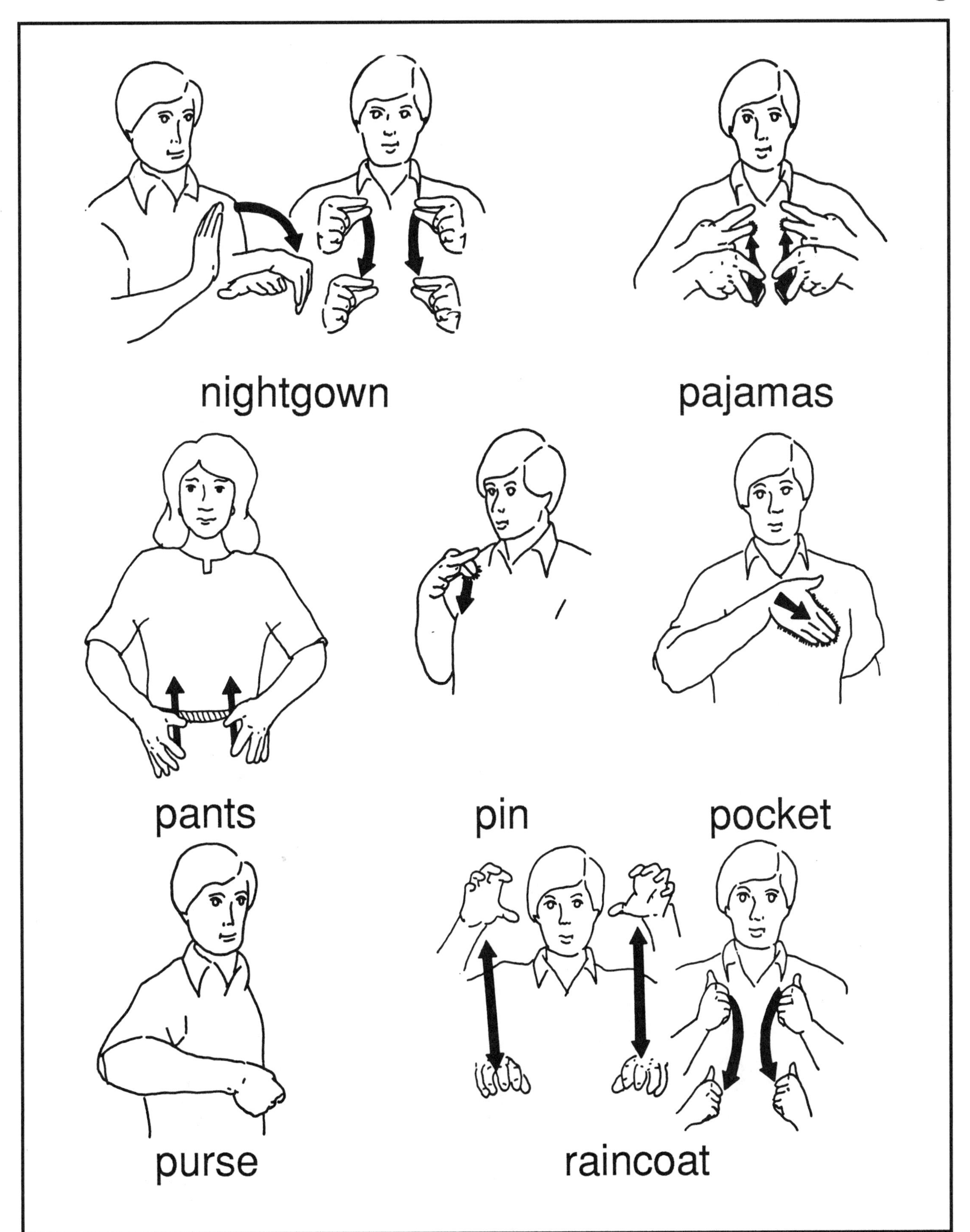
nightgown
pajamas
pants
pin
pocket
purse
raincoat

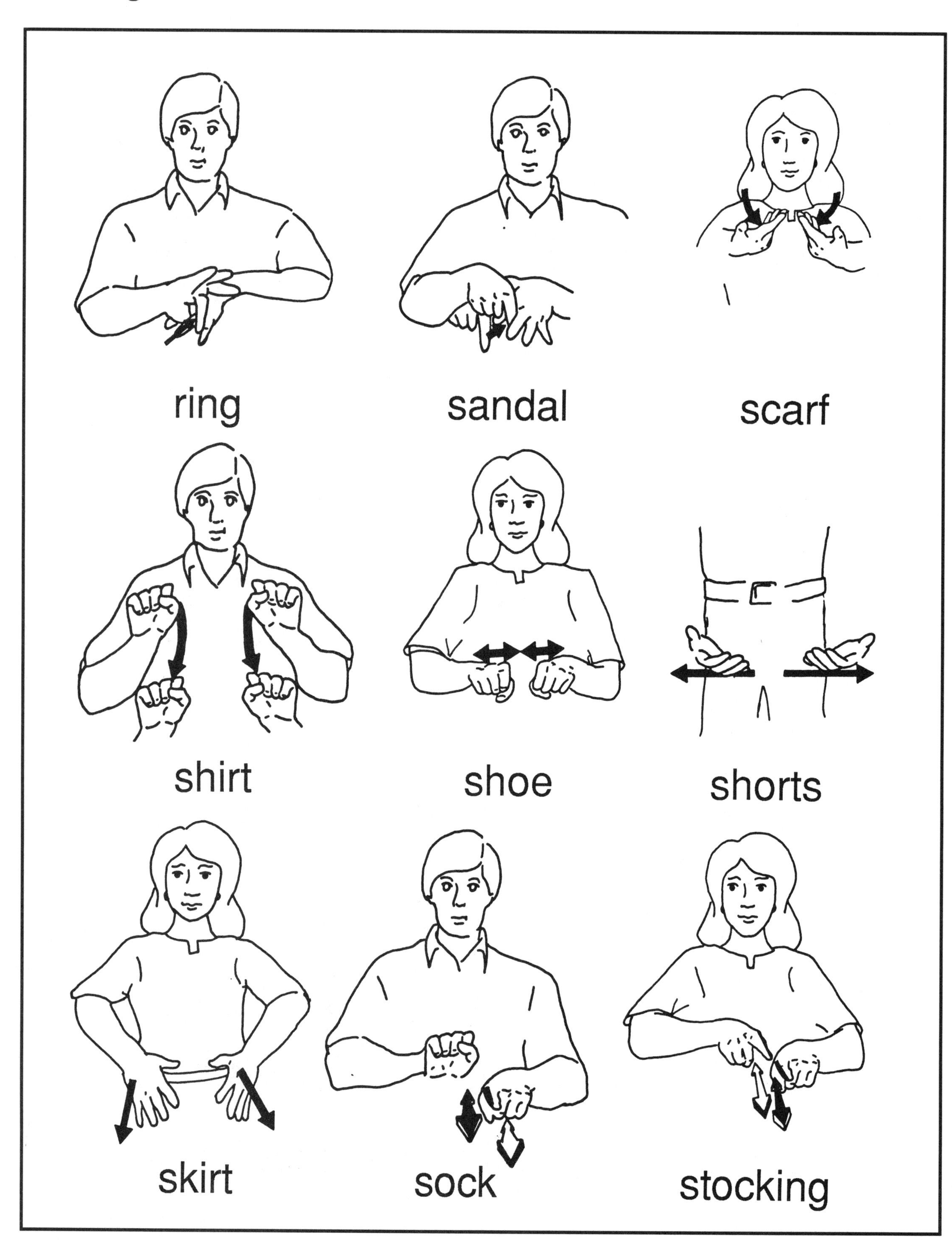
ring
sandal
scarf
shirt
shoe
shorts
skirt
sock
stocking

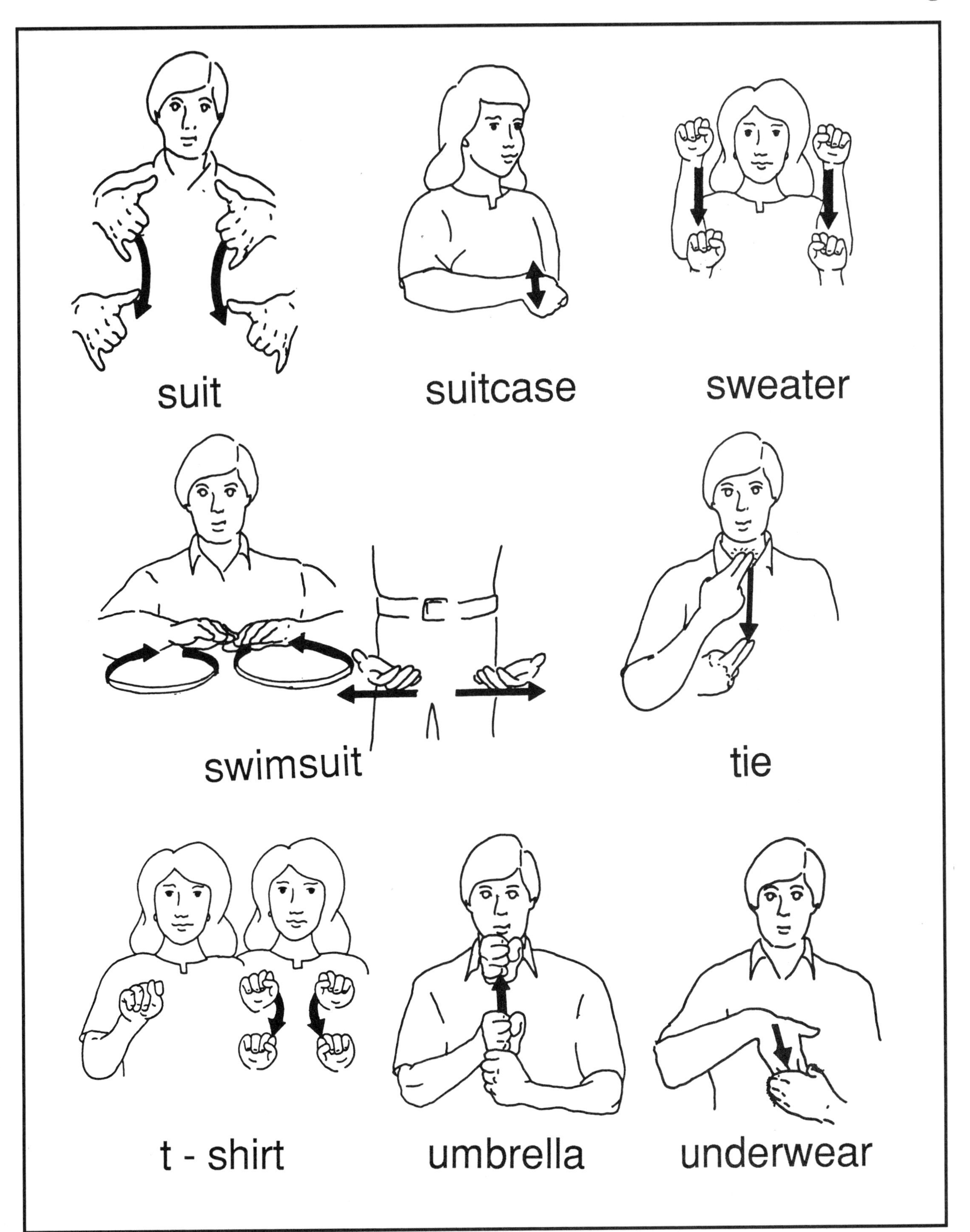
suit
suitcase
sweater
swimsuit
tie
t - shirt
umbrella
underwear

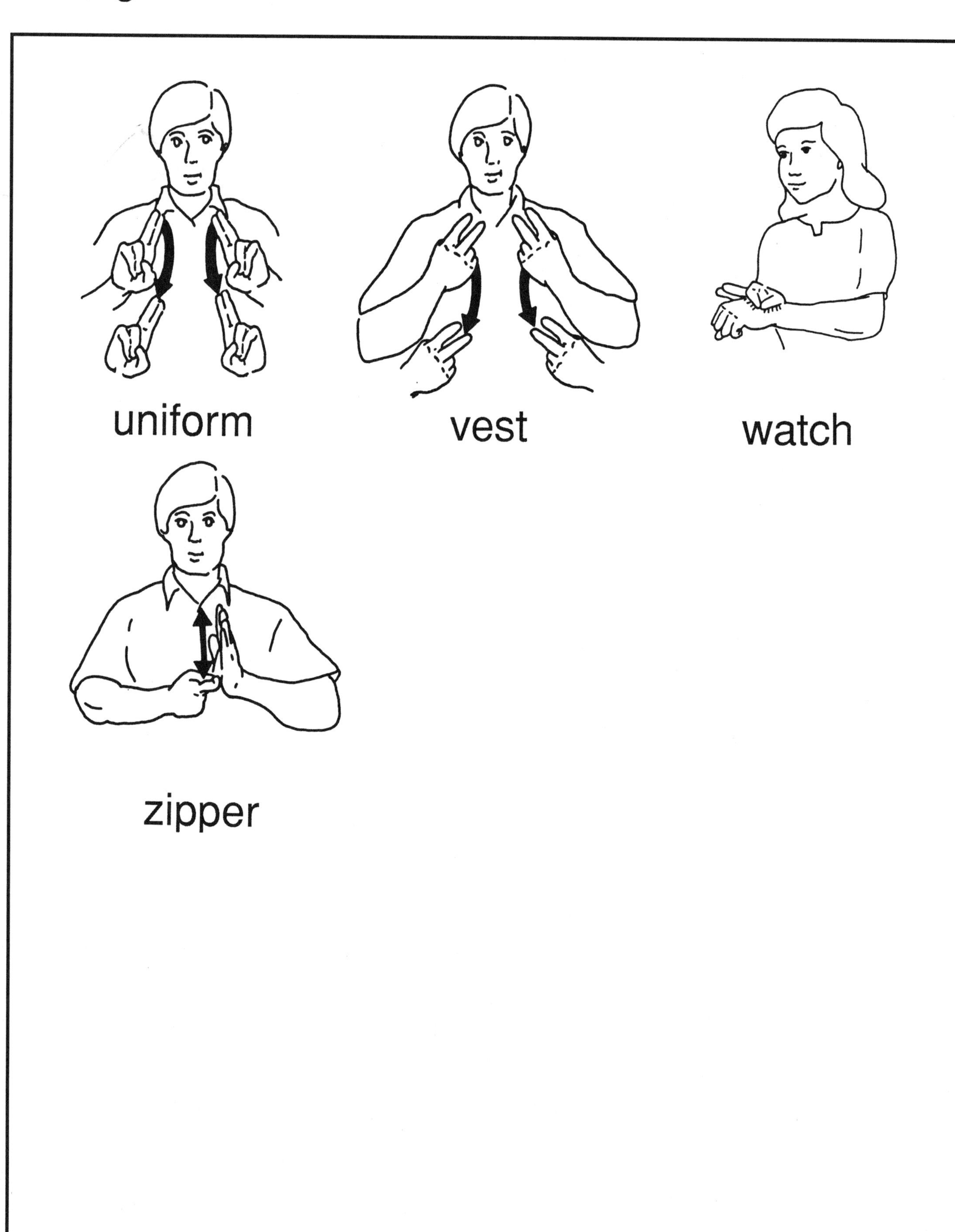
uniform
vest
watch
zipper

COLORS[1]

black [2]
blue [2]
brown [2]
gold
gray
green [2]
orange
pink
purple
red [1]
silver
tan
white
yellow [2]

ACTIVITY - COLORS

Purpose: To identify different colors.

Materials: Beanbag; different colored construction paper cut into large circles; tape.

Procedure:

1. Child places colored circles on floor.
2. Adult puts tape on floor for child to stand behind several feet from the circles.
3. Child stands behind tape and throws beanbag onto colored circles.
4. Adult signs/says , "What color is this?"
5. Child signs/says color and removes it from the floor.
6. Repeat procedures 3, 4, and 5 until all the circles are identified and removed by child.

Variations: Put a number on each piece of colored paper and have child identify only the number or both the color and number; cut the paper into different shapes and the child can identify the shape, color and /or number on each throw of the beanbag.

COLORS

1. My favorite color is ______.

2. What color is your ______?

3. Show me the ______ one.

4. Can you spell ______?

COLORS

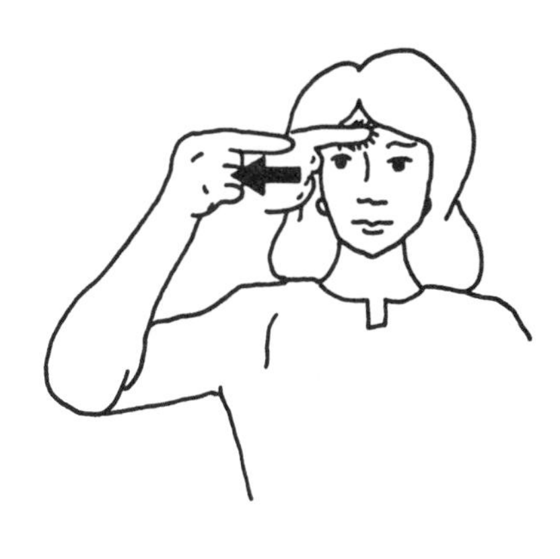

black

blue

brown

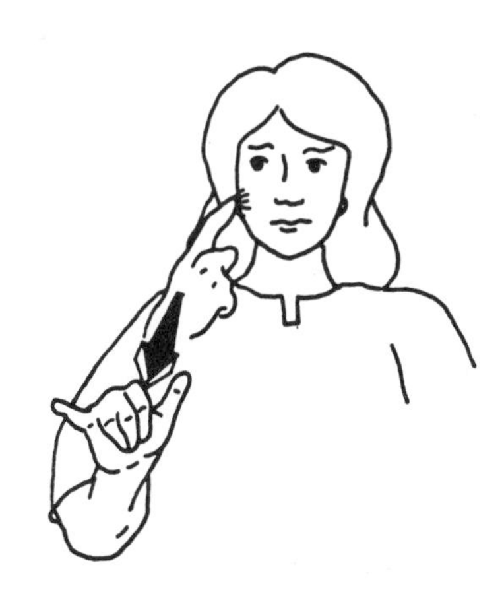

gold

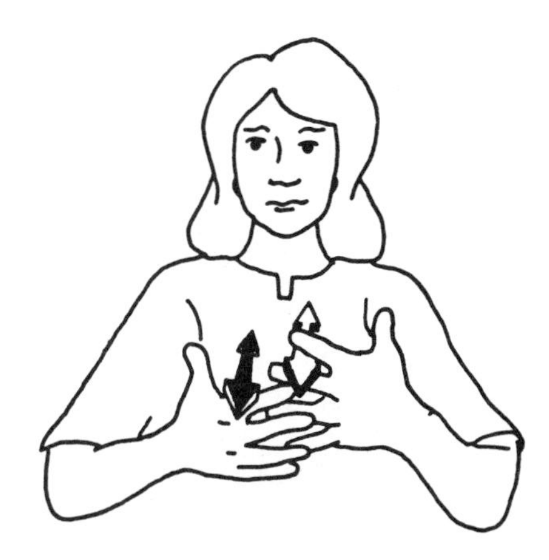

gray

green

orange
pink
purple
red
silver
tan
white
yellow

THINGS WITH CORNERS

block
book 2
box 2
card 1
certificate
check
cube
dollar 2
door 1
flag
frame

house 1
license
magazine
map
paper 2
picture 2
pocket
poster
rectangle
refrigerator
room 1

sign
square
stamp
street 2
suitcase
table
television 1
ticket
window 2
yard

THINGS WITH CORNERS

1. Can you spell ______?

2. Where is the corner?

3. Count the corners.

4. Draw something with corners.

THINGS WITH CORNERS

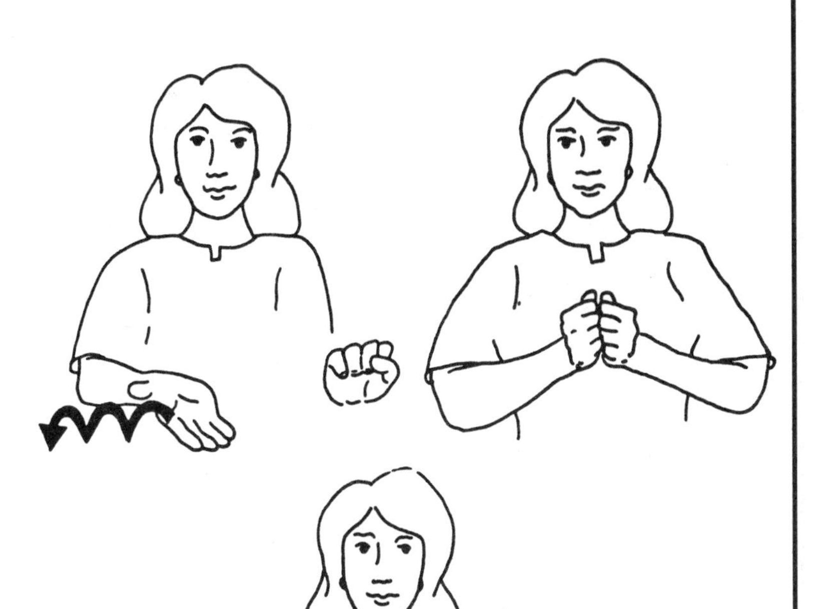

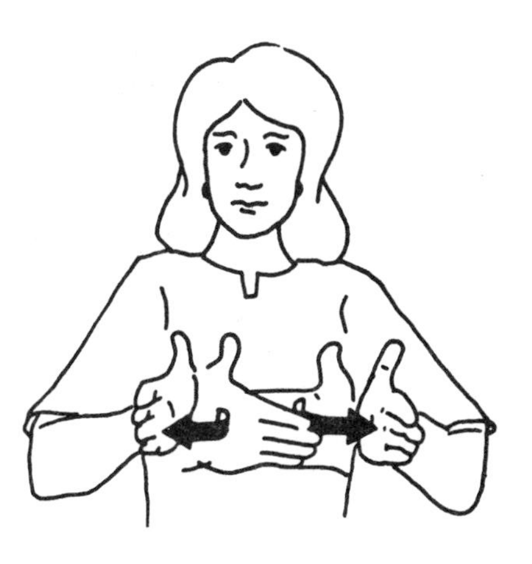

block book box

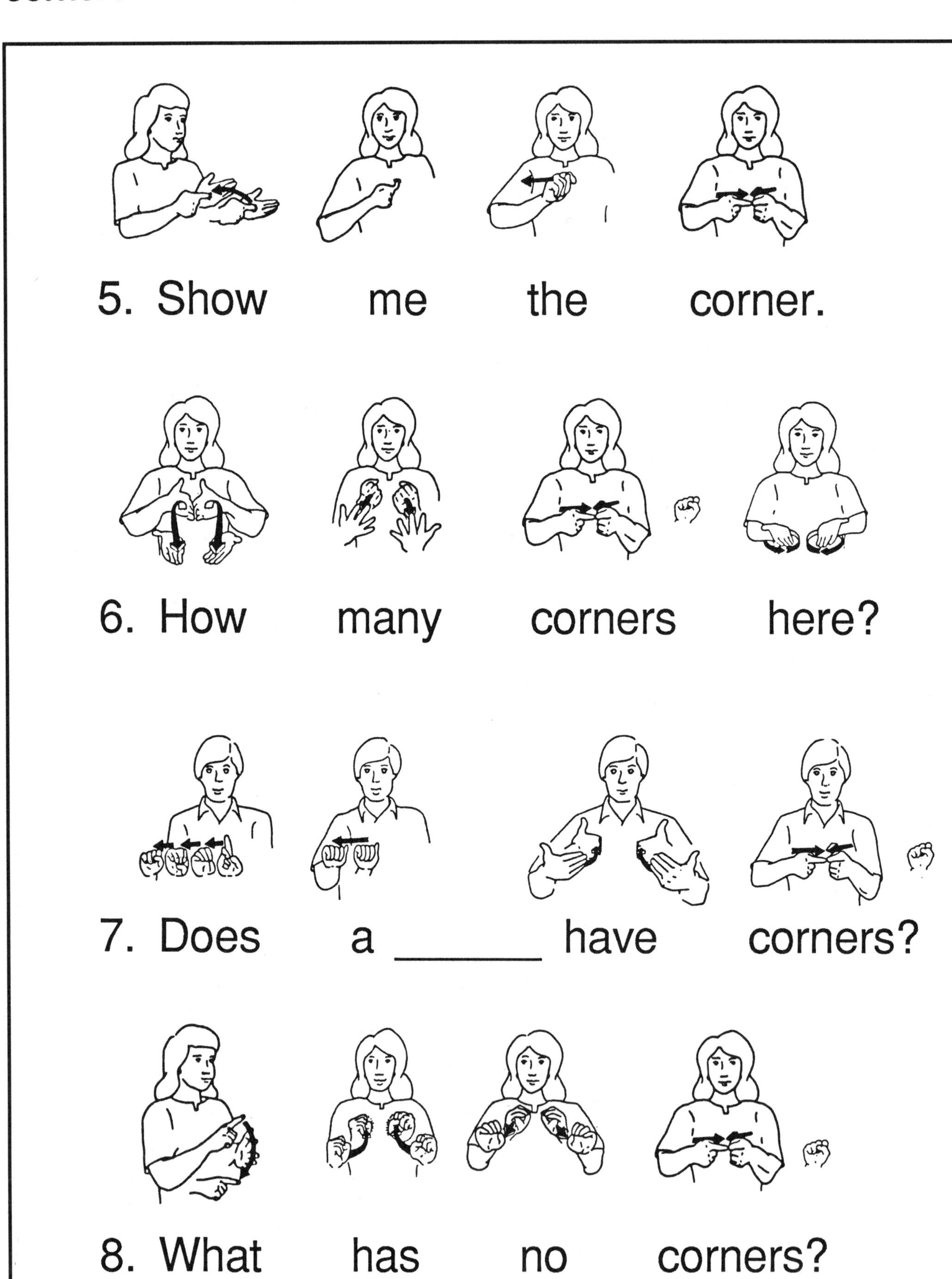
5. Show me the corner.
6. How many corners here?
7. Does a ______ have corners?
8. What has no corners?

card
certificate
check
cube
dollar
door
flag
frame
house

corners

license
magazine
map
paper
picture
pocket
poster
rectangle
refrigerator

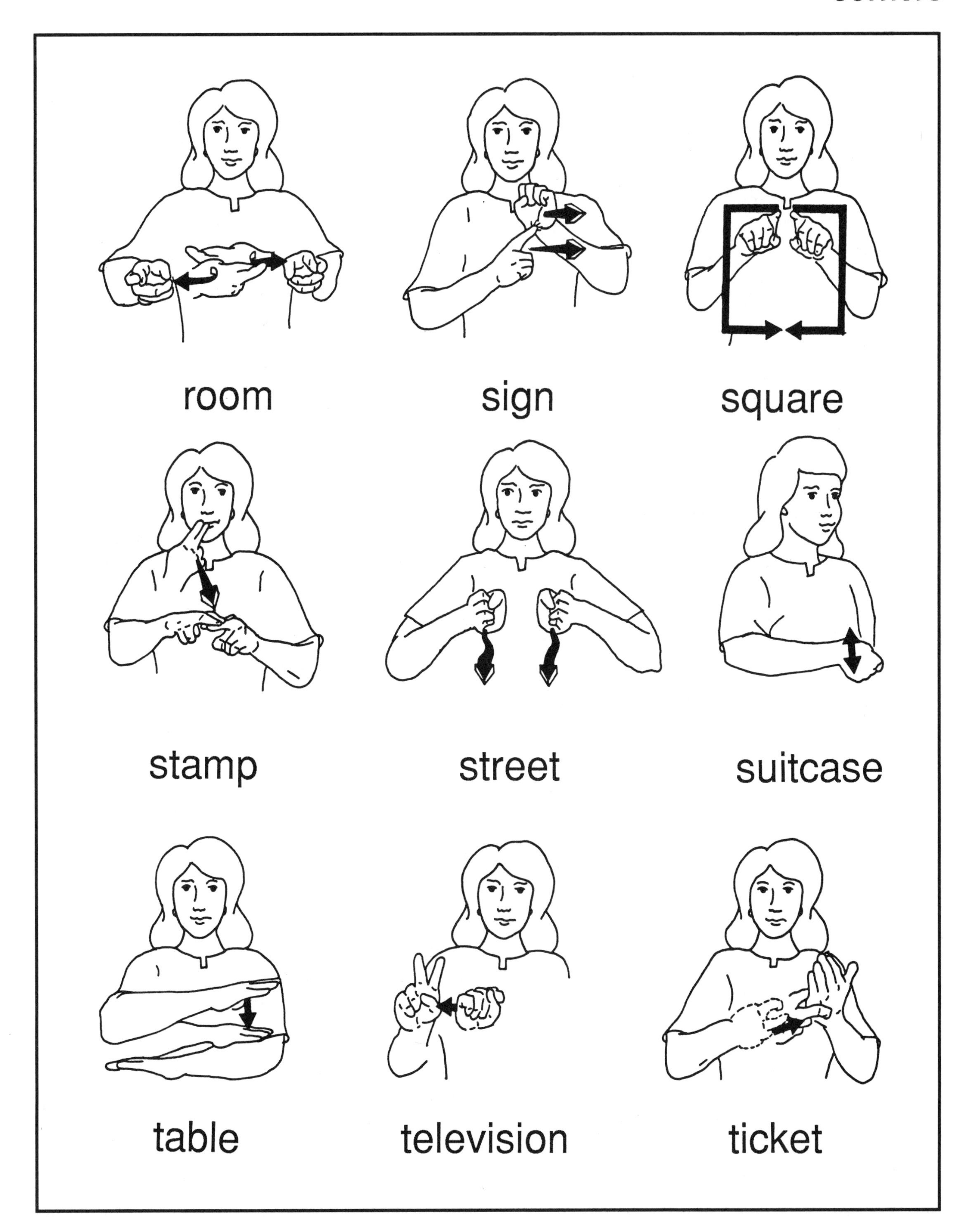
room
sign
square
stamp
street
suitcase
table
television
ticket

corners

yard

ACTIVITY - THINGS WITH CORNERS

Purpose: To identify things that have corners.

Materials: Paper bag; various objects that have corners: matchbook, card, comb, letter, dice, block, etc., all put into another bag.

Procedure:

1. Adult shows child a box signing/saying corner while pointing to each corner.
2. Child signs/says corner while pointing to each corner.
3. Adult signs/says that the child is to feel in the paper bag and identify what the object is (demonstrate).
4. Child puts hand in bag, feels object, signs/says what it is.
5. Child takes object from bag and points to each corner signing/saying corner (how many?).
6. Adult puts a different object in the bag and continues with procedures 4 and 5.
7. All identified objects are put together to sign/say and identify how many corners after all objects are pulled from the bag.

Variations: Instead of one object at a time, several objects with and without corners can be put into the bag and pulled out one at a time to be identified and the corners counted, if any.

COUNTRY THINGS

axe
barn
beehive
bird house
crop
farm
fence
field
forest
garden
grain
grass
ground [2]
gun
hatchet
hay
hill [2]
land [2]
meadow
mine
oat
orchard
picnic
pig pen
plow
ranch
rifle
road
rock [2]
silo
soil
stable
tractor
well
wheelbarrow

ACTIVITY - COUNTRY THINGS

Purpose: To identify different things found in the country.

Materials: Large picture of a farm.

Procedure:

1. Adult puts farm picture on board or on floor.
2. Adult signs/says, "I see a ___." Then fingerspells an object seen in the picture.
3. Child points to the object and then signs/says what the object is.
4. Continue activity pointing to different farm objects in the picture.

Variations: Adult signs the object while the child fingerspells it.

COUNTRY THINGS

1. Show me the ______.

 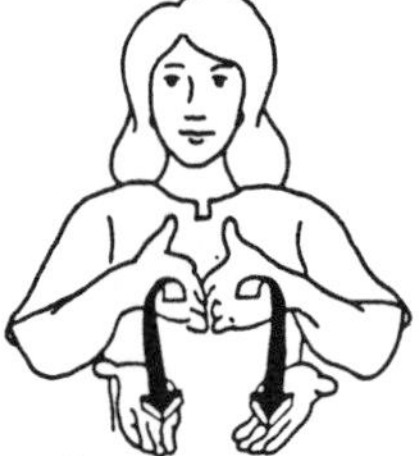  

2. Count how many ______.

3. Yes, that is a ______.

4. Where are the ______?

COUNTRY THINGS

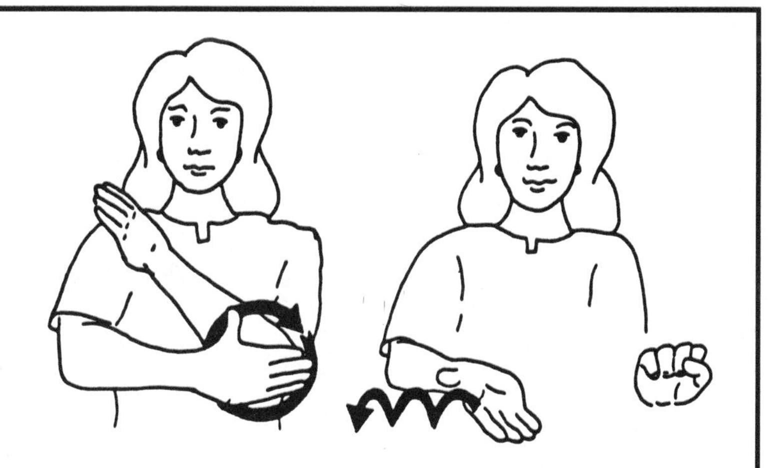

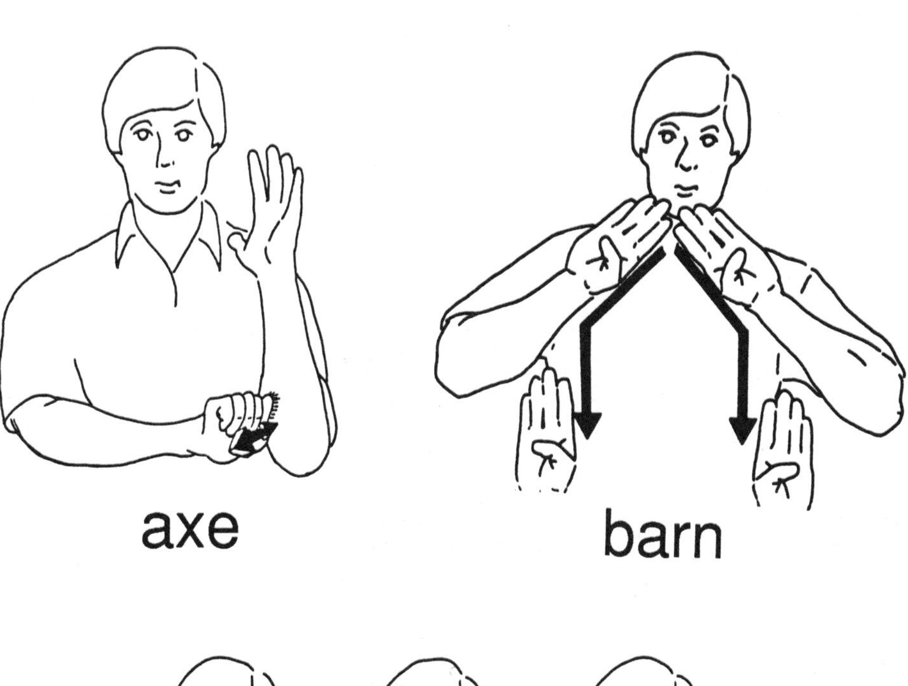

axe

barn

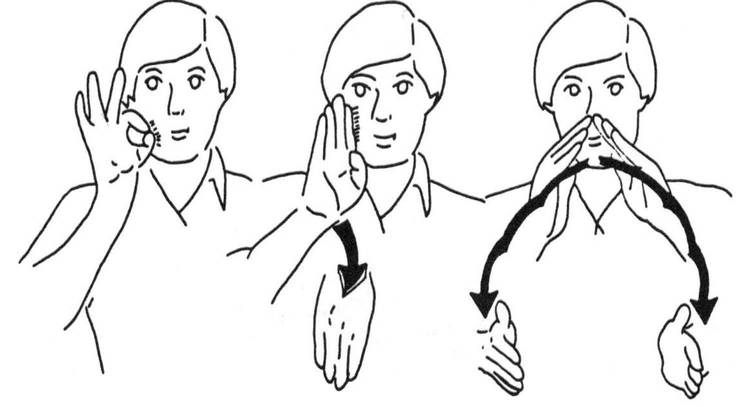

beehive

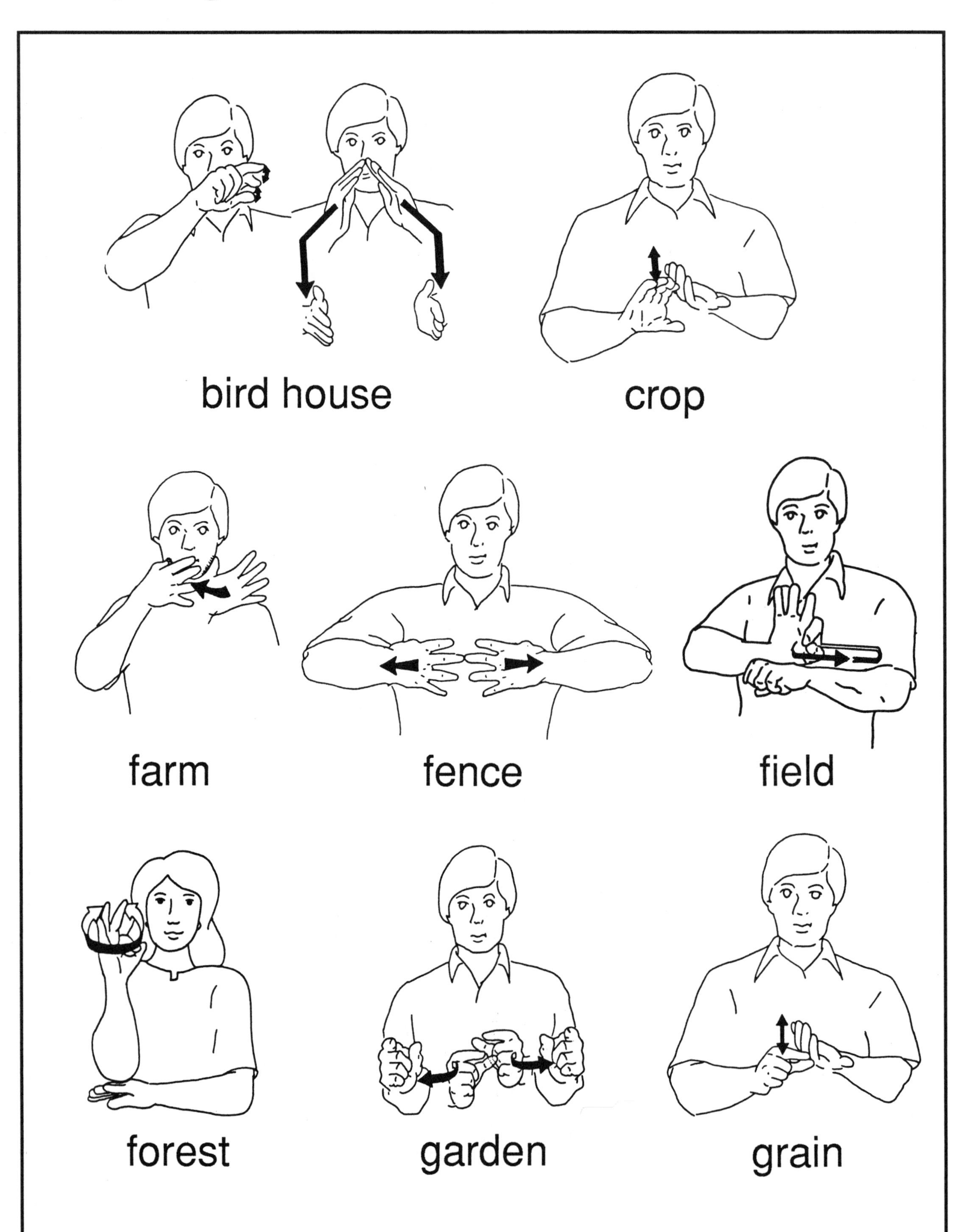
bird house
crop
farm
fence
field
forest
garden
grain

grass
ground
gun
hatchet
hay
hill
land
meadow
mine

oat
orchard
picnic
pig pen
plow
ranch
rifle

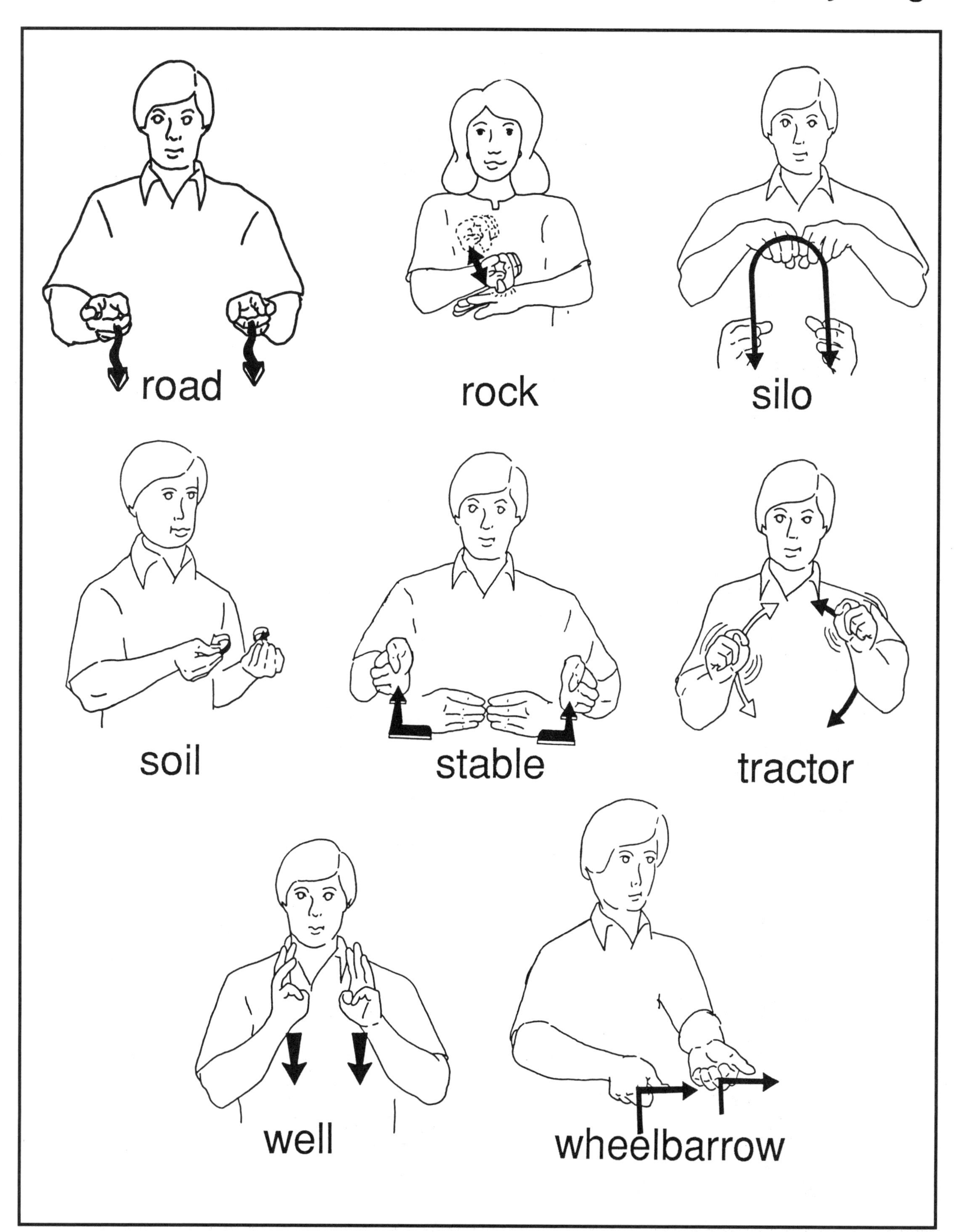
road
rock
silo
soil
stable
tractor
well
wheelbarrow

DEAFNESS

ASL (American Sign Language)
audiogram
audiology
battery
blind
caption
deaf
deaf (traditional)
decoder
ear mold
Gallaudet
hard of hearing
headphone
hear
hearing (person)
hearing aid
hearing impaired
hearing test
I love you
institution (school for the deaf)
interpret
language
mainstream
manual alphabet
method
noise
oral
regular
sign
sign language
simultaneous communication
sound
speech
speechread
spell (fingerspell)
system
TDD (telecommunication device for the deaf)
therapy
total communication
translate
voice

DEAFNESS

ASL
(American Sign Language)

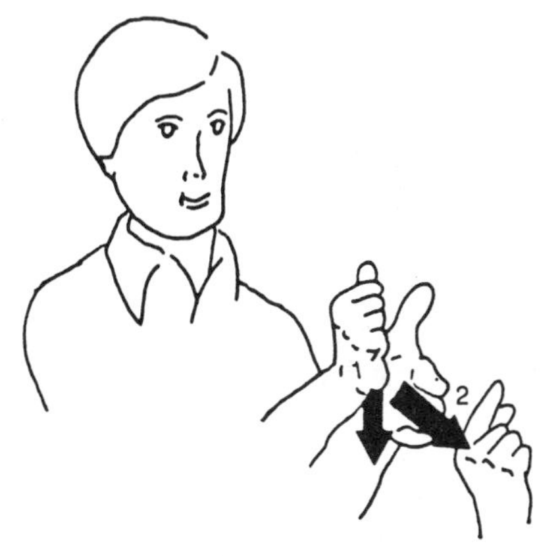

audiogram

audiology

battery

blind

DEAFNESS

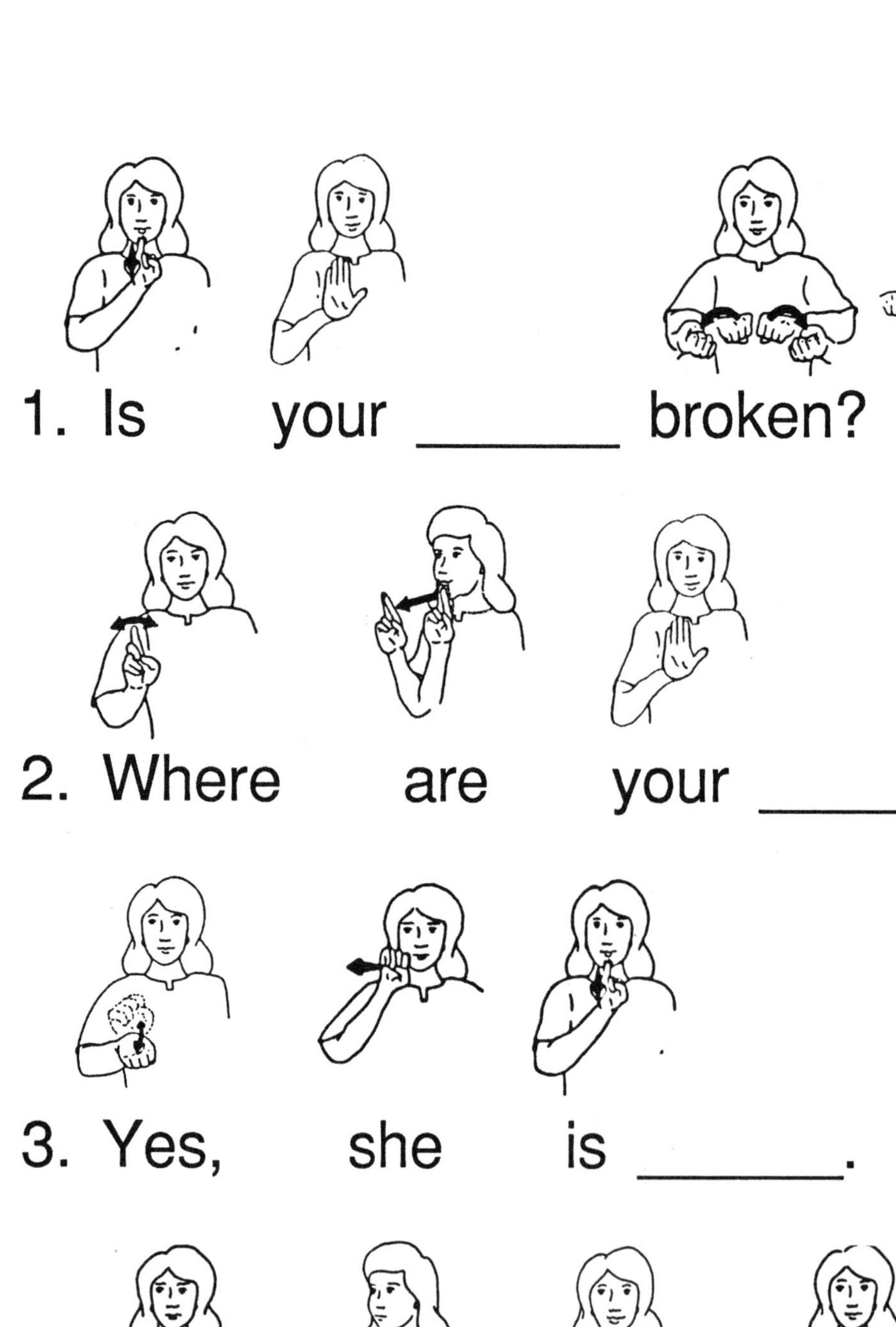

1. Is your ______ broken?

2. Where are your ______?

3. Yes, she is ______.

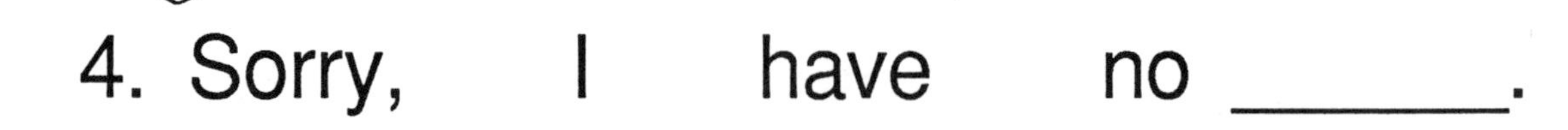

4. Sorry, I have no ______.

caption
deaf
deaf (traditional)
decoder
ear mold
Gallaudet
hard of hearing
headphone
hear

5. Can you ______ that?

6. Please say that again.

7. Let me see your ______.

8. Can you spell ______?

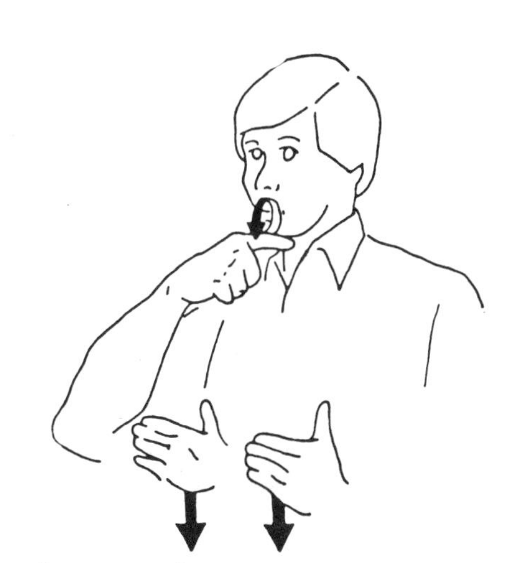
hearing (person)

hearing aid

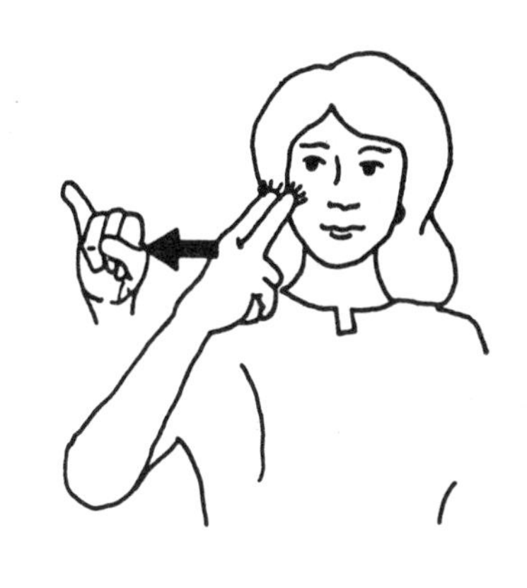
hearing impaired

hearing test

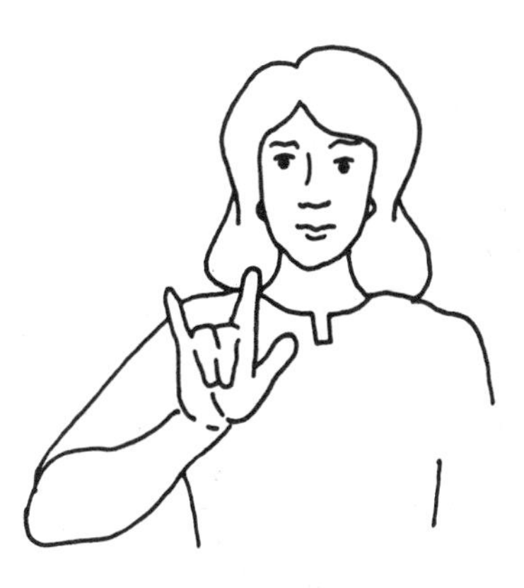
I love you

institution
(school for the deaf)

interpret

language

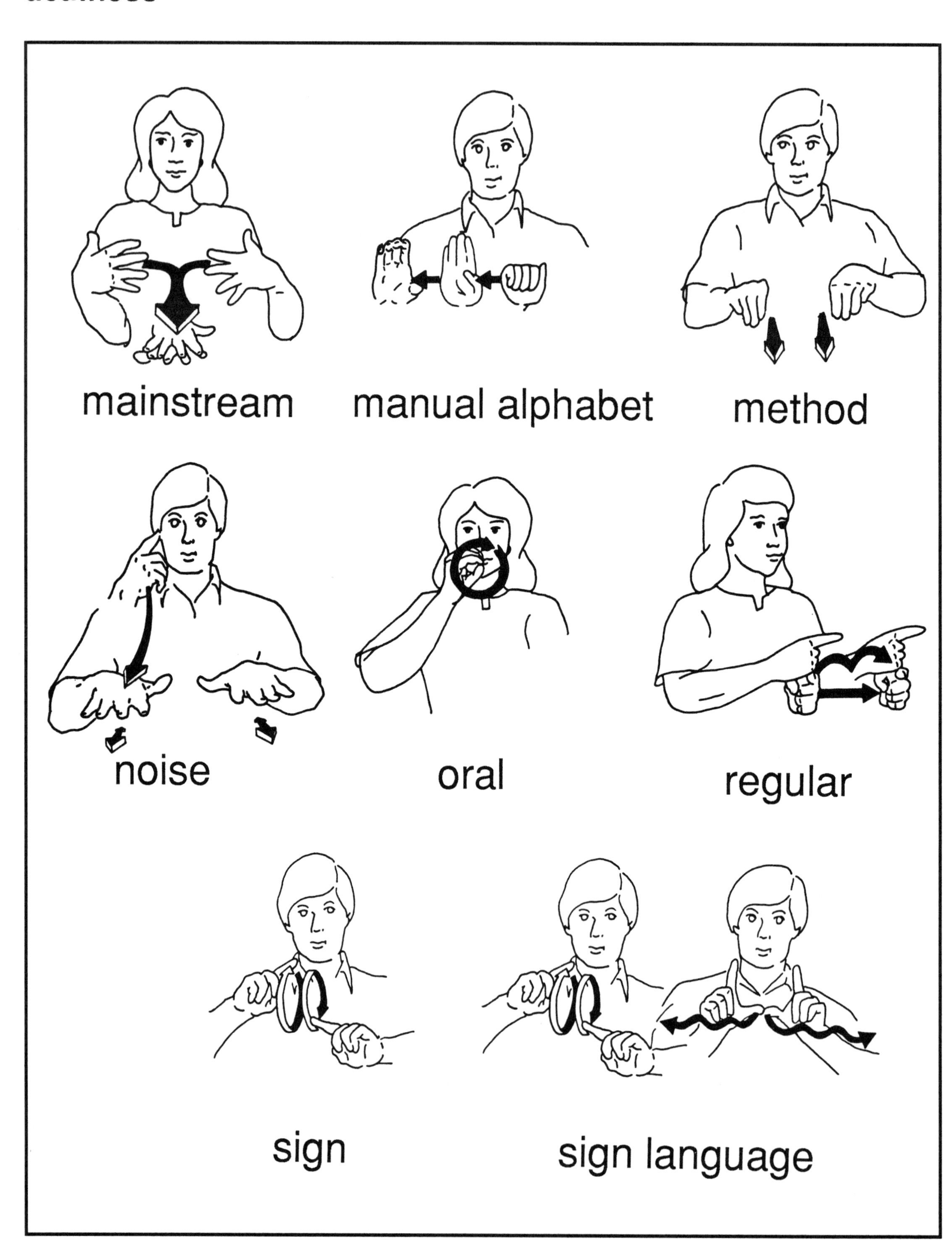
mainstream
manual alphabet
method
noise
oral
regular
sign
sign language

simultaneous communication

sound

speech

speechread

spell (fingerspell)

system

TDD
(Telecommunication Device for the Deaf)

therapy

total communication

translate

voice

DEFINITIONS

Deaf — A hearing loss so severe that a person cannot hear or understand speech through the ear alone, with or without a hearing aid.

Hard of Hearing — A mild hearing loss which makes the understanding of speech difficult, with or without a hearing aid.

Hearing Impaired — A general term which describes all types of hearing impairements, including deaf and hard of hearing.

Total Communication — A philosophy that endorses the right of every hearing-impaired child to communicate using whatever mode is most beneficial, including, signs, fingerspelling, speech, gestures, writing, facial expressions, fingerspelling and amplification.

TDD (telecommunication device for the deaf) — Any of several devices used to assist deaf individuals in communicating over the telephone.

Manual Alphabet — The representation of each of the 26 letters of the written alphabet with a specific handshape.

DIRECTIONS

across [2]
again
against
ahead
among
around
back
behind
beneath
beside
between
down [1]
east
enter
far [2]
first [1]
from [1]
front
high
hurry
immediate
in [1]
inside [2]
into [1]
last
left [2]
low
near
north
off [1]
on [1]
out [1]
outside [2]
over [1]
right
south
stop
through [2]
to [1]
together
toward
under [2]
up [1]
upon [2]
west
with [1]
without

ACTIVITY - DIRECTIONS

Purpose: To teach child to follow directions correctly.

Materials: Objects which child already signs/says: box, hat, glass, pan, small ball, baby doll, pencil.

Procedure

1. Adult sits across from child on floor or table with objects already known by child between them, e.g., hat, glass, pan.
2. Adult signs/says to child, "Ball in hat."
3. Child puts ball in hat. Adult praises.
4. Adult signs/says to child, "Ball in pan."
5. Child puts ball in pan. Adult praises.
6. Continue procedure using different objects, e.g., "Pencil in glass.", "Baby doll in box.", etc.
7. After child exhibits mastery of concept "in" introduce another direction word, "Ball on hat.", etc. while occasionally reviewing the concept "in", e.g., "Pencil in box."

Variations: Child can perform different activities, e.g., "Stand <u>near</u> a chair.", "Walk <u>near</u> me."; adult can sign/say activities and child can sign/say what was done.

DIRECTIONS

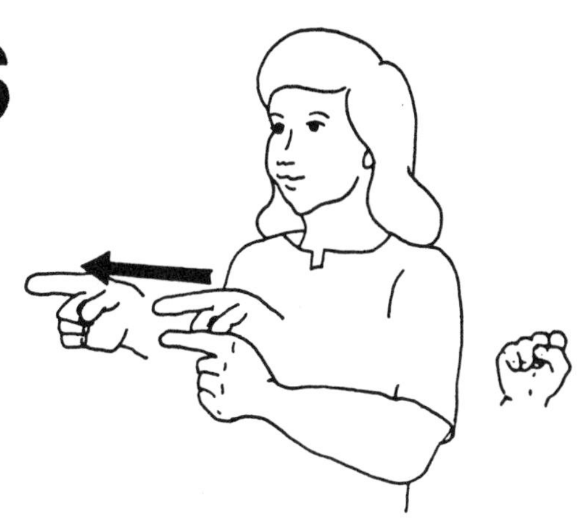

across

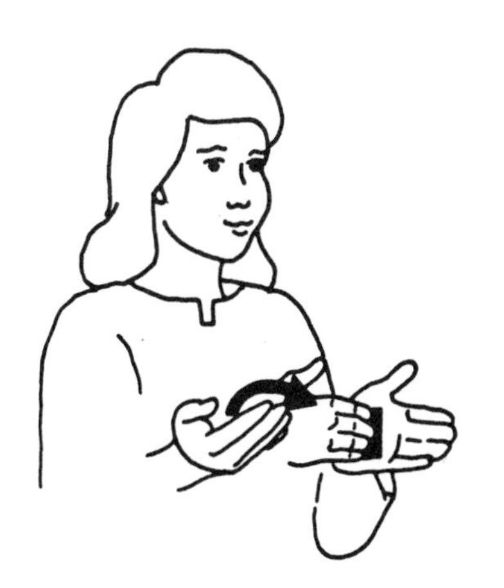

again

against

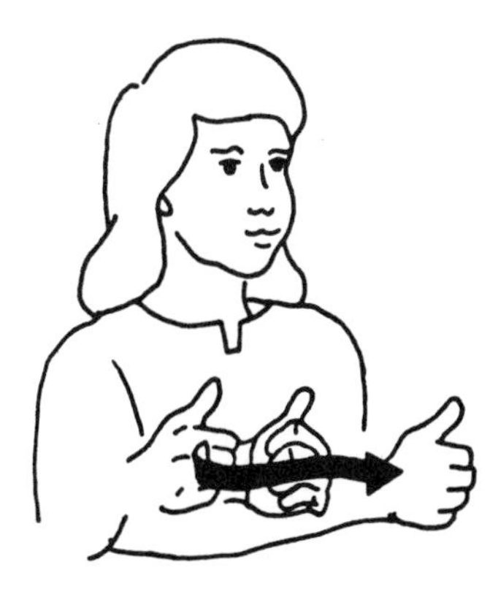

ahead

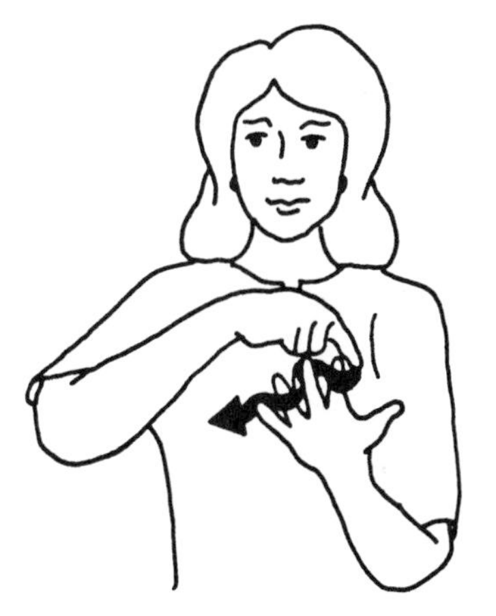

among

around

DIRECTIONS

1. Walk around the _____.

  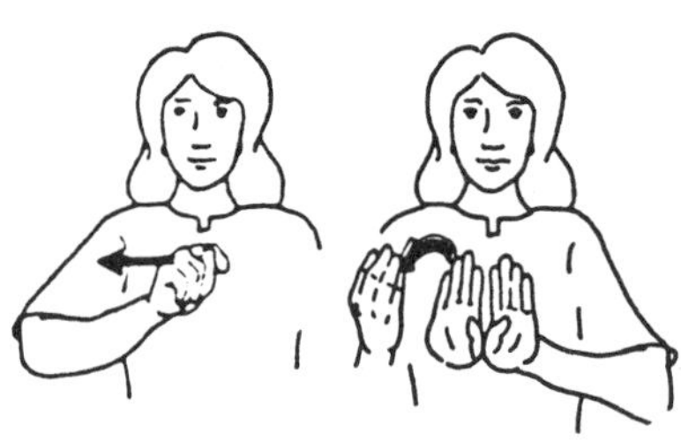

2. Please go _____ the door.

  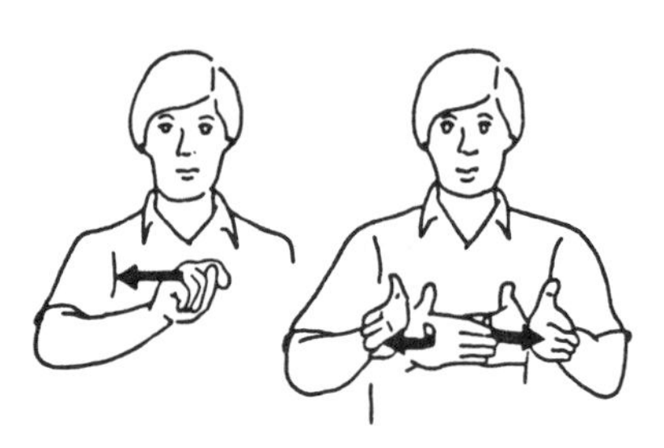

3. Put the _____ _____ the box.

 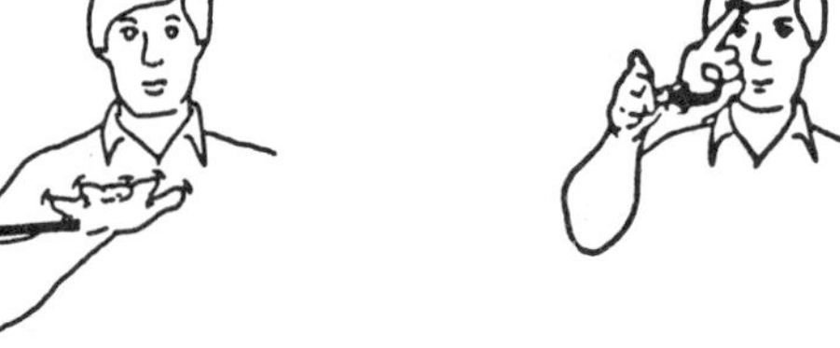 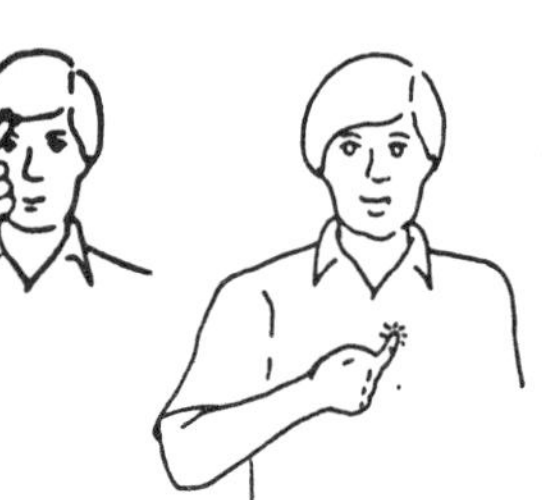

4. Spell _____ for me.

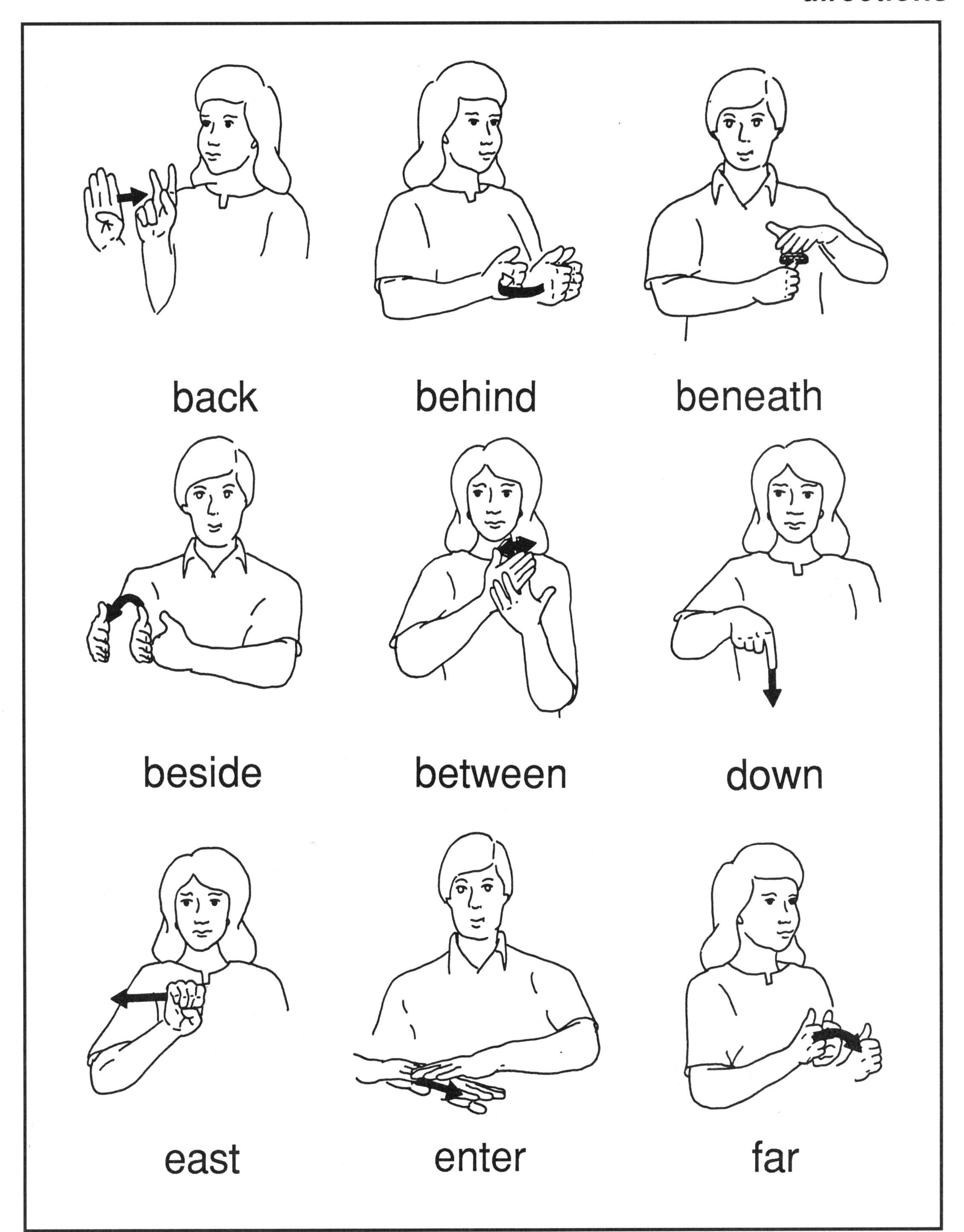
back
behind
beneath
beside
between
down
east
enter
far

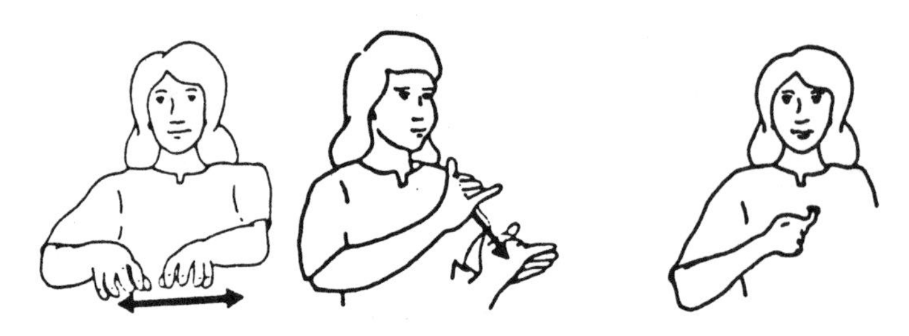

5. Do that _____ me.

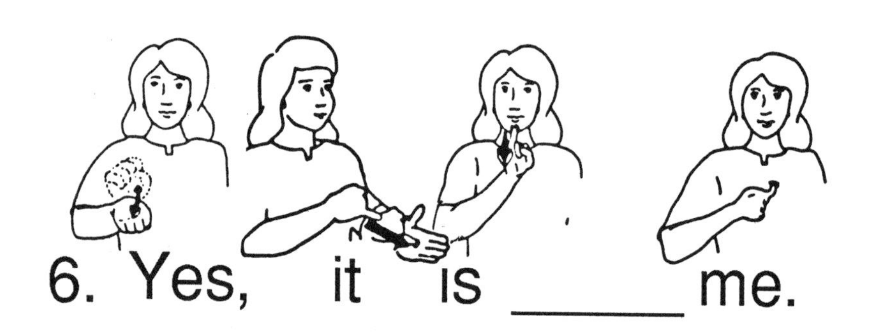

6. Yes, it is _____ me.

7. Put the paper _____ the table.

8. Can you run _____ that?

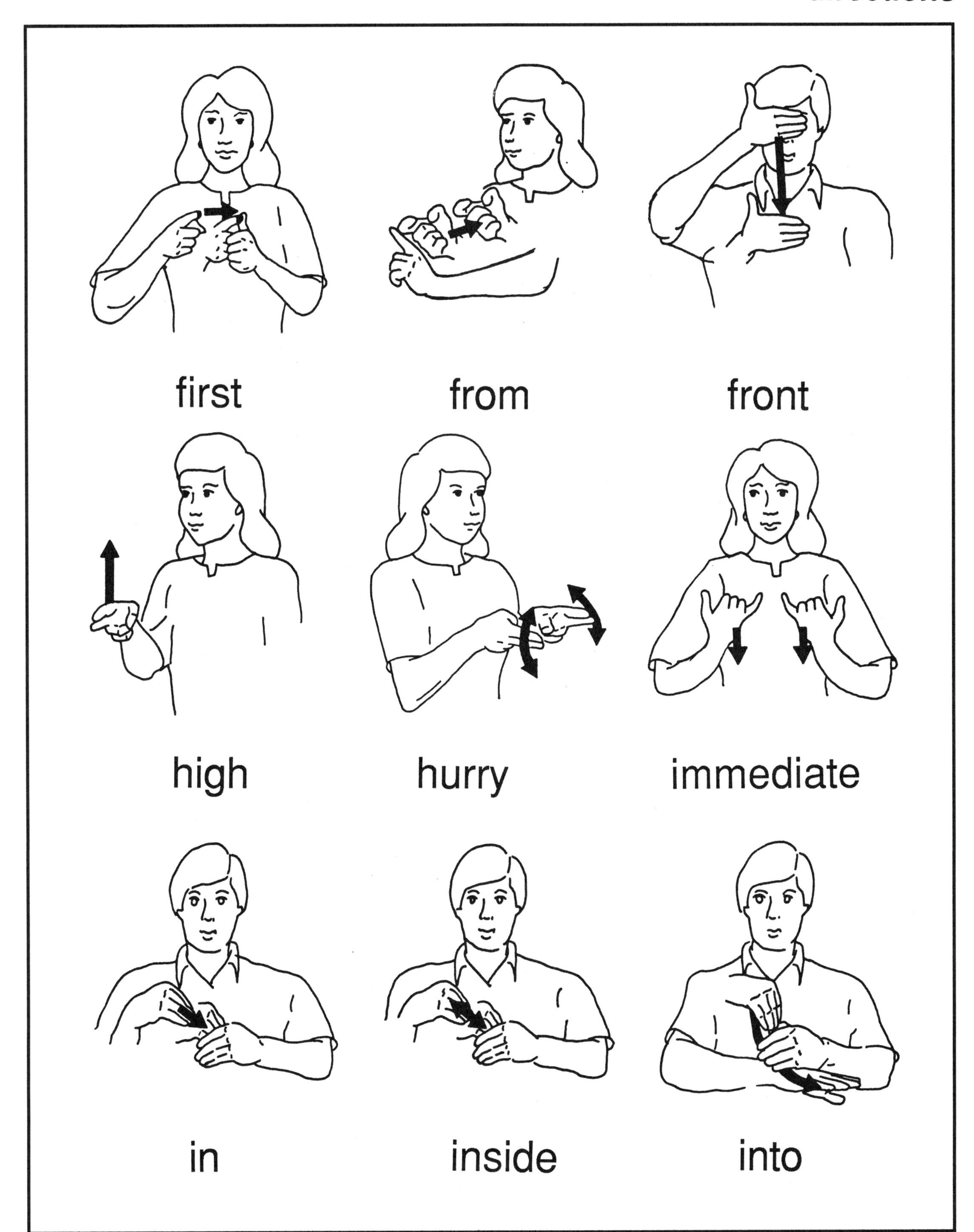
first
from
front
high
hurry
immediate
in
inside
into

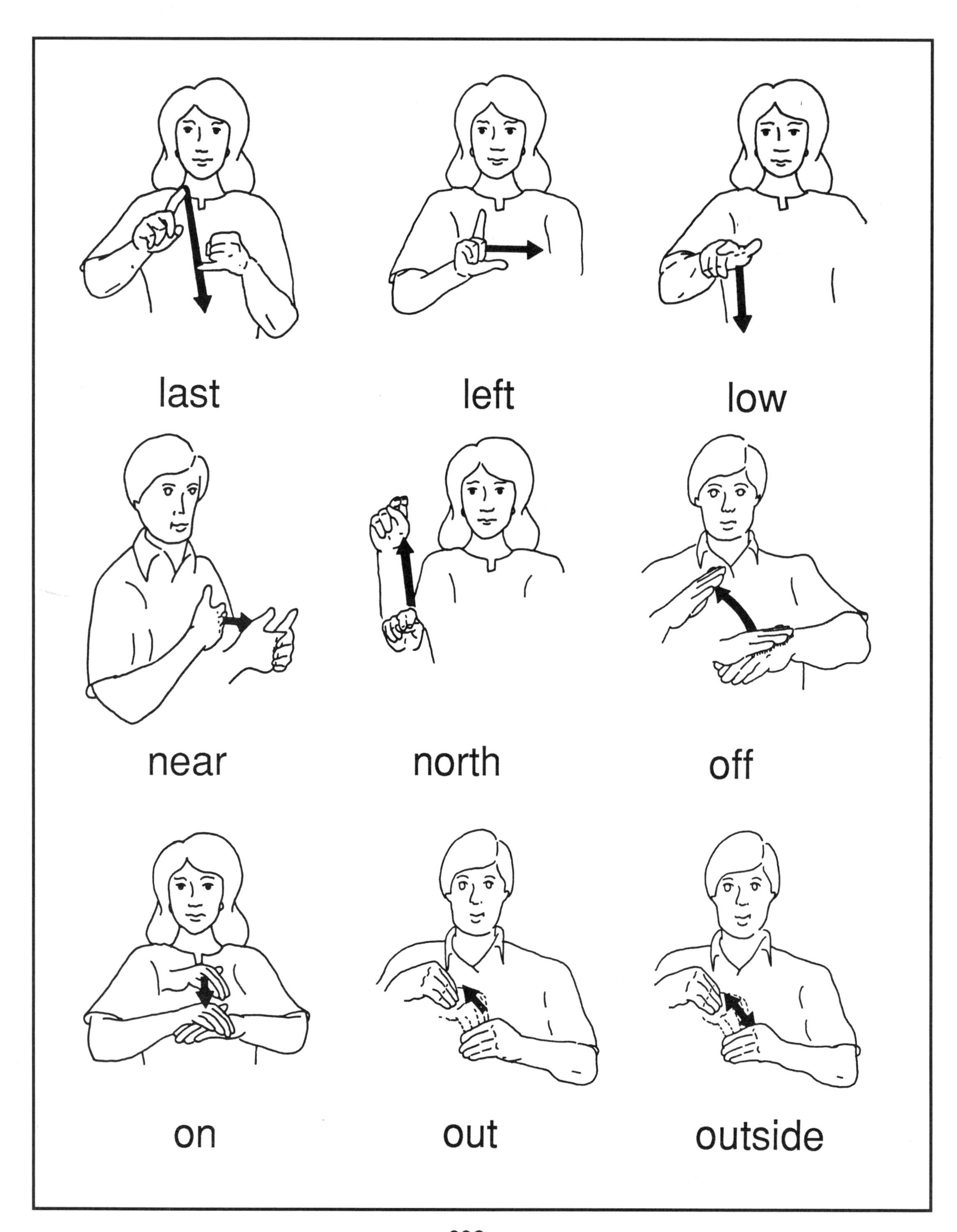
last
left
low
near
north
off
on
out
outside

over
right
south
stop
through
to
together
toward
under

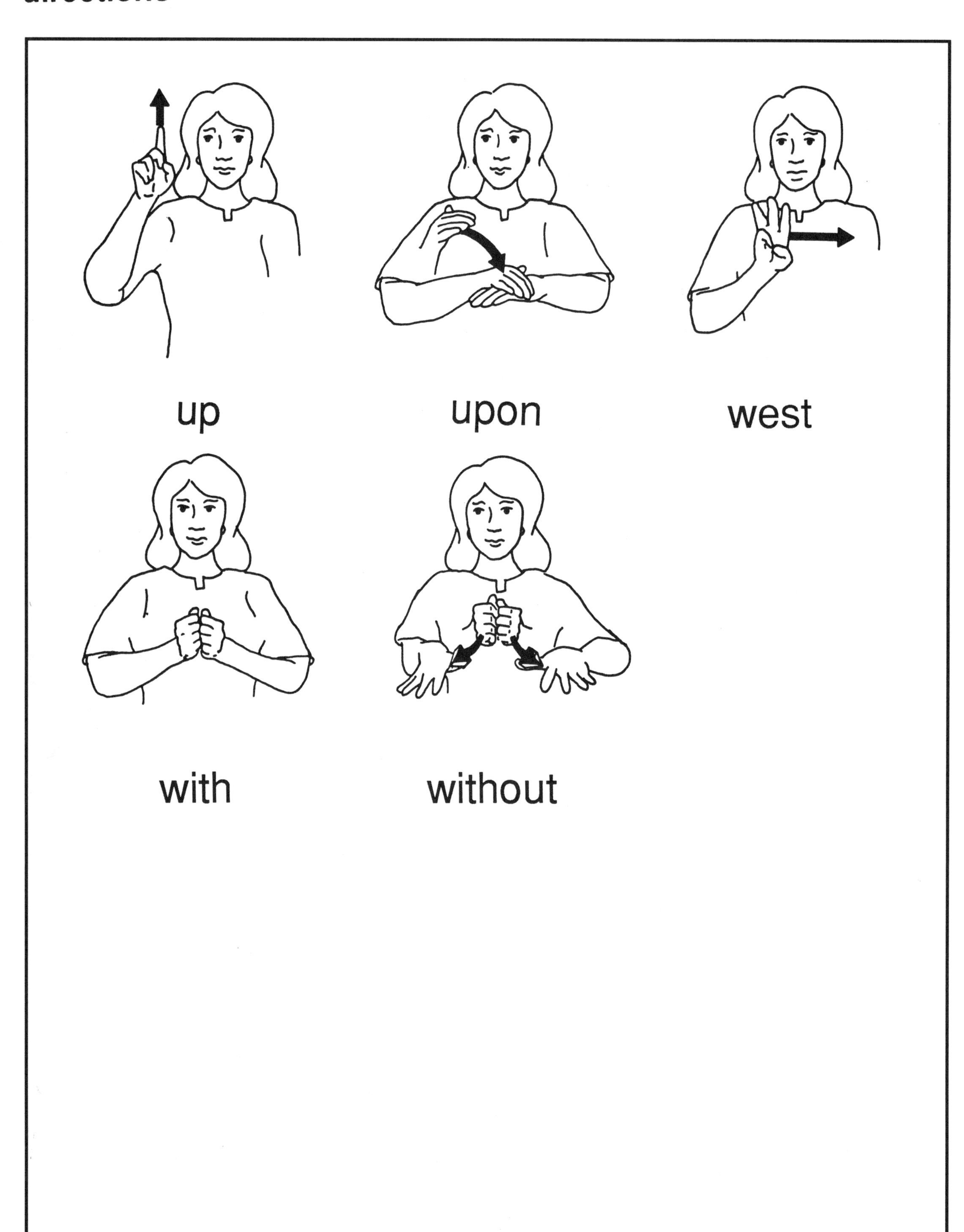
up
upon
west
with
without

FEELINGS / EMOTIONS

afraid
apologize
believe
bored
brave
calm
calm down
celebrate
clever
concentrate
cry
curious
disappoint
discourage
dizzy
don't believe
don't care
don't know
don't like
dream
dumb
embarrass
enjoy
enthusiasm
excite
expect
expression
faith
feel
forget [1]
friendly
frighten
full
gentle
get even
good [1]
guess
guilty
happy
hate
hope
hungry
idea
interest
jealous
kind [1]
know
laugh
lazy
like [1]
lonesome
love [2]
luck
mad
manner
mind
miss
misunderstand
mood
nervous
odd
pity
please
polite
private
promise
proud
realize
reason
relax
relieve
remember [1]
rest [2]
sad
satisfy
scared
secret
selfish
serious
shame
shy
silly
smart
sorry
stingy
strange
stubborn
stupid
suffer
surprise
tendency
thank
think [1]
think over
tired
trouble
trust
understand
well
willing
wise
wish
worry

FEELINGS / EMOTIONS

1. Are you ______?

2. You look very ______.

3. Yes, I ______ that.

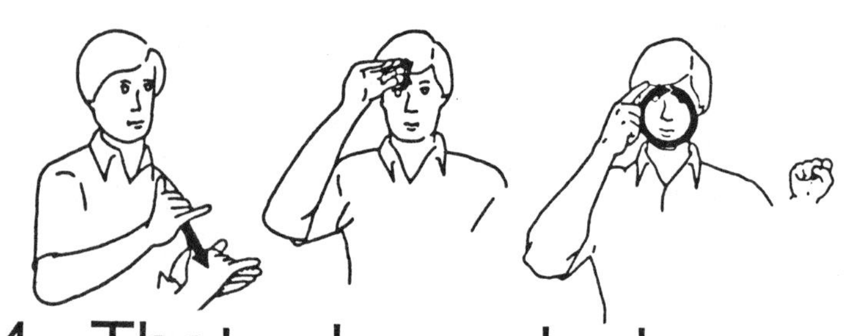

4. That boy looks ______.

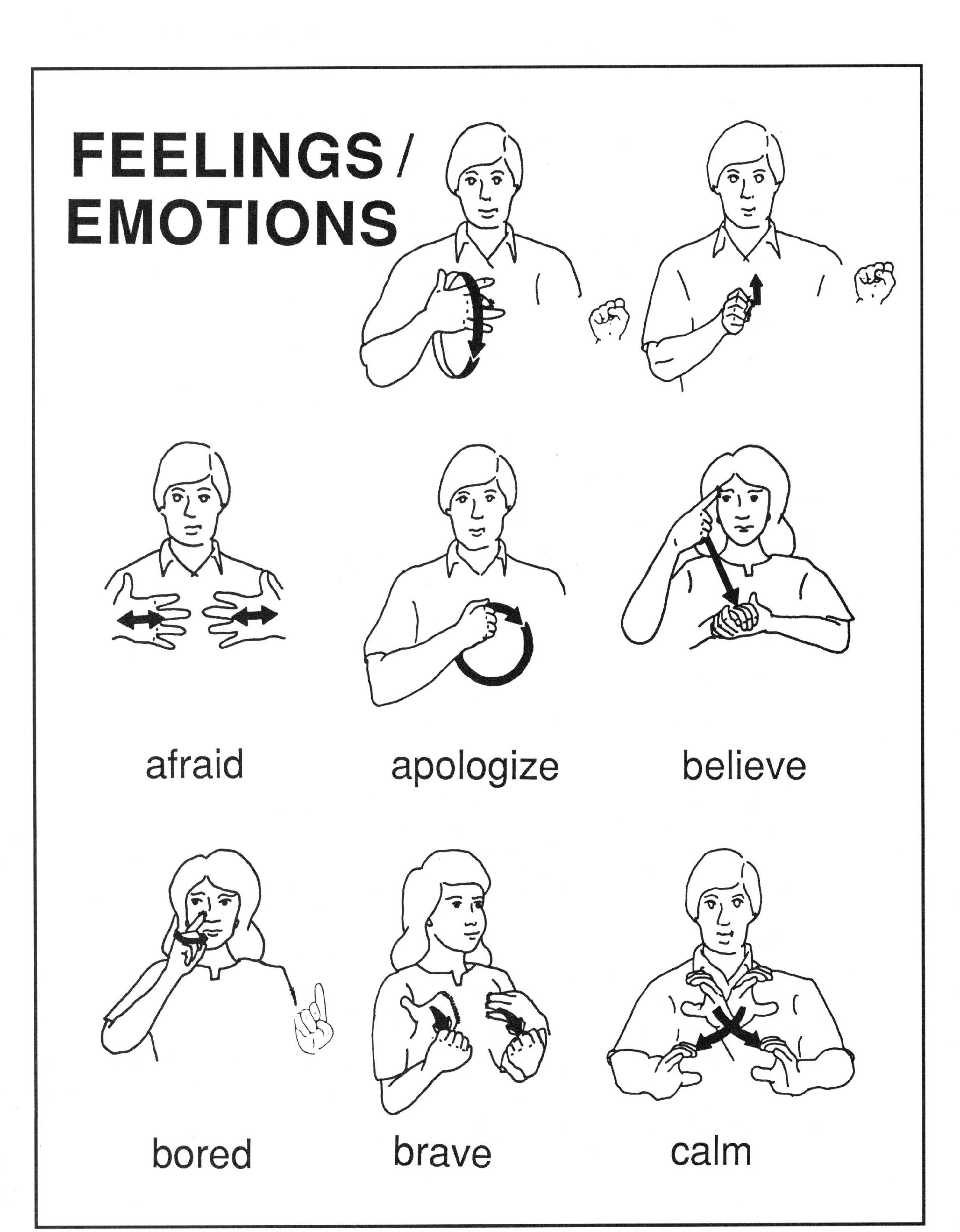
FEELINGS / EMOTIONS
afraid
apologize
believe
bored
brave
calm

5. Please don't become _____.

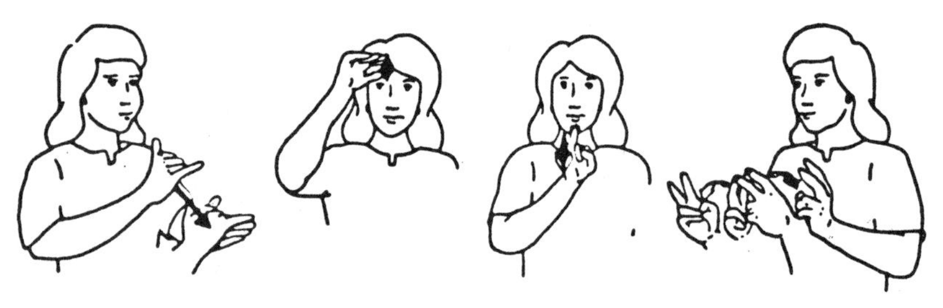

6. That boy is very _____.

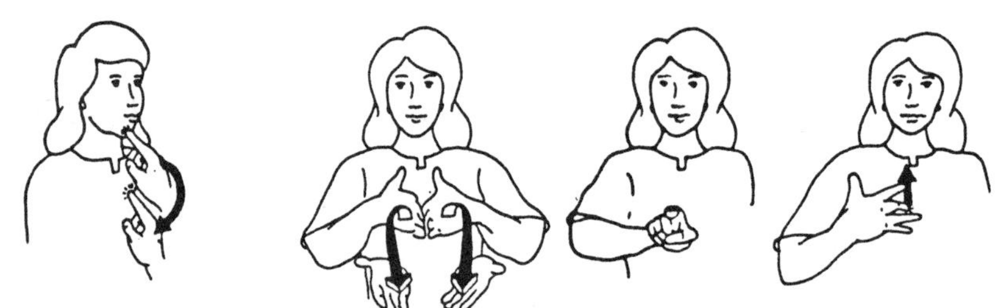

7. Tell me how you feel?

8. I like you to be _____.

calm down
celebrate
clever
concentrate
cry
curious
disappoint
discourage
dizzy

don't believe
don't care
don't know
don't like
dream
dumb
embarrass
enjoy
enthusiasm

excite
expect
expression
faith
feel
forget
friendly
frighten
full

gentle
get even
good
guess
guilty
happy
hate
hope
hungry

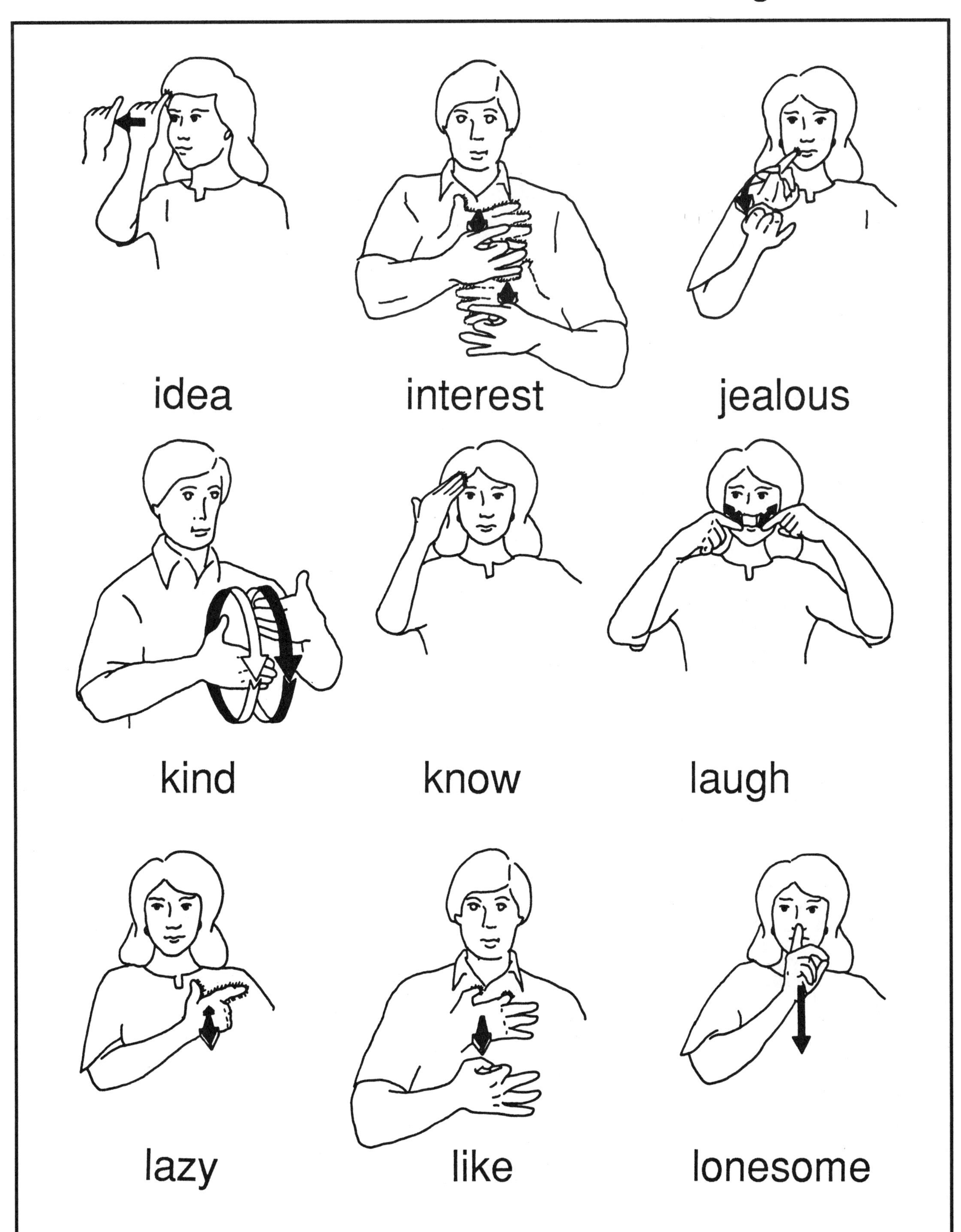
idea
interest
jealous
kind
know
laugh
lazy
like
lonesome

love
luck
mad
manner
mental
mind
miss
misunderstand
mood

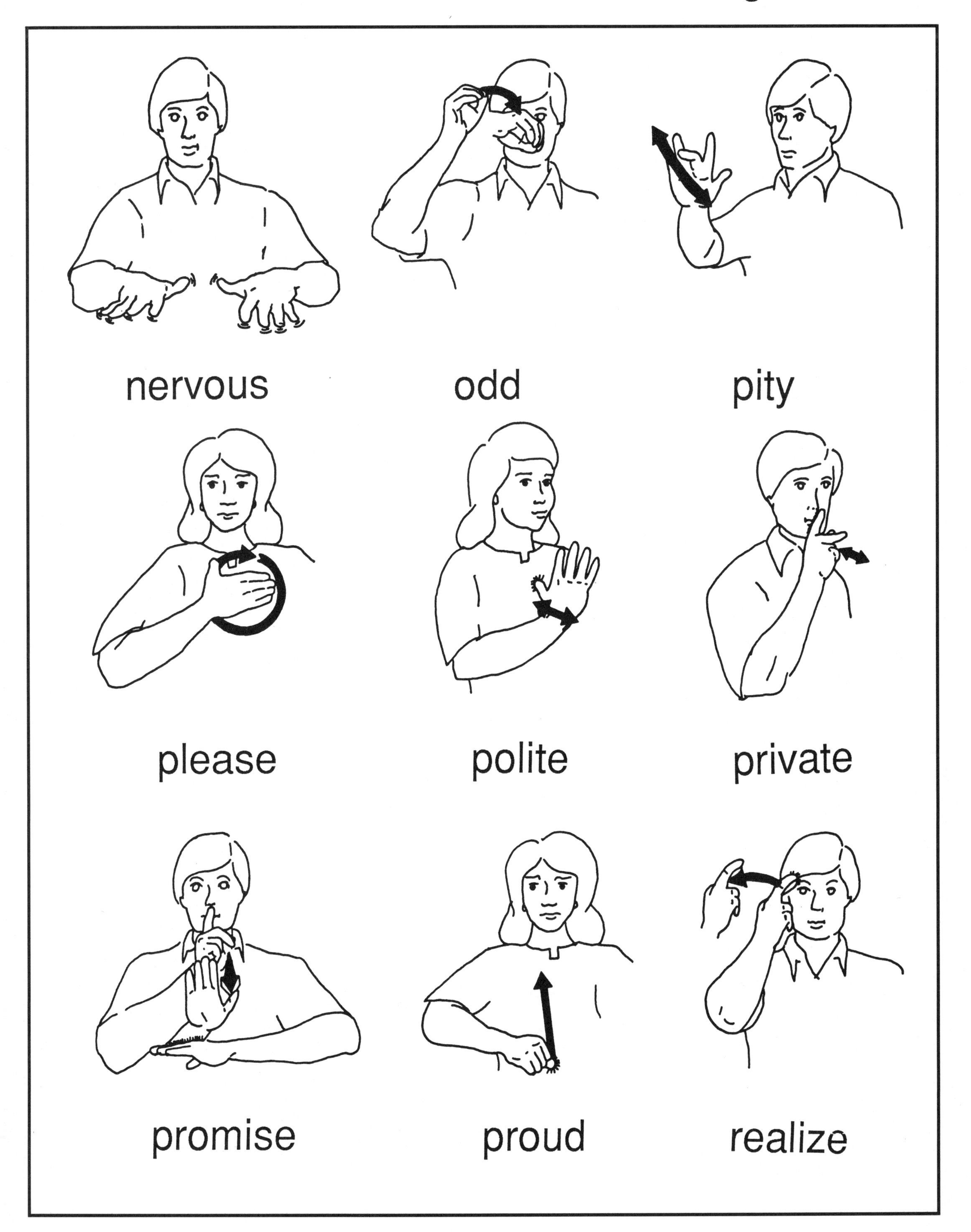
nervous
odd
pity
please
polite
private
promise
proud
realize

reason
relax
relieve
remember
rest
sad
satisfy
scared
secret

selfish
serious
shame
shy
silly
smart
sorry
stingy

strange
stubborn
stupid
suffer
surprise
tendency
thank
think

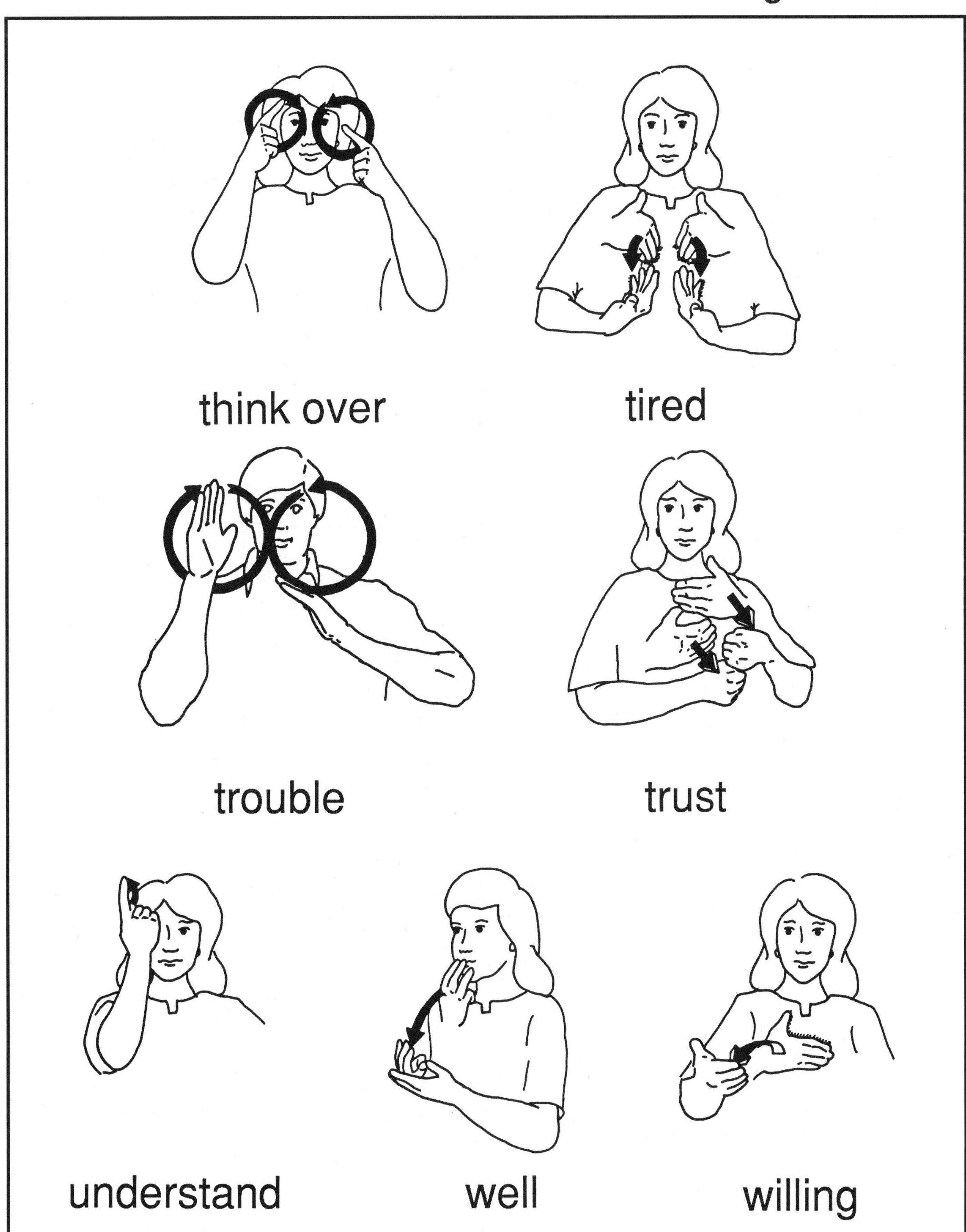
think over
tired
trouble
trust
understand
well
willing

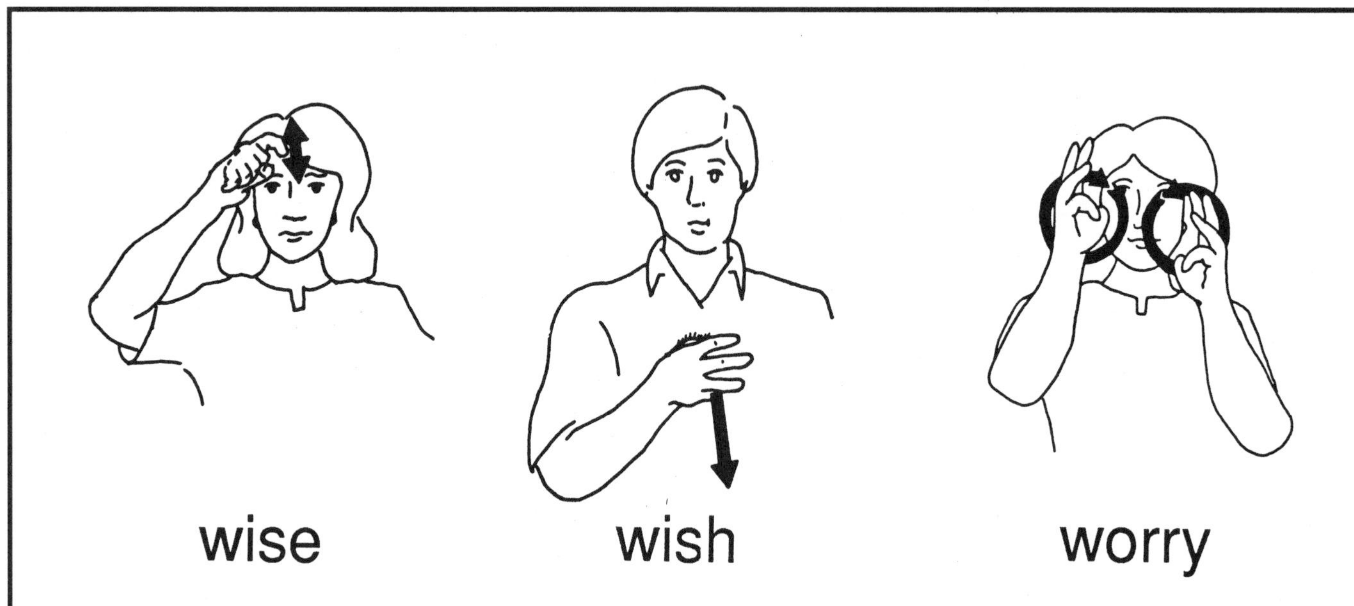

ACTIVITY - FEELINGS

Purpose: To enable child to identify different feelings expressed by by children and adults.

Materials: Pictures of children and adults showing different feelings; chalkboard and chalk or flashcards with different feeling words written on them.

Procedure:

1. Adult shows child three feelings on the board or on flashcards, e.g., mad, happy, sad, then signs/says each.
2. Child signs/says each of the feelings shown.
3. Adult shows child a picture which expresses one of the written feelings and asks, "How does the (girl) feel?"
4. Child responds by signing/saying the correct feeling shown.
5. Adult signs/says, "Yes, the (girl) is very (sad)."
6. Child imitates what adults signs/says above, procedure 5.
7. Adult repeats procedures beginning with number 1 and three different feelings.

GENERAL FOODS[2]

bacon
beef
bologna (baloney)
bread
butter
catsup (ketchup)
cereal
cheese
chicken
coffee
coleslaw
dessert
egg
fish
ham

hamburger
hot dog
jelly
lasagna
macaroni
mayonnaise
meat
milk
mustard
noodles
pepper
pickle
pork
ravioli
rice

salad
salad dressing
salami
salt
sandwich
sausage
soup
spaghetti
sugar
taco
toast
veal

GENERAL FOODS

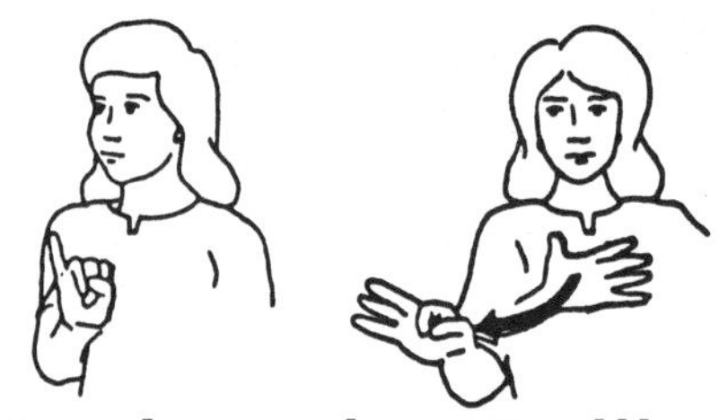

1. I don't like ______.

2. What is your favorite food?

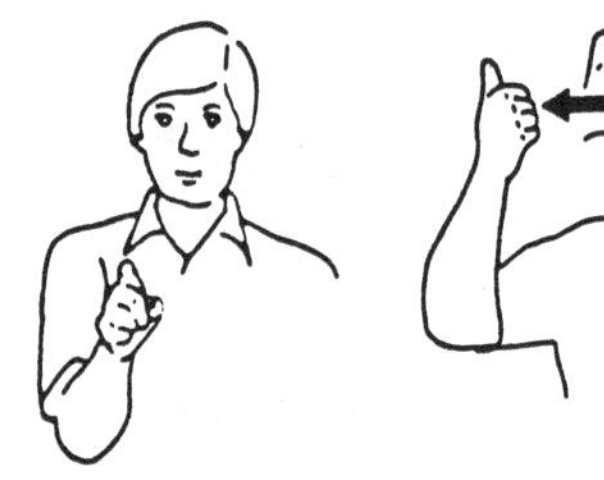  

3. You forgot the ______.

4. Will you buy the ____ tomorrow?

GENERAL FOODS

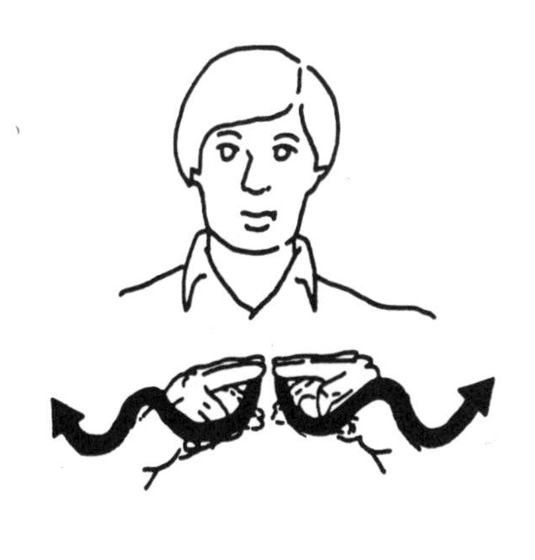

bacon

beef

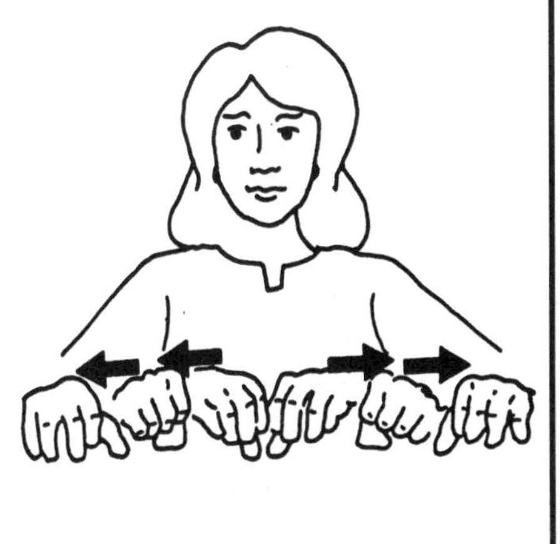

bologna (baloney)

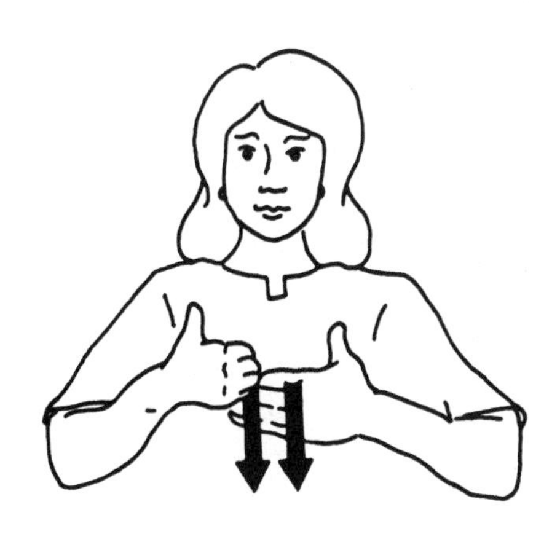

bread

butter

catsup (ketchup)

5. Your _____ is very good.
6. Why don't you like _____?
7. What would you like to eat?
8. My favorite food is _____.

cereal
cheese
chicken
coffee
coleslaw
dessert
egg
fish
ham

hamburger
hot dog
jelly
lasagna
macaroni
mayonnaise
meat
milk

mustard
noodles
pepper
pickle
pork
ravioli
rice
salad

salad dressing
salami
salt
sandwich
sausage
soup
spaghetti
sugar

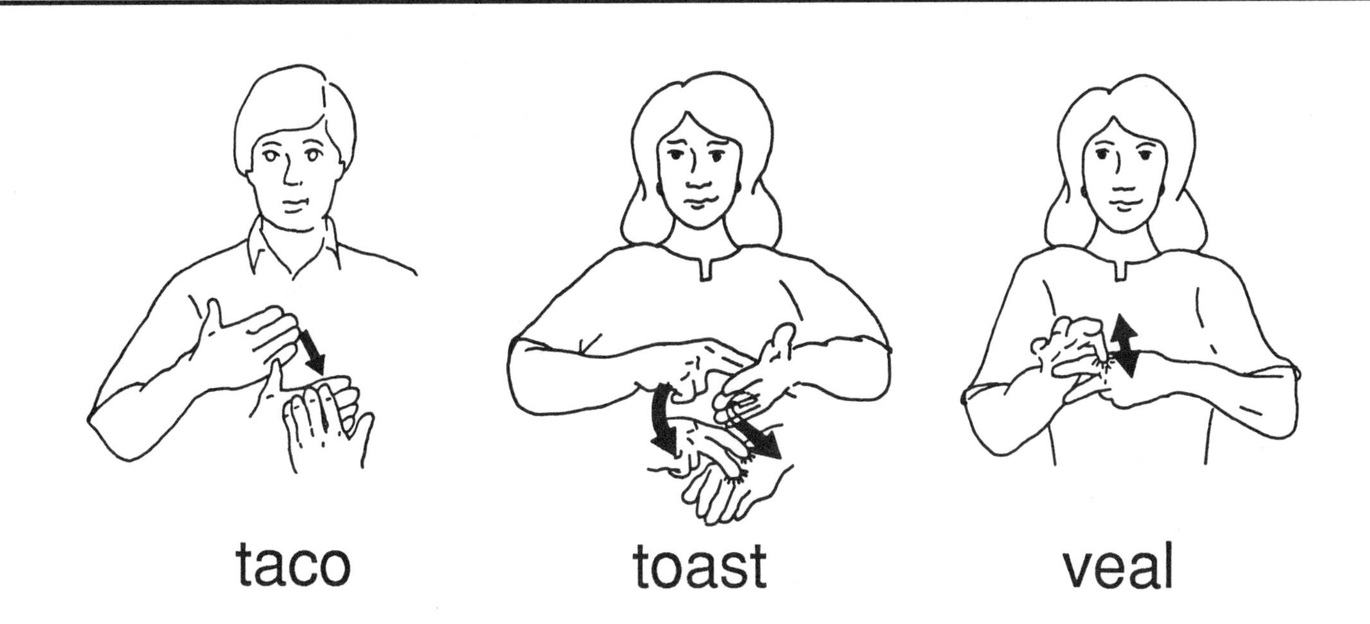

ACTIVITY - FOODS

Purpose: To identify different foods that we eat, and to improve visual memory.

Materials: Empty cereal boxes, vegetable cans, milk cartons, bottles, wax fruit and vegetables, ice cream cartons, frozen food boxes, etc.; grocery bags; paper and pencil.

Procedure:

1. Adult sets aside an area where the empty containers can be placed.
2. Adult shows child that she is making out a grocery list, signing/saying each item as it is written.
3. Adult gives child a grocery bag.
4. Adult signs/says an item from the grocery list, one item at a time, and child gets item and puts it into bag.
5. After all items are collected by child, adult takes one item out at a time, child signs/says item and returns it to shelf.

Variations: Adult takes child to grocery store and signs/says each item put into shopping cart while child repeats what is signed/said; Adult may sign two or more items at a time for child to gather and put into bag.

FRUITS

apple
apricot
banana
berry
blackberry
blueberry
cantaloupe
cherry
coconut
grape
grapefruit
lemon
lime
melon
nectarine
orange
peach
pear
pineapple
plum
prune
raspberry
strawberry
watermelon

ACTIVITY - FRUITS

Purpose: To identify different fruits through the sense of taste.

Materials: A variety of different fruits, e.g., banana, apple, pear, orange, grapefruit, etc.

Procedure:

1. Adult signs/says the name of a fruit, e.g., banana, then gives child small piece to eat.
2. Child signs/says banana.
3. Adult signs/says the name of another fruit, e.g., apple, then gives child small piece to eat.
4. Child signs/says apple.
5. Adult continues activity until three fruits have been signed/said and eaten by child.
6. Adult has child close eyes and puts a piece of fruit, already introduced, into child's mouth.
7. Child opens eyes and signs/says name of fruit being eaten.
8. Repeat procedures 1 and 2, and 6 and 7 in a random fashion.

FRUITS

apple

apricot

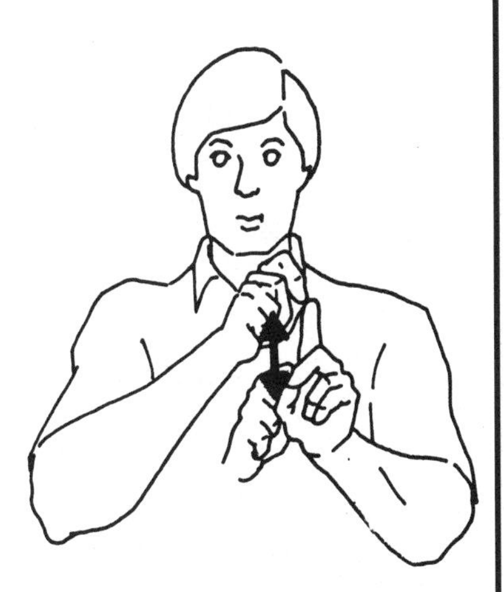

banana

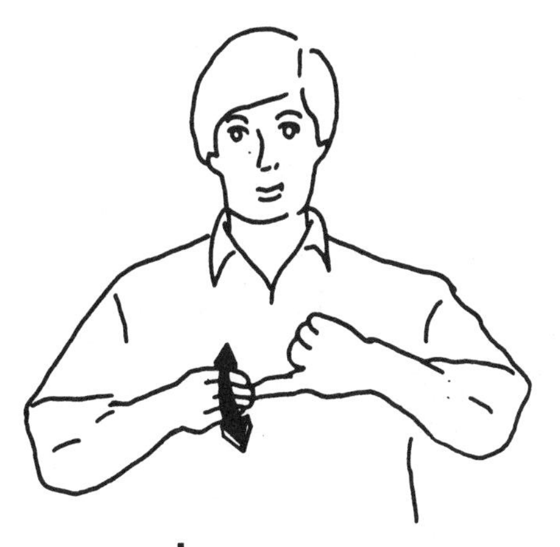

berry

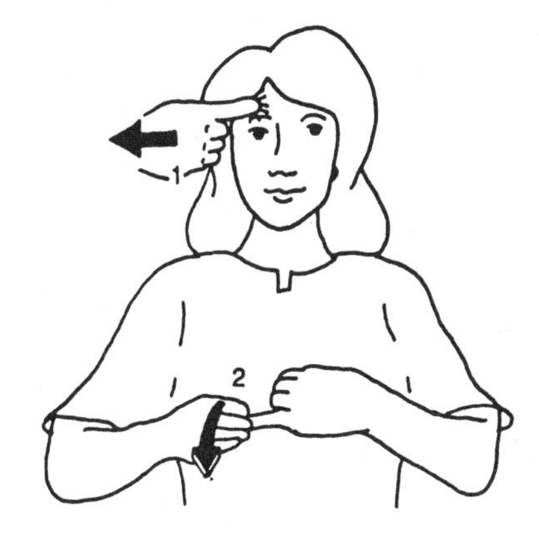

blackberry

FRUITS

1. What color is a ______?

2. Do you like eating ______?

3. We ate many ______.

4. Show me the ______.

blueberry
cantaloupe
cherry
coconut
grape
grapefruit
lemon
lime

melon
nectarine
orange
peach
pear
pineapple
plum
prune

raspberry strawberry

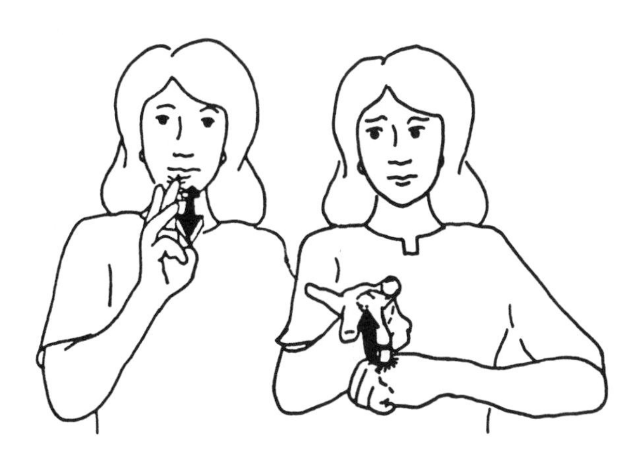

watermelon

NOTE:

American Sign Language has a general rule that when a sign is made with both hands, only the dominant hand moves if the two handshapes are different. If both handshapes are similar then both hands move. This does not hold true in Manual English as one can see in the Insects/Bugs category where both hands move on most of the signs regardless of the handshapes.

GAMES[1] / TOYS[2] / SPORTS

airplane [2]
ball [1]
balloon
baseball [2]
basketball
bicycle [2]
boat
bounce
bowling
car
catch [1]
checkers
dance
dice
doll [1]
football (game)
football [1]
golf
hockey
hopscotch
ice skate
jump rope
kickball
kite
magnifying glass
ping pong
play [1]
puzzle
racket
roller skate
run [1]
ski
sled
sleigh
slide
soccer
swim [1]
swing [2]
tag [1]
tennis
train [2]
tricycle
truck [2]
volleyball
wagon
wrestle
yoyo

ACTIVITY - GAMES

Purpose: To have child learn a new games along with the rules.

Materials: Whatever materials are required for the game selected.

Procedure:

1. Adult explains that a new game will be played.
2. Adult and child begin playing game. Rules are explained as game progresses.
3. Adult determines if child understands game based on participation.

GAMES / TOYS / SPORTS

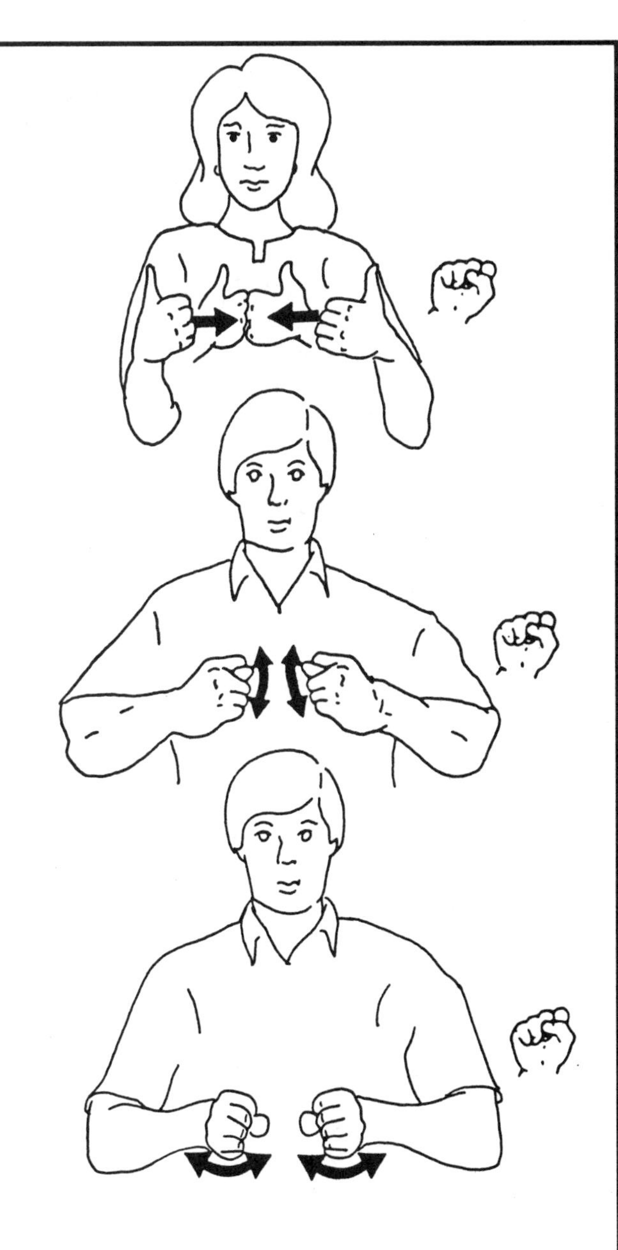

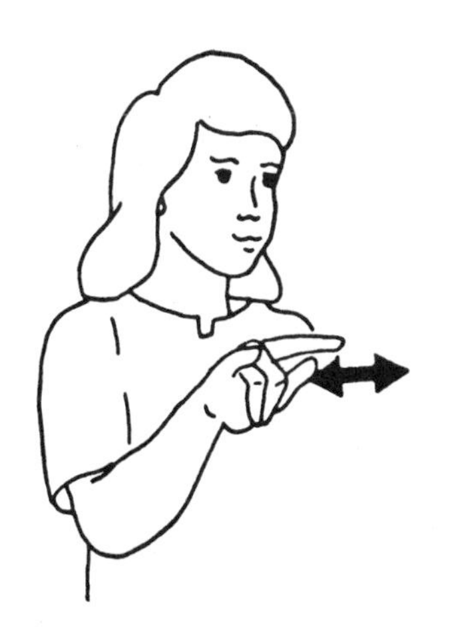

airplane

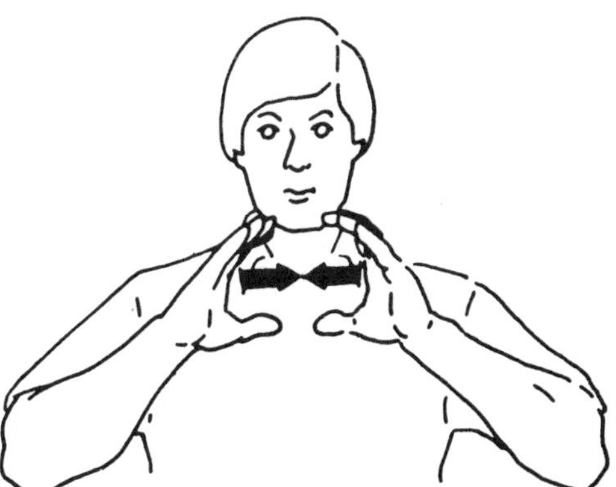

ball

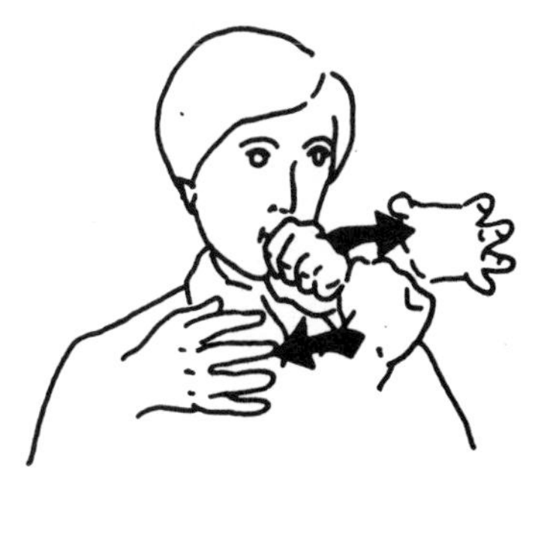

balloon

GAMES / TOYS / SPORTS

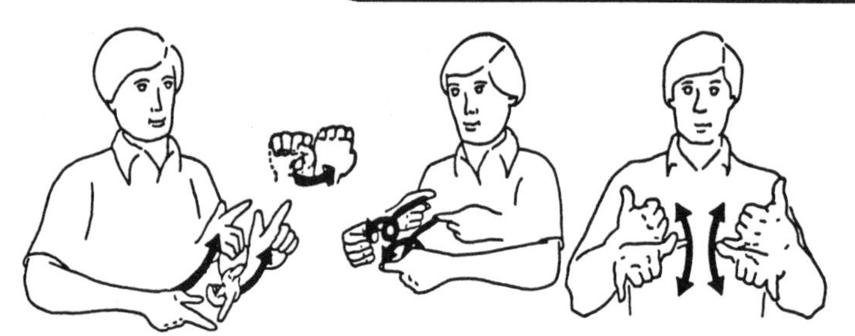

1. Let's go play ______.

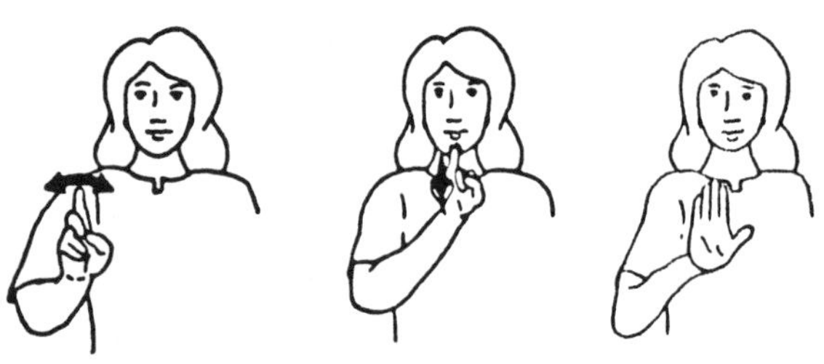

2. Where is your ______?

3. Put your ______ away.

4. Please pick up the ______.

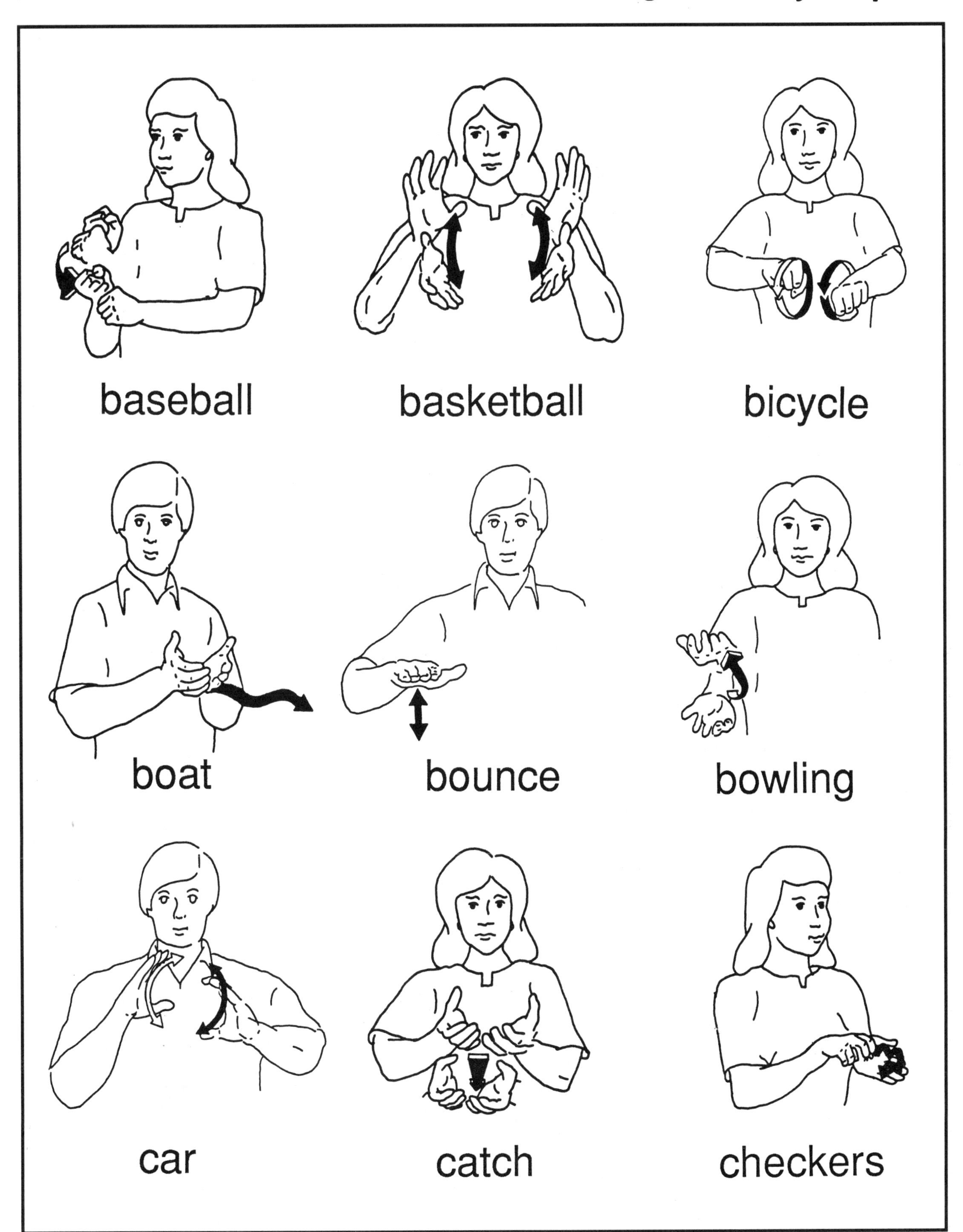

baseball
basketball
bicycle
boat
bounce
bowling
car
catch
checkers

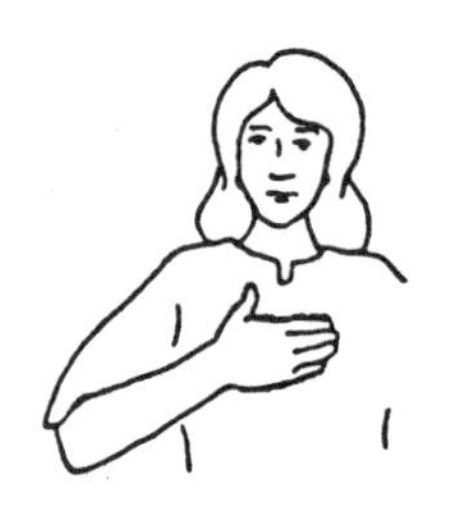  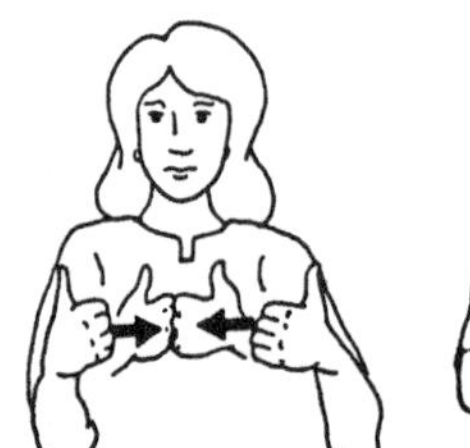 

5. My favorite game is ______.

6. Can you play ______?

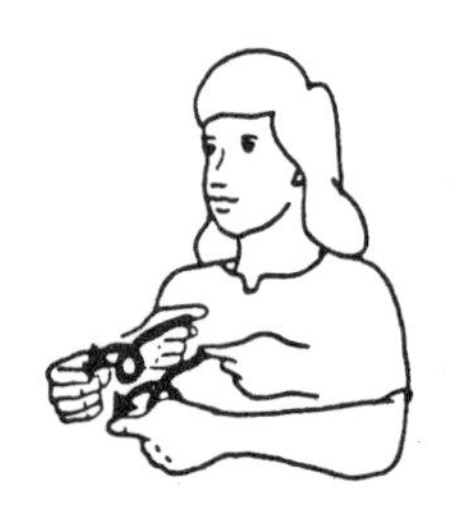 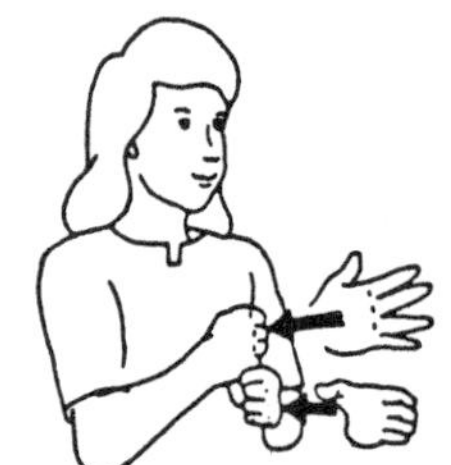 

7. Go get your ______.

8. Be careful, you will break that.

dance
dice
doll
football (game)
football
golf
hockey
hopscotch
ice skate

jump rope
kickball
kite
magnifying glass
ping pong
play
puzzle
racket

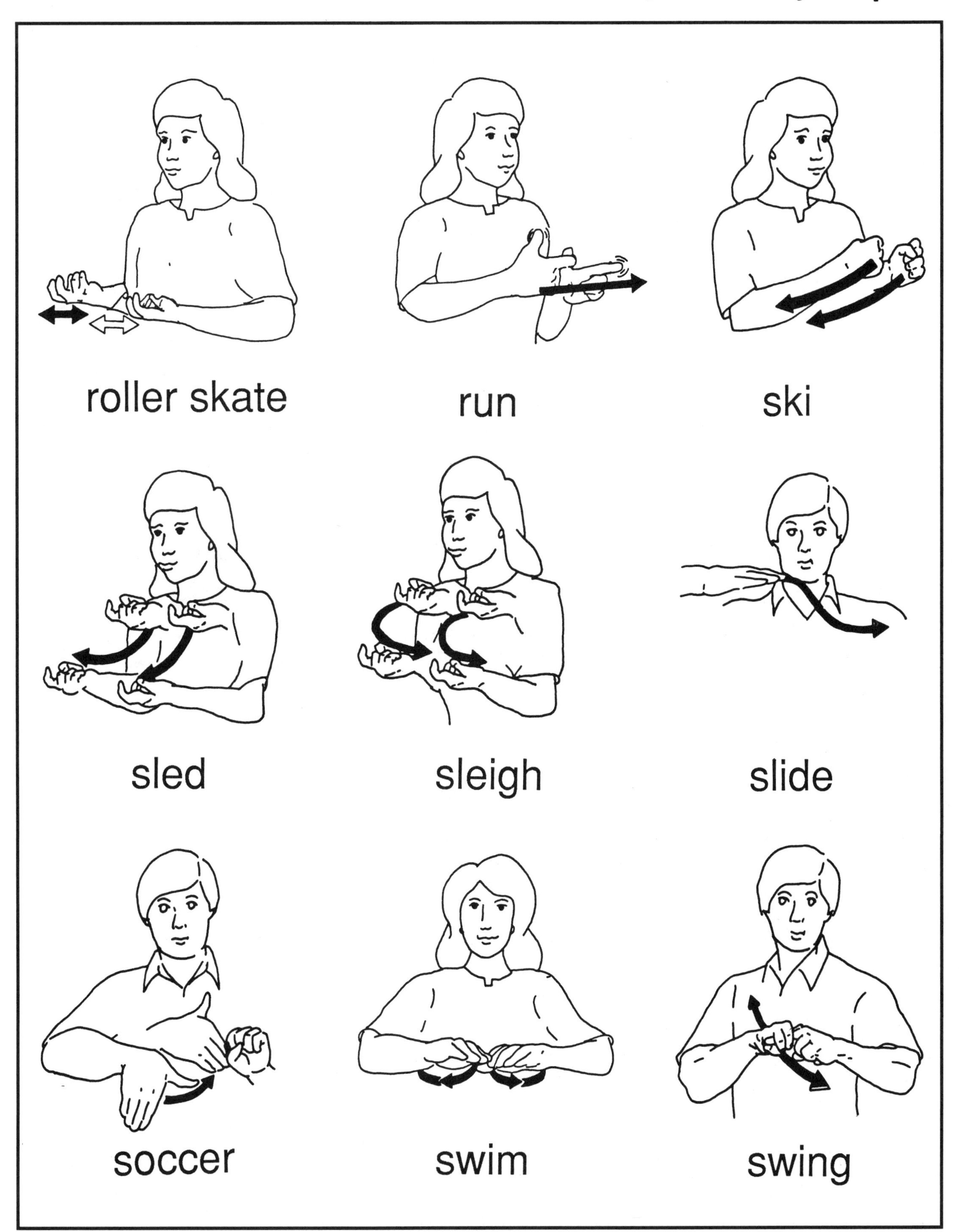

roller skate
run
ski
sled
sleigh
slide
soccer
swim
swing

tag
tennis
train
tricycle
truck
volleyball
wagon
wrestle
yo yo

HEALTH

ache
age
all right
appointment
bandage
Band Aid
blood
birth
bm (bowel movement)
breath
breathe
bruise
choke
clean
cold [2]
confuse
cough
cramp
crazy
dentist
depressed
die
dirty
disabled
disease
dizzy
doctor
drown
drug
earache
emergency
examination
faint
fat
feel
fever
fine
flu
glasses
haircut [2]
handicap
headache
heart
heart attack
hospital
hurt [2]
ill
improve
infection
infirmary
lump
measles
medicine
mental
mentally retarded
mind
mumps
nauseous
nervous
normal
nosebleed
nurse
ointment
old [1]
operation
pain
patient
physical
pill
pneumonia
poison
pregnant
prescription
psychiatrist
psychiatry
runny nose
sex
sick
slim down
spread
stomach ache
strong
therapy
thin
thirsty
unconscious
upset
urinate
vaccination
vomit
weak
well
worse

ACTIVITY - HEALTH

Purpose: To demonstrate knowledge of vocabulary related to health.

Materials: none

Procedure:

1. Adult fingerspells a vocabulary item from the Health category, e.g., headache.
2. Child signs/says headache.
3. Child "acts out" how an individual with a headache might behave.
4. Repeat procedures 1 through 3 using a variety of health vocabulary that can be "acted out", e.g., vomit, stomachache, pain, faint, etc.

Variations: Adult "acts out" health vocabulary while child signs/says correct responses.

HEALTH

ache

age

all right

appointment

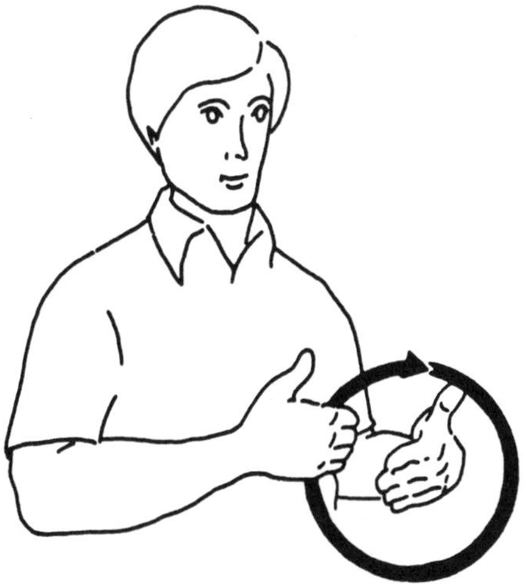

bandage

Band Aid

HEALTH

  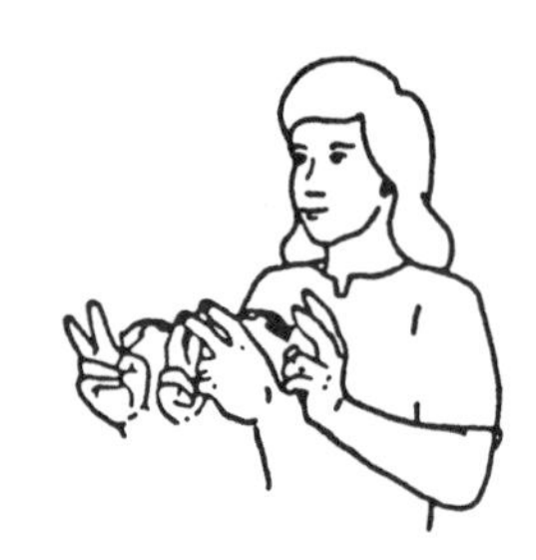

1. You look very ______.

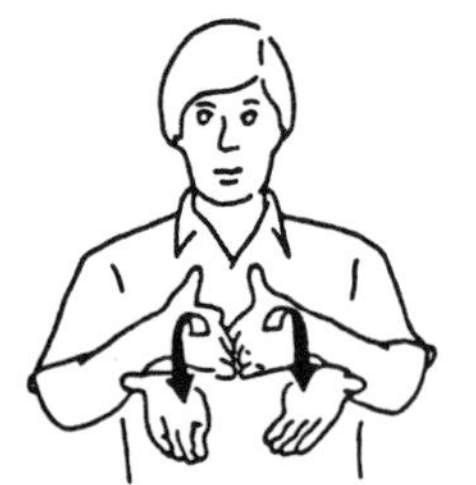   

2. How do you feel?

3. Do you have a ______?

4. Remember, take your medicine.

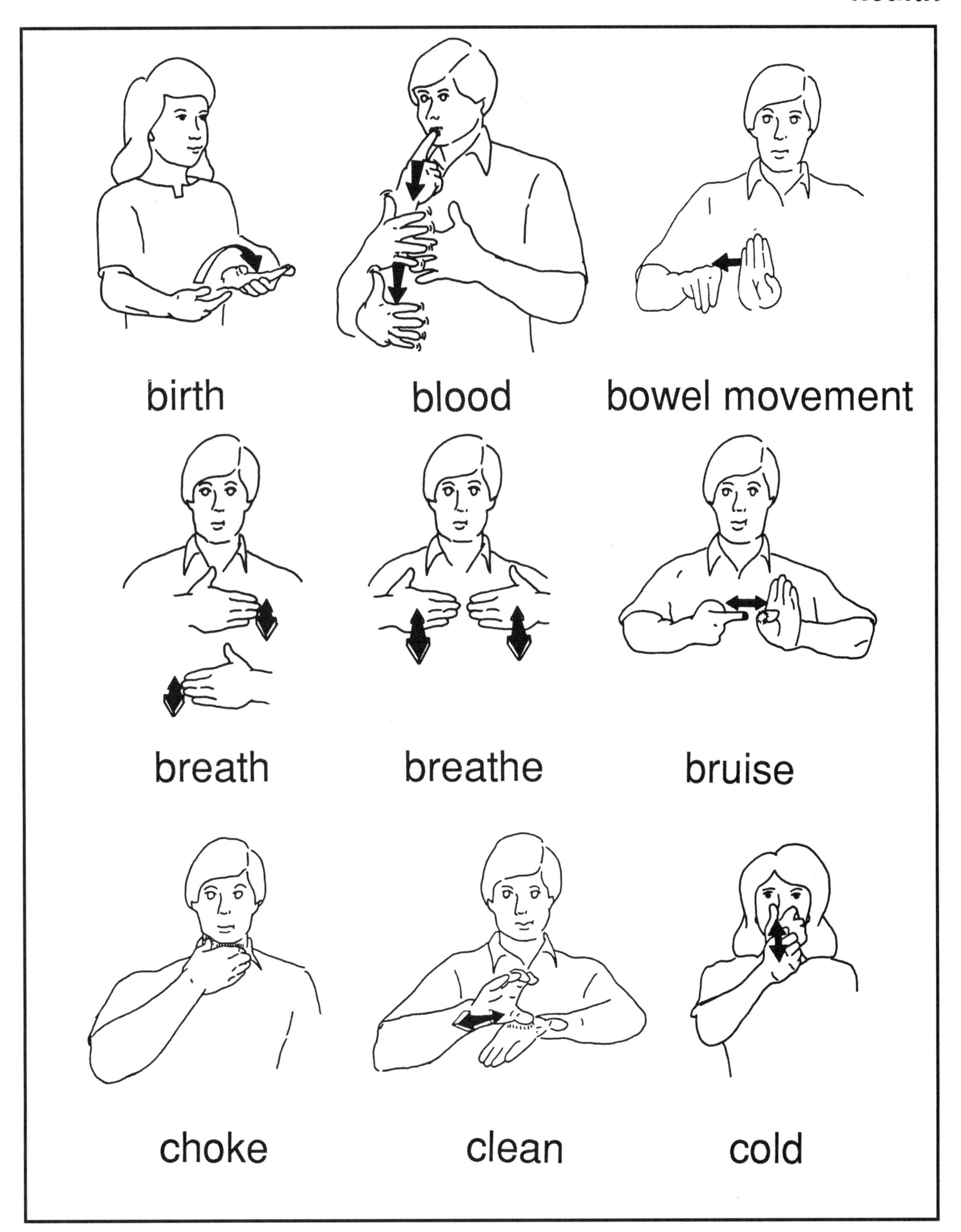
birth
blood
bowel movement
breath
breathe
bruise
choke
clean
cold

5. Please don't become _____.

6. Are you ______?

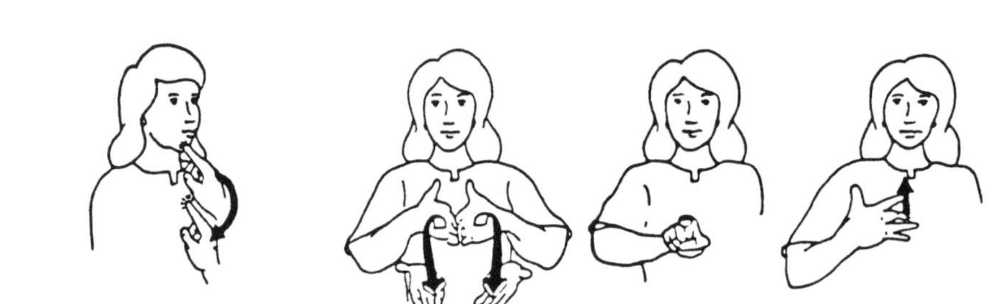

7. Tell me how you feel?

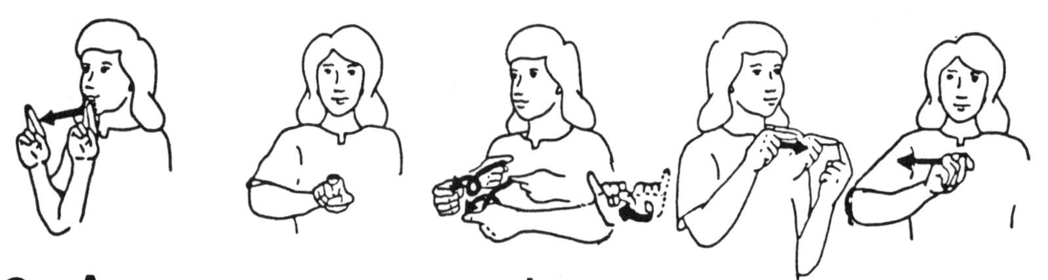

8. Are you going to the_____?

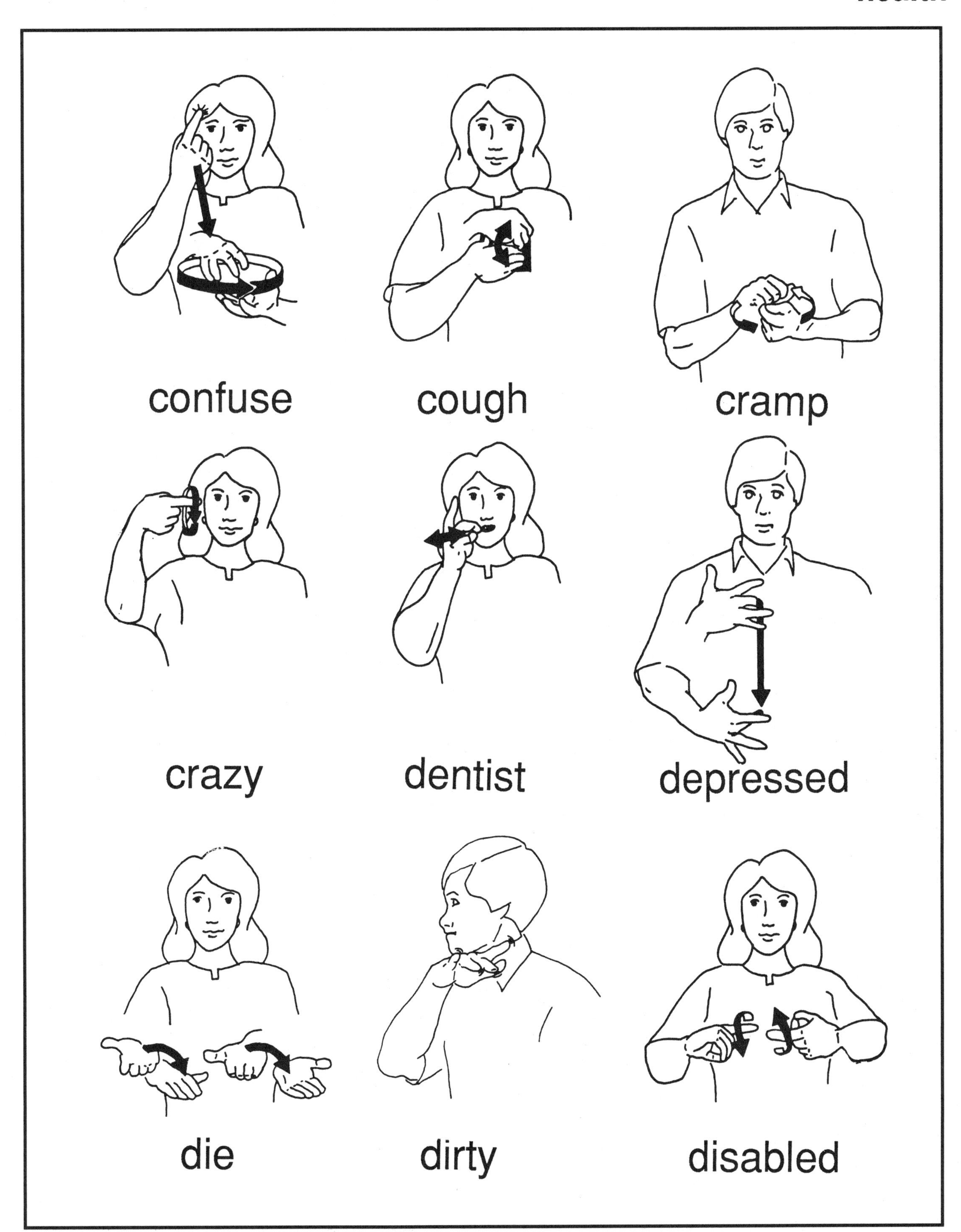
confuse
cough
cramp
crazy
dentist
depressed
die
dirty
disabled

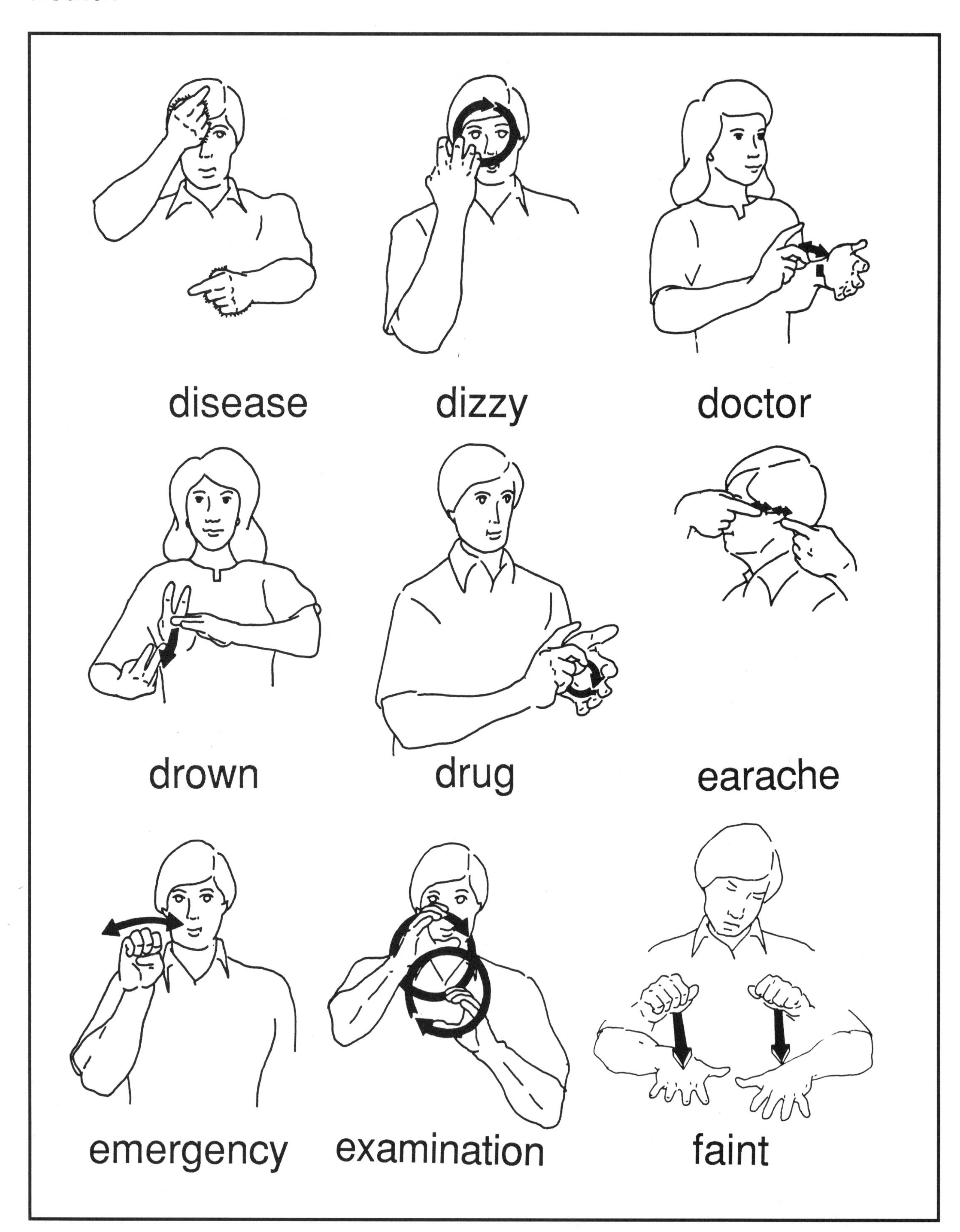
disease
dizzy
doctor
drown
drug
earache
emergency
examination
faint

fat
feel
fever
fine
flu
glasses
haircut
handicap
headache

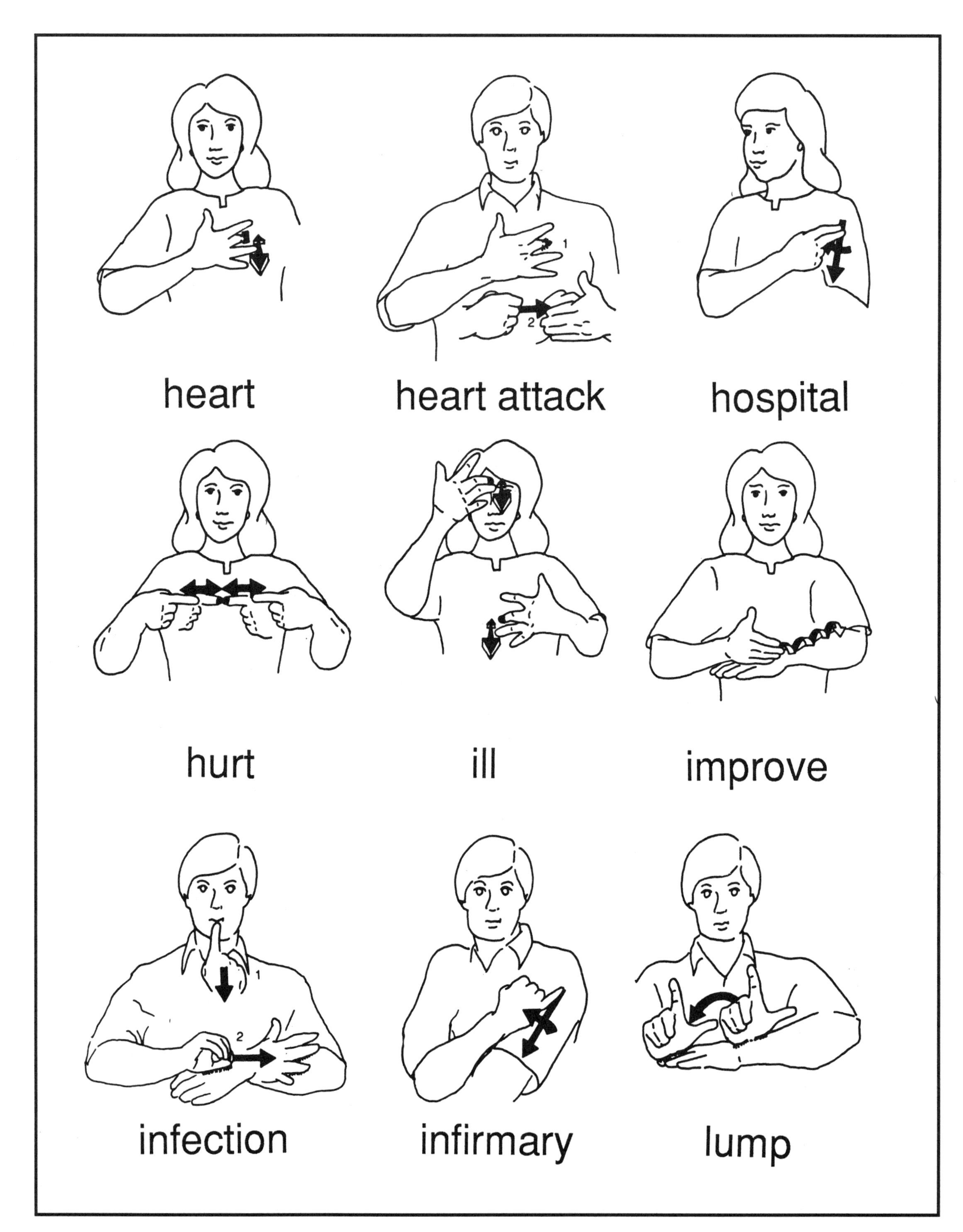

heart

heart attack

hospital

hurt

ill

improve

infection

infirmary

lump

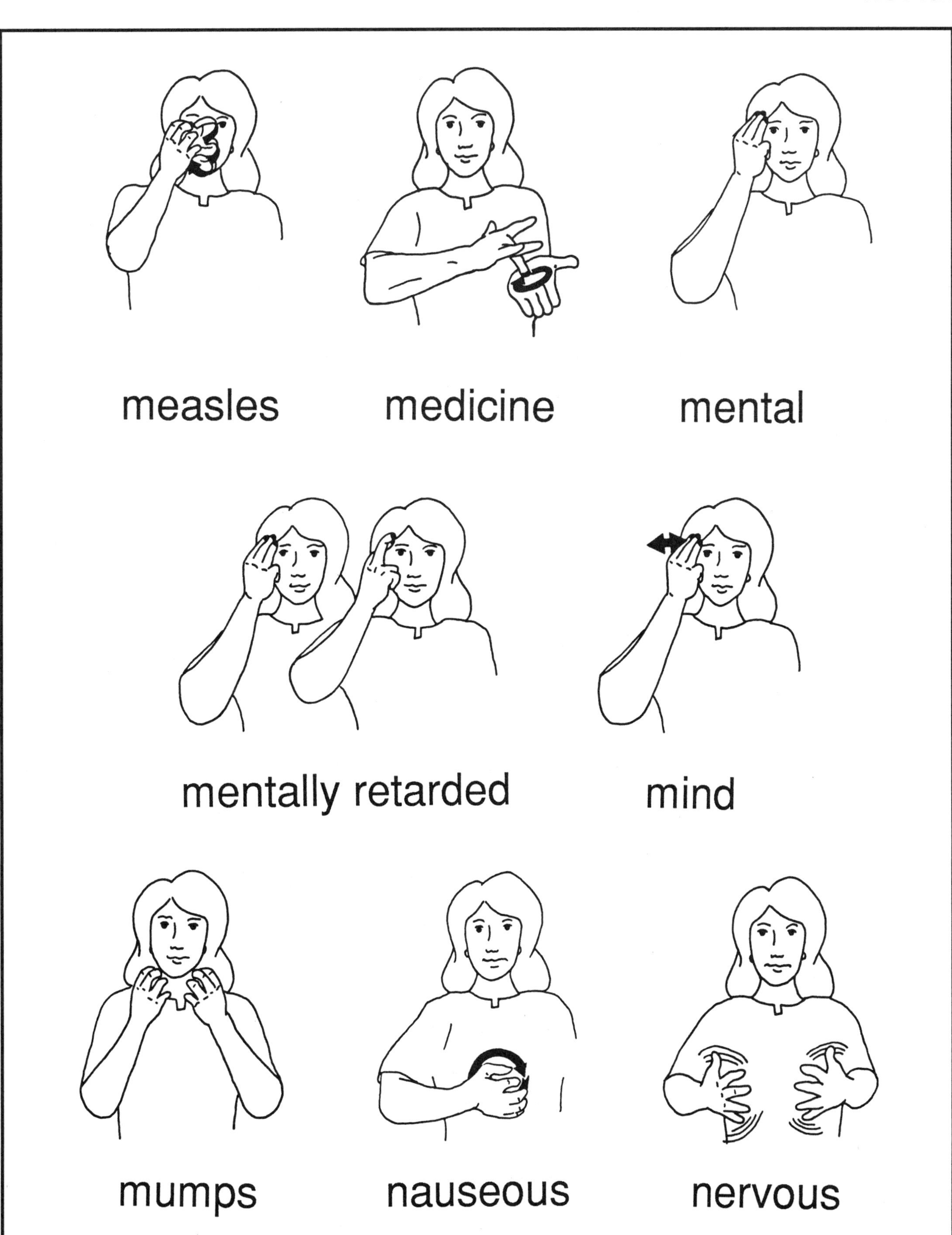
measles
medicine
mental
mentally retarded
mind
mumps
nauseous
nervous

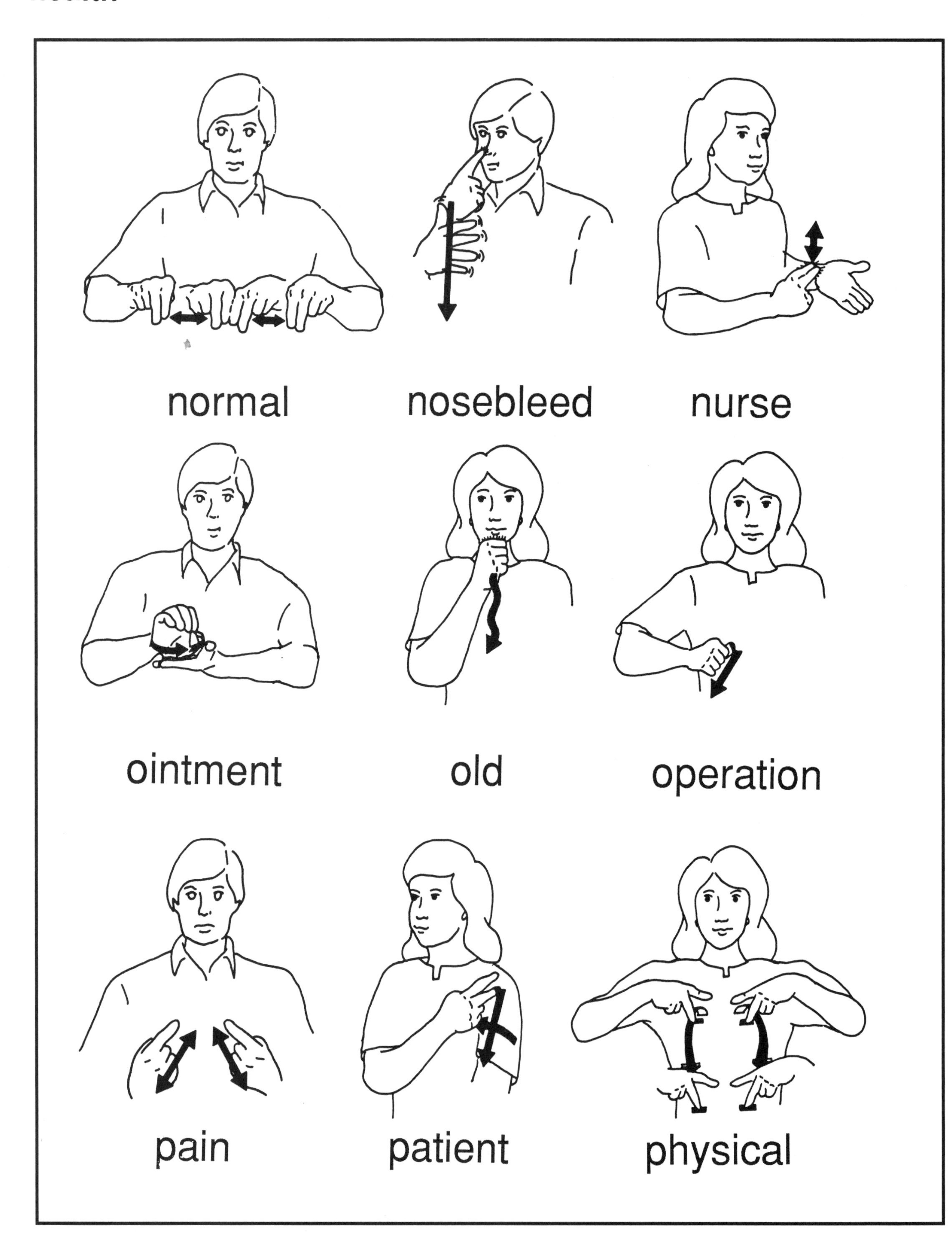
normal
nosebleed
nurse
ointment
old
operation
pain
patient
physical

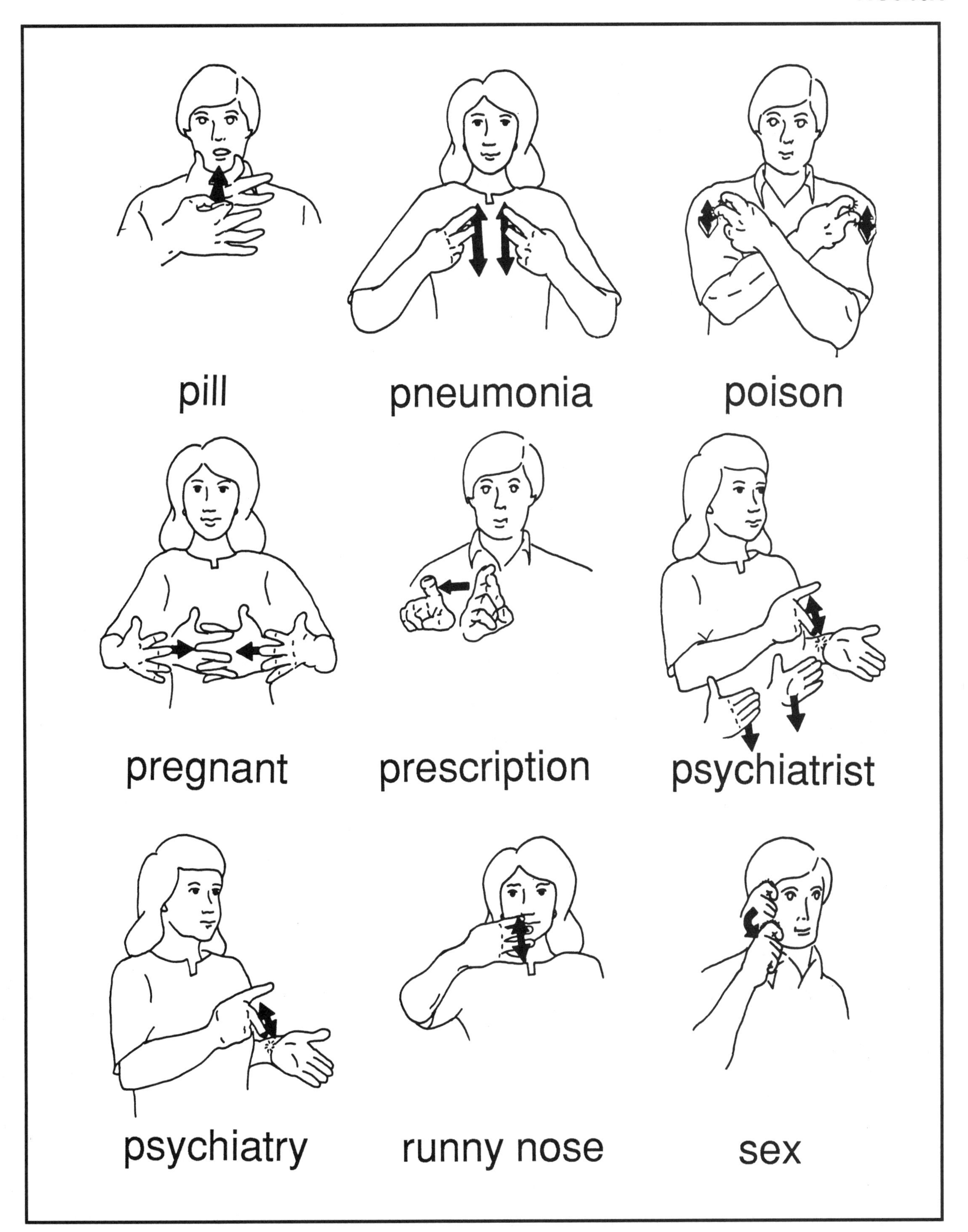
pill
pneumonia
poison
pregnant
prescription
psychiatrist
psychiatry
runny nose
sex

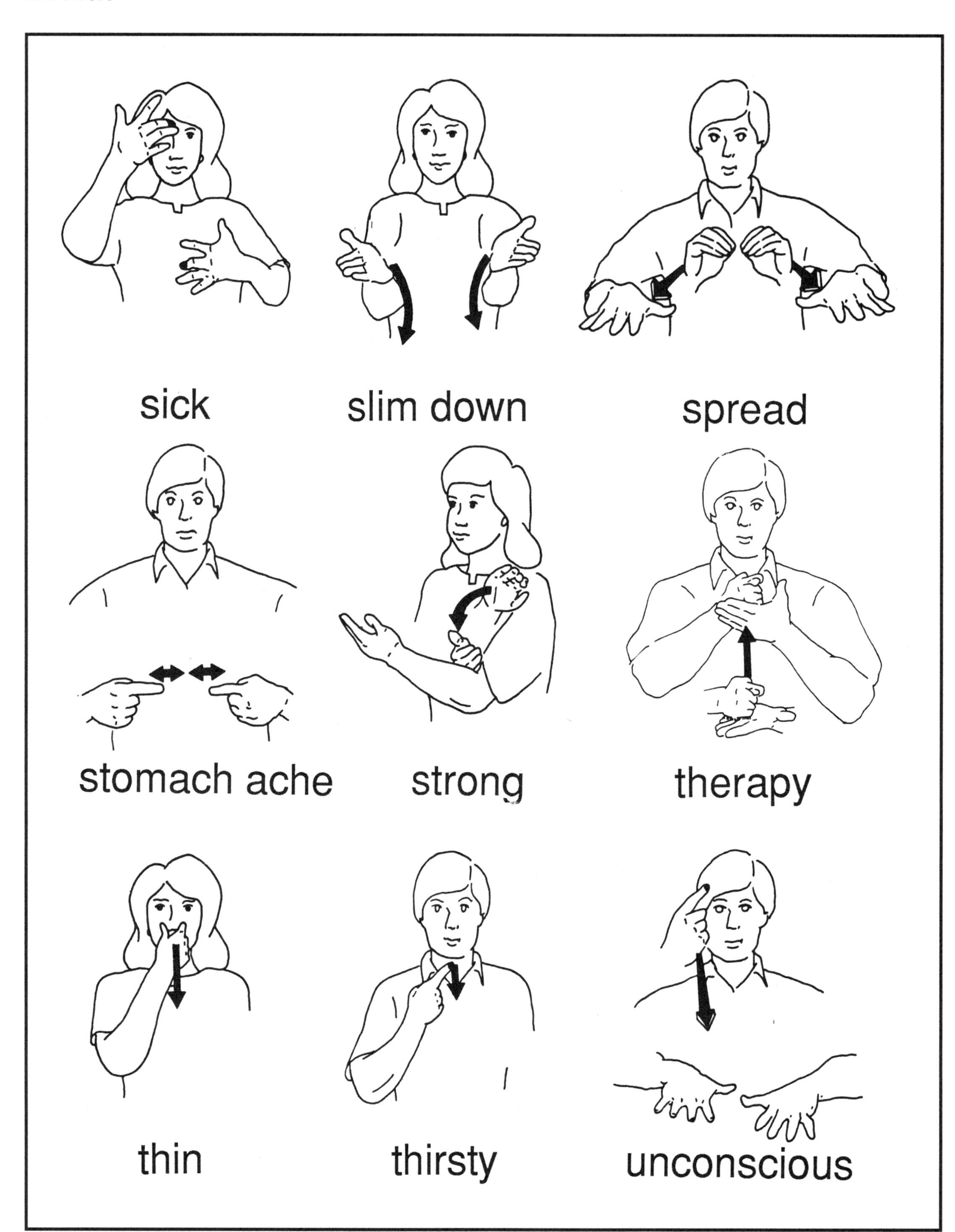
sick
slim down
spread
stomach ache
strong
therapy
thin
thirsty
unconscious

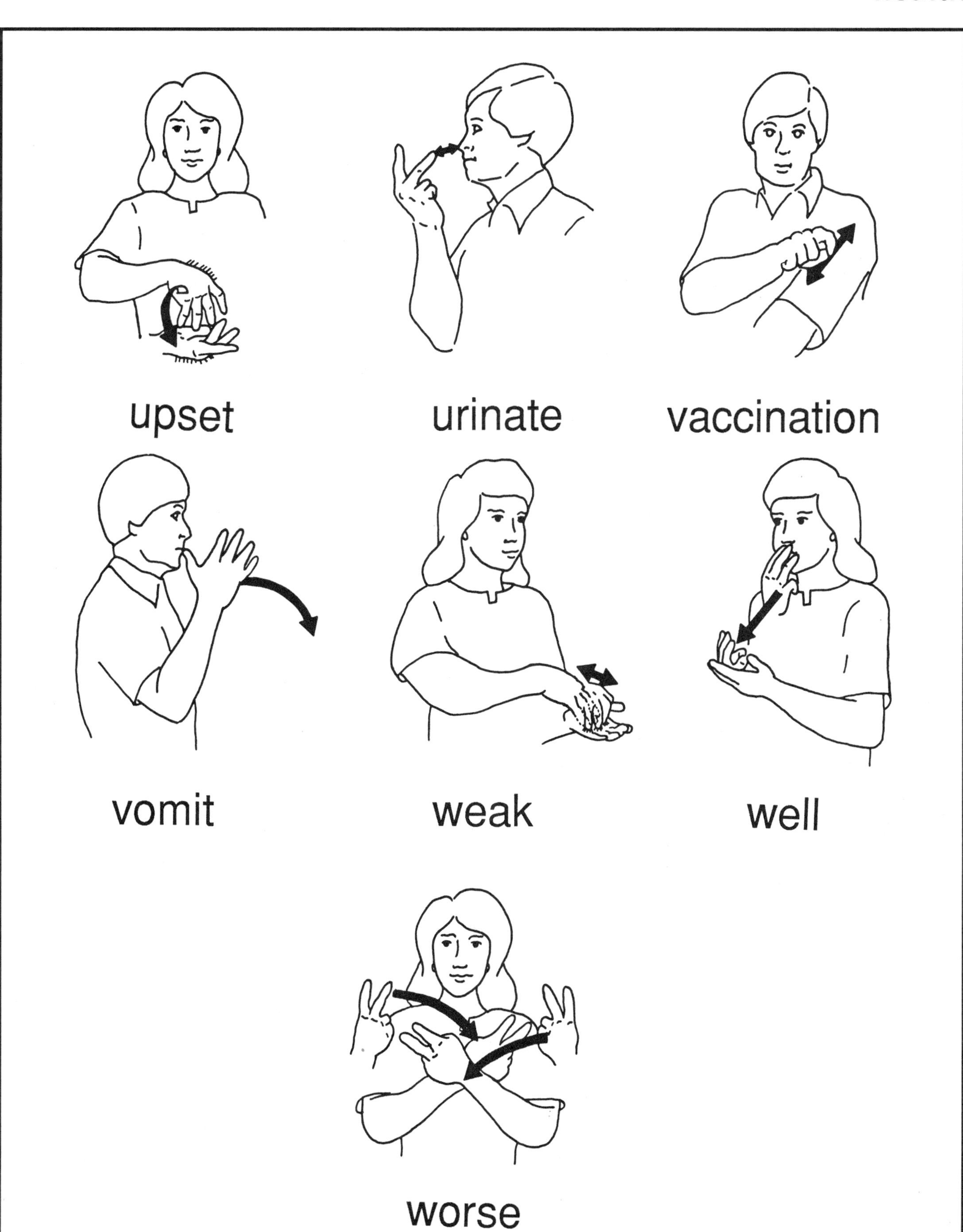
upset
urinate
vaccination
vomit
weak
well
worse

HOUSE THINGS

air conditioner
apron
basement
basket
bath
bathtub
bed [1]
bedroom
blanket
bottle
box
broom
cabinet
carpet
ceiling
chair [1]
clock
closet
couch
curtain
dining room
door
doorbell
downstairs
drawer
dresser
dryer
electric
faucet
fireplace
floor
flower [1]
fork
furniture
garage
gift
glass
hair dryer
heater
home [1]
key
kitchen
knife
lamp
laundry
letter
light
living room
machine
magazine
mail
match
microwave
mirror
motor
napkin
newspaper
oven
pan
pet
picture
pillow
pot
present
radio
refrigerator
roof
room
rug
saucer
sewing machine
sheet
shelf
shower
sink
soap
spoon
step
string
table
television
toaster
toilet
toothbrush
toothpaste
towel
toy
upstairs [2]
vacuum
VCR (video cassette recorder)
wall [2]
washing machine
window

ACTIVITY - HOUSE THINGS

Purpose: To identify different items found in specific rooms in a house.

Materials: House and items typically found in specific rooms; pencil and paper.

Procedure:

1. Child and adult go to a specific room in the house, e.g., bedroom, kitchen, living room, etc.
2. Adult signs/says to child, "Write the name of any item in this room on the paper."
3. Adult signs/says that child can only answer "yes" or "no" to the questions that are asked.
4. Adult signs/says questions about what item he thinks the child has wrtten on the paper, e.g., "Is it yellow?", "Is it big?", "Is it high?", etc.
5. Adult should write questions down to avoid confusion and for review.
6. Adult signs/says ten questions then stops, unless item has been identified before ten questions.
7. Adult selects some item in the room and child signs/says questions.

HOUSE THINGS

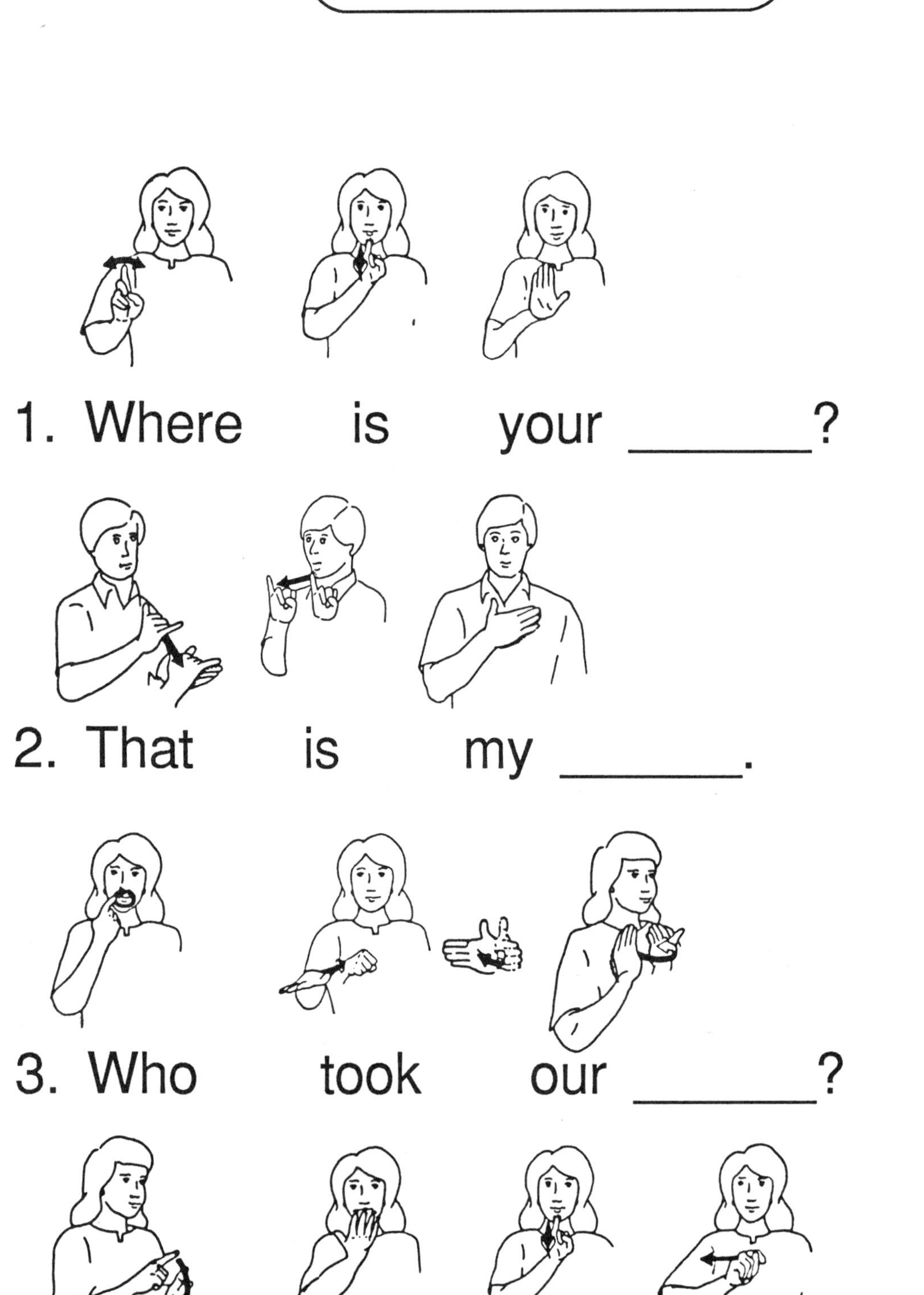

1. Where is your ______?

2. That is my ______.

3. Who took our ______?

4. What color is the ______?

HOUSE THINGS

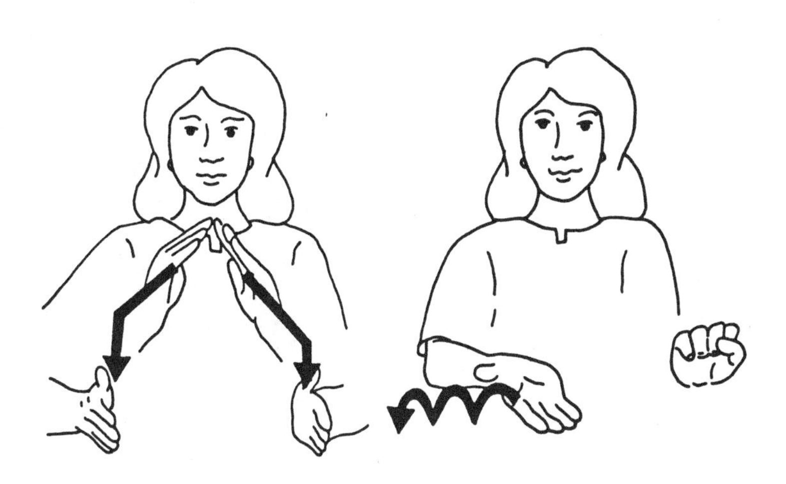

air conditioner

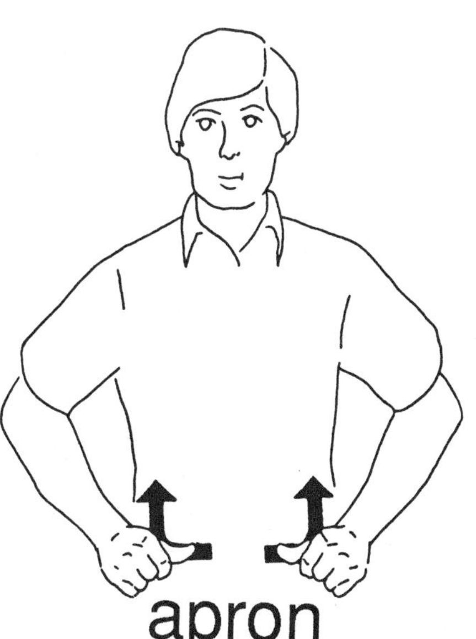

apron

basement

basket

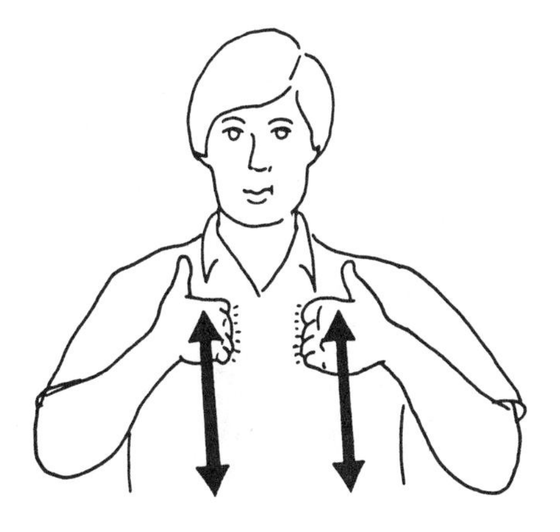

bath

5. Who broke the ______?
6. Put the ______ away.
7. Can you find my ______?
8. Where did you put the_____?

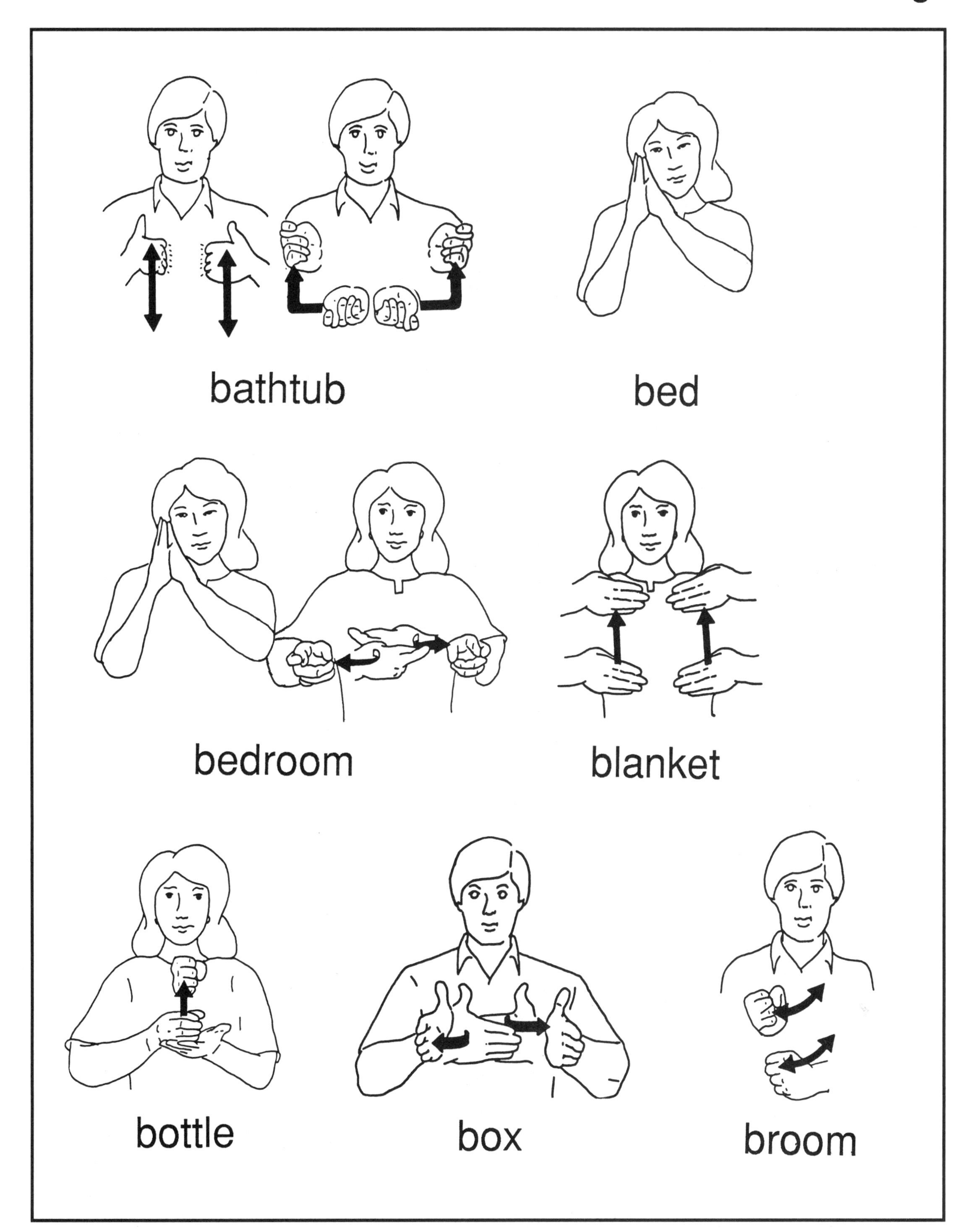
bathtub
bed
bedroom
blanket
bottle
box
broom

cabinet
carpet
ceiling
chair
clock
closet
couch
curtain

dining room
door
doorbell
downstairs
drawer
dresser
dryer
electric

faucet
fireplace
floor
flower
fork
furniture
garage
gift

glass
hair dryer
heater
home
key
kitchen
knife
lamp
laundry

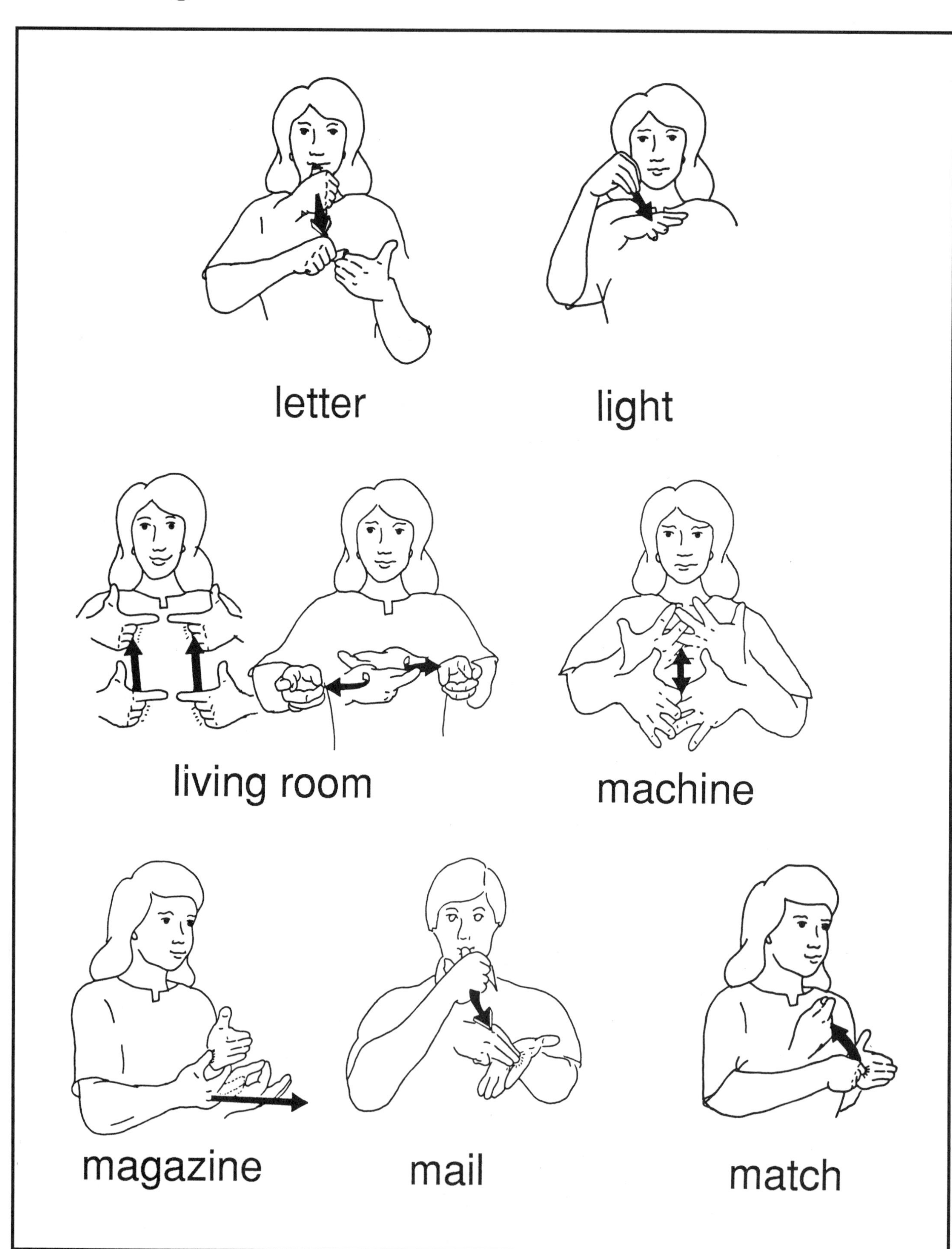
letter
light
living room
machine
magazine
mail
match

microwave
mirror
motor
napkin
newspaper
oven
pan
pet
picture

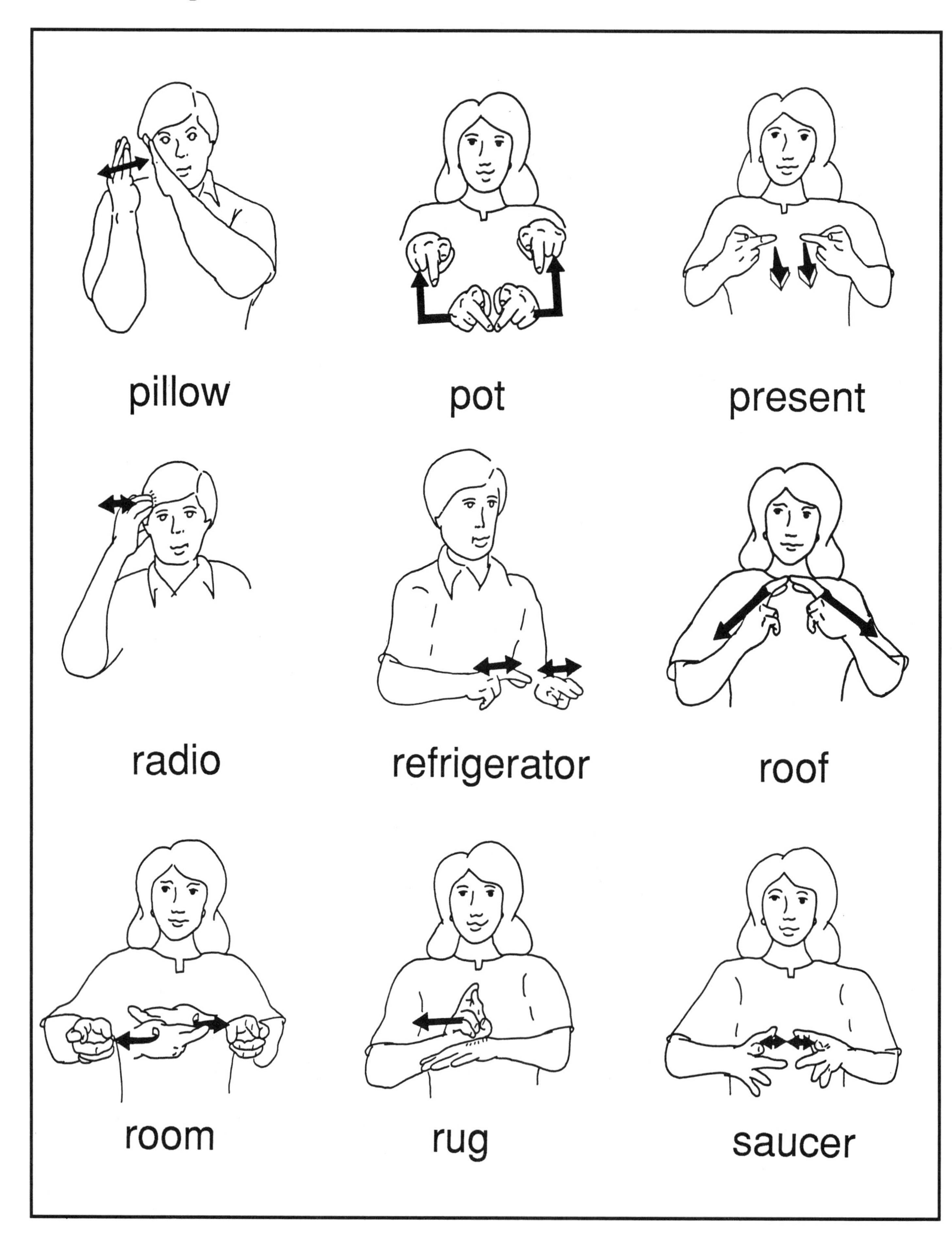
pillow
pot
present
radio
refrigerator
roof
room
rug
saucer

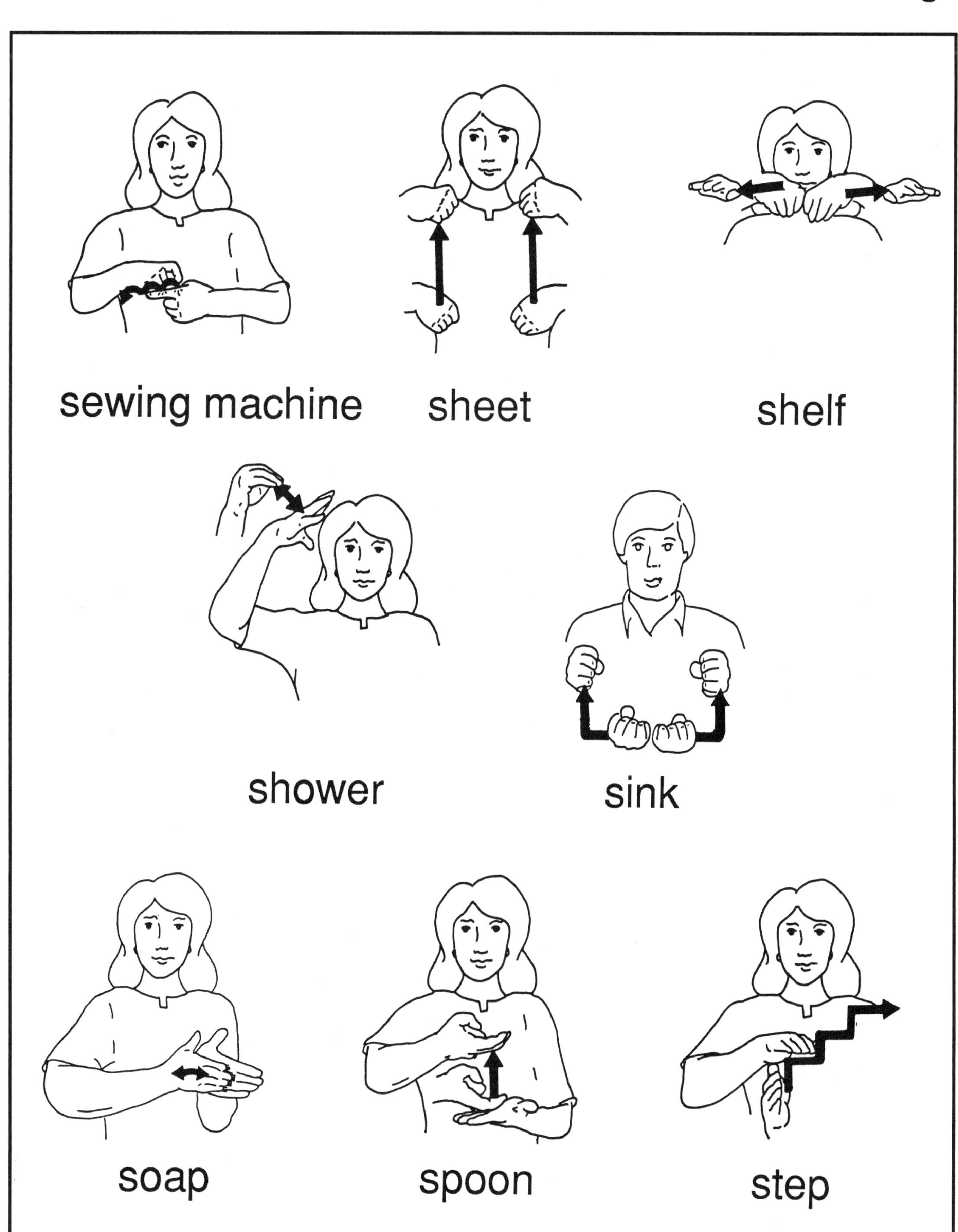
sewing machine
sheet
shelf
shower
sink
soap
spoon
step

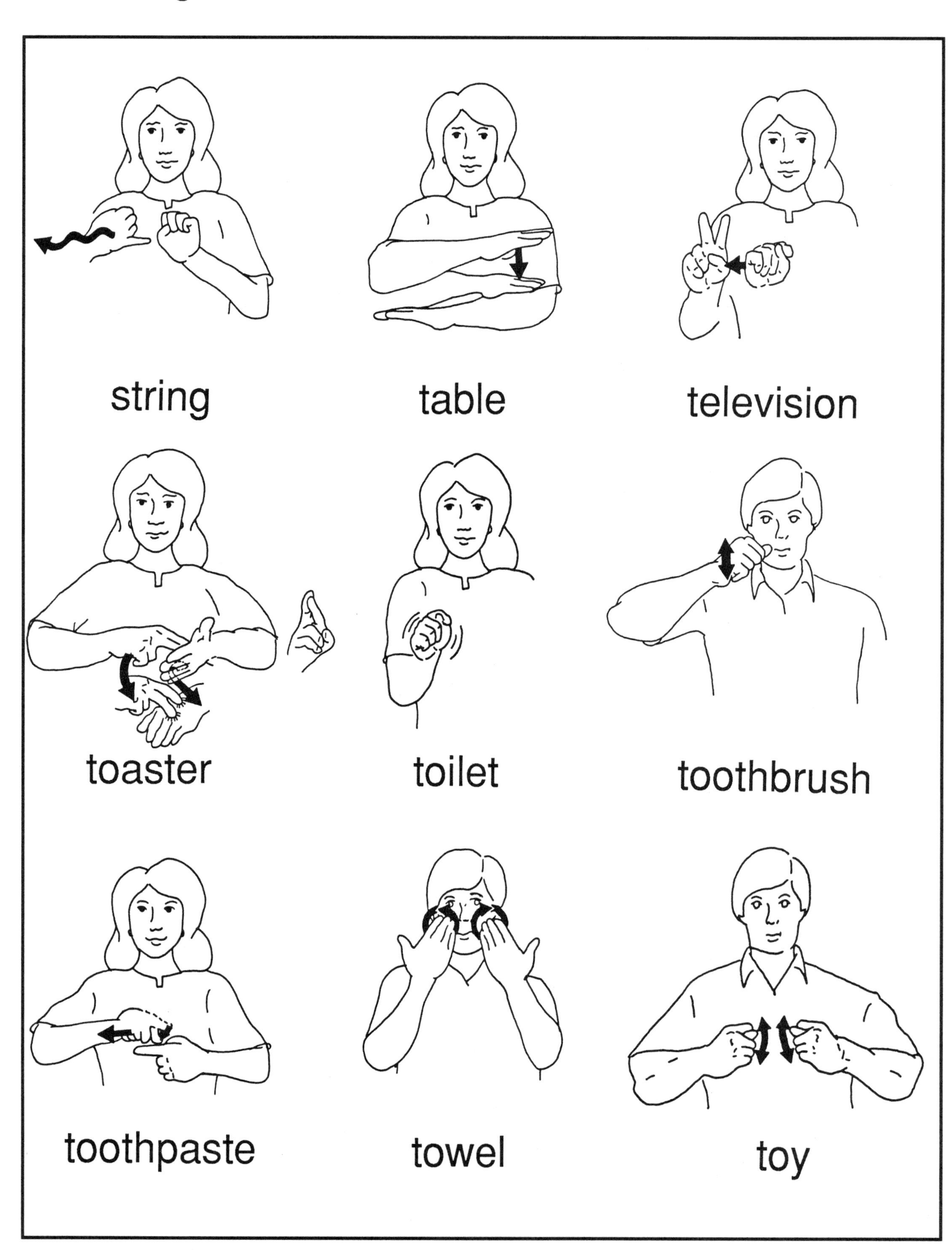
string
table
television
toaster
toilet
toothbrush
toothpaste
towel
toy

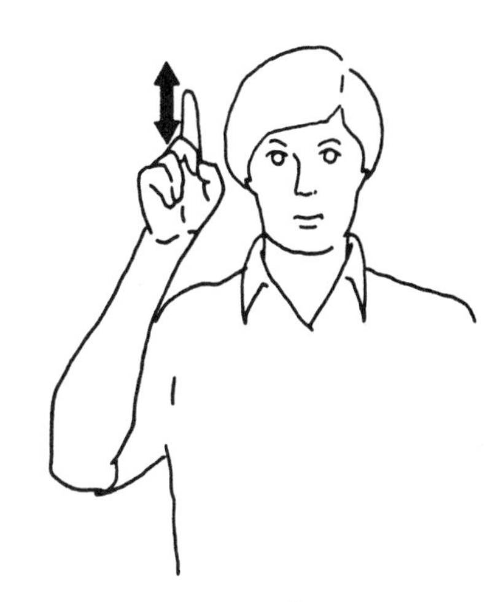

upstairs

vacuum

VCR
(video cassette recorder)

wall

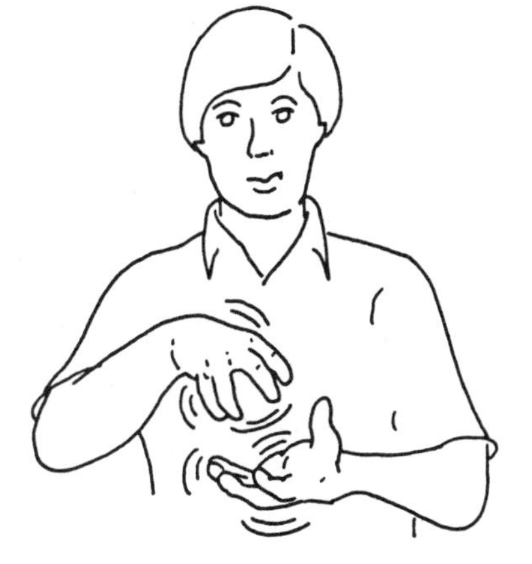

washing machine

window

INSECTS / BUGS[2]

ant
bee
beetle
butterfly
caterpillar
cricket
flea
fly
grasshopper
katydid
locus
mantis(praying)
mosquito
moth
roach
snail
spider
termite
wasp

ACTIVITY - INSECTS / BUGS

Purpose: To identify and be able to spell the names of several insects/bugs.

Materials: Pictures of insects/bugs; chalkboard and chalk.

Procedure:

1. Adult shows picture of insect/bug and asks its name sign.
2. Adult asks child to spell the name of the insect/bug in the picture.
3. Child either spells the name correctly or not. If correct, go to next picture, procedures 1 through 3. If not spelled correctly , continue to procedure 4.
4. Adult first puts blanks on board corresponding to the letter in the insect/bug's name, e.g., _ _ _ _ _ _ _ _ (mosquito).
5. Adult writes m on the first blank, m _ _ _ _ _ _ _, and asks child to write the rest of the name.
6. Adult continues to fill in blanks until child is able to write the rest of the name himself.
7. Adult erases the complete name from the board and repeats procedures 4 and 5 until child is able to write the insect/bug's name by himself with out any cues (spaces for letters).
8. Repeat procedures 1 through 7 with a new picture.

Variations: Child can catch insects/bugs and put them into containers labeling them with proper names or name signs.

INSECTS / BUGS

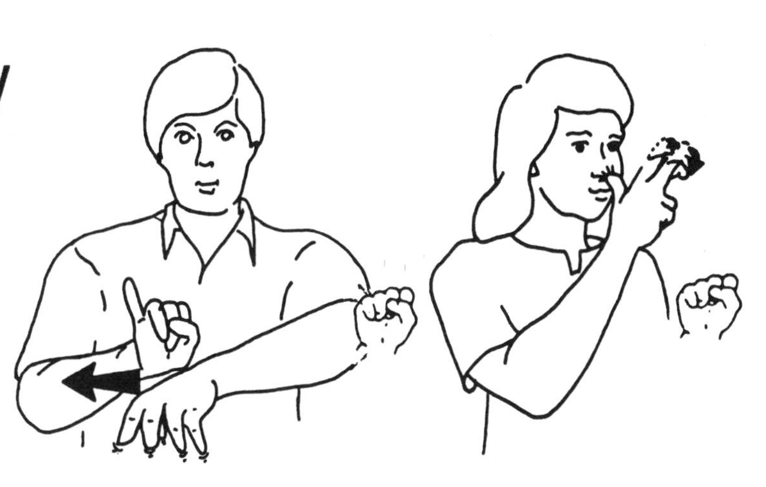

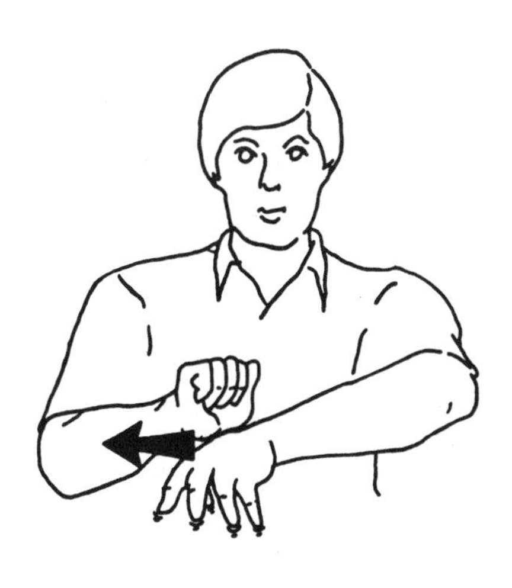

ant

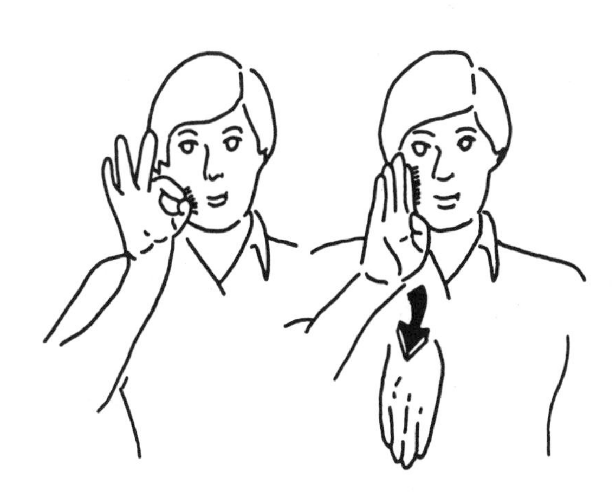

bee

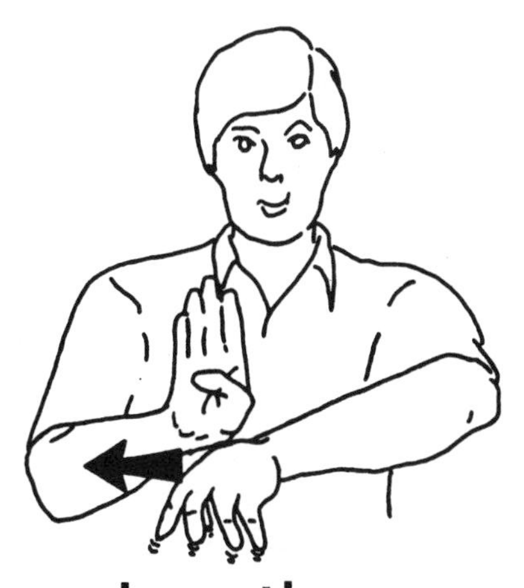

beetle

butterfly

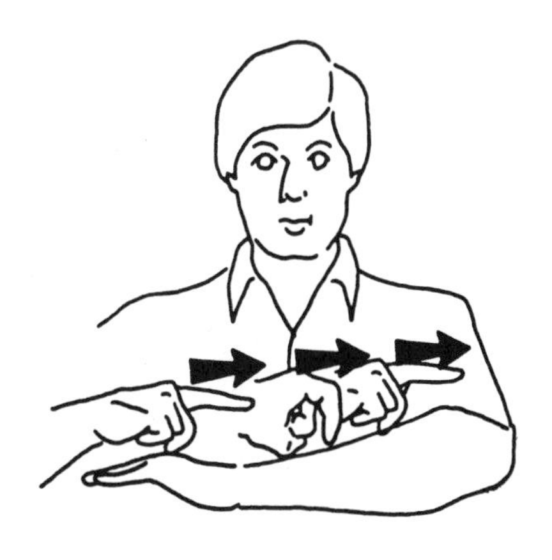

caterpillar

INSECTS / BUGS

1. What color is the ______?

2. Show me the ______.

3. The ______ is very ugly.

4. A ______ is pretty.

cricket
flea
fly
grasshopper
katydid
locus
mantis (praying)
mosquito

moth
roach
snail
spider
termite
wasp

INTERROGATIVES

are	don't[1]	when [1]
can[1]	how [1]	where [1]
could	is [1]	which [2]
did [1]	may	will [2]
didn't	should	who [1]
do[1]	was [1]	why [2]
does[2]	were	won't [2]
doesn't	what [1]	would

ACTIVITY - INTERROGATIVES

Purpose: To have child learn that the interrogative <u>who</u> represents a person.

Materials: Photographs of family members; chalkboard and chalk or large sheet of paper and pencil.

Procedure:

1. Adult shows child a picture of family member signing/saying, "Who is this?" (<u>this</u> would be signed by pointing to the picture). Adult writes it on chalkboard.
2. If child responds correctly, e.g., papa, adult writes on chalkboard, "This is papa.", right under, "who is this?"
3. Adult draws a circle around "who" and "papa" then draws a line connecting the circled words.
4. Adult repeats procedures one through three with another family member.
5. Adult puts both pictures in front of child and signs/says, "Who is this?" Child responds appropriately. Repeat.
6. Child put pictures in front of adult signing/saying, "Who is this?" When mastery is achieved, add other family members one at a time.

Variations: This activity can be done using other interrogatives with some minor changes. Have child write sentences on chalkboard.

INTERROGATIVES

1. What is your name?

2. When are you going?

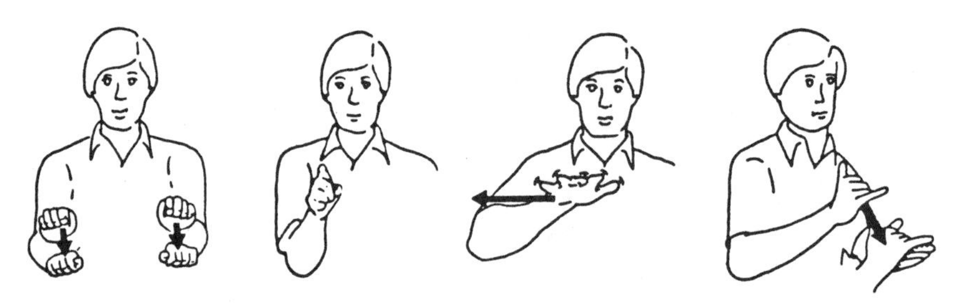

3. Can you spell that?

4. Who is your brother?

INTERROGATIVES

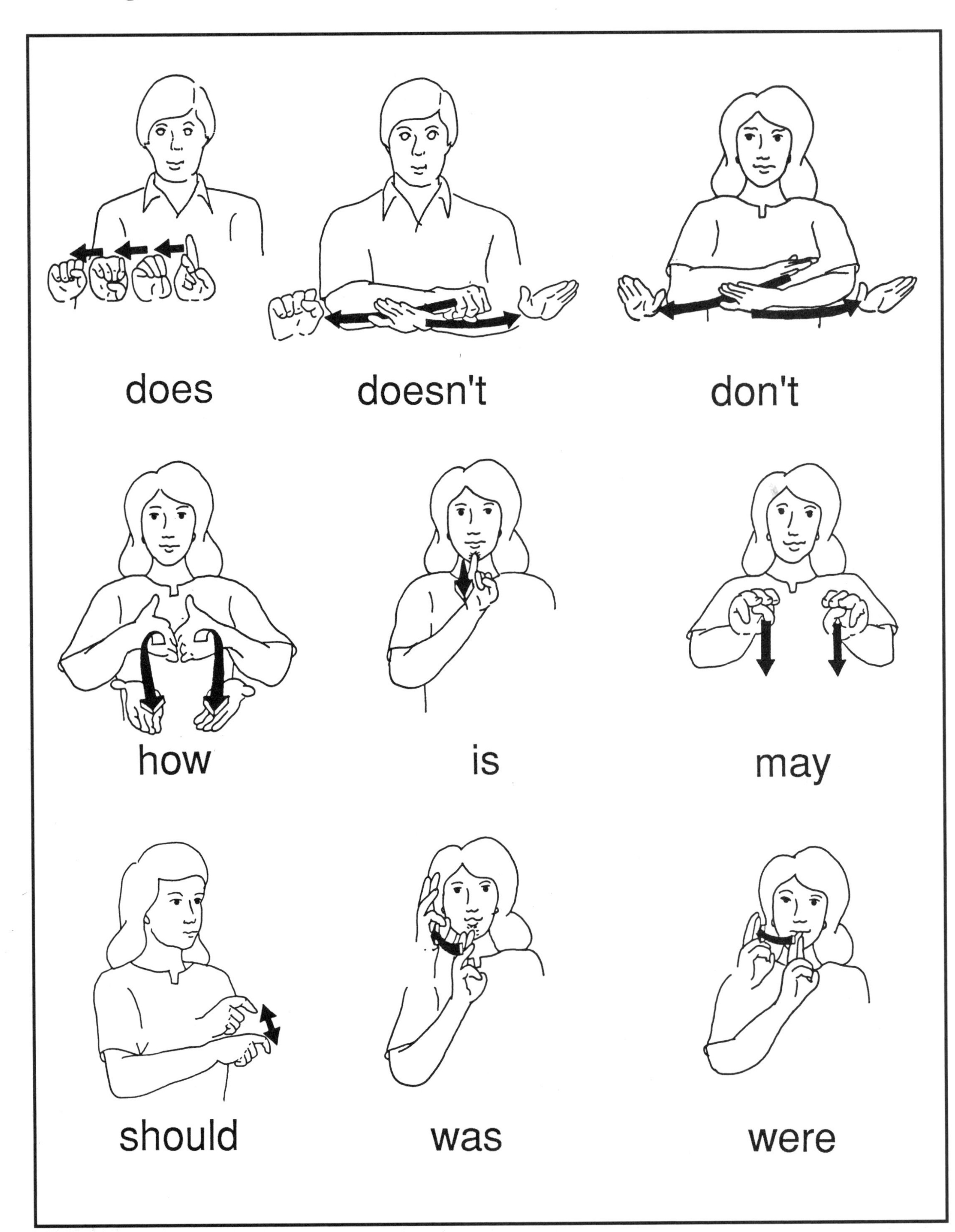
does
doesn't
don't
how
is
may
should
was
were

what
when
where
which
who
why
will
won't
would

LIQUIDS

alcohol
beer
blood
cider
cocoa
coffee
coke (Coca-Cola)
cough syrup
gasoline
gravy
grease
honey
juice
Kool Aid
lemonade
liquor
milk
oil
Pepsi
perfume
pop
salad dressing
sauce
shampoo
soda
soup
syrup
tea
vinegar
water
whiskey
wine

ACTIVITY - LIQUIDS

Purpose: To show that liquids take the shape of the container into which they are poured.

Materials: Pie pan, bottle, tall glass, short glass, cup, water.

Procedure:

1. Adult sets up all the containers on a table in front of child with water in the short glass.
2. Adult signs/says, "See the the water in the short glass?" Child responds with a yes.
3. Adult signs/says, "The water is the shape of the glass."
4. Adult signs/says to pour water from short glass into the tall bottle.
5. Adult praises child and signs/says, "Look, the water is not small and round, it is now round and tall. The water is the shape of the tall bottle."
6. Continue with procedures 4 and 5 until all of the containers have had water in them and each of the shapes identified.
7. Adult emphasizes the concept that water (a liquid) takes the shape of the container that it is in.

Variations: Freeze several different liquids, e.g., lemonade, cider, Pepsi, etc. in different shaped containers. Show that the frozen liquid has taken the shape of its container. Let the frozen shape melt in pie pan to again illustrate that a liquid takes the form of its container. Let the child drink each of the liquids and identify each.

LIQUIDS

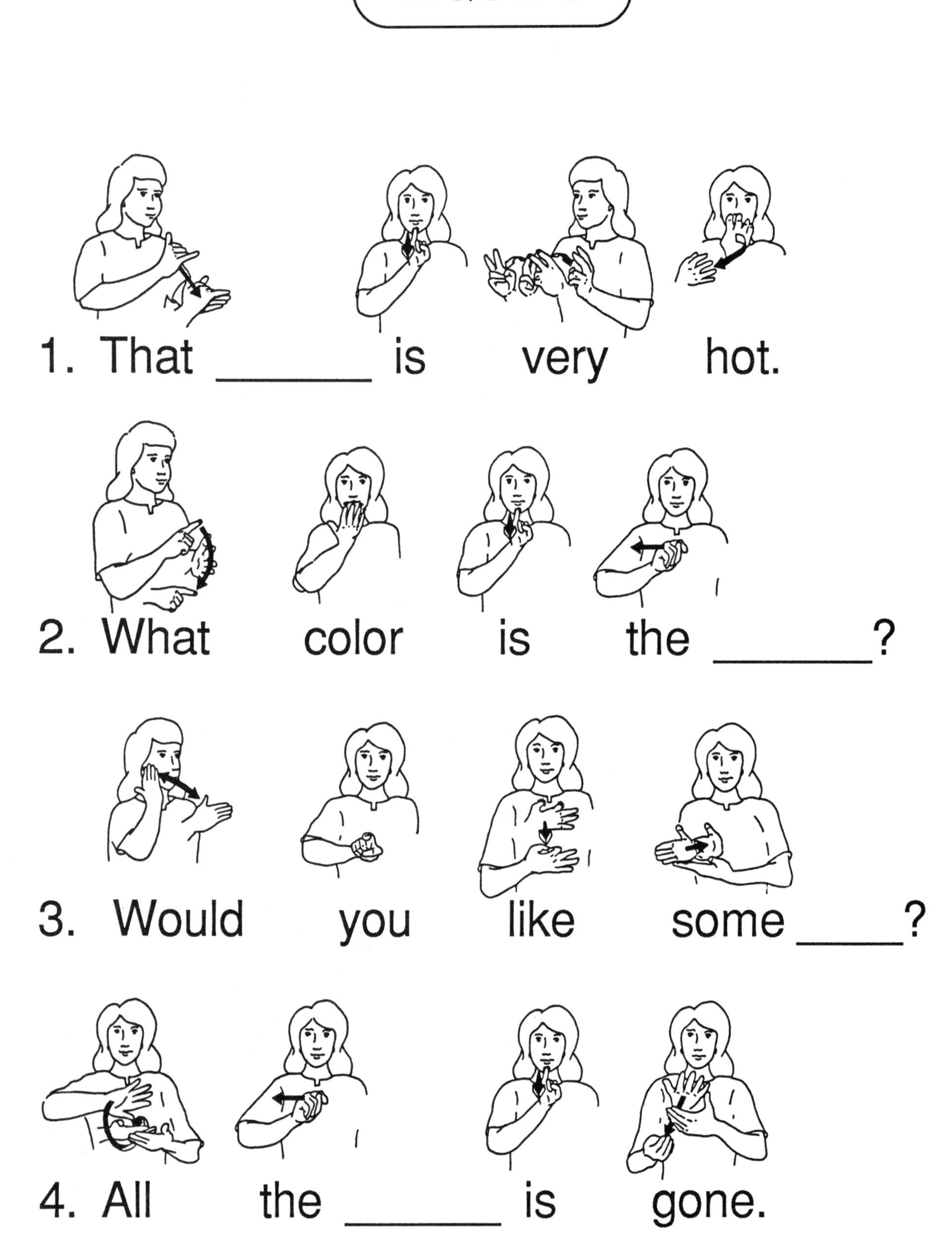
1. That ______ is very hot.
2. What color is the ______?
3. Would you like some _____?
4. All the ______ is gone.

LIQUIDS

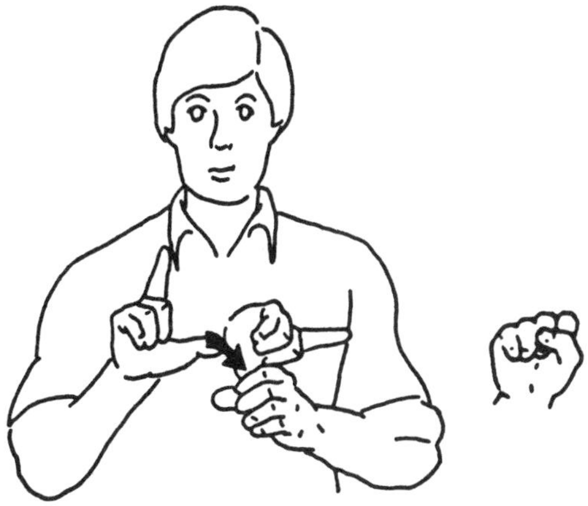

alcohol

beer

blood

cider

cocoa

coffee

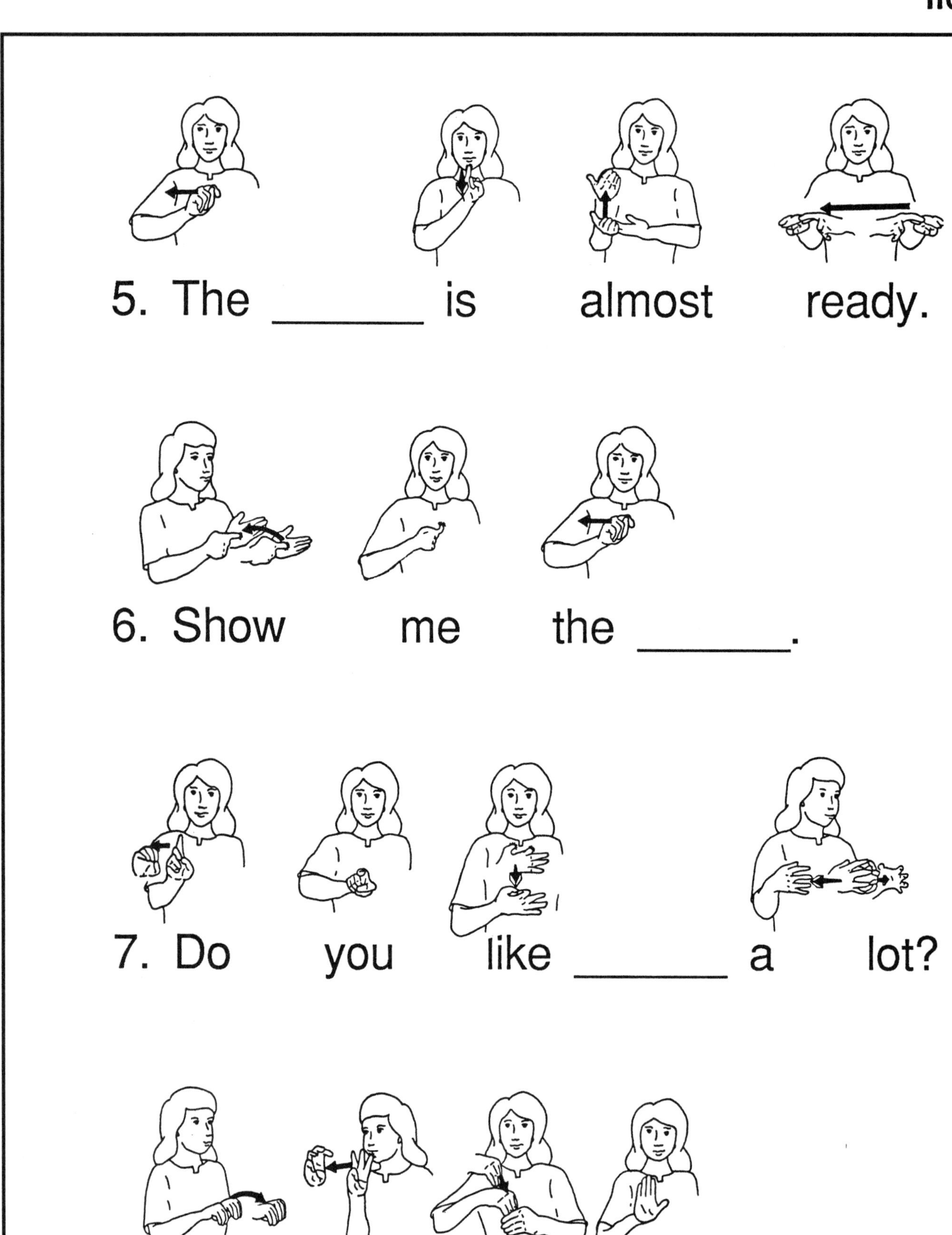
5. The ______ is almost ready.
6. Show me the ______.
7. Do you like ______ a lot?
8. Put ice in your ______.

Coke (Coca-Cola)

cough syrup

gasoline

gravy

grease

honey

juice

Kool Aid

lemonade
liquor
milk
oil
Pepsi
perfume
pop
salad dressing
sauce

shampoo
soda
soup
syrup
tea
vinegar
water
whiskey
wine

LITTLE THINGS

ant
bead
bug
button
caterpillar
chip
cotton
dust
earring
eyelash
feather
flea
french fry
insect
key
leaf
mouse
nut
paperclip
peanut
pin
raisin
rice
sand
seed
smoke
tack
thimble
worm

ACTIVITY - LITTLE THINGS

Purpose: To get across the concept of little.

Materials: Items around the house; paper bag.

Procedure:

1. Adult picks up something little, e.g., pencil, signing/saying "little".
2. Child signs/says, "little".
3. Adult gives pencil to child to put into bag.
4. Adult, walking through house, picks up something little, signing/saying, "little".
5. Child signs/says, "little", and puts object into bag.
6. Adult continues activity occasionally picking up something that will not fit into the bag, then signing/saying, "Not little".
7. Adult allows child to try putting "Not little" object into bag signing/saying, "Not little" when child fails.
8. Child signs/says, "Not little".
9. Continue activity until child is able to look at a variety of things identifying them as "little"and "Not little".

Variations: Do the same activity with the concept of big. If the object does not fit into the bag, it is big, if it goes into the bag the object is little (That is if the concept of little has been learned, if not, the object is "Not big").

LITTLE THINGS

1. Show me something little.

2. Can you find a little ________?

3. Where did you put the ______?

4. Can you see the ________?

LITTLE THINGS

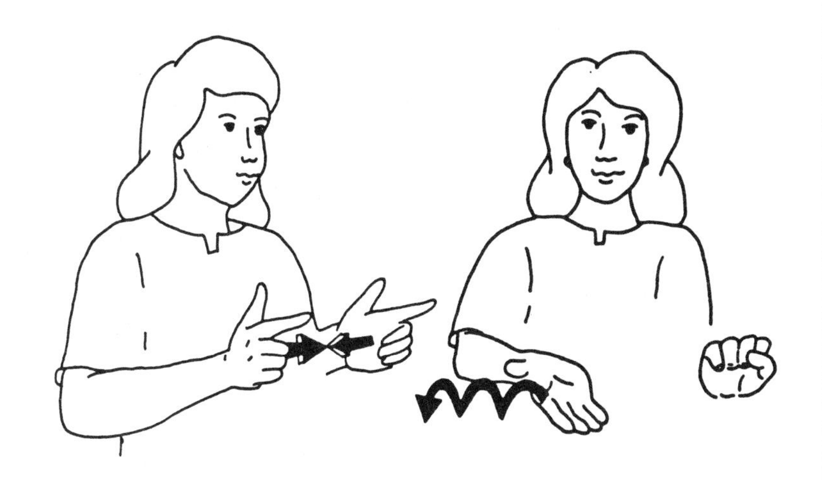

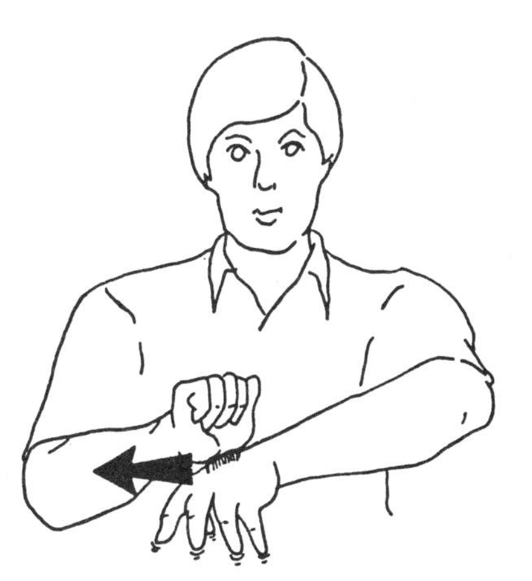

ant

bead

bug

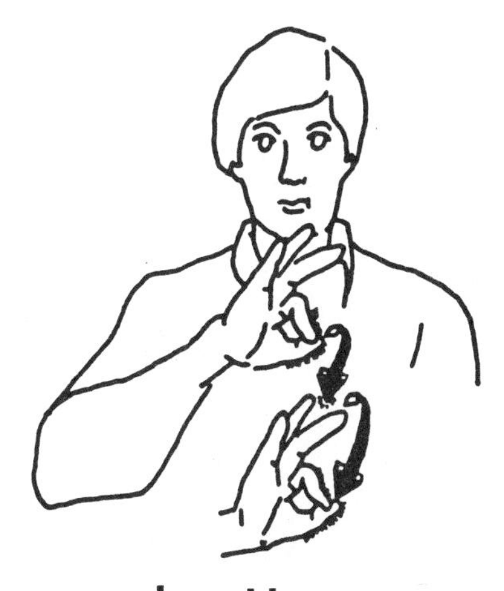

button

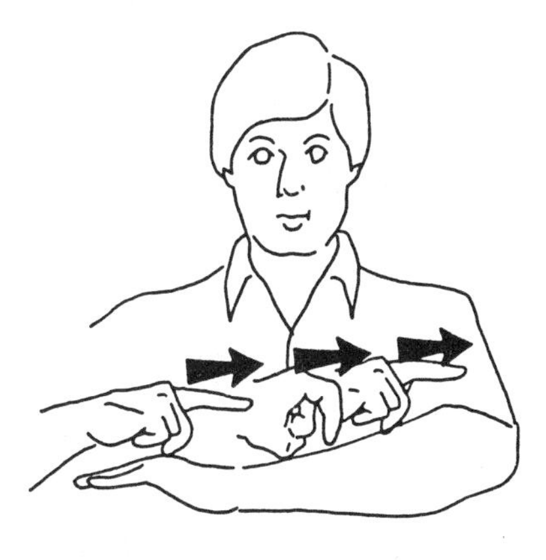

caterpillar

chip

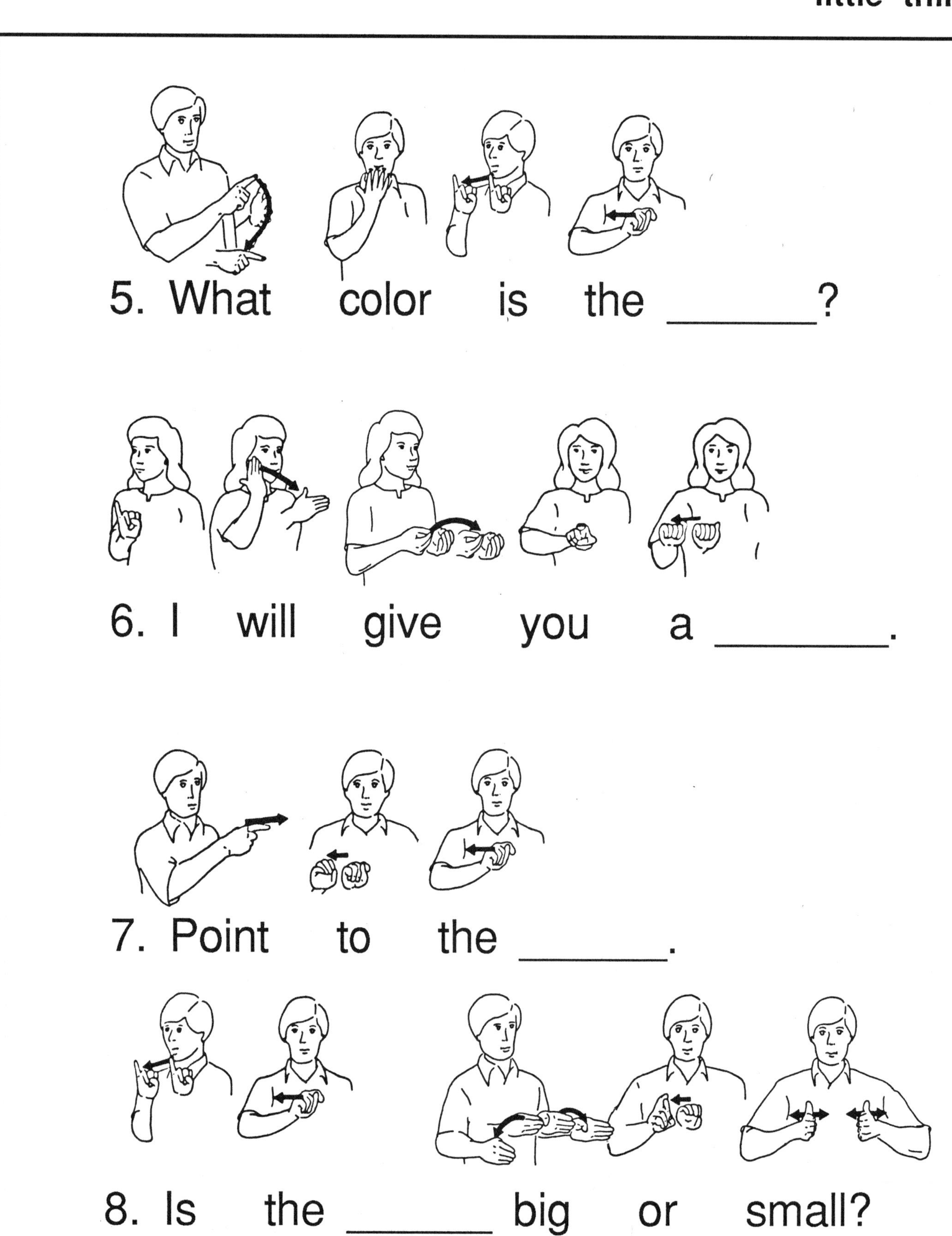
5. What color is the ______?
6. I will give you a ______.
7. Point to the ______.
8. Is the ______ big or small?

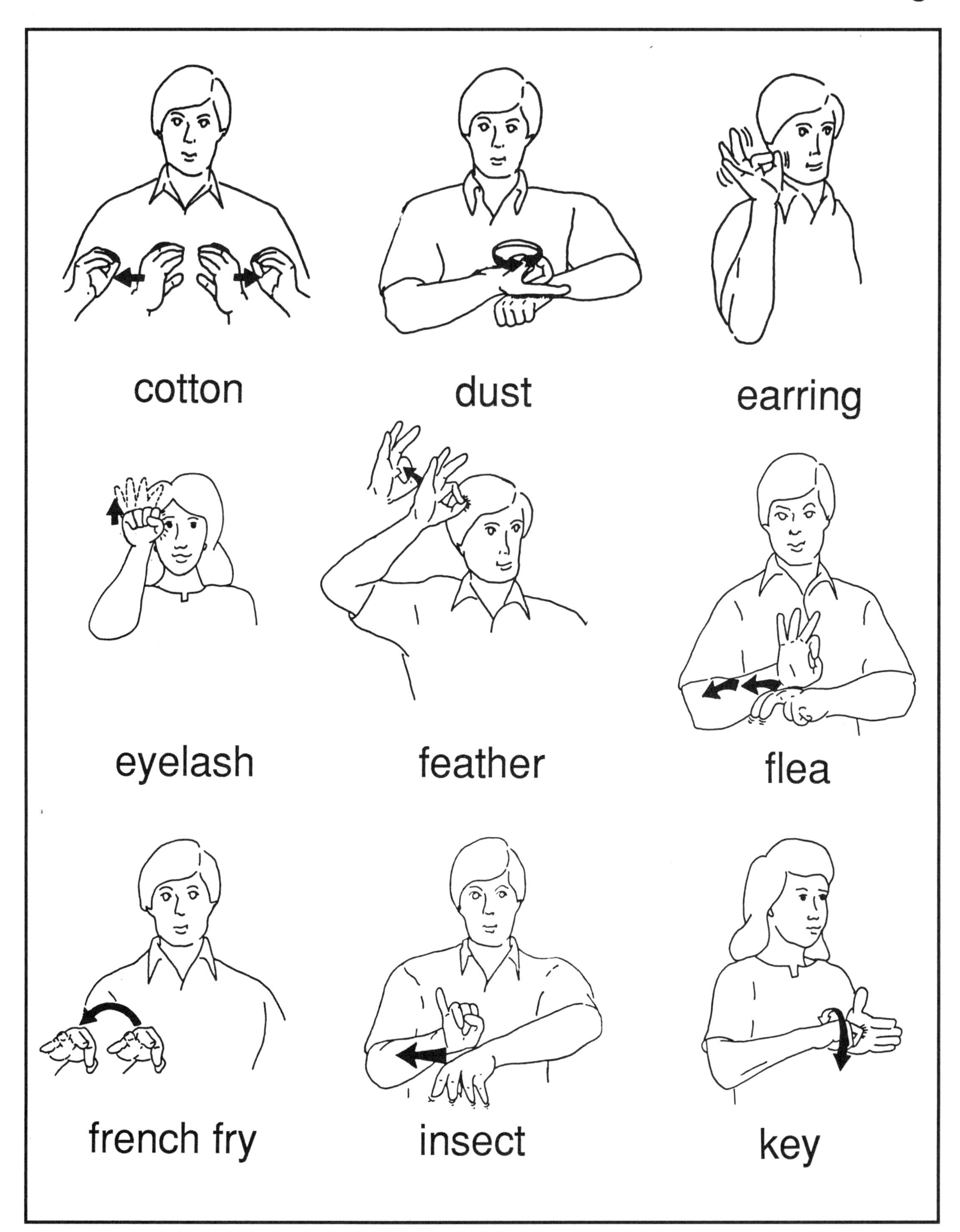
cotton
dust
earring
eyelash
feather
flea
french fry
insect
key

leaf
mouse
nut
paper clip
peanut
pin
raisin
rice

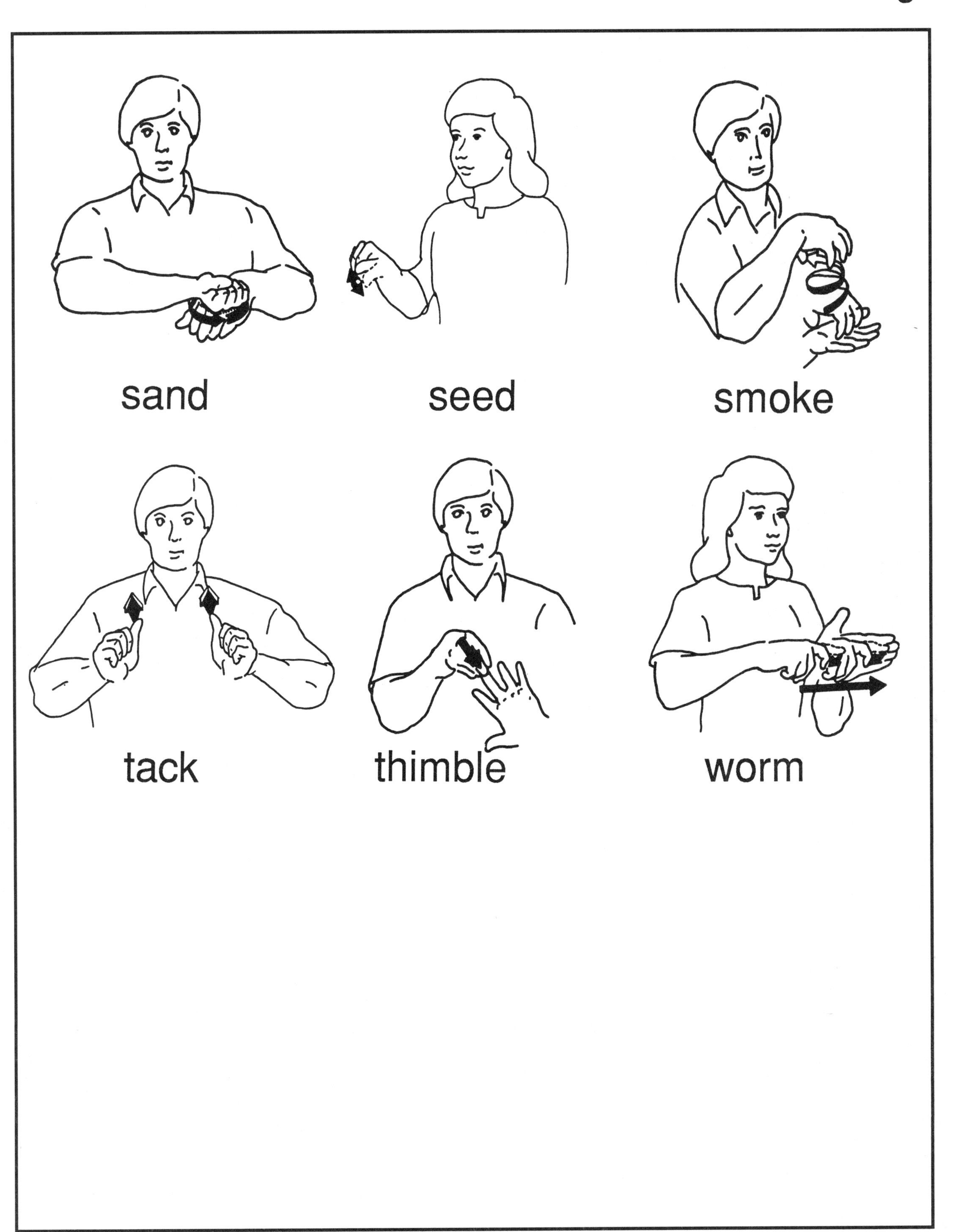
sand
seed
smoke
tack
thimble
worm

MELTING THINGS

butter
candle
candy
chocolate
crayon
gold
ice
ice cream
icicle
marshmallow
plastic
popscicle
silver
snow
snowball
snowman
soap
sugar

ACTIVITY - THINGS THAT MELT

Purpose: To identify things that melt and things that do not melt.

Materials: Hot plate; skillet; chalk and chalkboard; variety of different objects, e.g., shoe, butter, spoon, wood, pencil, plastic, ice cube, paper, crayon, etc.

Procedure:

1. Adult writes on chalkboard:

   <u>**Things that melt**</u>   <u>**Things that do not melt**</u>

2. Adult puts skillet on hot plate and turns on hot plate, signing/saying names of each.
3. Adult picks each object from a bag, child signs/says each object, and puts each on table.
4. Adult signs/says, "What do you think will melt?"
5. Child signs/says an object and hands it to adult.
6. Adult puts it into skillet for several minutes.
7. Child signs/says whether object melted or did not melt.
8. Child writes name of object under appropriate heading on chalkboard.
9. Child signs/says all objects on board after each has been classified, "Wood will not melt.", "Butter will melt," etc.

Variations: Make a cake with child to show which ingredients melt and which do not; make smores to show the marshmallows and chocolate melting; bring in snow from outdoors.

MELTING THINGS

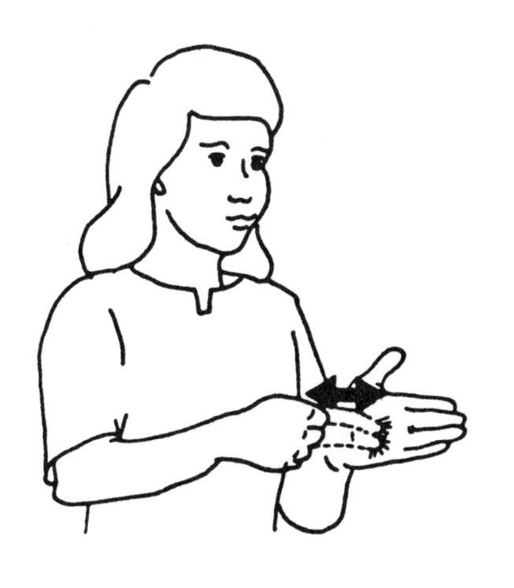

butter

candle

candy

chocolate

crayon

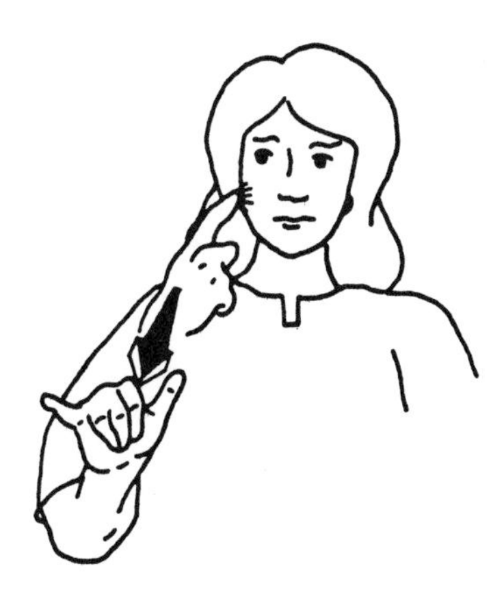

gold

MELTING THINGS

1. What color is the ______?

2. The sun melted the ______.

3. Is the ______ sticky now?

4. ______ is a liquid.

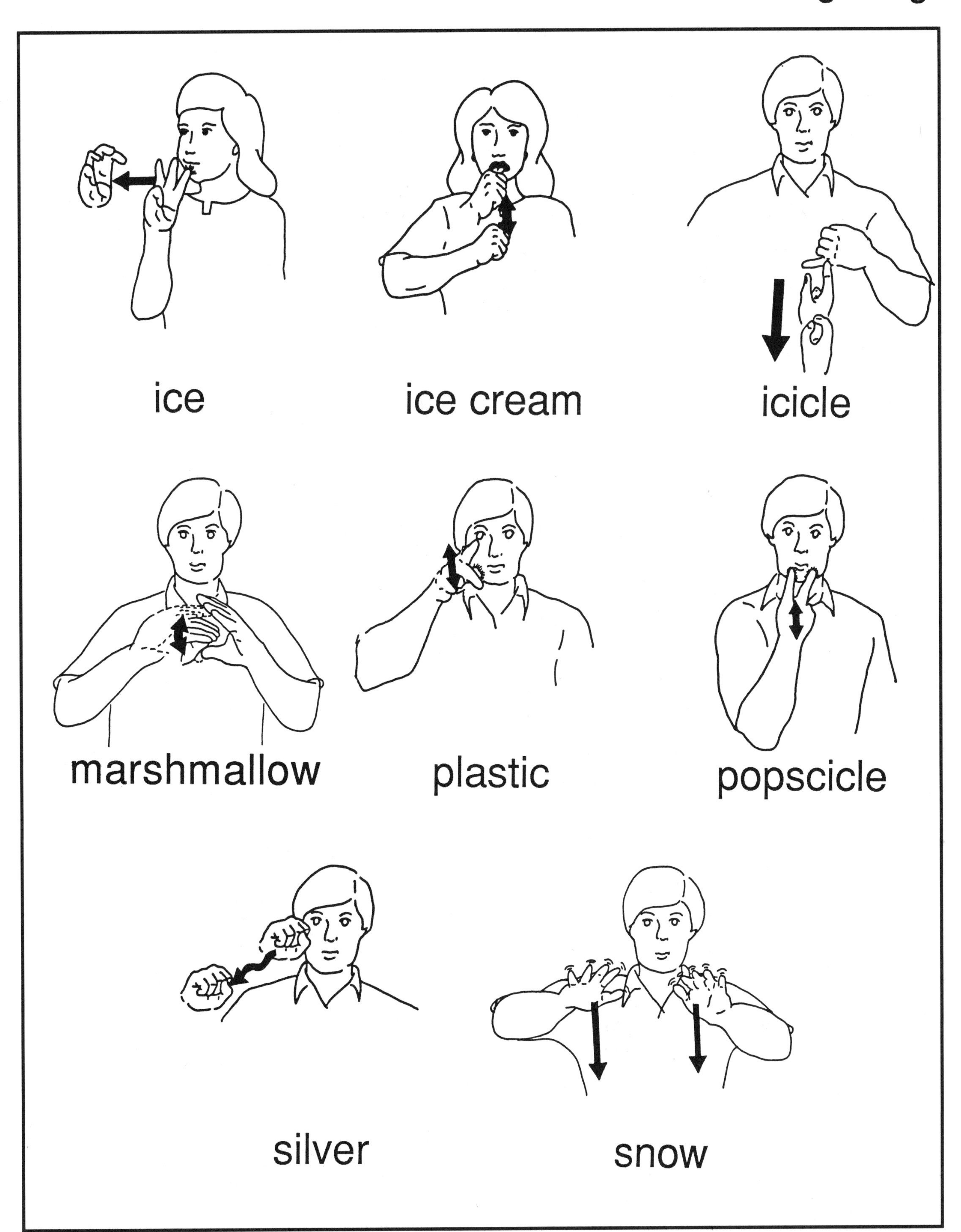
ice
ice cream
icicle
marshmallow
plastic
popscicle
silver
snow

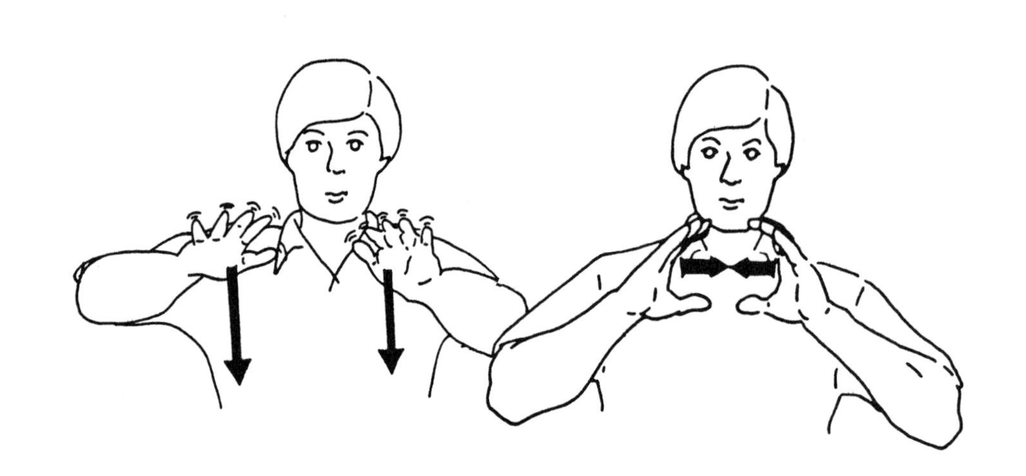

snowball

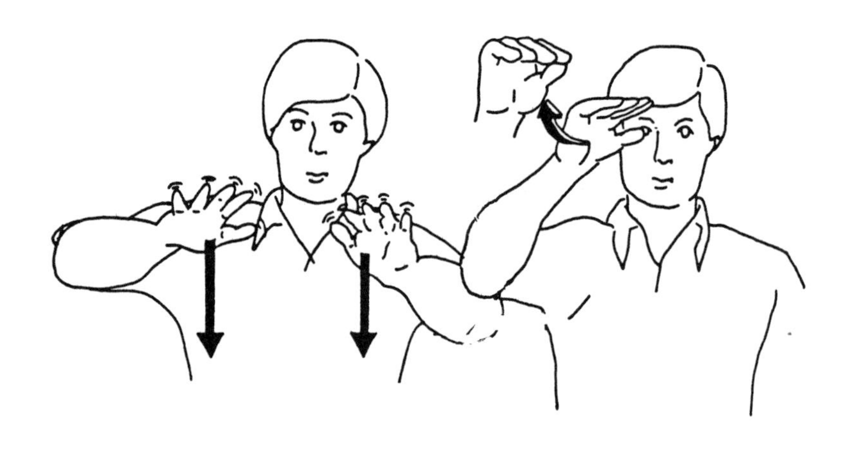

snowman

soap

sugar

MISCELLANEOUS

a [1]
about [1]
already [2]
an [2]
and
another [1]
as
because [1]
better [2]
break [2]
but [1]
buy [2]
cartoon [2]
close [2]
for [1]
gas
good bye [1]
hi [2]
hole [2]
let [1]
line [2]
middle [2]
Mr. [1]
Mrs. [1]
much [2]
other [1]
own [2]
part [2]
piece [2]
place [1]
privilege
real [1]
shape
suppose [2]
than [2]
the
wave
while [2]

NOTE:

The following words are generally fingerspelled:

as [2] at [1] by [1] if [1] of [1] or [1] so [1]

MISCELLANEOUS

a

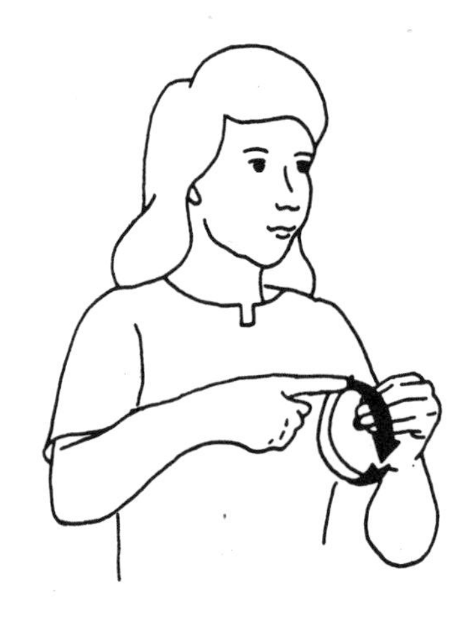

about

already

an

and

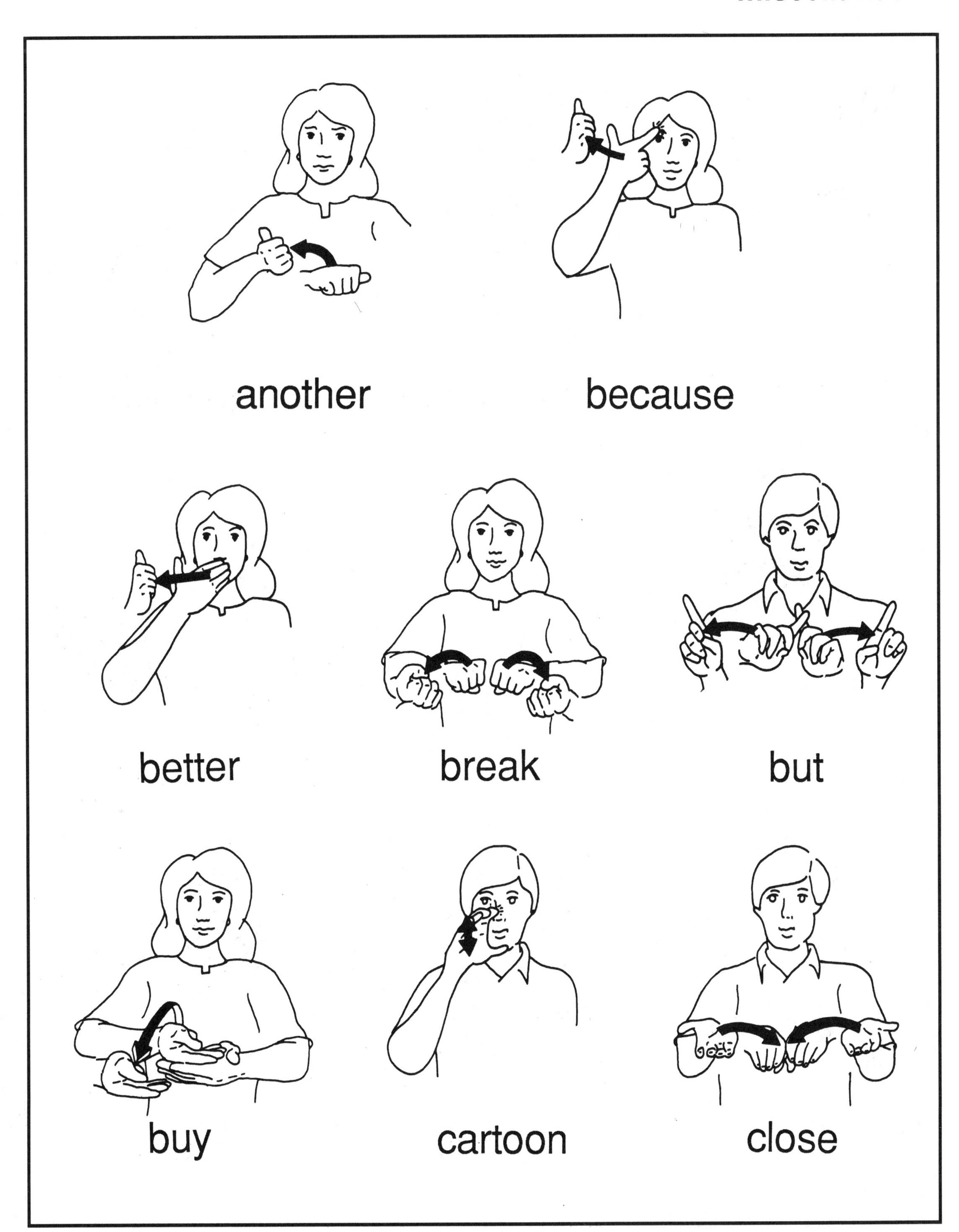
another
because
better
break
but
buy
cartoon
close

for
gas (vapor)
good bye
hi
hole
let
line
middle
Mr.

Mrs.
much
other
own
part
piece
place
privilege
real

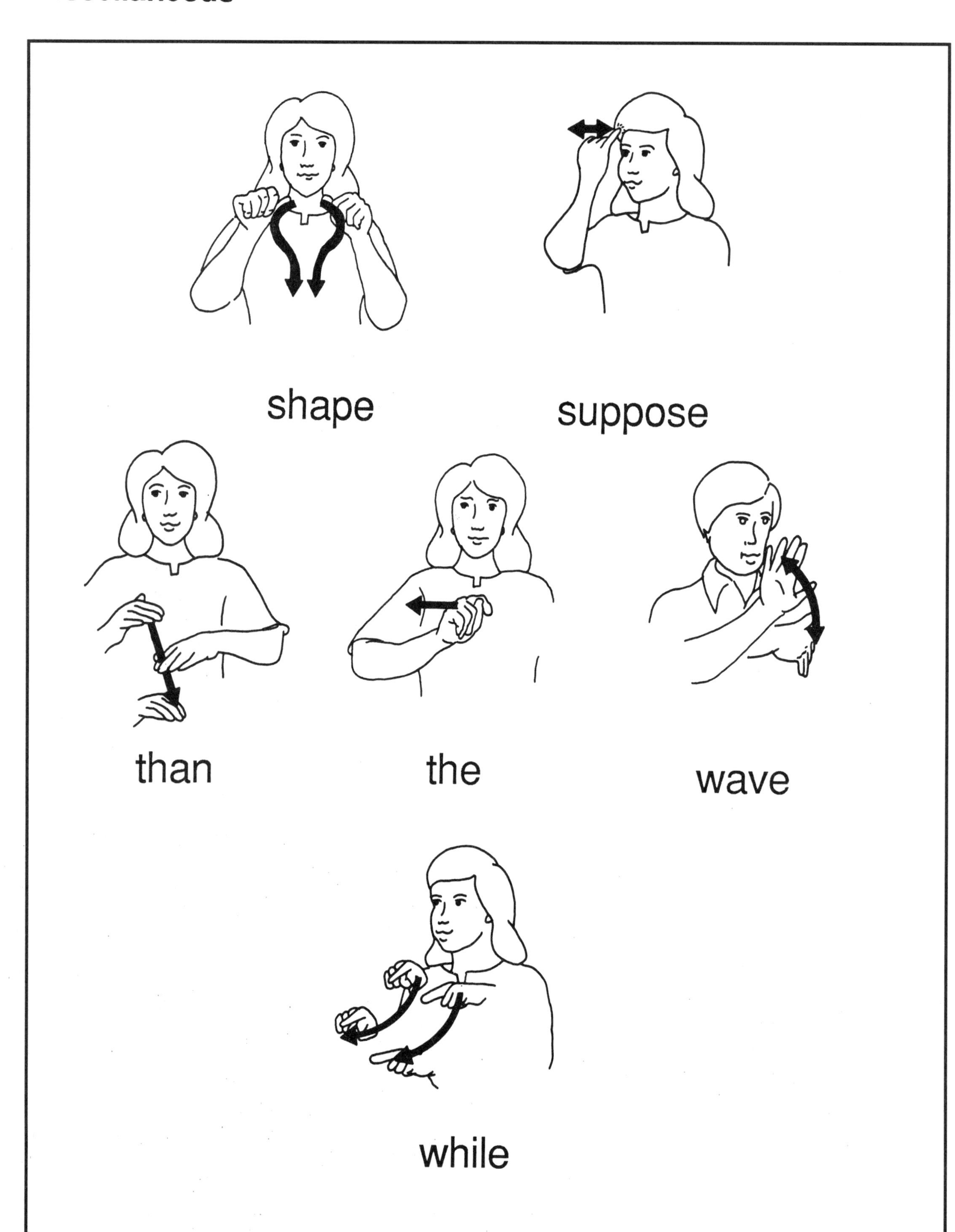
shape
suppose
than
the
wave
while

OCCUPATIONS

actor
actress
aide
artist
astronaut
audiologist
author
baker
barber
bus driver
butcher
carpenter
clown
congressman
cook
counselor
cowboy
custodian
dancer
dentist
detective
doctor
driver
electrician
factory worker
farmer
fireman
fisherman

garbage man
gardner
general
governor
grocer
guard
judge
lawyer
legislator
librarian
magician
mailman
mechanic
milkman
miner
minister
musician
nun
nurse
paperboy
pilot
pirate
police
politician
preacher
president
priest

prince
princess
principal
printer
psychiatrist
psychologist
rancher
referee
sailor
salesman
scientist
secretary
singer
soldier
speech therapist
superintendent
supervisor
teacher
thief
trashman
truck driver
veterinarian
vice president
waiter
waitress
wrestler
writer

OCCUPATIONS

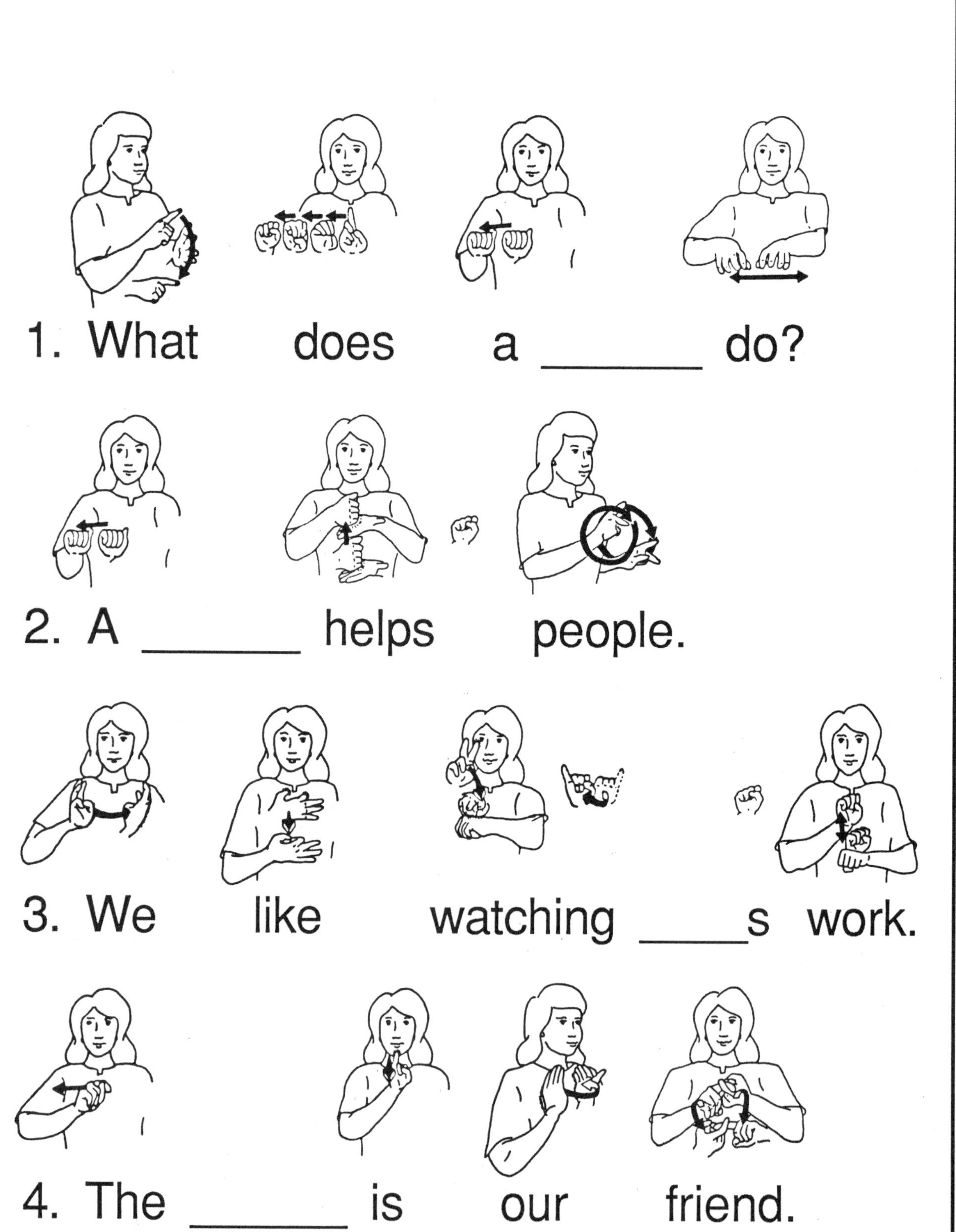

1. What does a _______ do?
2. A _______ helps people.
3. We like watching _____s work.
4. The _______ is our friend.

OCCUPATIONS
actor
actress
aide
artist
astronaut

5. Will a ______ hurt us?

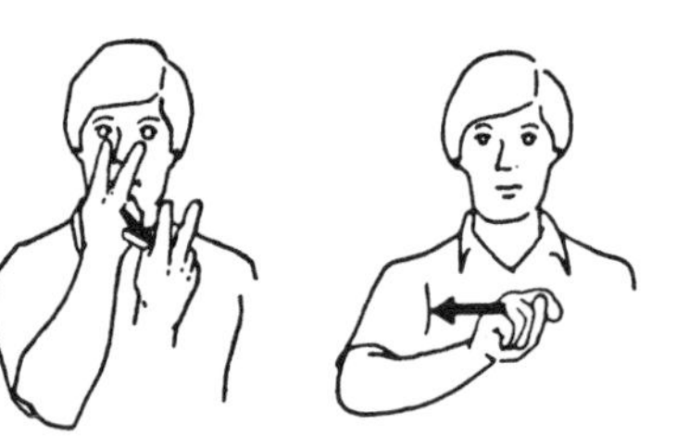

6. You see the ______ sometimes.

7. Are you going to the______?

8. I want to become a ______.

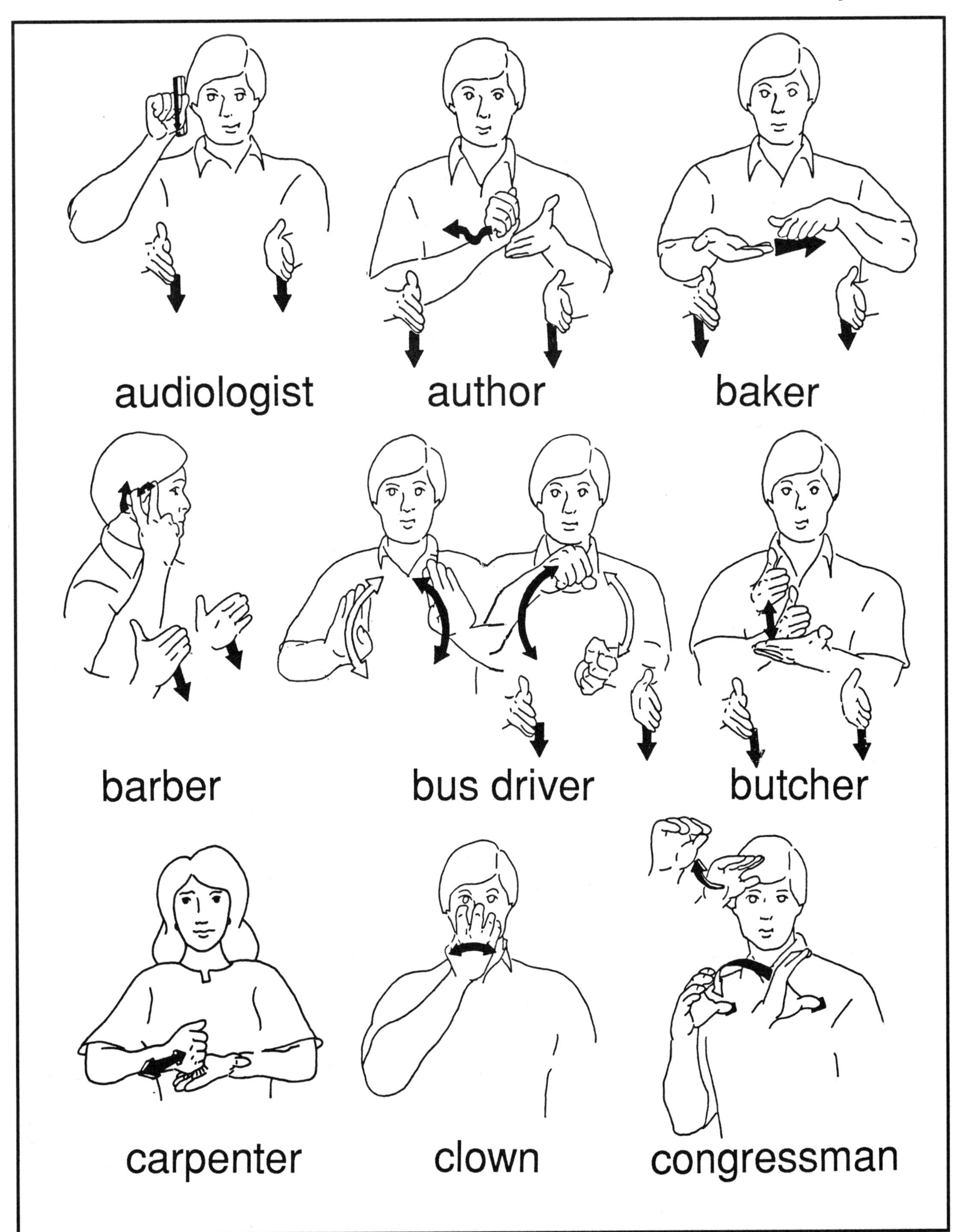
audiologist
author
baker
barber
bus driver
butcher
carpenter
clown
congressman

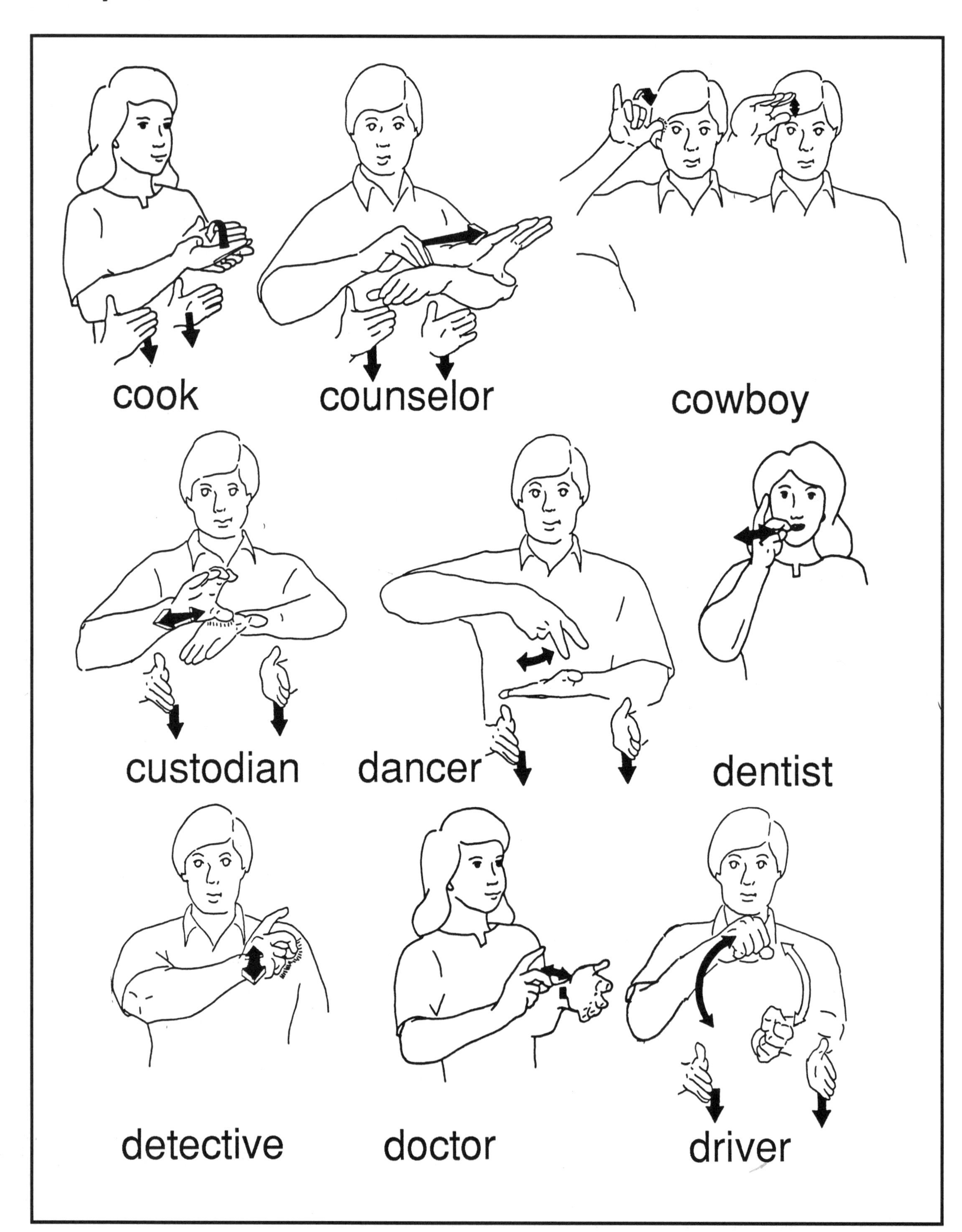
cook
counselor
cowboy
custodian
dancer
dentist
detective
doctor
driver

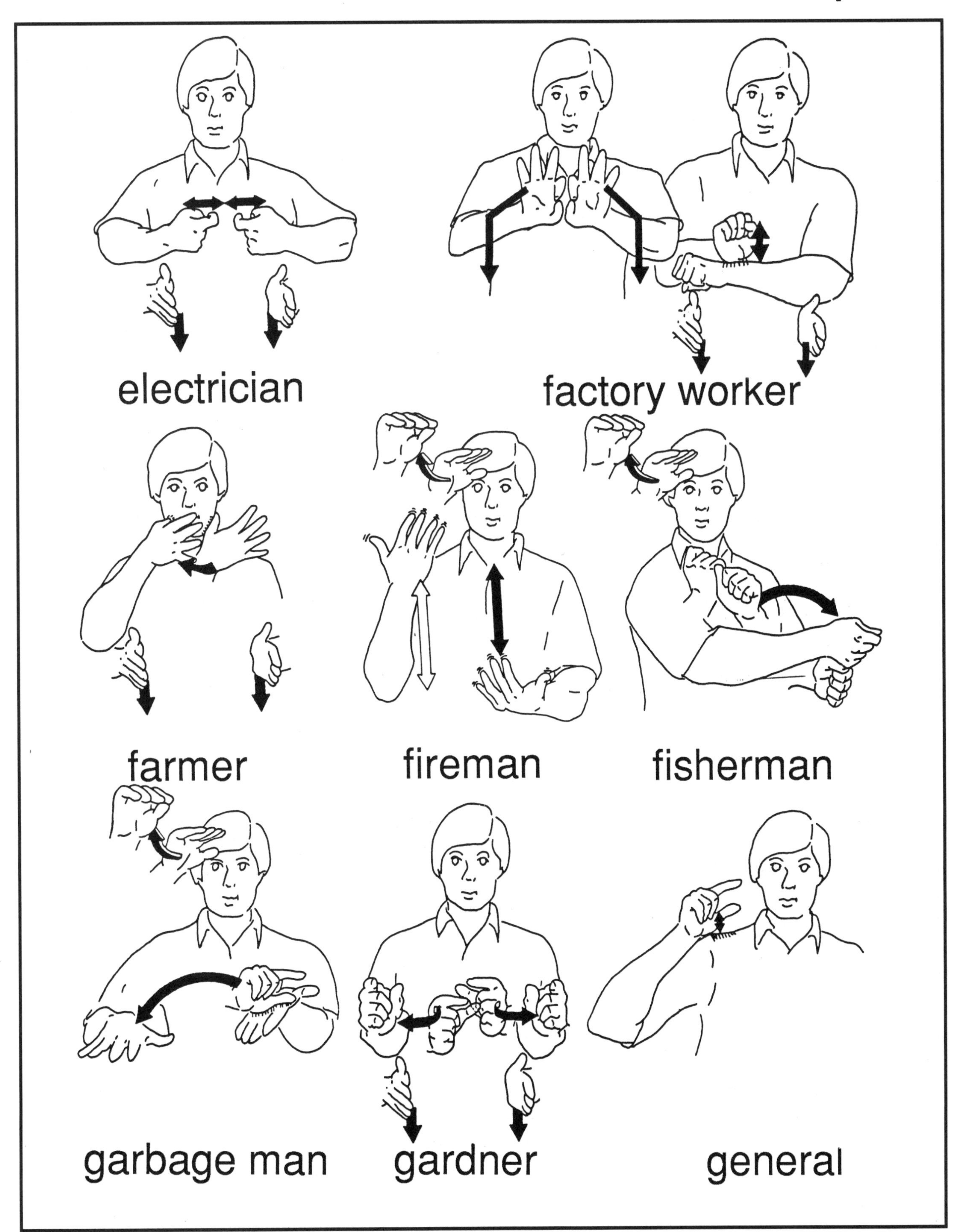
electrician
factory worker
farmer
fireman
fisherman
garbage man
gardner
general

governor
grocer
guard
judge
lawyer
legislator

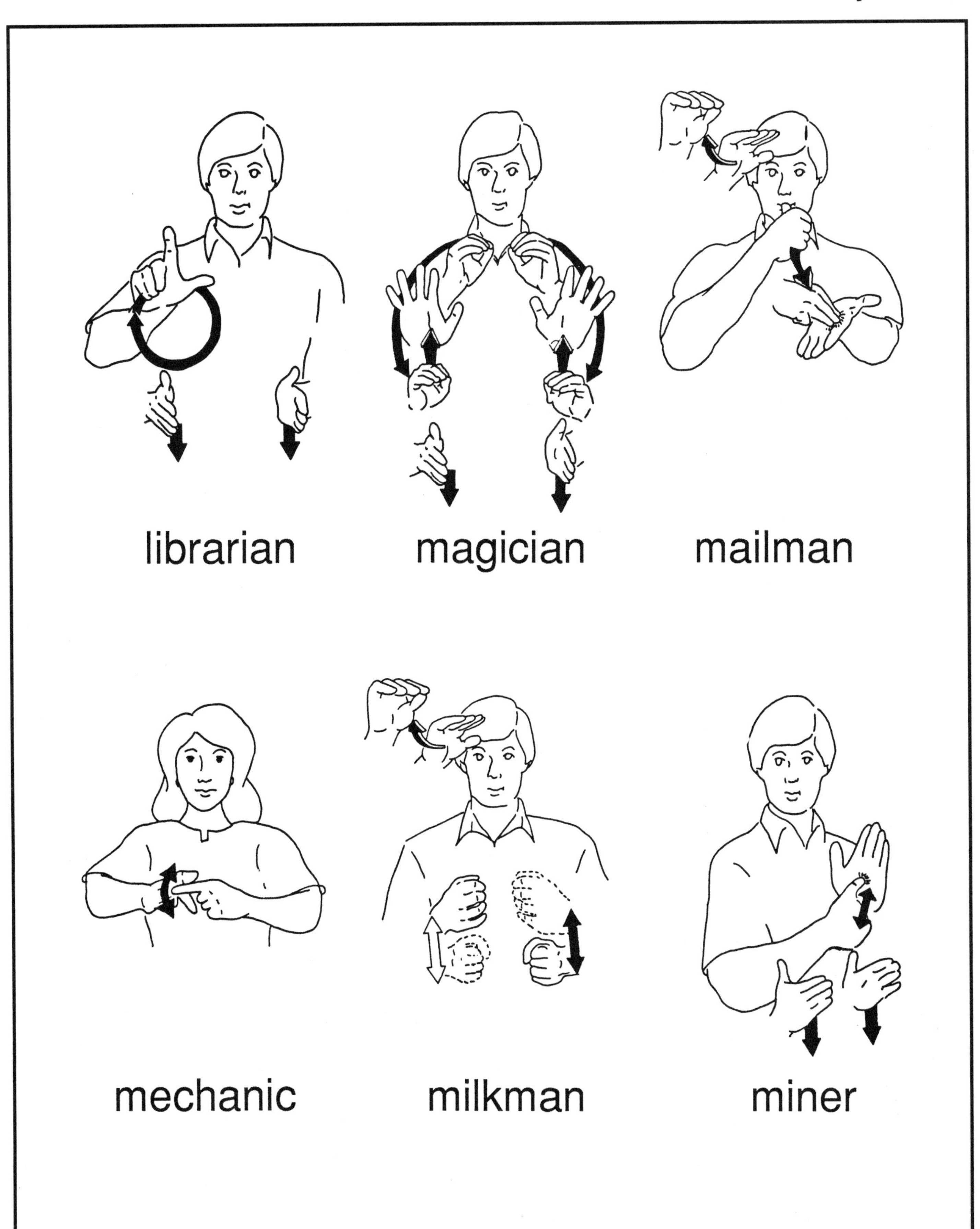
librarian
magician
mailman
mechanic
milkman
miner

minister
musician
nun
nurse
paperboy
pilot
pirate
police
politician

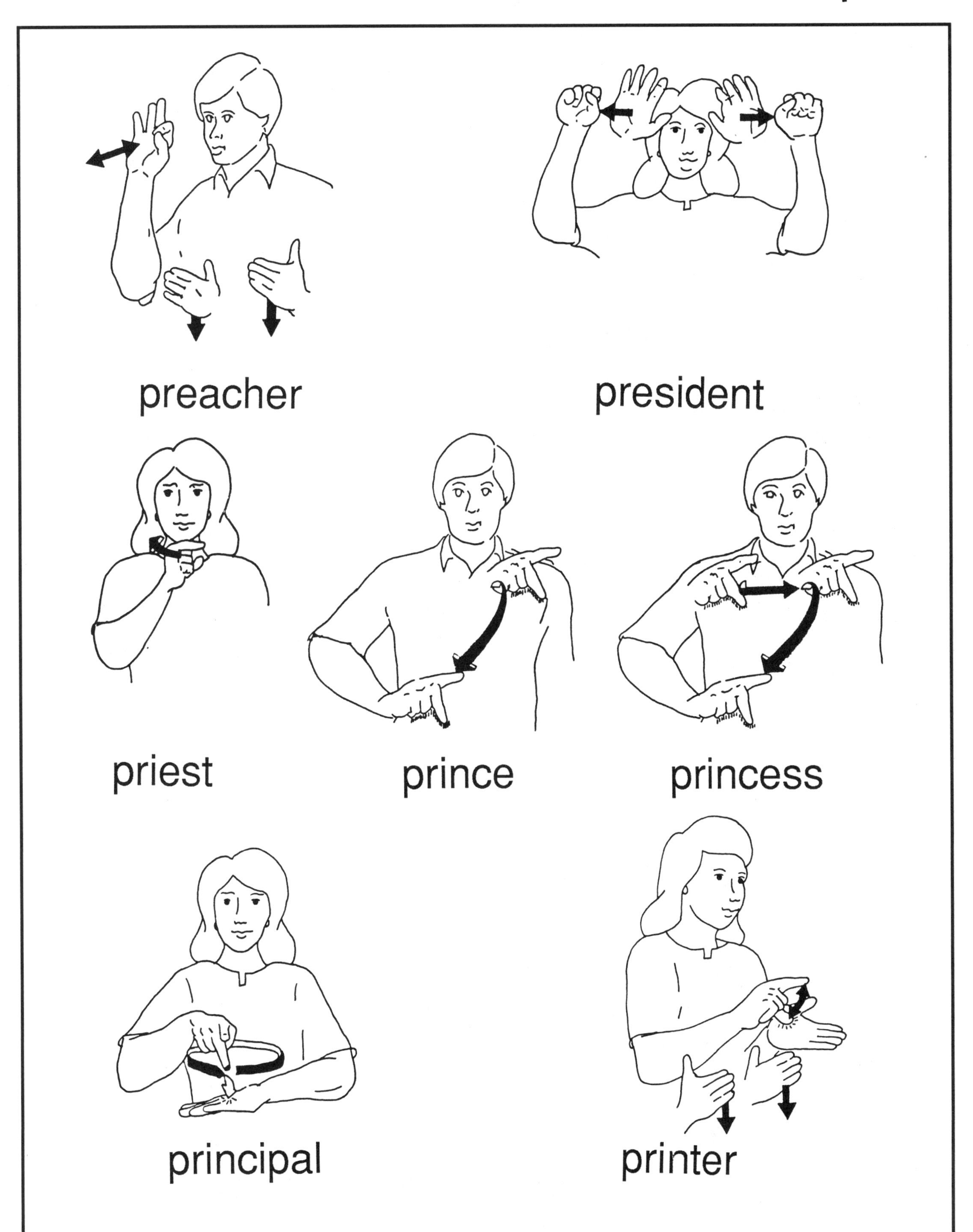
preacher
president
priest
prince
princess
principal
printer

psychiatrist
psychologist
rancher
referee
sailor
salesman
scientist
secretary
singer

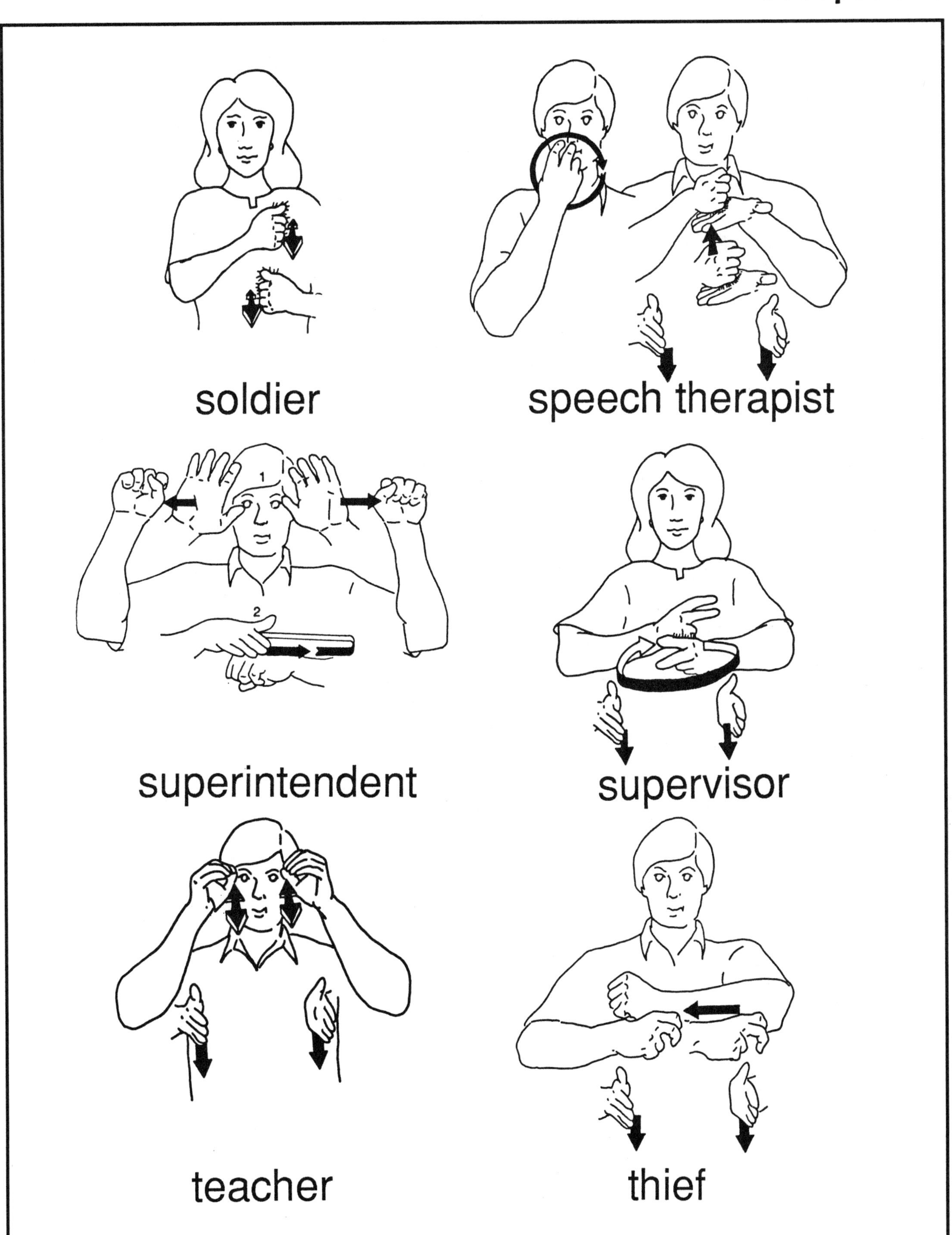

soldier

speech therapist

superintendent

supervisor

teacher

thief

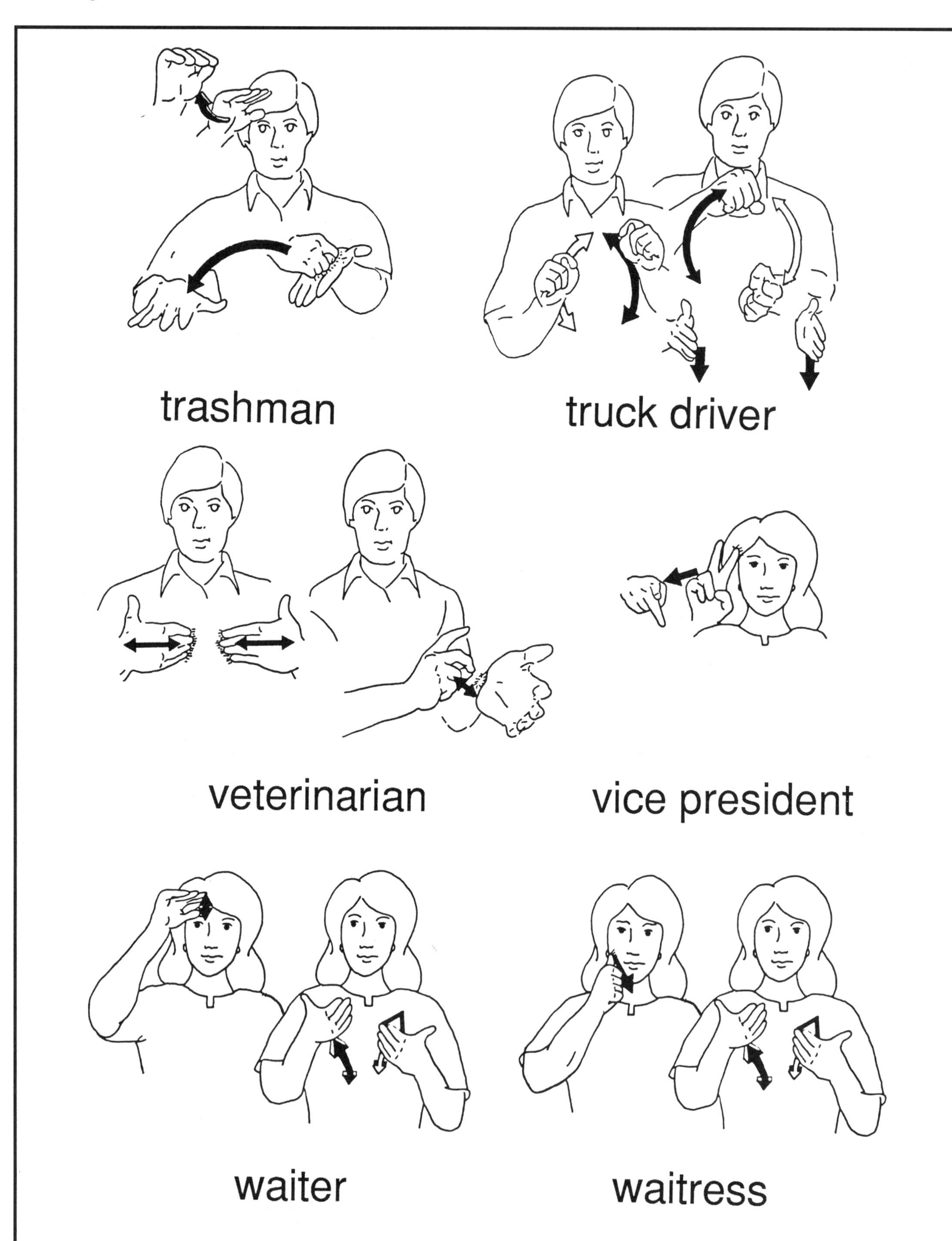
trashman
truck driver
veterinarian
vice president
waiter
waitress

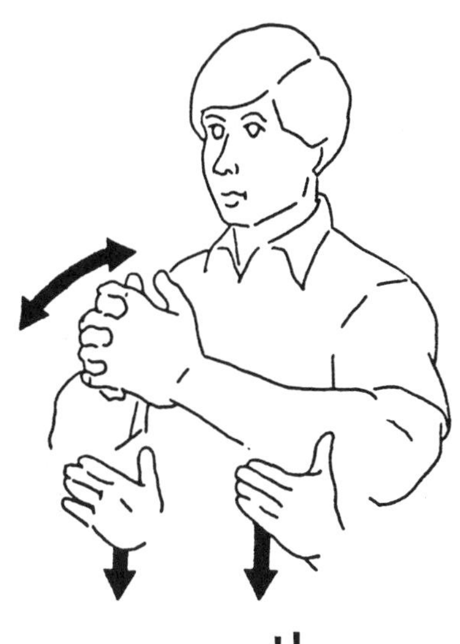

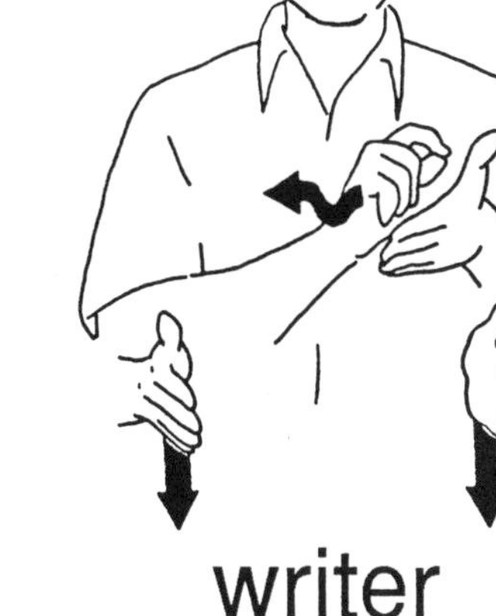

ACTIVITY - OCCUPATIONS

Purpose: To identify different occupations of people based on their clothing or activities.

Materials: Scissors; old magazines; sheets of paper; glue; crayons

Procedure:

1. Adult shows child an old magazine.
2. Adult demonstrates how to cut out pictures of people shown in the magazine.
3. Child imitates cutting out pictures of people from the magazine (five pictures).
4. Adult writes the occupations of people in pictures at top of sheets of paper in crayon (one sheet of paper per occupation).
5. Adult signs/says occupation for each picture while child imitates (duplicate occupations are fine).
6. Adult glues an occupation picture onto appropriate sheet of paper.
7. Child glues remaining pictures onto appropriately marked sheets of paper.
8. Child continues cutting and pasting other occupations to make a scrapbook of occupations.

Variations: Other scrapbooks of other categories can be put together by the child, e.g., body parts, big things, colors, etc.

PEOPLE

adult
association
athlete
audience
aunt[2]
baby[1]
bachelor
board[2]
boss
boy[1]
brother[1]
captain
chief
children
child
committee
cousin[2]
customer
daddy[1] (dada)
daughter
Democrat
enemy
Eskimo
family
father[2]
friend[1]
girl[1]
graduate
grandchild
grandfather
grandmother[1]
grouch
group
guest
human
hunter
husband
Indian
individual
in-law
king[2]
man[1]
member
mommy[1] (mama)
mother[1]
neighbor
nephew
niece
officer
pal
parent
passenger
patient
person[1]
player
queen
relative
Republican
Santa Claus
Scout
sister[1]
son
spinster
stepfather
stepmother
student
sweetheart
team
teenager
twin
uncle[2]
wife
woman[2]

ACTIVITY - PEOPLE

Purpose: To identify different family members.

Materials: Photographs of individual family members.

Procedure:

1. Adult shows child picture of grandmother and signs/says, "grandmother".
2. Adult puts picture of grandmother on table next to picture of another family member, signs/says, "Where is grandmother?".
3. Child responds by pointing appropriately.
4. Adult puts picture of grandmother on table next to two other family members, signs/says, "Where is grandmother?".
5. Child responds appropriately by pointing.
6. Adult continues showing grandmother's picture along with other family member's pictures until child identifies grandmother's picture correctly consistently.
7. Adult shows child picture of another family member, following procedures 1 through 7. Occasionally show grandmother's picture to reinforce that concept which has already been learned.

PEOPLE

1. I don't know your ______.

2. Where does your ______ live?

3. Do you have a ______?

 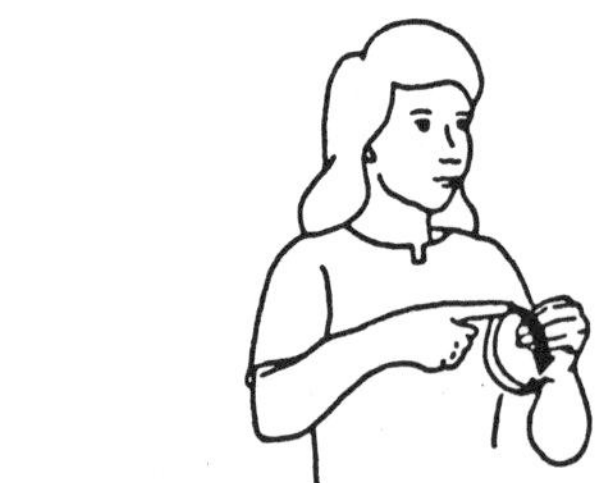 

4. Tell me about your ______.

PEOPLE

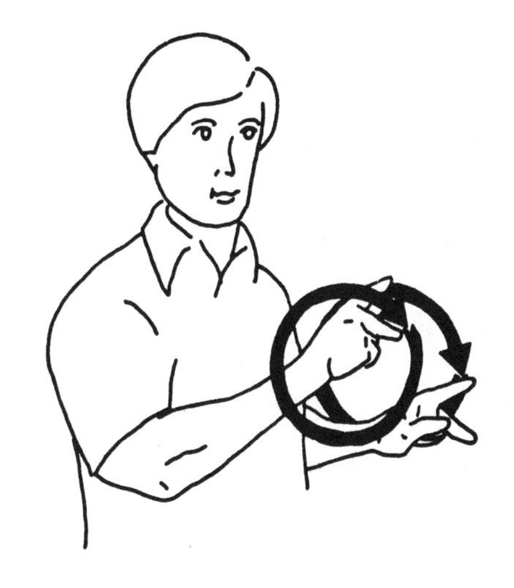

adult

association

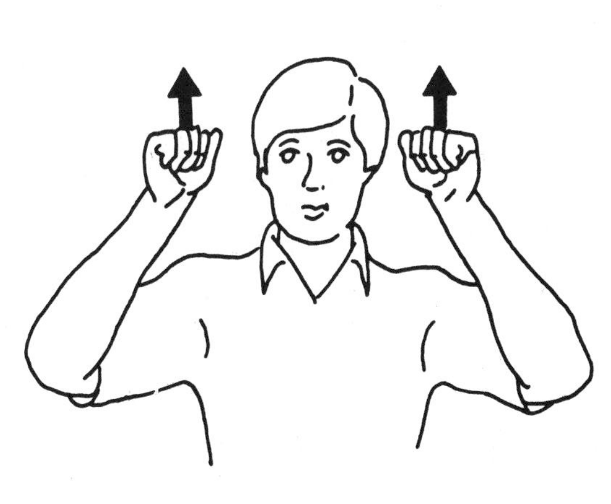

athlete

audience

aunt

baby

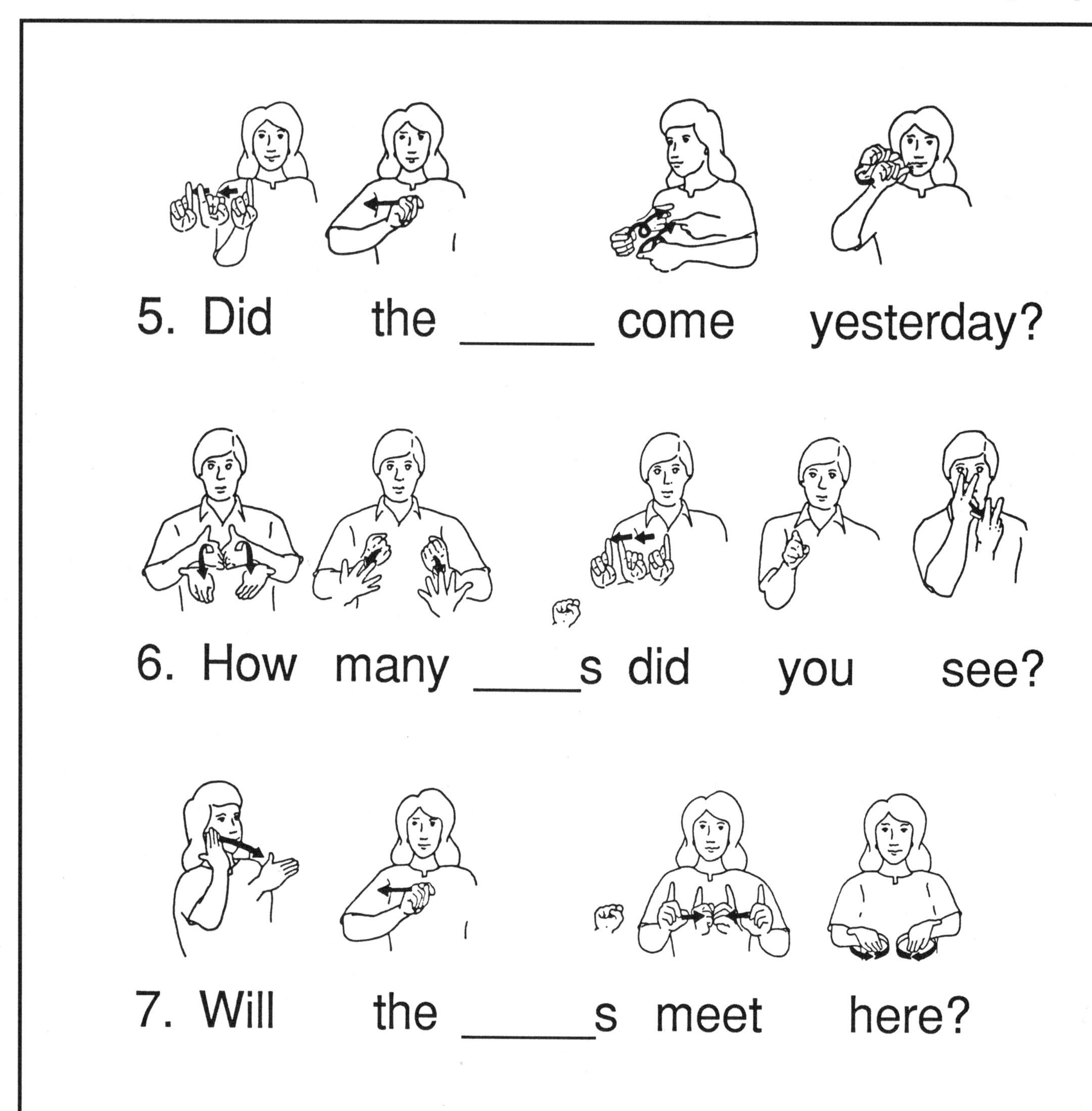

5. Did the ______ come yesterday?

6. How many _____s did you see?

7. Will the ______s meet here?

  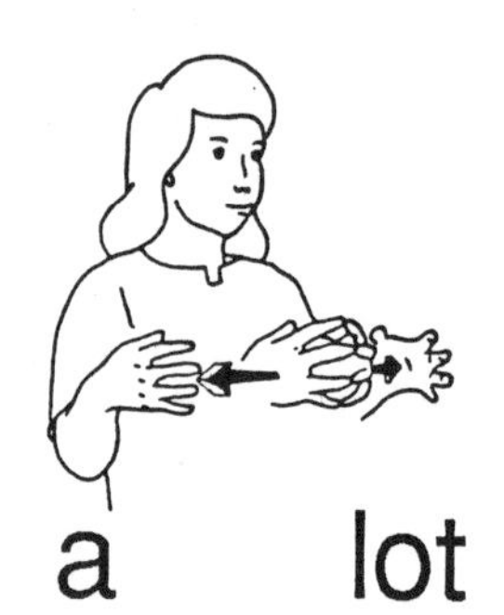 

8. There are a lot of_____.

bachelor
board
boss
boy
brother
captain
chief
child
children

committee
cousin
customer
daddy(dada)
daughter
Democrat
enemy
Eskimo
family

father
friend
girl
graduate
grandchild
grandfather
grandmother
grouch
group

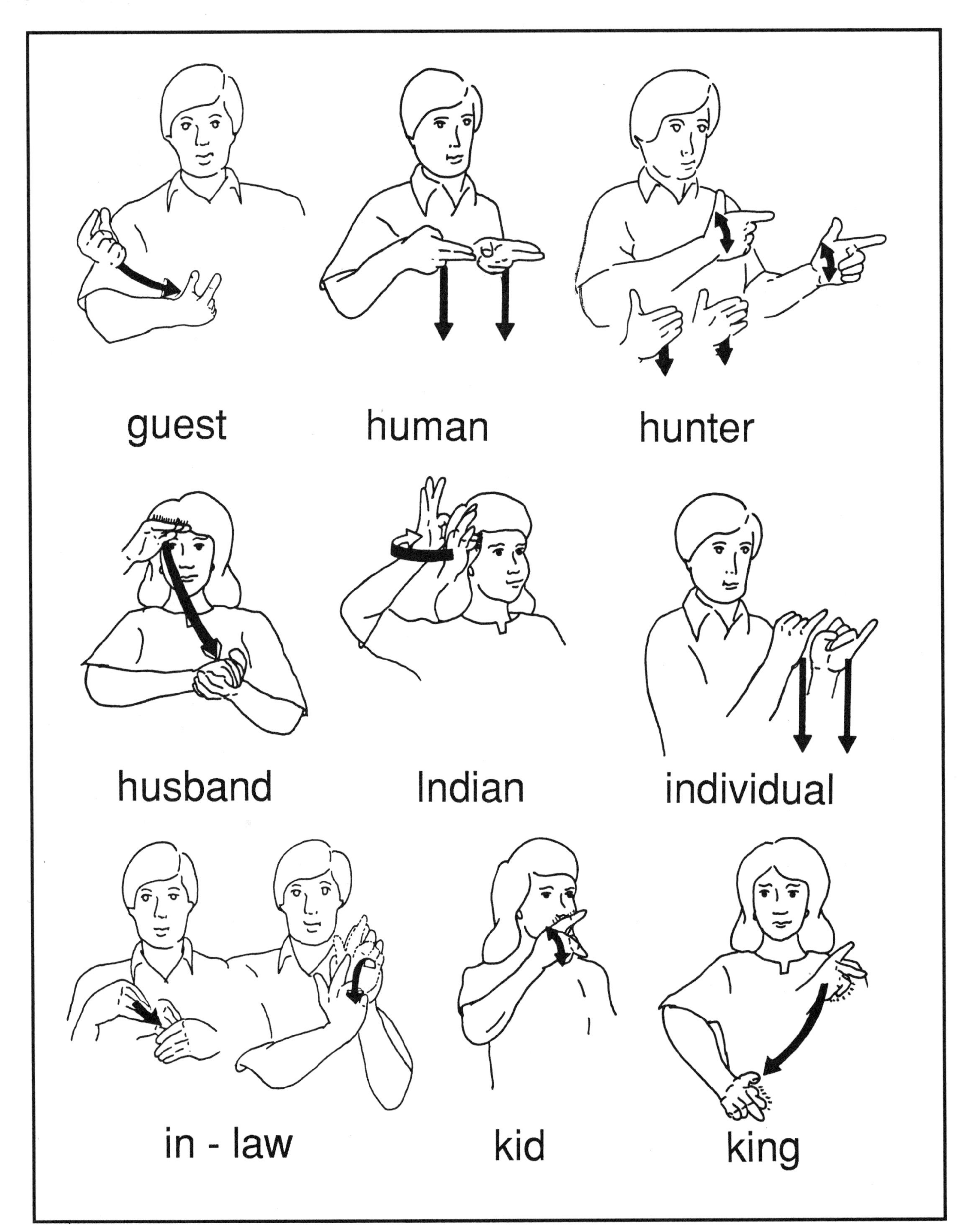
guest
human
hunter
husband
Indian
individual
in - law
kid
king

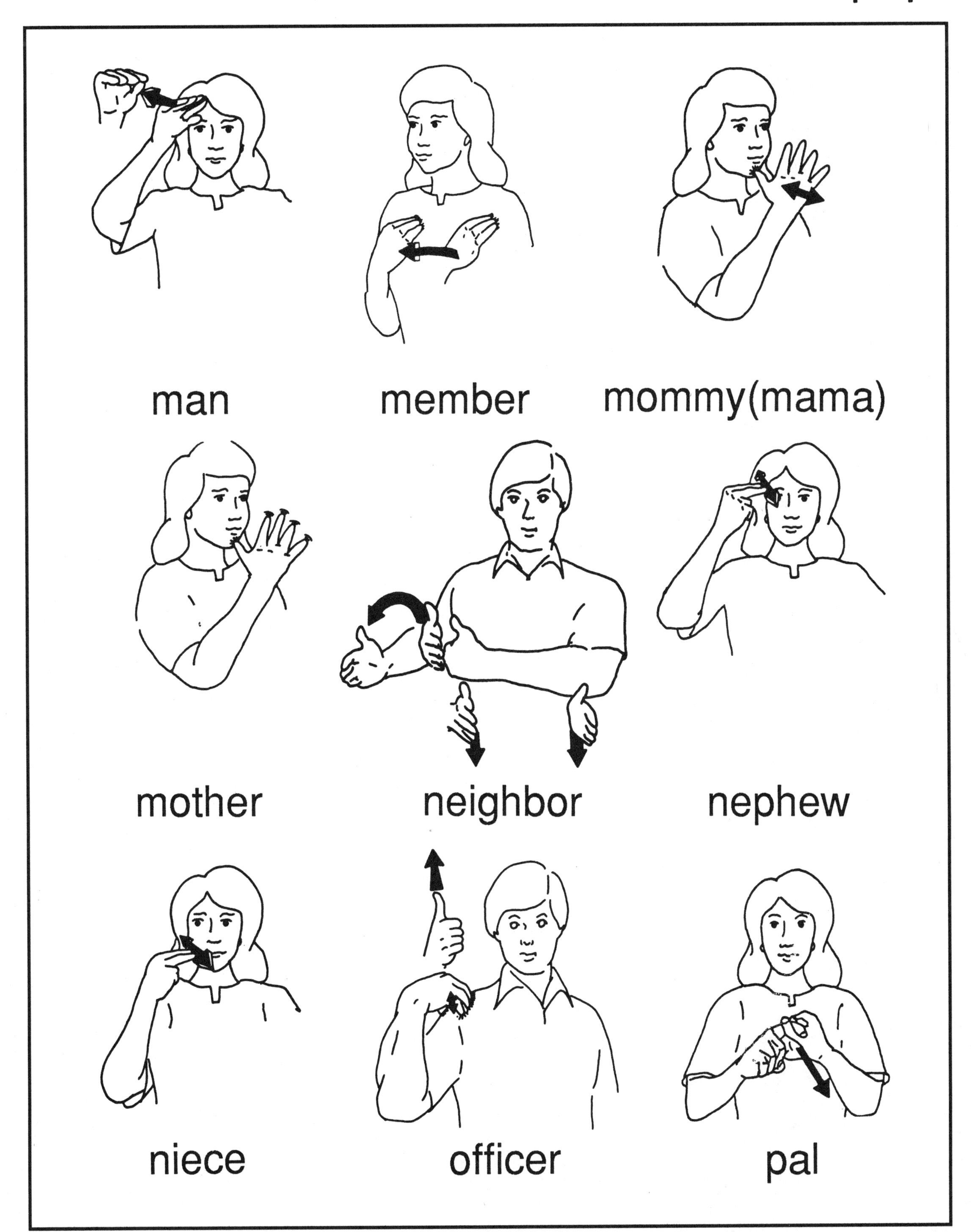
man
member
mommy(mama)
mother
neighbor
nephew
niece
officer
pal

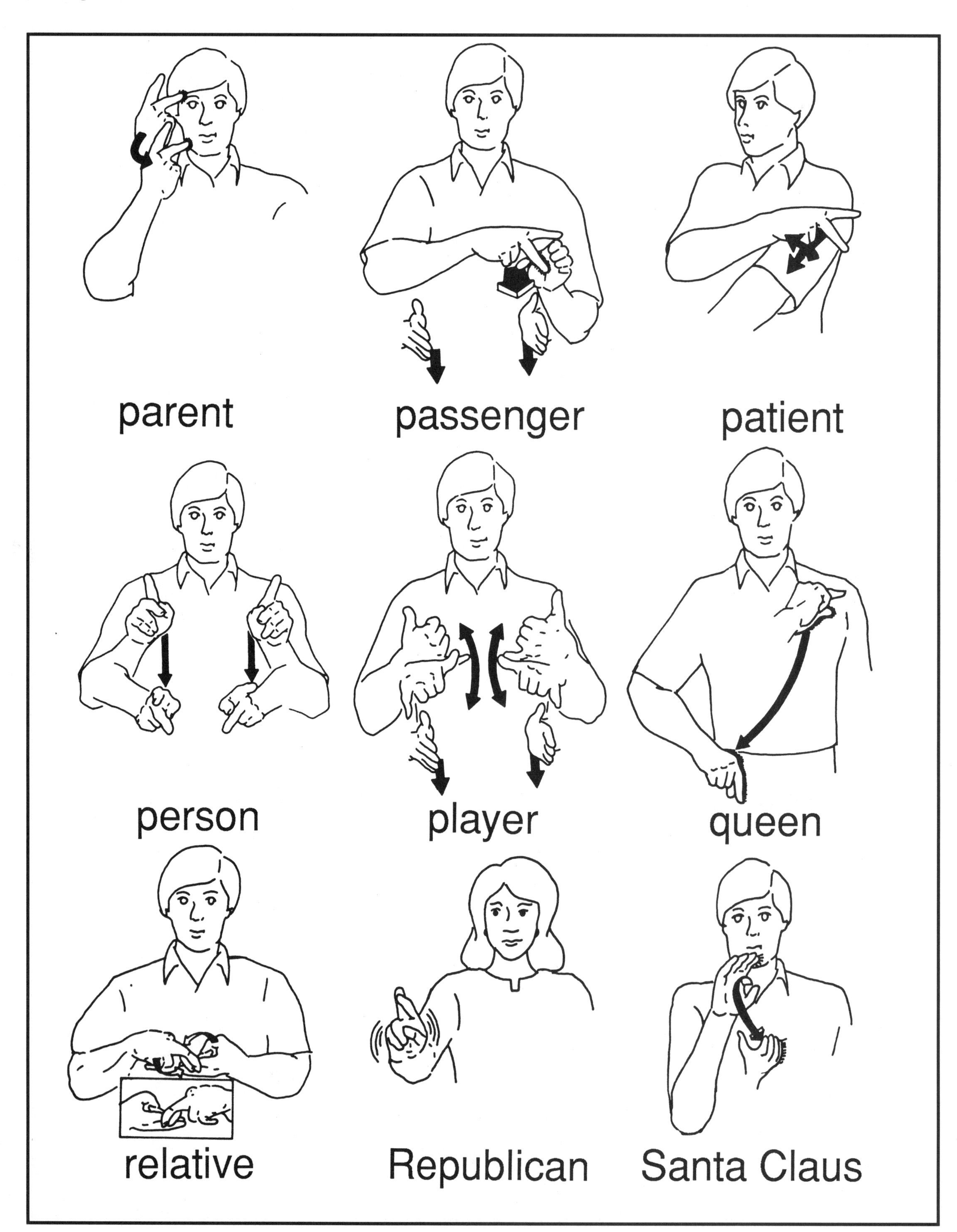
parent
passenger
patient
person
player
queen
relative
Republican
Santa Claus

Scout
sister
son
spinster
stepfather
stepmother
student
sweetheart
team

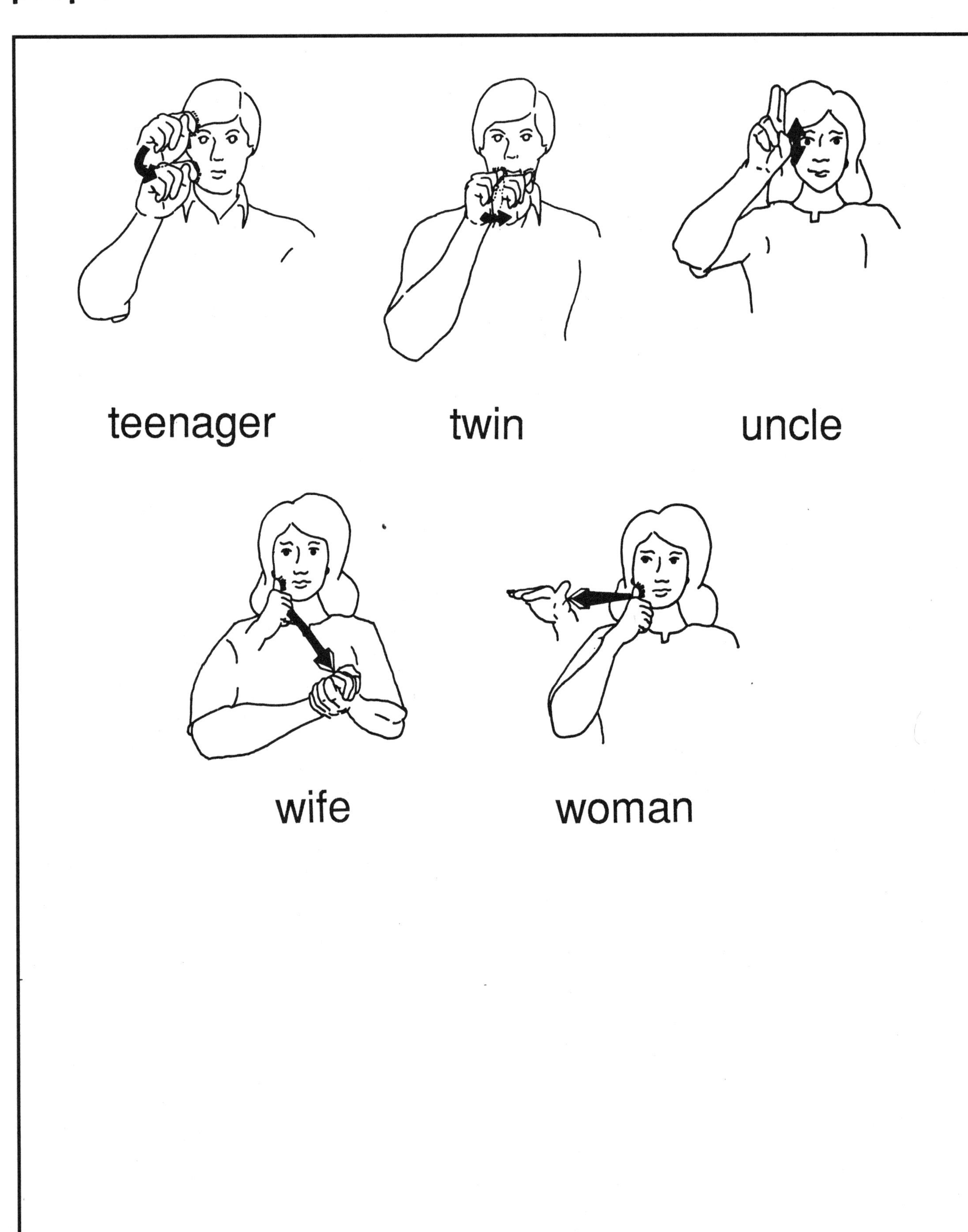
teenager
twin
uncle
wife
woman

PRONOUNS

anybody
anyone
anything [1]
everybody [2]
everyone
everything [1]
he [1]
her [1]
hers
herself
him [1]
himself
his [1]
I [1]
it [1]
me [1]
mine [2]
my [1]
myself
nobody [1]
no one
nothing [1]
our [1]
ours
ourselves
she [1]
somebody [1]
someone [1]
something [1]
that [1]
their [1]
theirs
them [1]
themselves
these
they [1]
this
those [1]
us [1]
we [1]
you [1]
your [1]
yours
yourself

NOTE:

Additional level 1 vocabulary:

he's	I'm	we're	you've
I'll	I've	they're	

ACTIVITY - PRONOUNS

Purpose: To learn the use of the pronoun she.

Materials: Pictures of females doing different activities; chalkboard and chalk or pencil and paper.

Procedure:

1. Adult shows child picture of a woman doing an activity, e.g., driving a car.
2. Adult writes on chalkboard, "The woman is driving a car".
3. Adult shows child another picture, then writes activity on chalkboard (child should write sentence if able).
4. Continue activity until five sentences are written.
5. Adult puts line through woman in first sentence and writes she.
6. Adult signs/says sentence to child using she. Child repeats sentence.
7. Follow procedures five and six with sentences two and three.
8. Adult allows child to change sentences four and five.
9. Adult shows child other pictures for child to write sentences using she with assistance as needed.

Variations: As the concept she is mastered move on to other common pronouns that child will need.

PRONOUNS

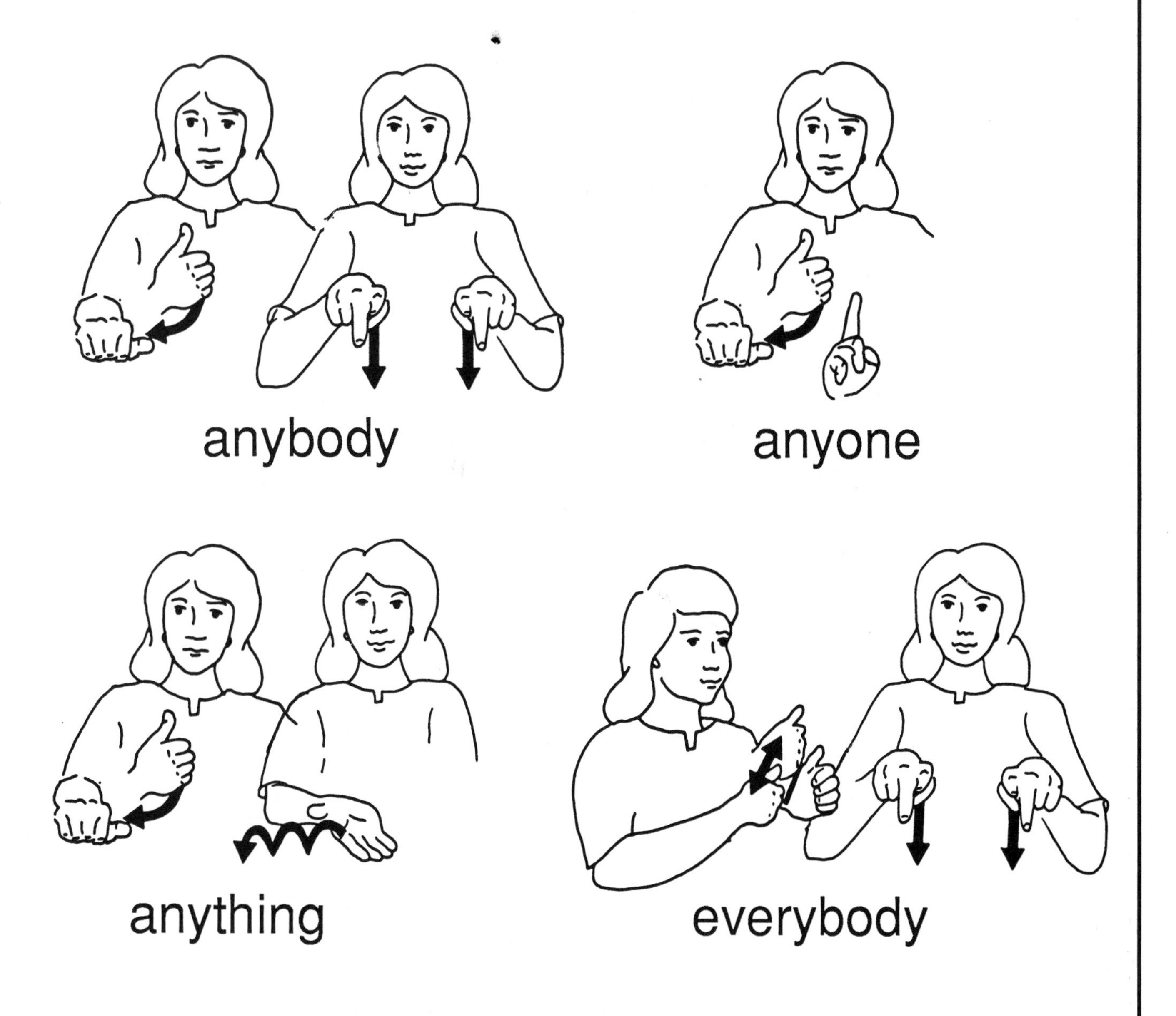
anybody
anyone
anything
everybody

PRONOUNS

1. ______ see ______.

2. Where is ______?

3. Can you find ______?

4. What are ______ doing?

1
2
1
2
everyone
everything
he
her
hers
herself
him
himself

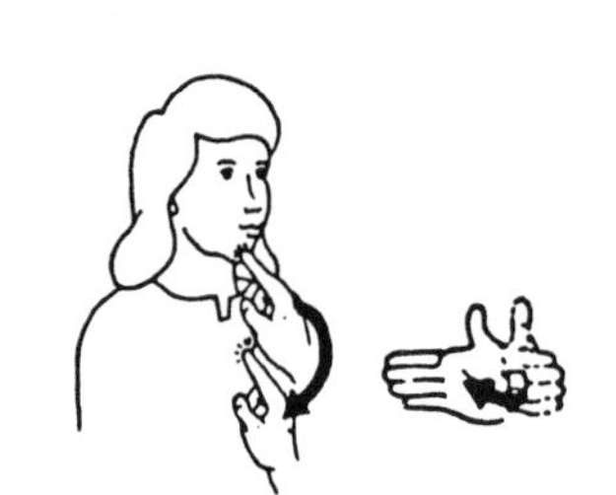

5. _______ told me.

6. _______ mother is here.

7. _______ is coming today.

8. Yes, _______ is playing.

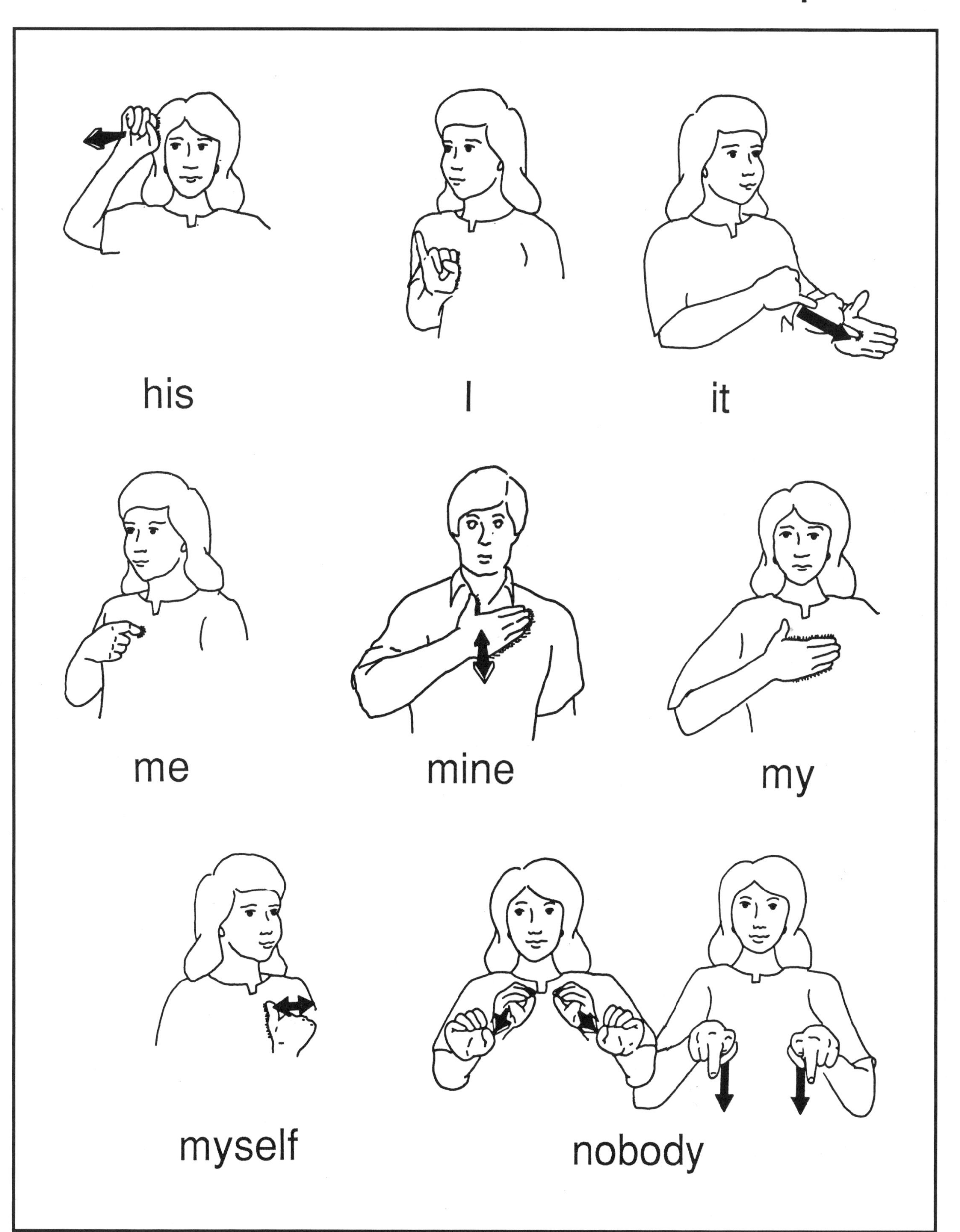
his
I
it
me
mine
my
myself
nobody

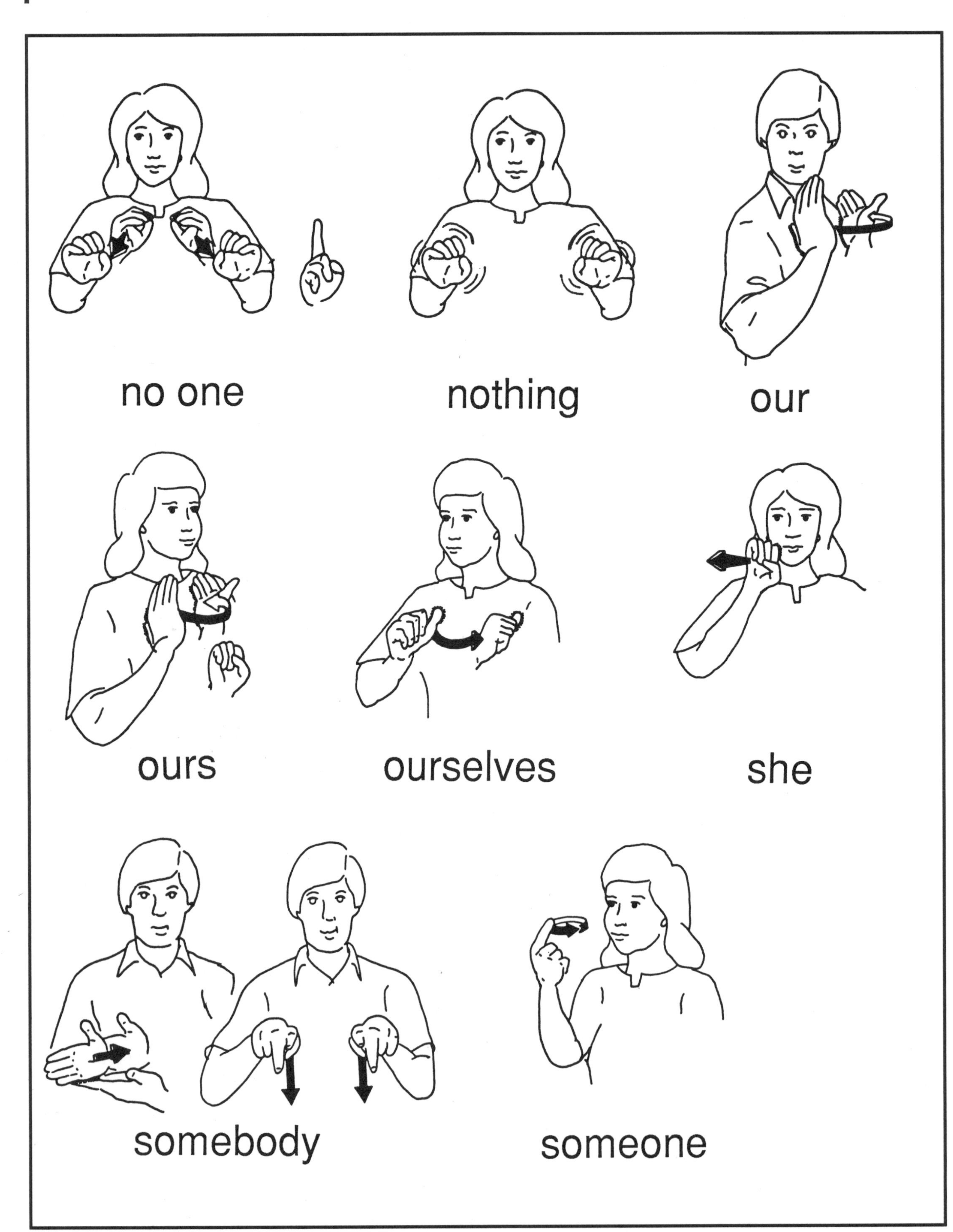
no one
nothing
our
ours
ourselves
she
somebody
someone

something
that
their
theirs
them
themselves
these
they
this

those
us
we
you
your
yours
yourself

ROUND THINGS

ball
balloon
blueberry
bowl
bracelet
bubble
button
can
cent
cherry
cigar
cigarette
circle [2]

clock
coin
cookie
cup
dime
donut
glass
grapefruit
half a dollar
marble
moon
nickel
orange

pancake
pea
penny
plate
quarter
ring
rope [2]
sun
tire
watch
wheel [2]

ACTIVITY - ROUND THINGS

Purpose: To identify the names of things that are round.

Materials: Flashcards with pictures of round objects on one side and objects' name on reverse side; bean bag; paper and pencil.

Procedure:

1. Adult assigns each picture points 1 to 10 based on child's familiarity with object pictured - familiar objects, 1 to 5 points, less familiar objects, 6 to 10 points.
2. Child scatters flashcards, picture side up, on the floor.
3. Adult and child stand back several feet taking turns throwing bean bag on flashcards.
4. After each throw, points are awarded upon signing/ saying the name of the pictured object hit by the bean bag.
5. Score is kept with pencil and paper.

Variations: Put picture side down with word only showing or randomize with both picture and word showing. Child has to spell/say, rather than sign/say, round object shown. Child has to tell function, use or purpose of round object shown in picture.

ROUND THINGS

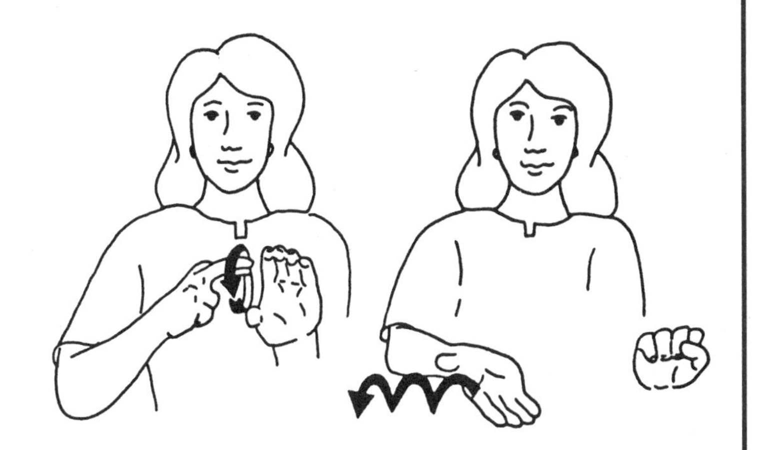

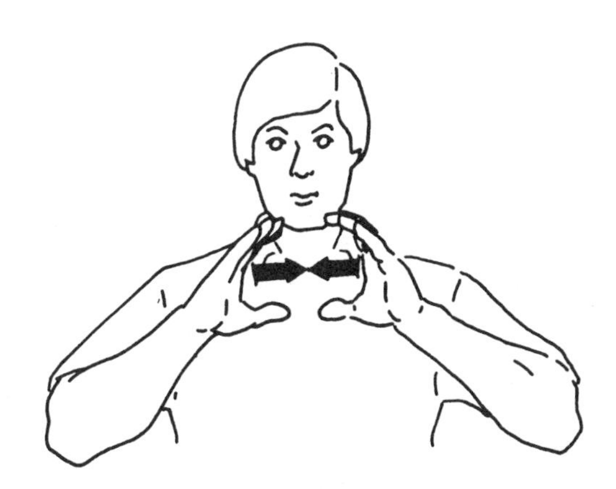

ball

balloon

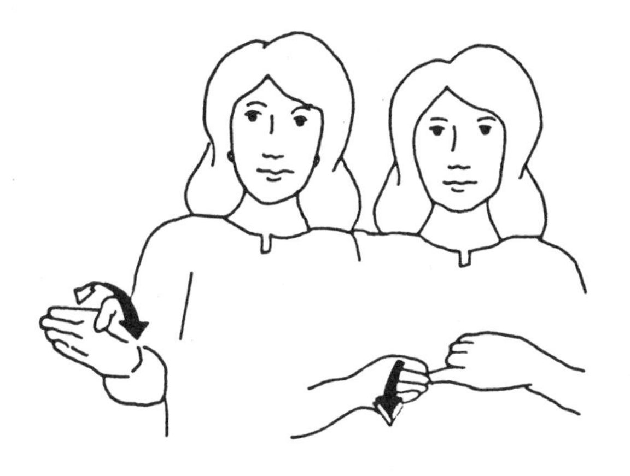

blueberry

bowl

ROUND THINGS

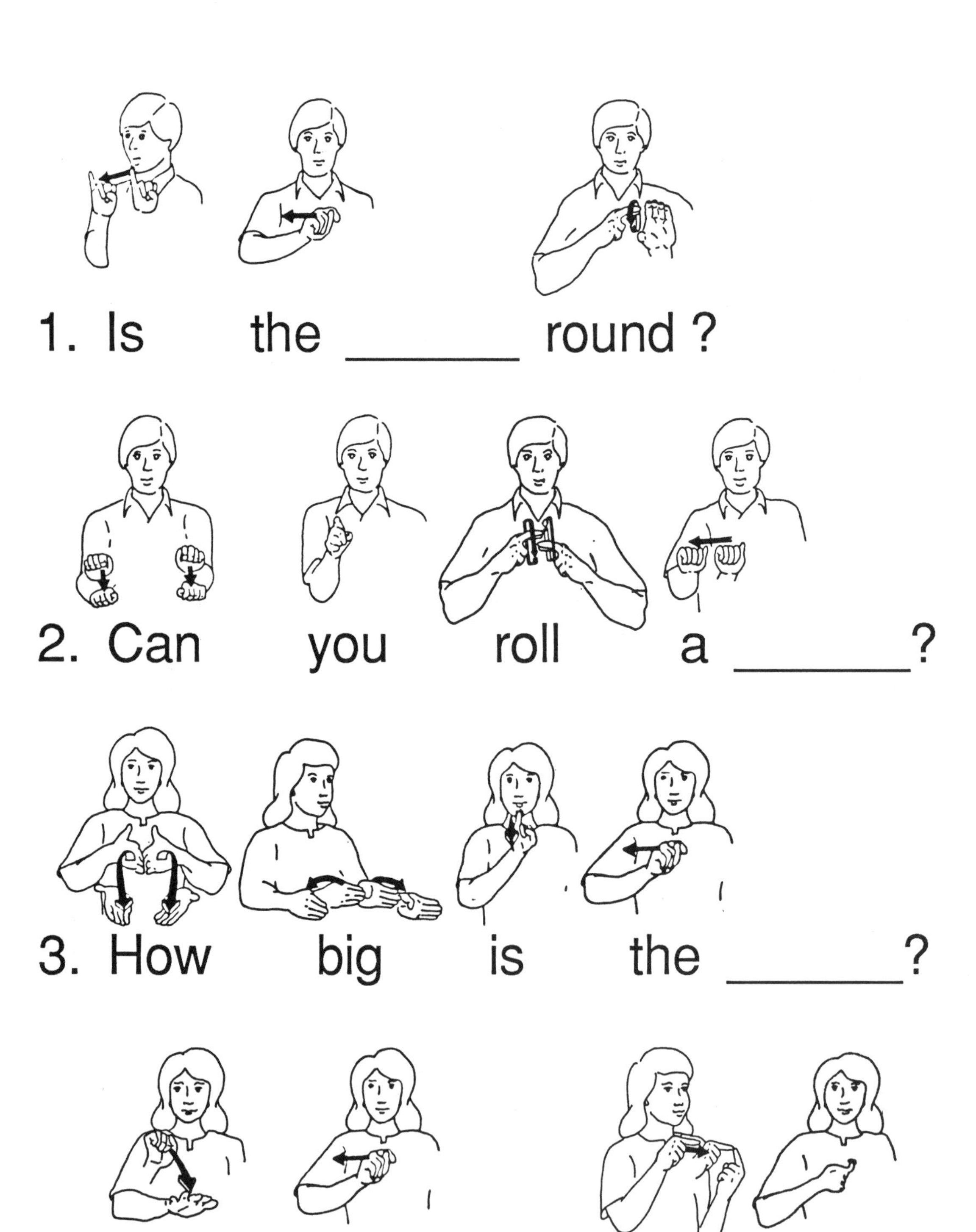

1. Is the ______ round ?
2. Can you roll a ______?
3. How big is the ______?
4. Throw the ______ to me.

bracelet
bubble
button
can
cent
cherry
cigar
cigarette
circle

clock
coin
cookie
cup
dime
donut
glass
grapefruit
half a dollar

marble
moon
nickel
orange
pancake
pea
penny
plate
quarter

round things

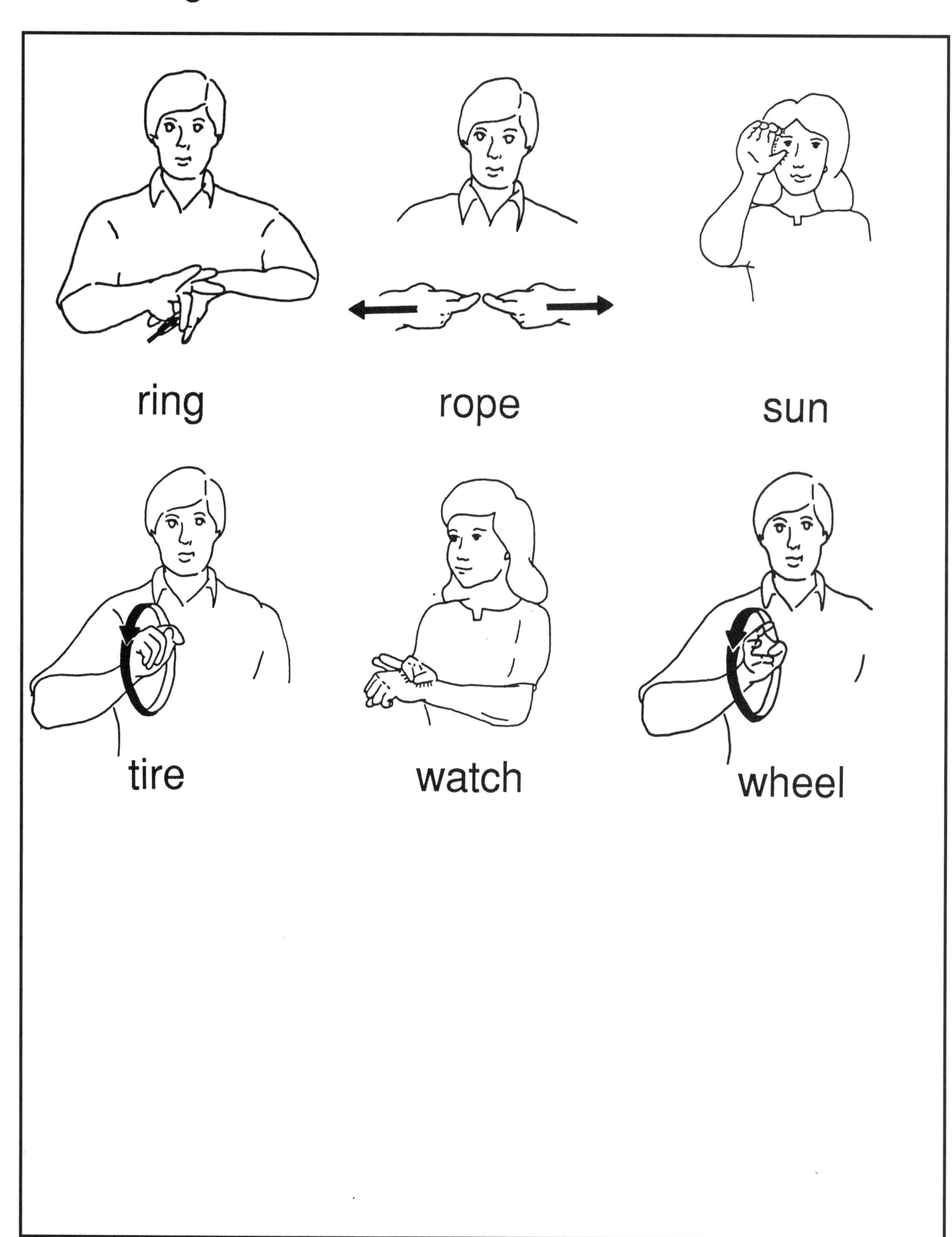

SCHOOL ACTIVITIES

add
announce
answer
ask [2]
begin
busy
call on
cancel
carry
change
check (correct)
clap
clean
come here
compare
converse
copy
count [2]
crayon
cut [2]
dance
discuss
dismiss
divide
draw [2]
educate
erase
excuse
exercise
explain
fail
get along
get up
give up (quit)
glue
graduate
hang (up)
help [2]
hit
hug
learn
leave
line up
list
listen
look up
make [1]
mean [1]
measure
memorize
miss (absent)
obey
paint [2]
paste
pay attention
play
point [2]
pour
practice
print
punch
push
read [2]
rehearse
remove
roll [2]
run off (duplicate)
search (look for)
show
sign (language)
sing
size
spill
spin [2]
start
stir
study
subtract
support
swing
teach
tear
tickle
train
visit
volunteer
wander
wipe
wrap
write

ACTIVITY - SCHOOL ACTIVITIES

Purpose: To identify different activities that children do in school.

Materials: Book, Signing English for Parents, Teachers and Clinicians.

Procedure:

1. Adult shows child vocabulary list under category, School Activities.
2. Adult points to one of the vocabualry items and asks child to sign, act out or mime the word.
3. Child points to one of the vocabulary items and adult signs, acts out or mimes the word.
4. Continue activity taking turns.

Variations: A sign can be shown from the School Activities Section with the word covered, child fingerspells sign's meaning.

SCHOOL
ACTIVITIES
add
announce
answer
apply
ask
begin

SCHOOL ACTIVITIES

1. We will ______ after music.

  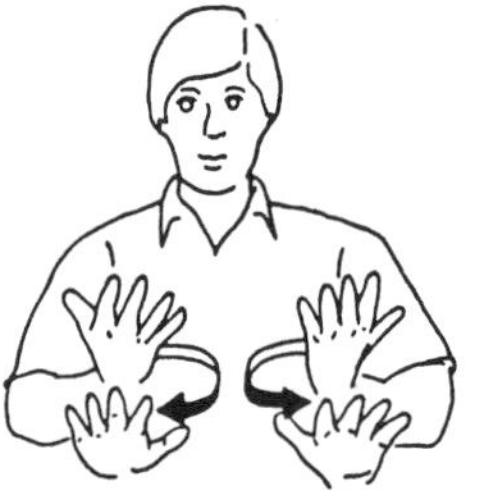 

2. Did you finish your ______?

3. Today we will ______.

4. You may make a ______.

busy
call on
cancel
carry
change
check (correct)
clap
clean
come here

5. ______ is my favorite activity.

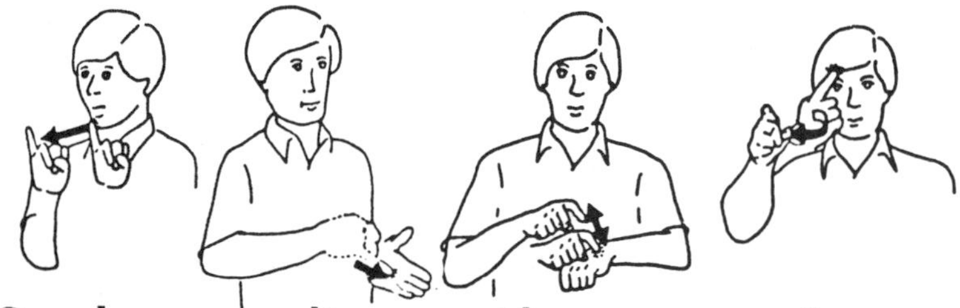

6. Is it time for _______?

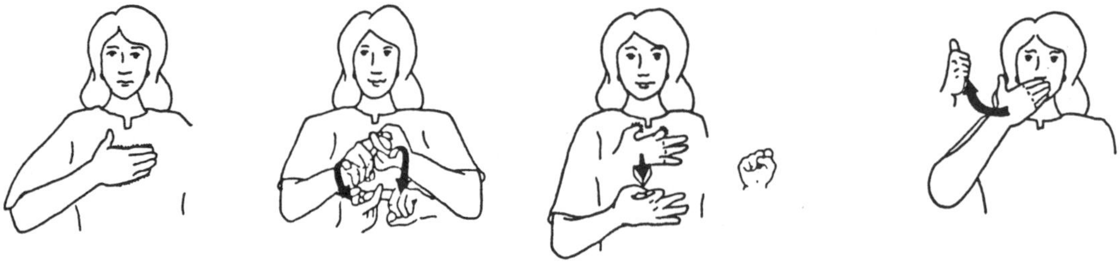

7. My friend likes _______ best.

8. Friday we will have _____.

compare
converse
copy
count
crayon
cut
dance
discuss
dismiss

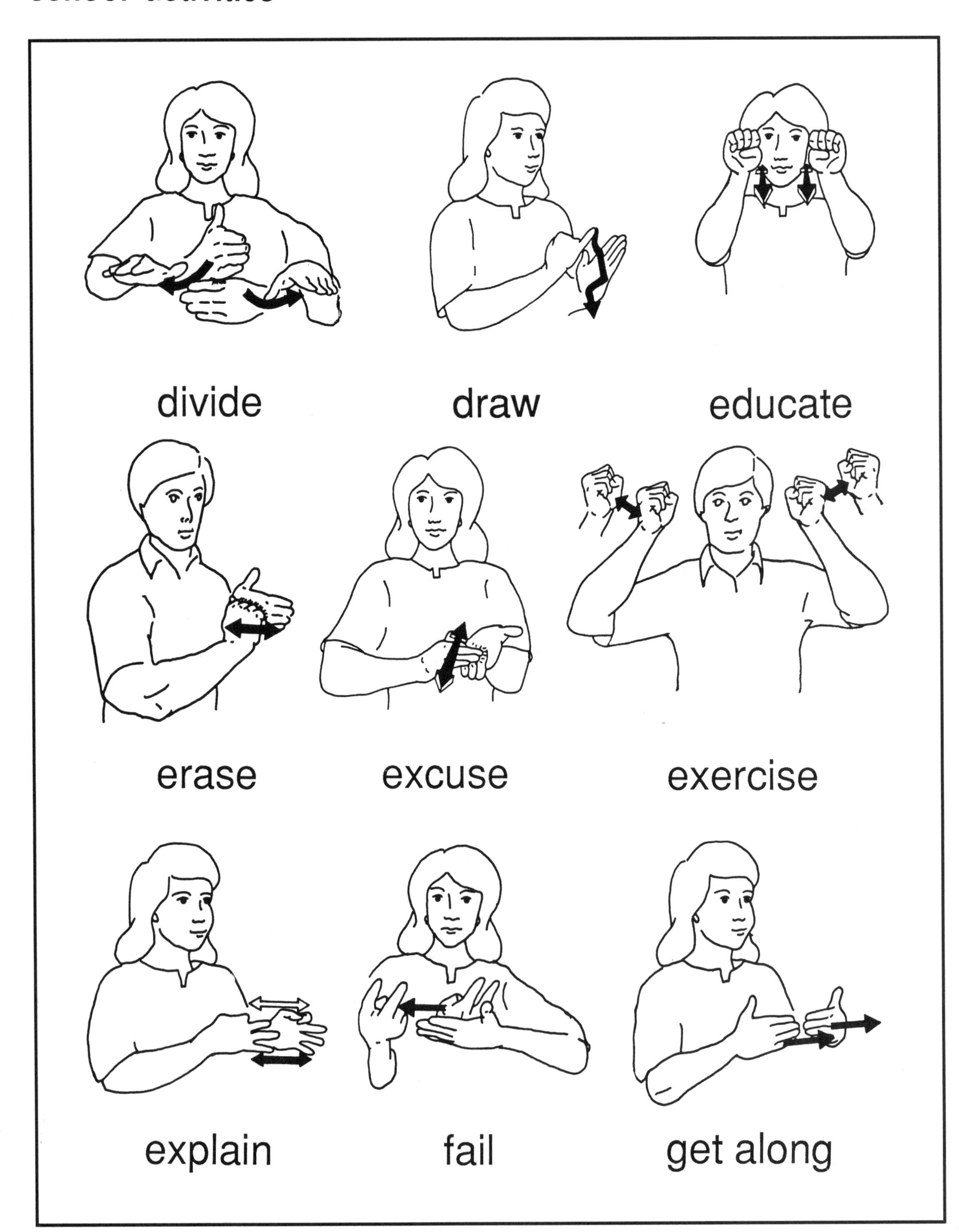
divide
draw
educate
erase
excuse
exercise
explain
fail
get along

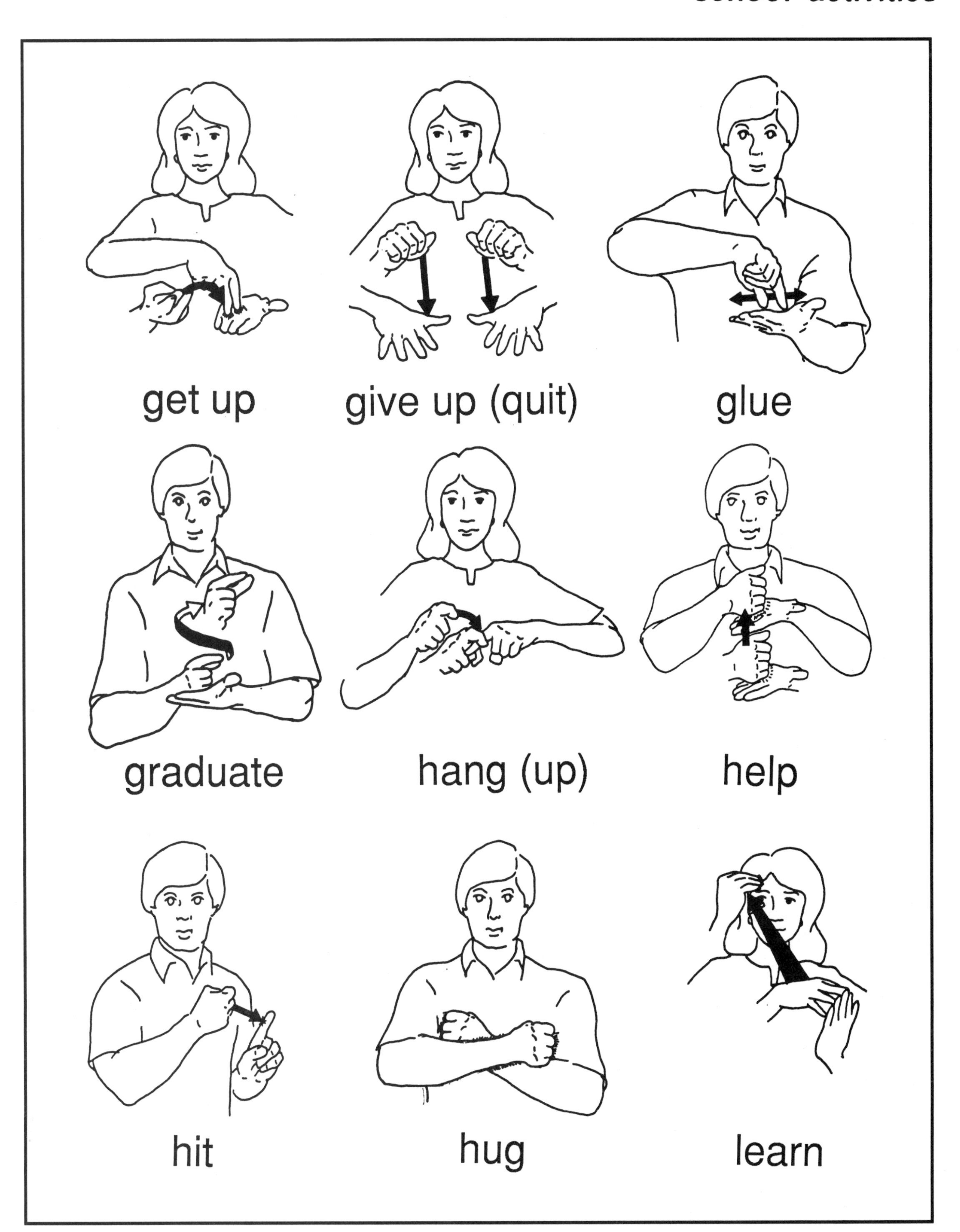
get up
give up (quit)
glue
graduate
hang (up)
help
hit
hug
learn

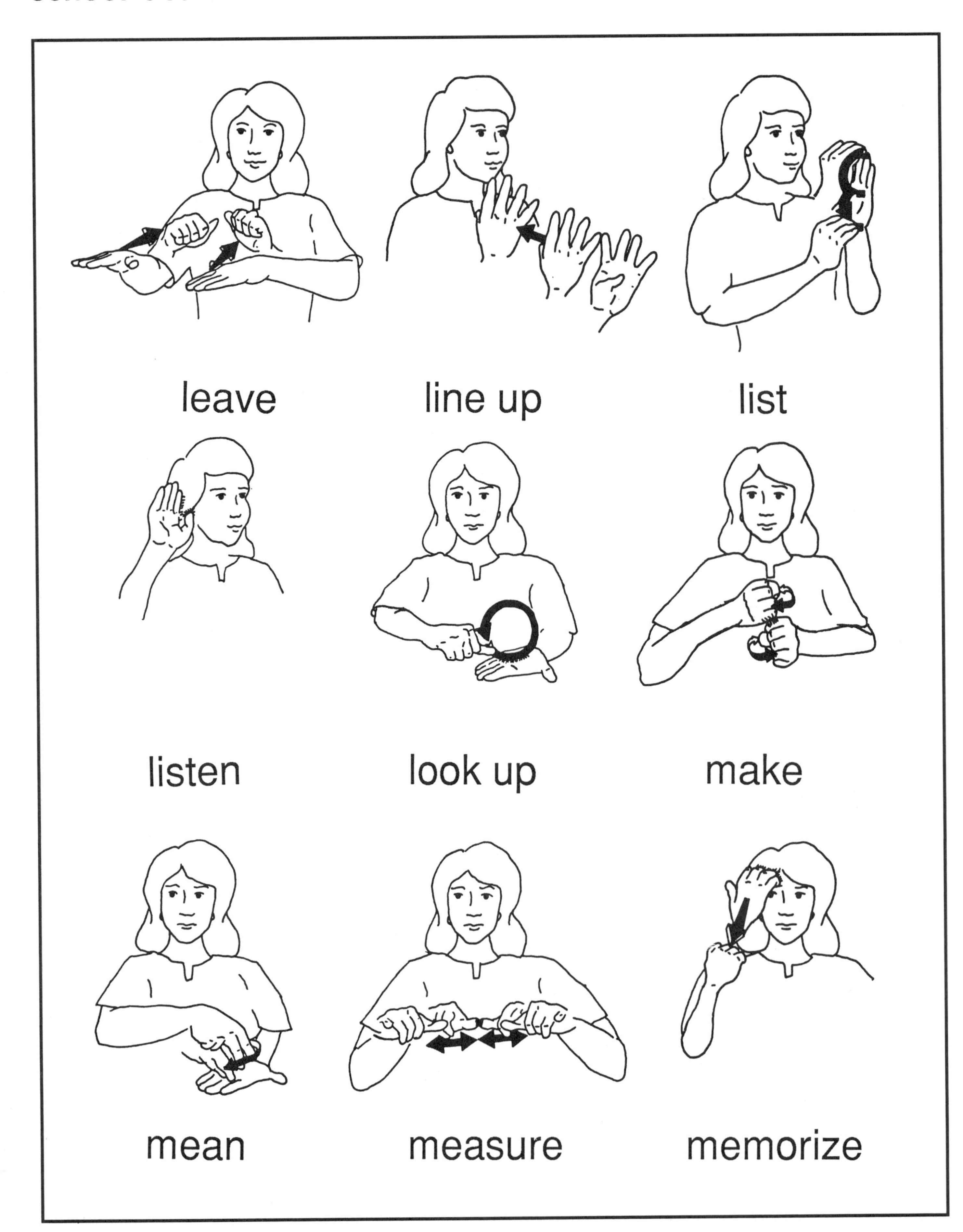
leave
line up
list
listen
look up
make
mean
measure
memorize

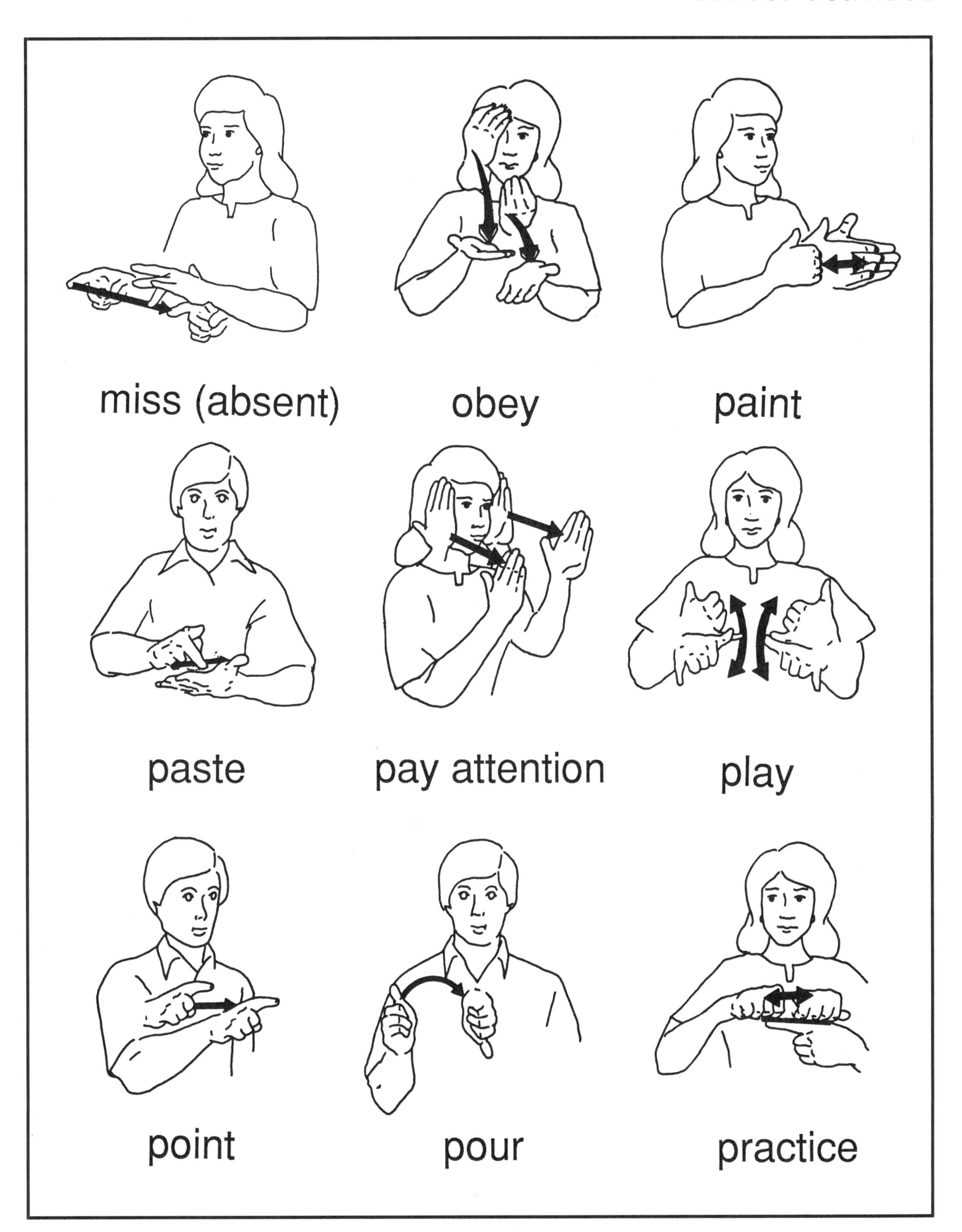
miss (absent)
obey
paint
paste
pay attention
play
point
pour
practice

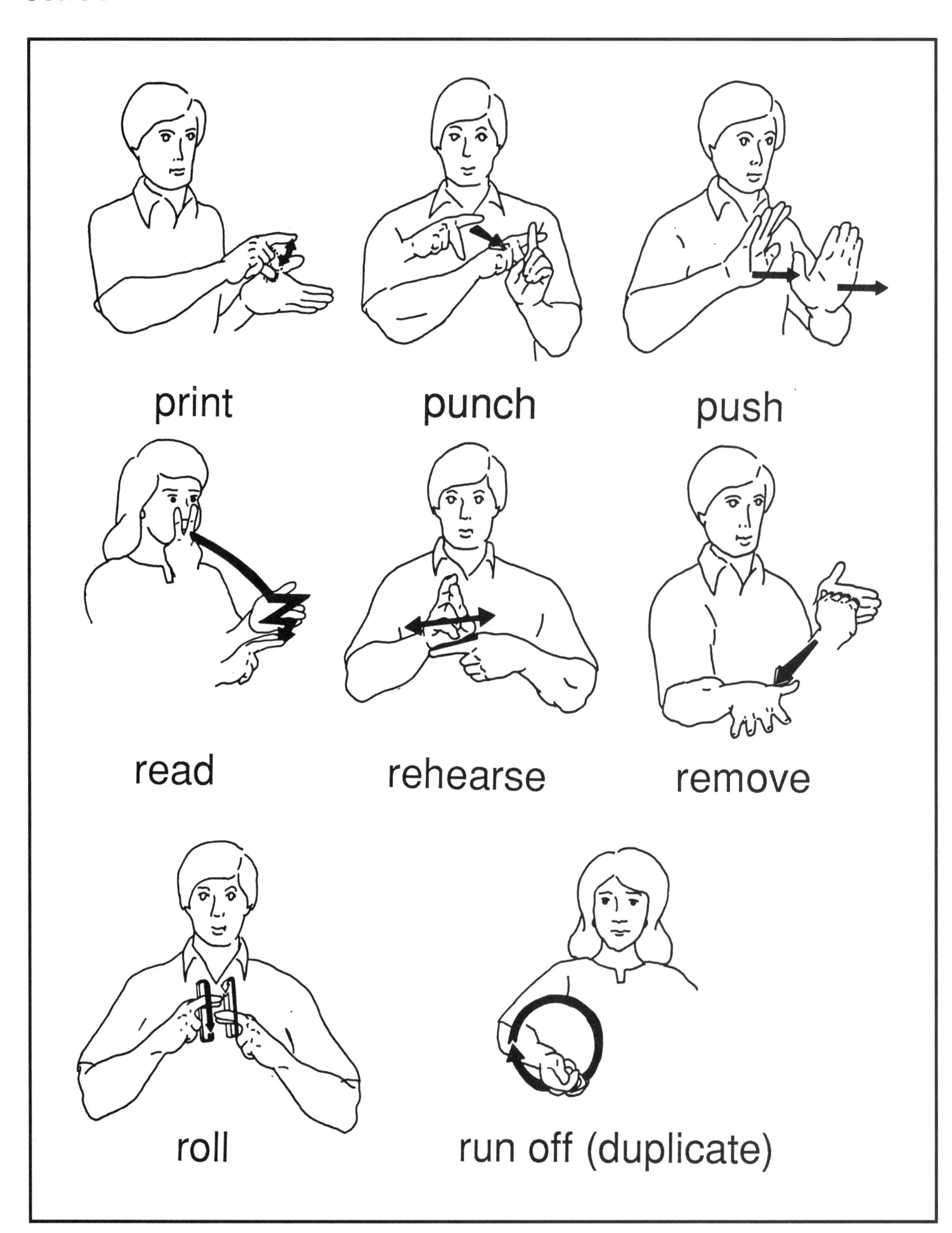
print
punch
push
read
rehearse
remove
roll
run off (duplicate)

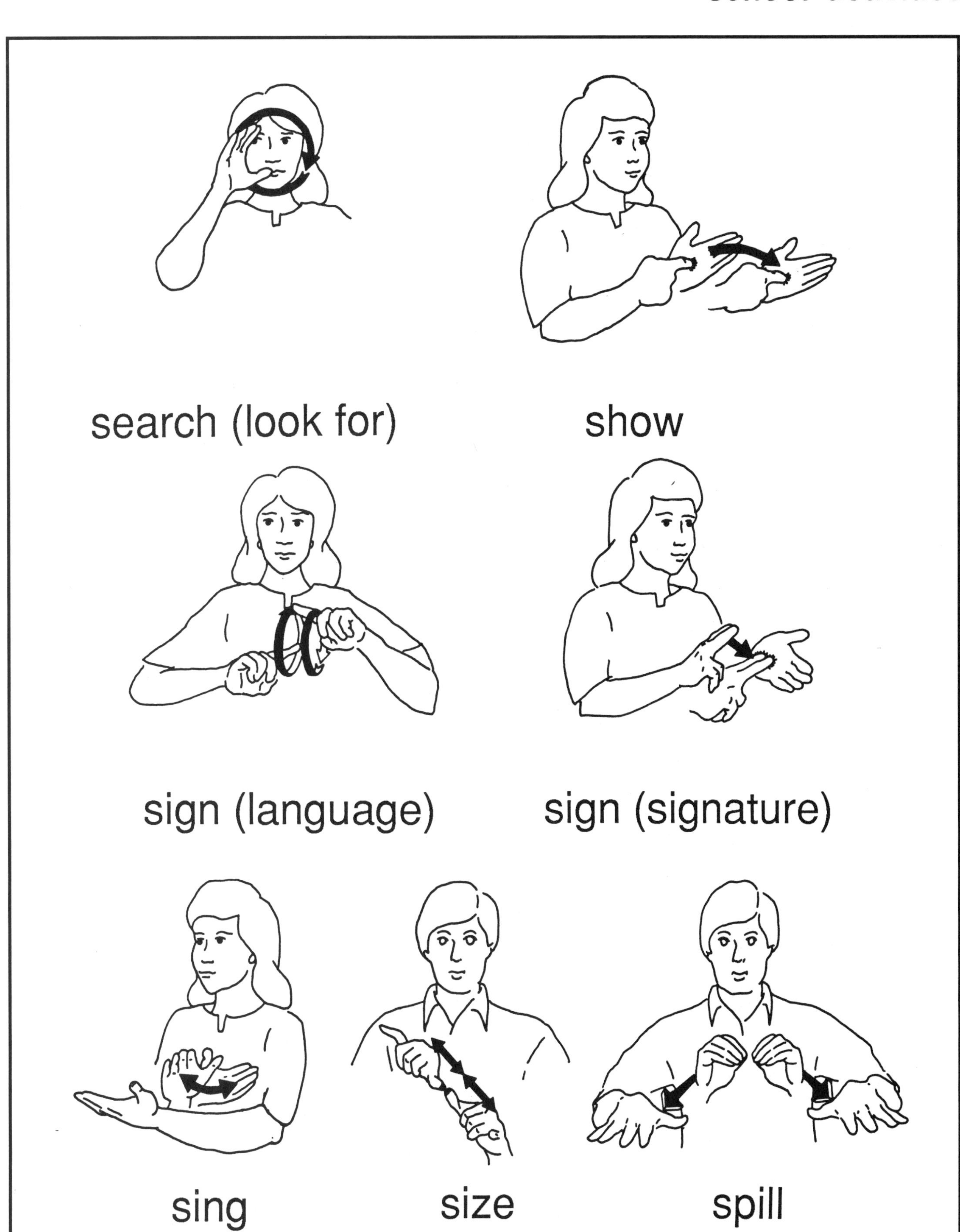
search (look for)
show
sign (language)
sign (signature)
sing
size
spill

spin
start
stir
study
subtract
support
swing
teach
tear

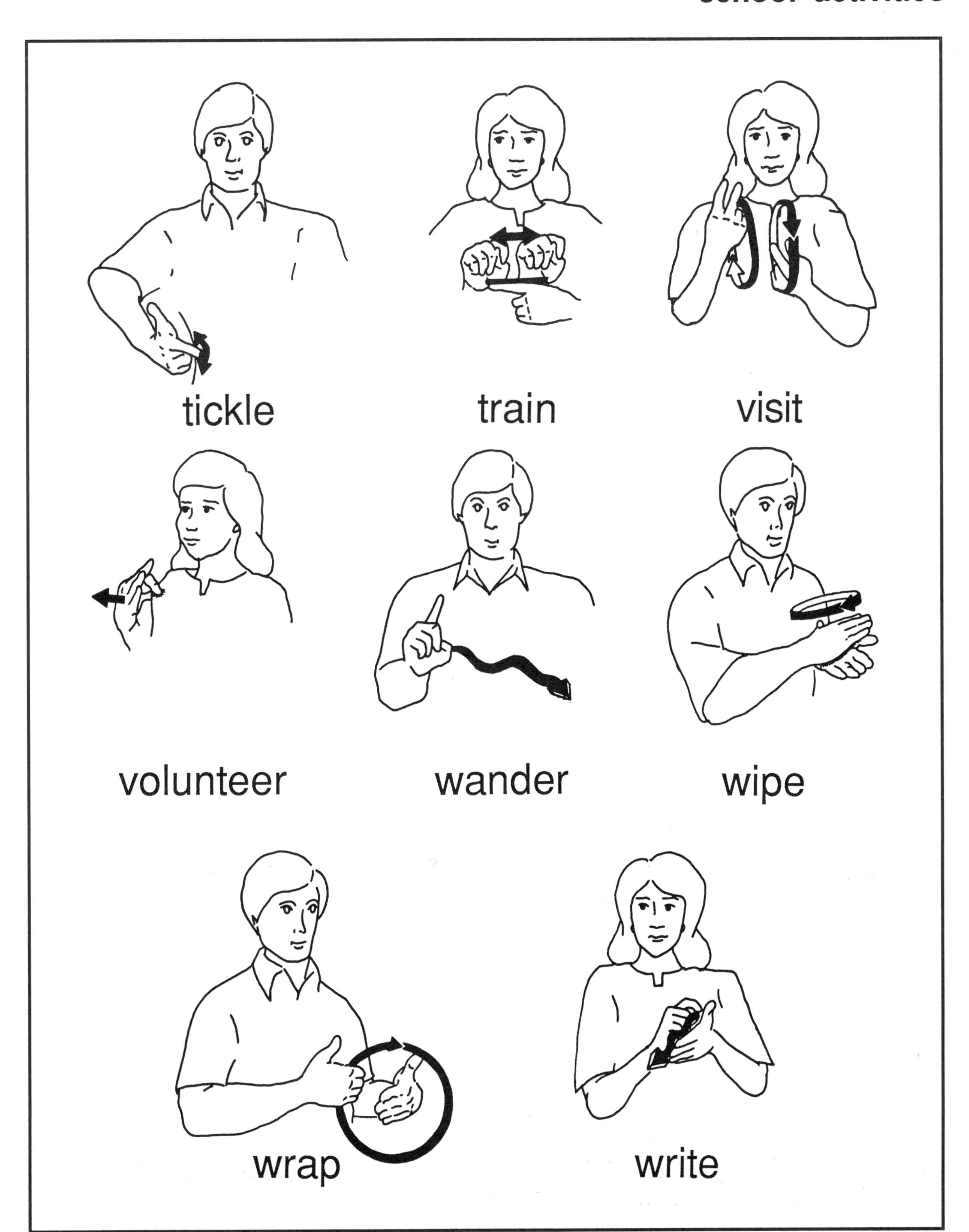
tickle
train
visit
volunteer
wander
wipe
wrap
write

SCHOOL SUBJECTS

arithmetic
art
audiology
biology
chemistry
English
geography
history
language
math
music
physical education
philosophy
psychology
reading
religion
science
sign
social studies
writing

ACTIVITY - SCHOOL SUBJECTS

Purpose: To learn how to spell different school subjects.

Materials: Pencil and paper or chalkboard and chalk.

Procedure:

1. Adult signs/says a school subject from list of School Subjects and child writes the correct name on chalkboard.
2. Adult assists child with subjects mispelled by putting lines and cues on chalkboard for child, e.g., s o c _ _ _ s t u _ _ _ _. (social studies)
3. Adult uses fading technique as child gains confidence in mastery, e.g., s _ _ _ _ l s _ _ _ _ _ _ _
   _ _ _ _ _ _ _ _ _ _ _ _ _
   ______ ______

Variations: Fading technique should be used frequently in a variety of areas to insure mastery.

SCHOOL SUBJECTS

arithmetic

art

audiology

biology

chemistry

English

SCHOOL SUBJECTS

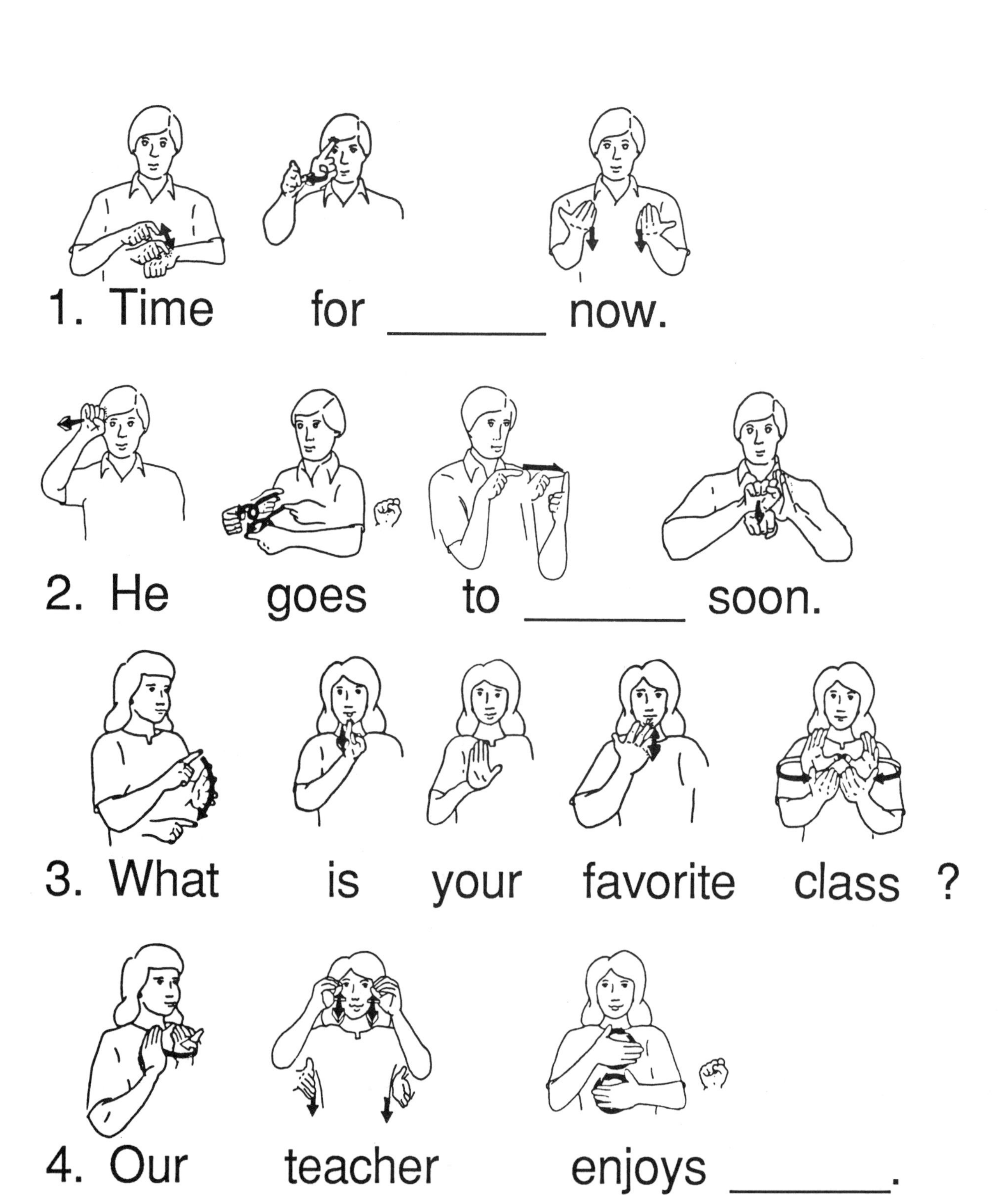

1. Time for ______ now.

2. He goes to ______ soon.

3. What is your favorite class ?

4. Our teacher enjoys ______.

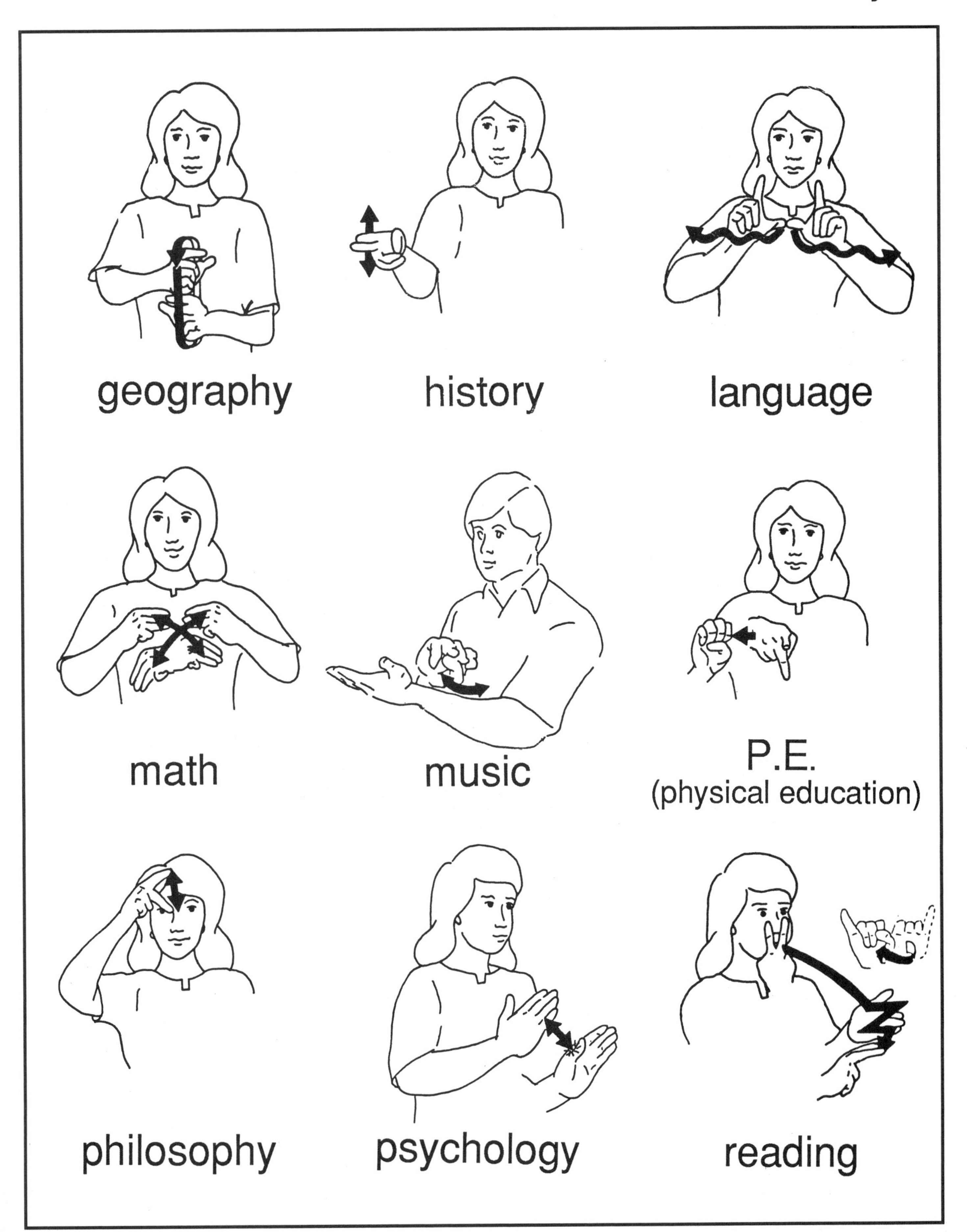
geography
history
language
math
music
P.E.
(physical education)
philosophy
psychology
reading

religion
science
sign
social studies
writing

SCHOOL[1] THINGS[1]

aide
alphabet
board [2]
book
bulletin board
bus area
cafeteria
chalk
chalkboard
chart
class
classroom
clay
clock
computer
course
crayon
desk
dictionary
dormitory
eraser
field (study)
field trip
furniture
game
goal
grade
gym
gynasium
homework
learning center
letter (alphabet)
mat
meeting
music
name
noise
note
notebook
paper
parking lot
partner
party
paste
pen
pencil
playground
policy
poster
pre-school
principal
problem
program
project
puzzle
question
quiet
quiet area
quiz
recess
reinforce
restroom
reward
room
rubber band
rule
ruler
schedule
scissors
sentence
sign (language)
sign (notice)
speech room
story [1]
student
table
tape [2]
teacher [2]
therapy
vocabulary
workshop

ACTIVITY - SCHOOL THINGS

Purpose: To collect and identify several items in the classroom as being hard or soft.

Materials: Items normally found in a classroom.

Procedure:

1. Adult writes the names of 10 items in the classroom on the chalkboard.
2. Adult explains that the items on the list have to be found and put on the table in five minutes.
3. Child puts as many of the items as possible, in five minutes, on the table.
4. Child feels each item and signs/says the name of each item in a sentence using hard or soft, e.g., The eraser is soft.
5. Child writes the sentence on the chalkboard.

Variations: If more than one child, make it a contest with different lists and shorter time limit; use different adjectives to describe items in the classroom, e.g., colors; use pictures for younger child rather than writing the names of items.

SCHOOL THINGS

aide

alphabet

board

book

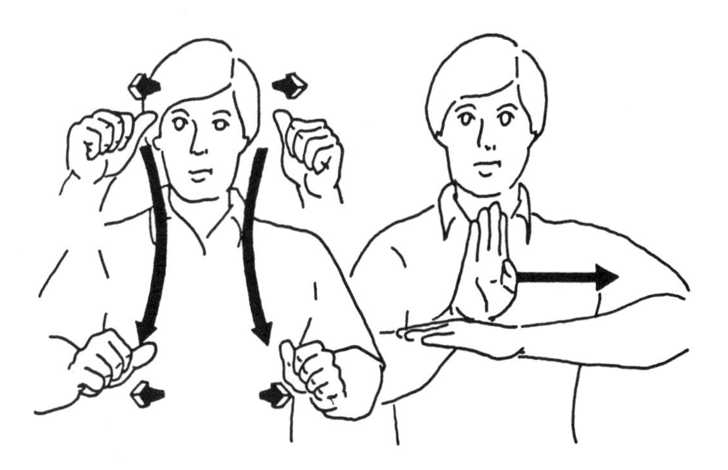

bulletin board

SCHOOL THINGS

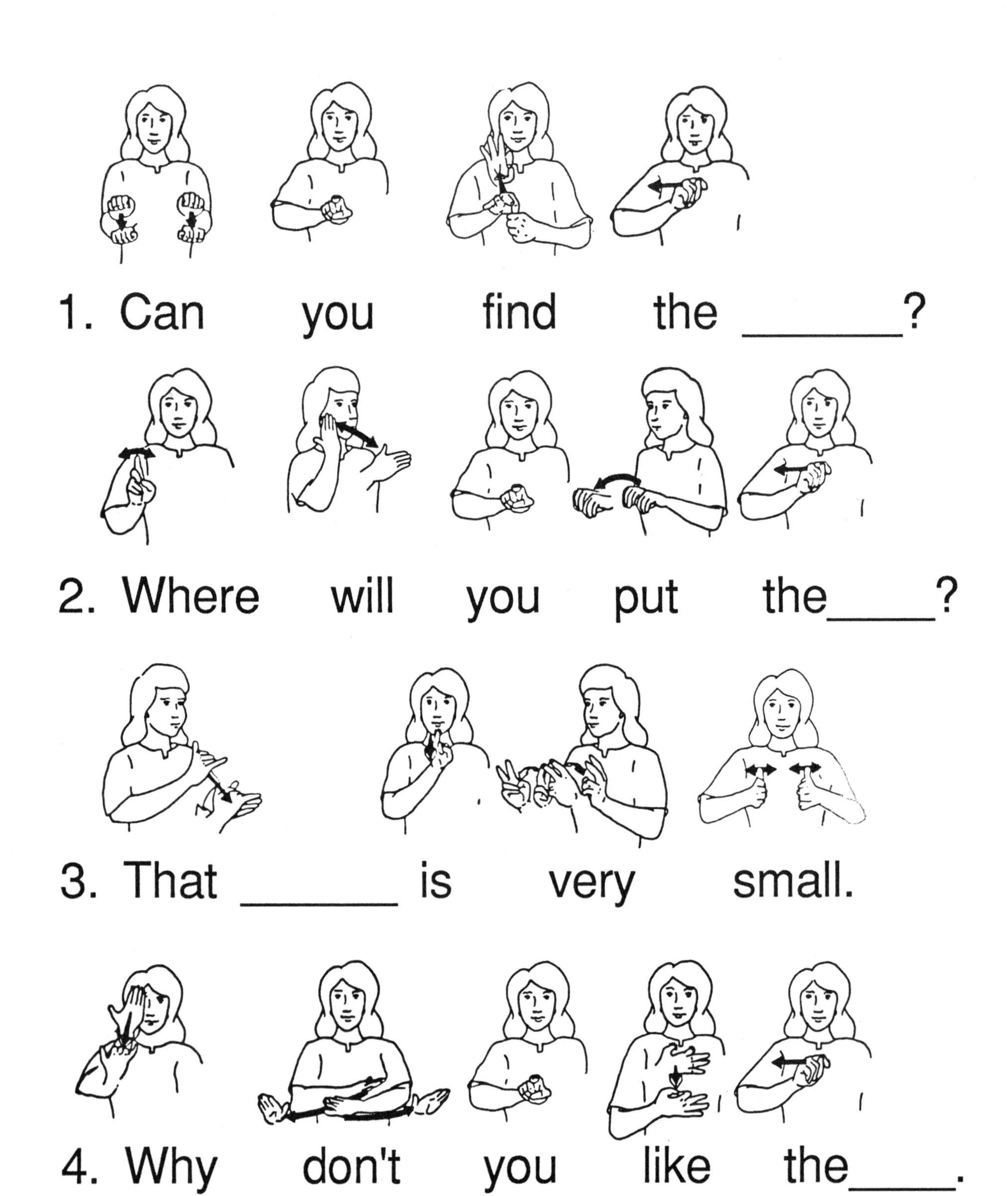
1. Can you find the ______?
2. Where will you put the_____?
3. That ______ is very small.
4. Why don't you like the_____.

bus area
cafeteria
chalk
chalkboard
chart
class

school things

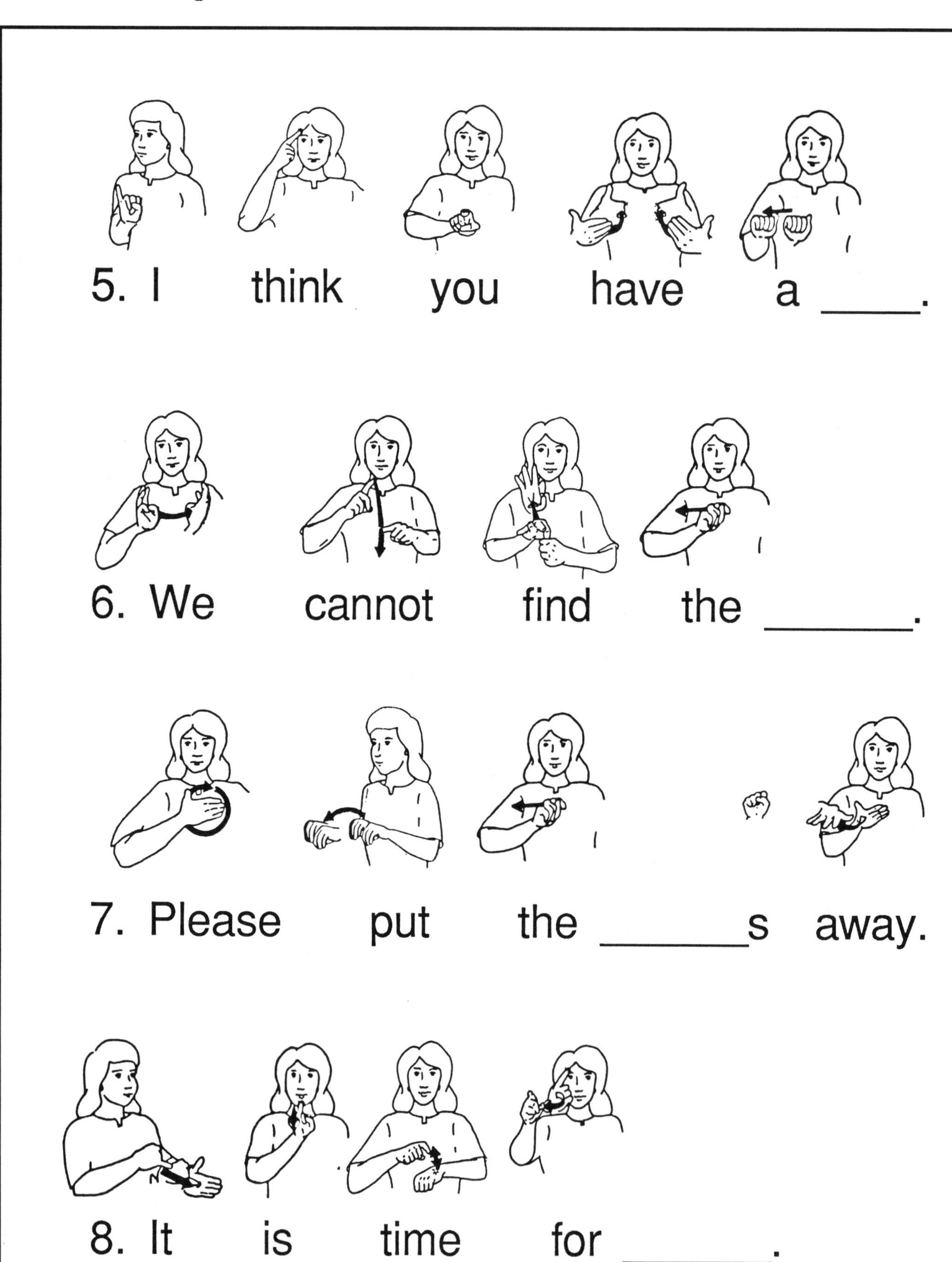
5. I think you have a ____.
6. We cannot find the ______.
7. Please put the ______s away.
8. It is time for ______.

classroom
clay
clock
computer
course
crayon
desk
dictionary

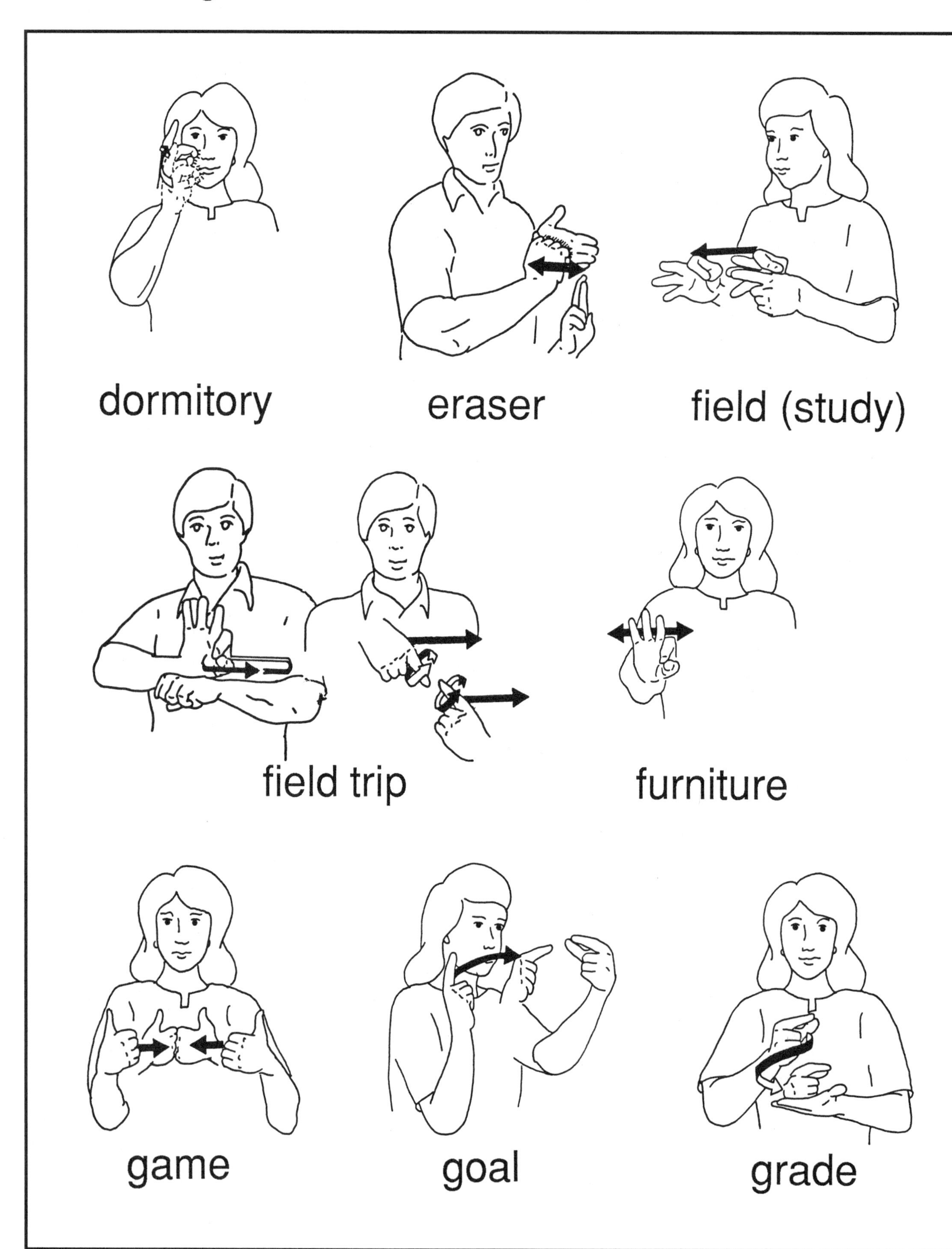
dormitory
eraser
field (study)
field trip
furniture
game
goal
grade

gym

gymnasium

homework

learning center

letter (alphabet)

mat

meeting

music
name
noise
note
notebook
paper
parking lot
partner

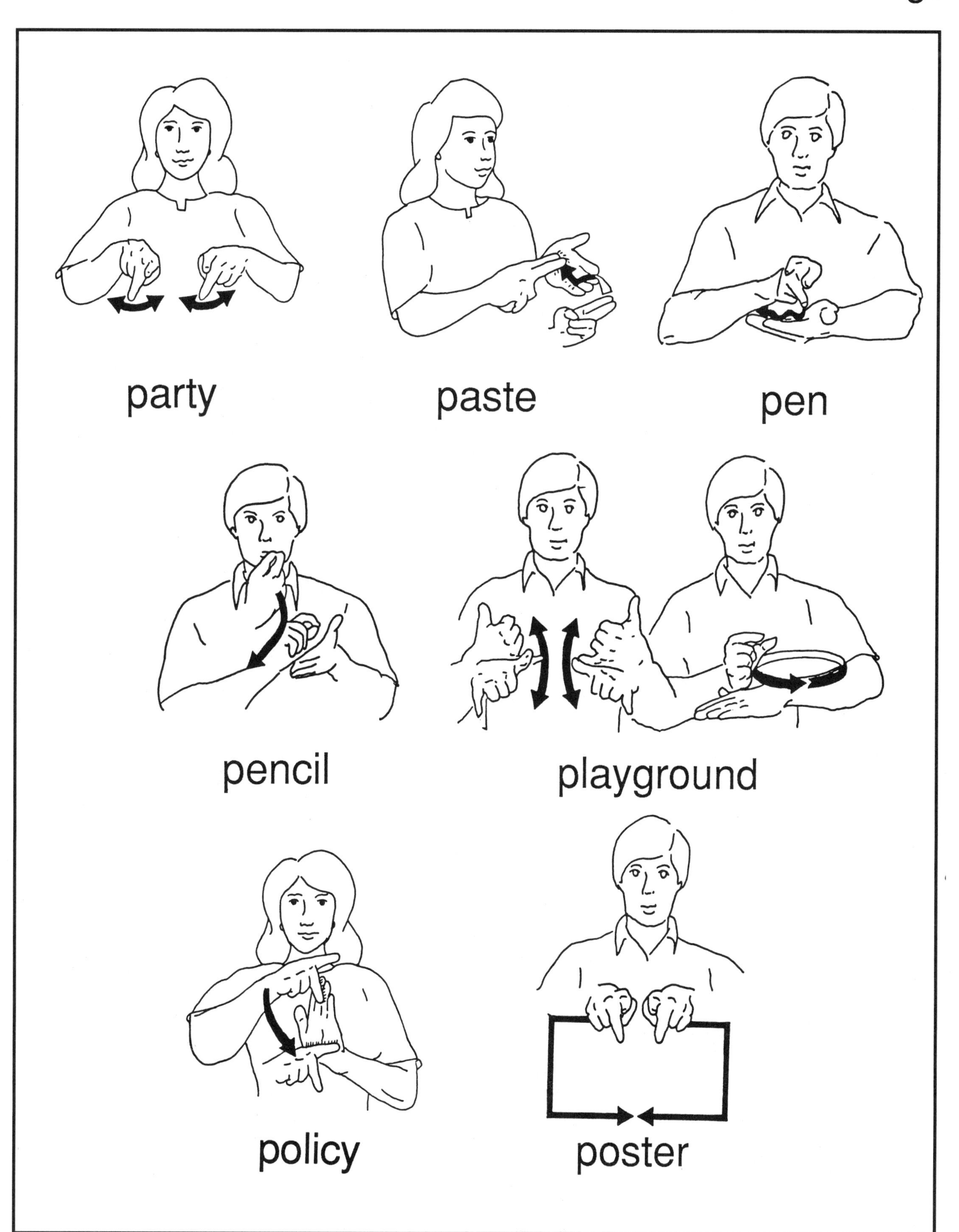
party
paste
pen
pencil
playground
policy
poster

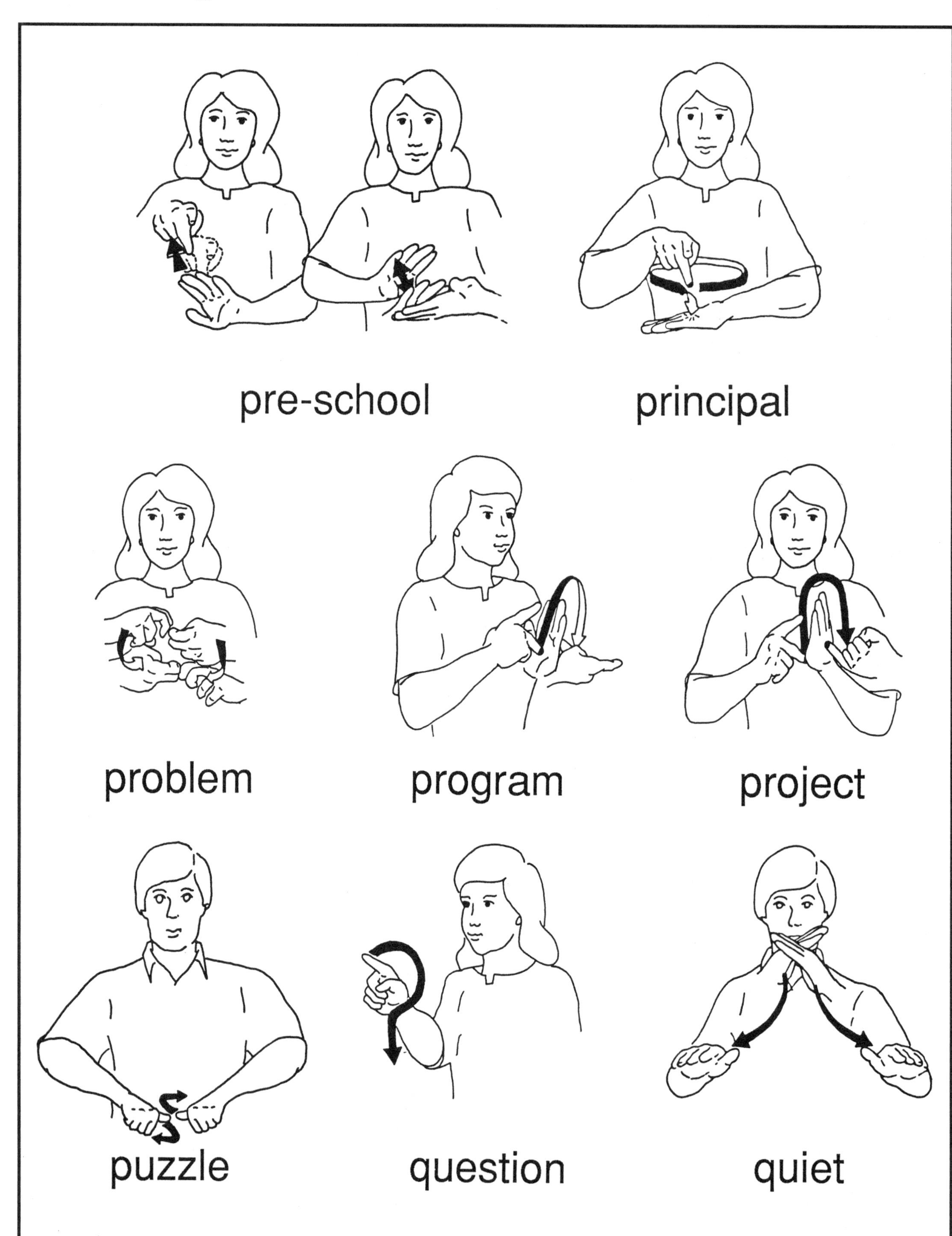
pre-school
principal
problem
program
project
puzzle
question
quiet

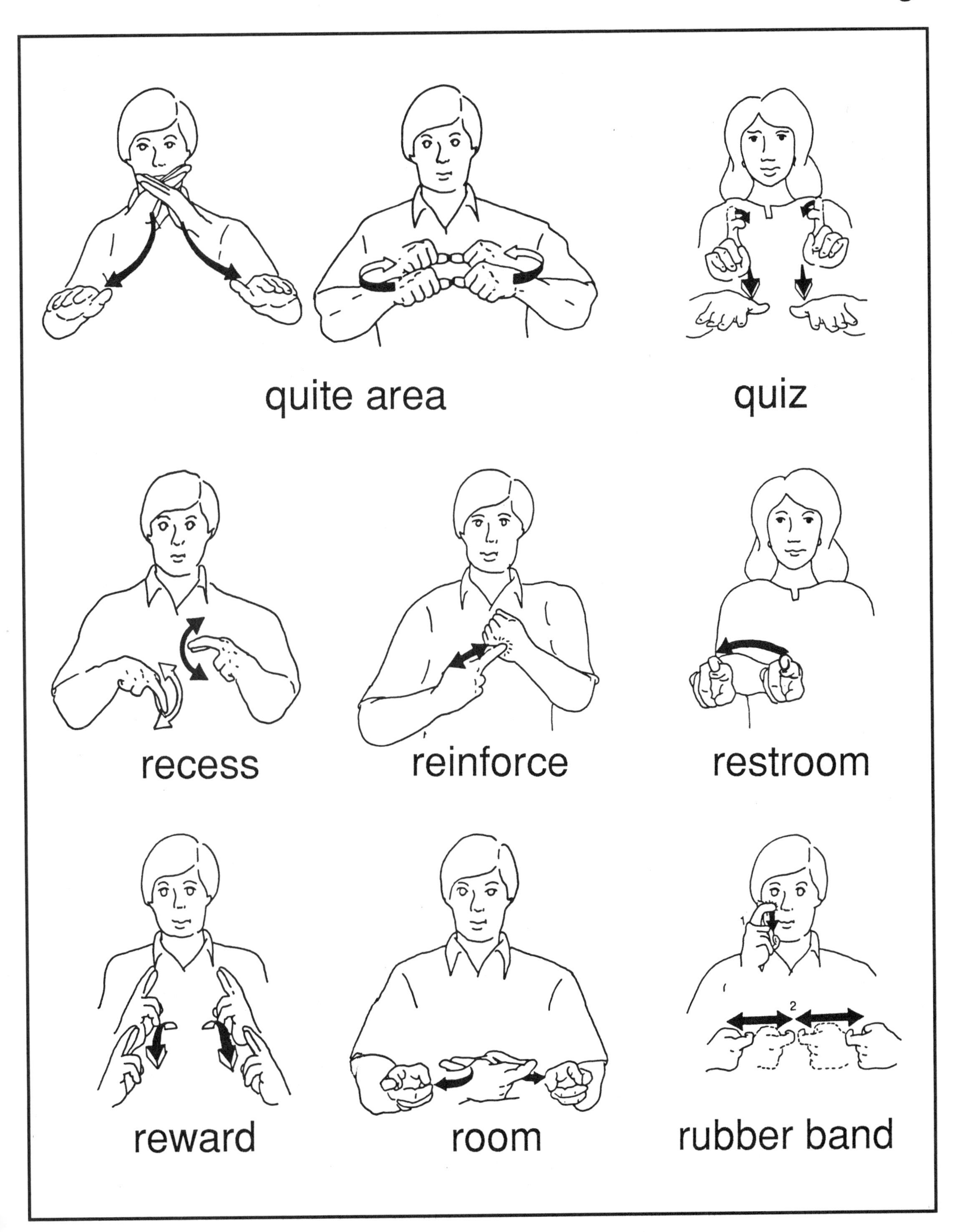

quite area

quiz

recess

reinforce

restroom

reward

room

rubber band

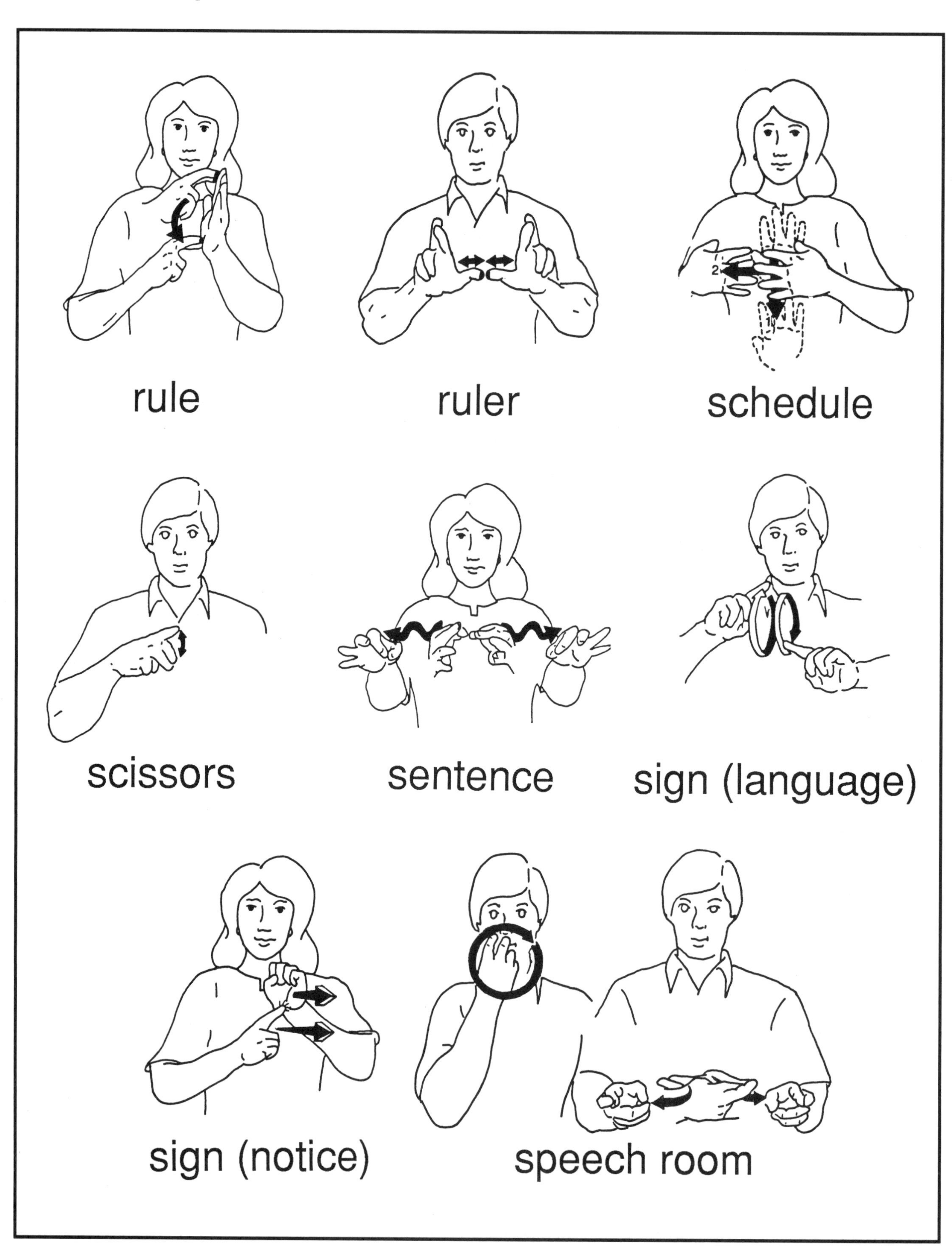

rule

ruler

schedule

scissors

sentence

sign (language)

sign (notice)

speech room

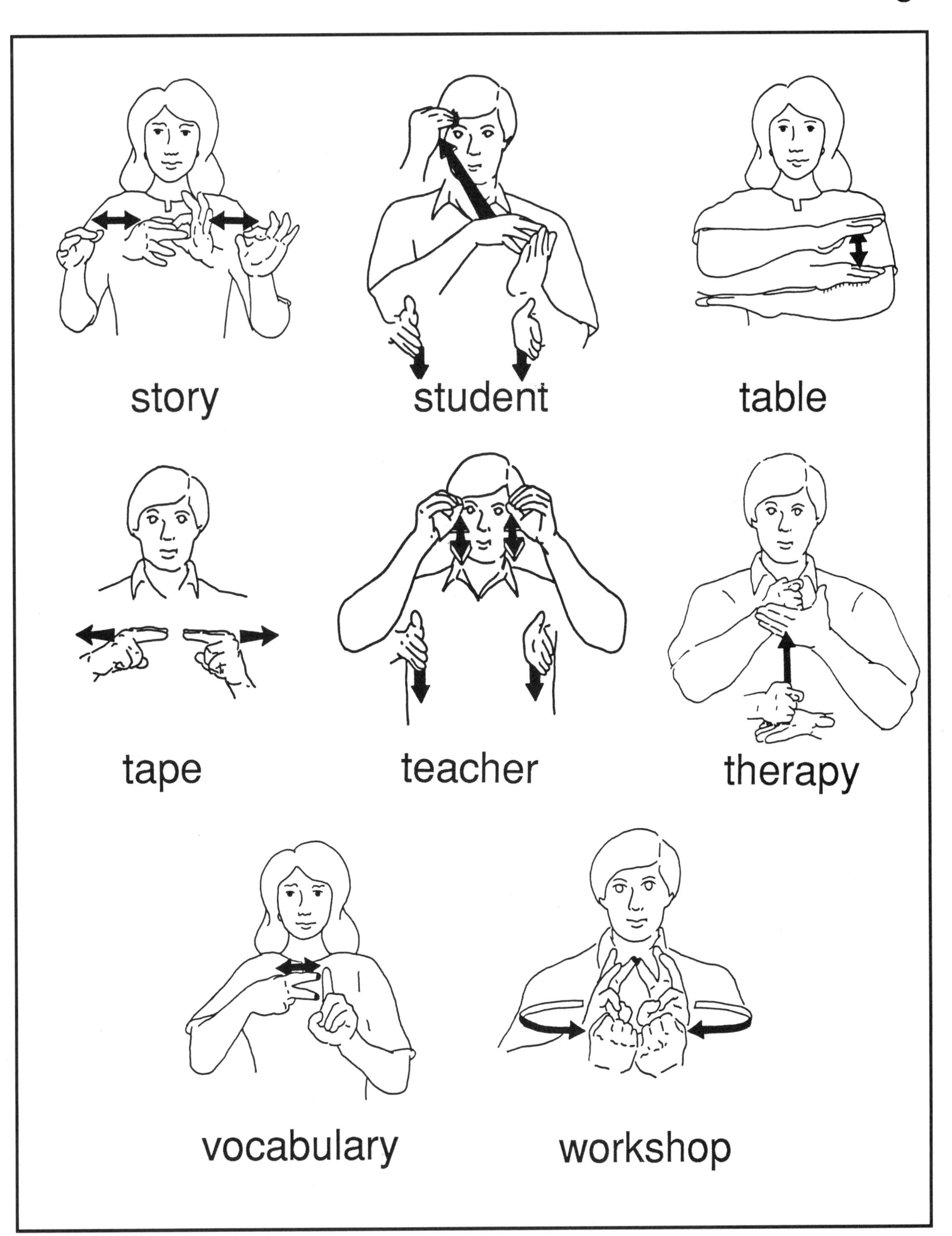
story
student
table
tape
teacher
therapy
vocabulary
workshop

SNACKS

apple
apple juice
banana
cake
candy [1]
cereal
cheese
chocolate
coke
cookie
cracker
donut
fruit
fudge
grape
ice cream [1]
jello
juice
Kool Aid
lemonade
lollipop
milk
nut
orange
orange juice
peanut
peanut butter
Pepsi
pie [2]
pizza
pop
popcorn
popscicle
potato chip
pretzel
pudding
raisin
soda
sundae
yogurt

ACTIVITY - SNACKS

Purpose: To identify and learn the names of different snacks.

Materials: Index cards; magic marker or pencil; table; three or four different snacks, e.g., raisins, apple pieces. cookies, cereal.

Procedure:

1. Adult writes name of each snack on an index card.
2. Adult puts index card (raisin) on table in front of child. Adult puts down one raisin for child to see and eat. Repeat procedure two.
3. Adult puts two index cards on table in front of child, raisin and apple.
4. Adult shows child raisin pointing to raisin card. Adult takes child's finger and points to raisin card. Adult gives child raisin.
5. Adult shows child another raisin indicating child should point to appropriate card. Child points to raisin card and gets raisin.
6. Adult continues activity until child masters raisin.
7. Adult repeats procedures two through six with another snack while occasionally referring back to raisin.

SNACKS

1. Do you like ______?

2. Don't eat too many ______.

3. Where are the ______?

4. Thank you, that is nice.

SNACKS

apple

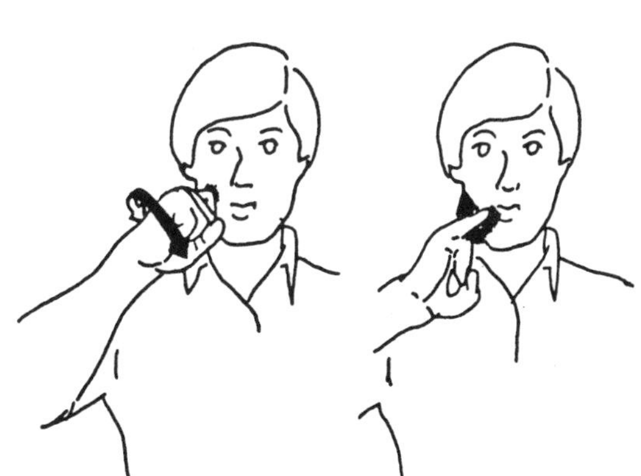

apple juice

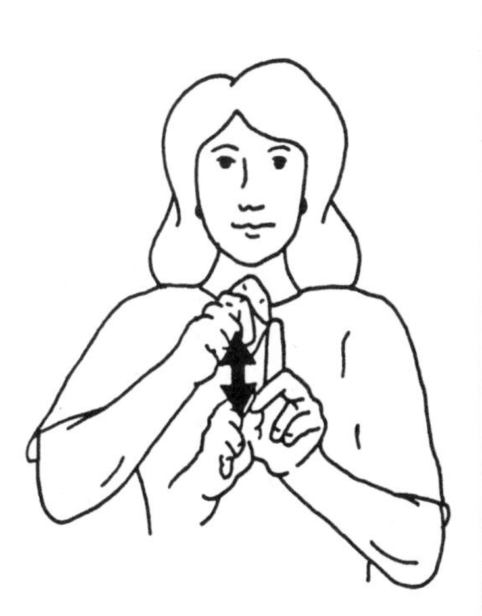

banana

cake

candy

cereal

5. The _______ tastes good.

6. Those ______s are old.

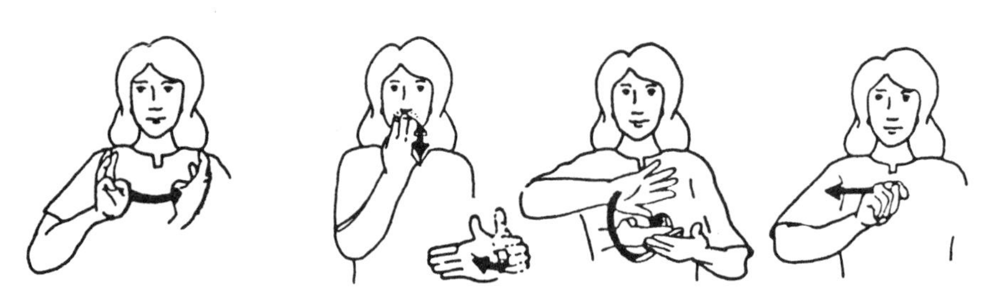

7. We ate all the _______.

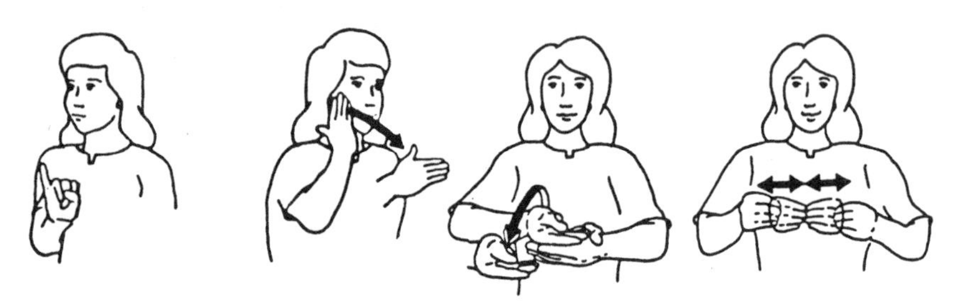

8. I will buy more _______.

cheese
chocolate
coke
cookie
cracker
donut
fruit
fudge
grape

ice cream

jello

juice

Kool Aid

lemonade

lollipop

milk

nut

orange

orange juice
peanut
peanut butter
Pepsi
pie
pizza
pop
popcorn
popscicle

potato chip
pretzel
pudding
raisin
soda
sundae
yogurt

TIME

a while ago
after [1]
after a while
afternoon
ago [2]
all night
before [1]
breakfast
daily
dawn
day
dinner
during
early
evening
every so often
fall
first
former
future
hour
last year
late
later
long
lunch
minute
month
monthly
morning [2]
nap
never
next [1]
next week
next year
night [1]
noon
now
often
once
once in awhile
past
period
postpone
recent
second [2] (time)
short
since
sometime
soon
spring
summer
sunrise
sunset
supper
third
time (clock)
today
tomorrow
until [2]
wait a minute
week [2]
weekend
winter
year [2]
yesterday

ACTIVITY - TIME

Purpose: To develop a sense of time relative to now, today, along with teaching the concept of future.

Materials: Flashcards with today, and yesterday written on them; chalkboard and chalk or pencil and paper.

Procedure:

1. Adult puts the flashcard on the floor and stands behind it.
2. Adult signs/says: "Today we will play outside". Write outside on the chalkboard. "Today we will eat ice cream". Write ice cream on the chalkboard. "Today we will make a cake". Write cake on the chalkboard.
3. Adult exchanges places with child and child points to ice cream , signing/saying, "Today we will eat ice cream". Adult prompts as necessary. Child signs/says other activities on the chalkboard.
4. Adult signs/says each of the activities again just before they are undertaken during the course of the day. Child signs/says the same thing.

Variations: After the concept of today is mastered, start with the concept of yesterday using the same procedure, e.g., "Yesterday we ate ice cream". Combine the two after the second is mastered.

TIME

time (period)

a while ago

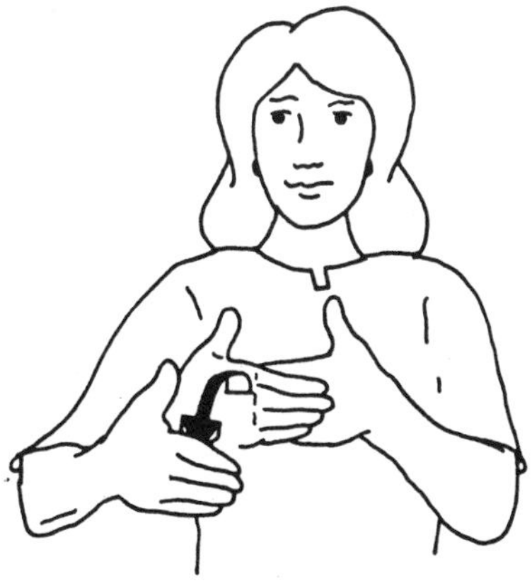

after

after a while

afternoon

ago

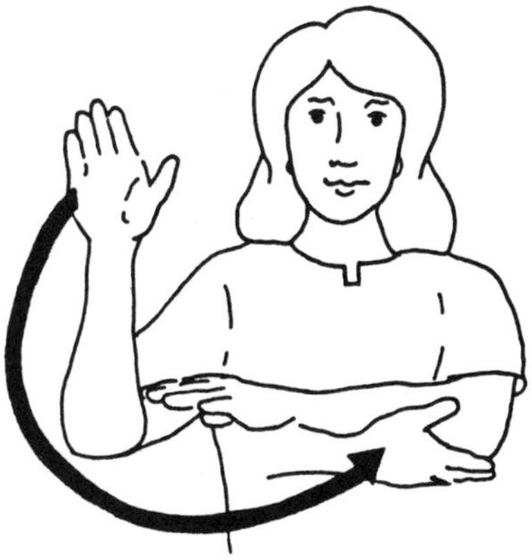

all night

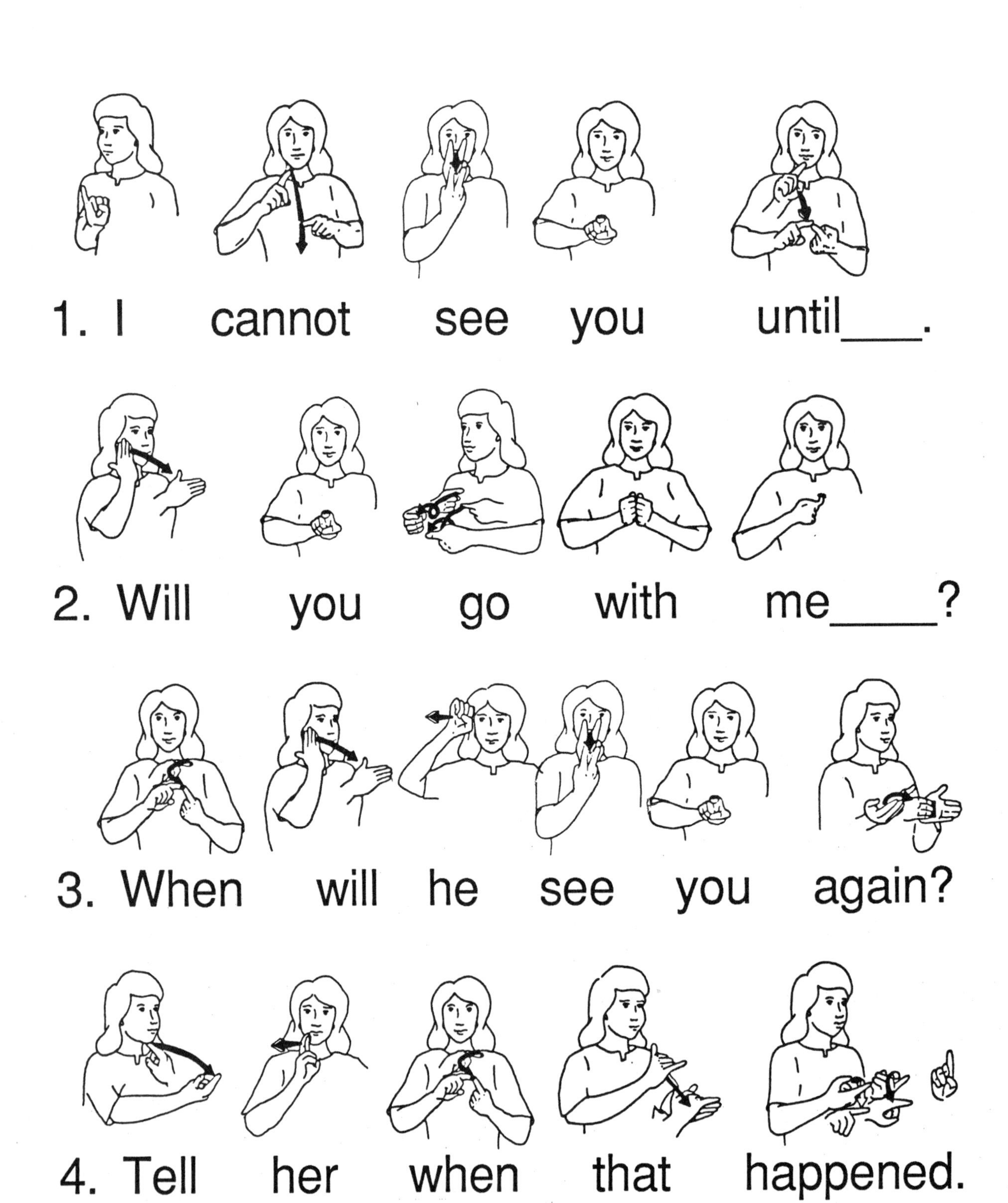
TIME
1. I cannot see you until___.
2. Will you go with me____?
3. When will he see you again?
4. Tell her when that happened.

before
breakfast
daily
dawn
day
dinner
during
early
evening

5. When will we go?
6. Can you wait here for ____?
7. ______ he will go ______.
8. How often does that happen?

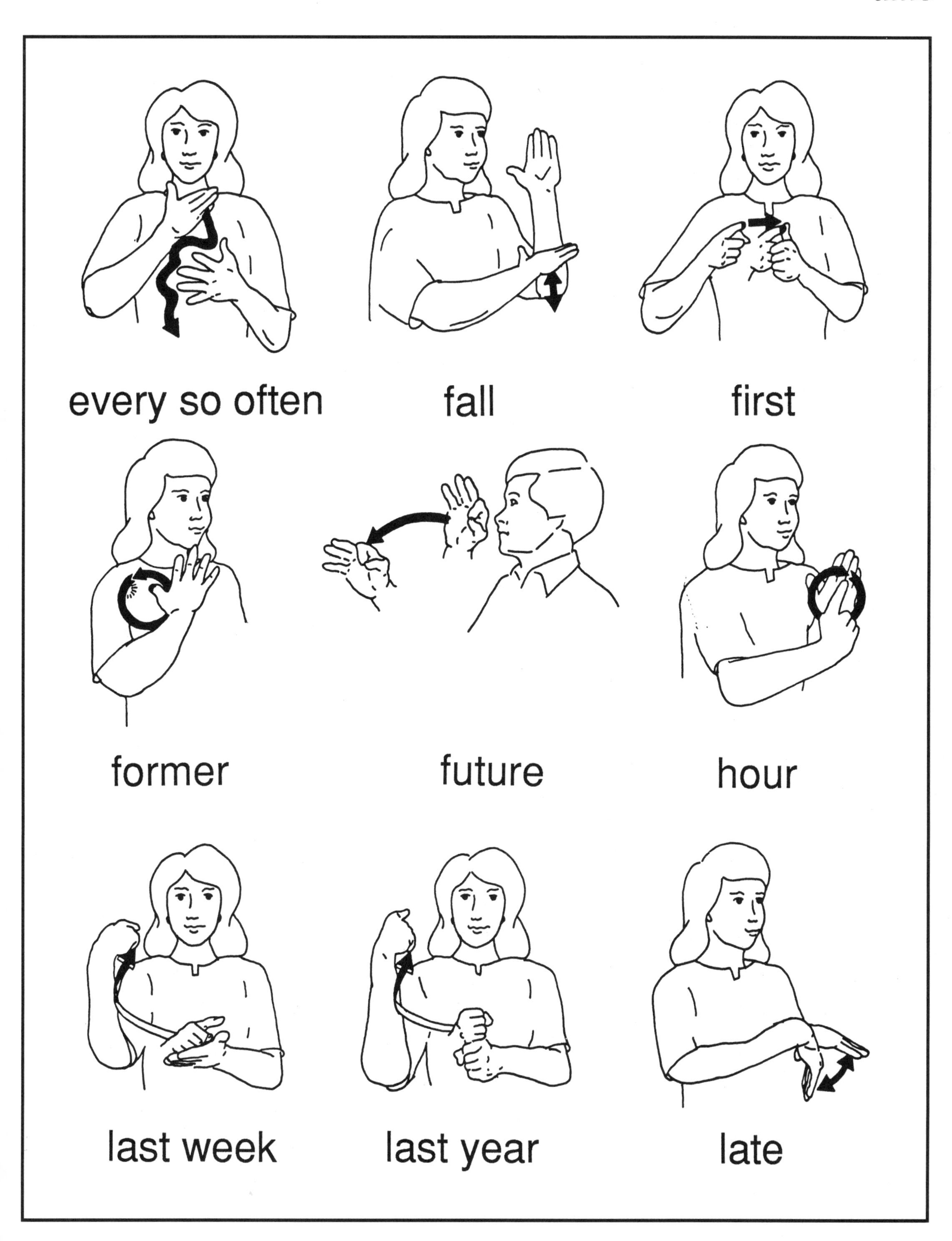
every so often
fall
first
former
future
hour
last week
last year
late

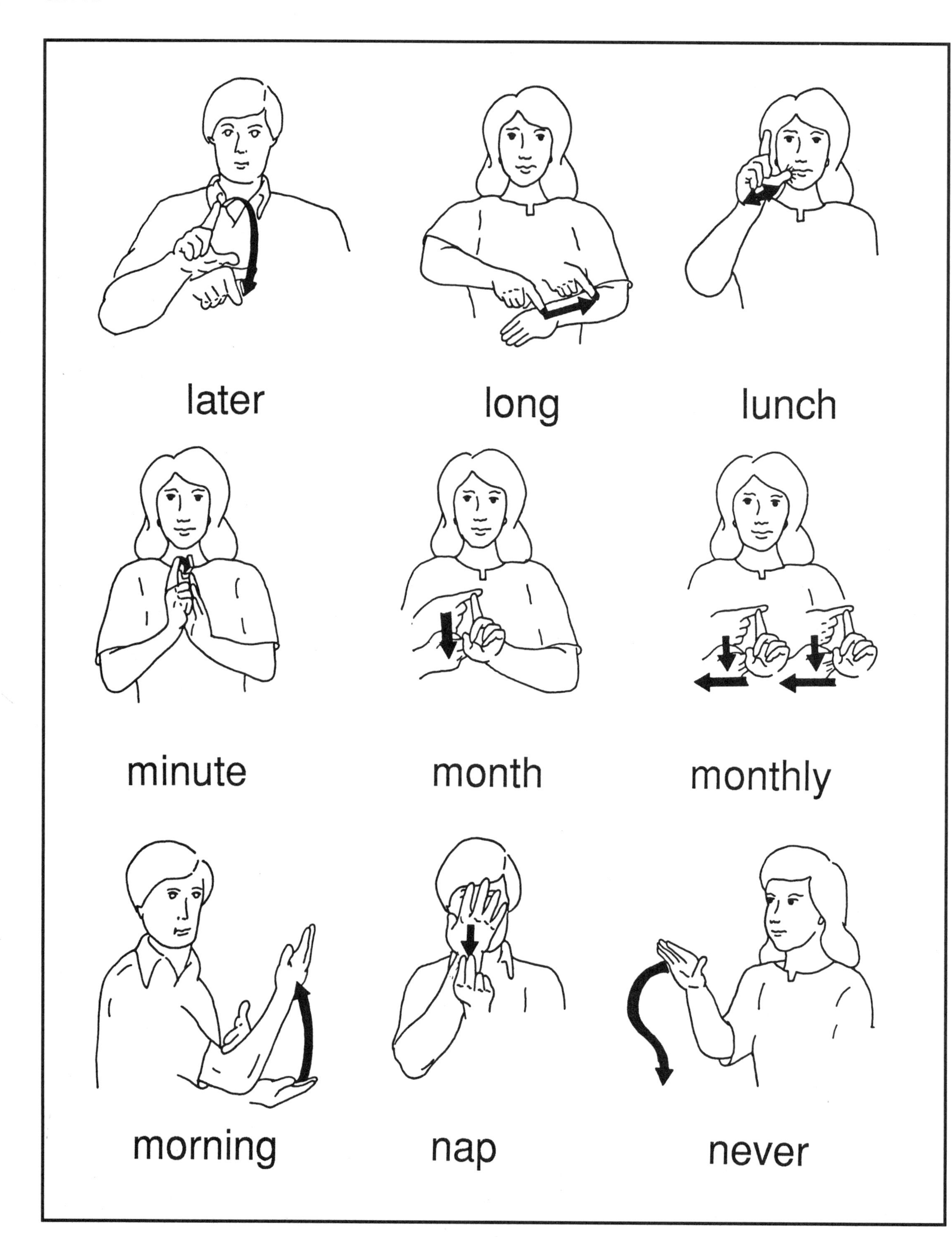
later
long
lunch
minute
month
monthly
morning
nap
never

next
next week
next year
night
noon
now
often
once
once in awhile

past
period
postpone
recent
second (time)
short
since
sometime
soon

spring
summer
sunrise
sunset
supper
third
time (clock)
today

tomorrow
until
wait a minute
week
weekend
winter
year
yesterday
use "Y" hand

TRANSPORTATION

airplane[2]
ambulance
barge
bicycle[1]
boat[2]
bus[2]
canoe
car[2]
donkey
fire truck
helicopter
horse
jet
motorboat
motorcycle
mule
police car
riverboat
rocket
rowboat
sailboat
ship
snowmobile
space ship
submarine
subway
taxicab
train[2]
tricycle
truck
van
wagon

ACTIVITY - TRANSPORTATION

Purpose: To be able to fingerspell different forms of transportation from A to Z.

Materials: none

Procedure:

1. Adult sits across from child and signs/says that they will take turns fingerspelling different forms of transportation that start with different lettters of the alphabet from A to Z.
2. Adult starts by signing/saying, "I fly in an airplane," fingerspelling airplane.
3. Child signs/says a sentence which has a form of transportation that begins with the letter b, e.g., "I like going in a boat."
4. Continue taking turns until the entire alphabet is done. If a form of transportation for a particular letter cannot be thought of, write the letter down and consult the dictionary later.

Variations: Instead of putting the form of transportation into a sentence, individual words may be fingerspelled. Child may individually use the dictionary to look for forms of transportation writing a list from A to Z. This activity can also be used with foods, animals, and some other categories.

TRANSPORTATION

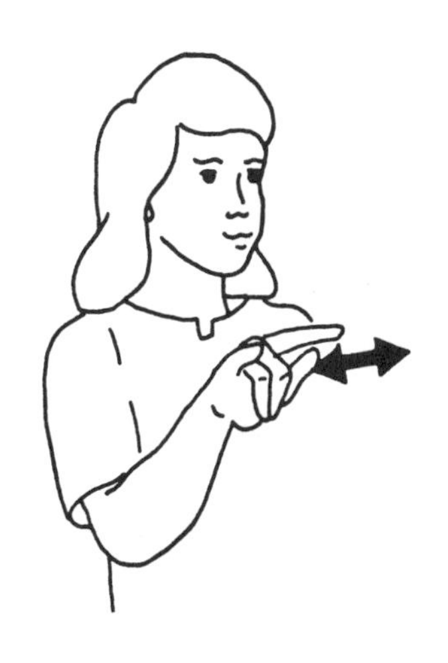

airplane

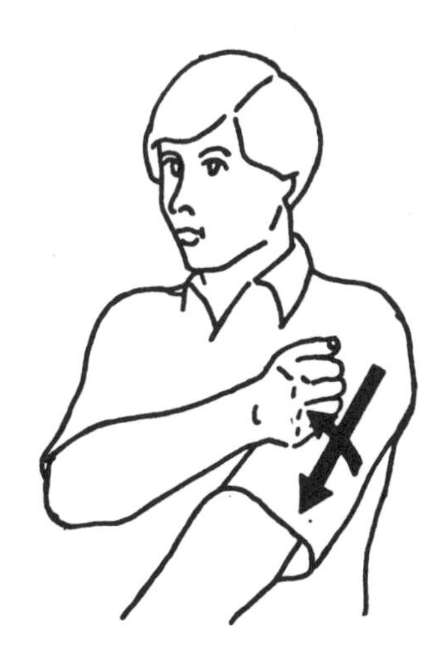

ambulance

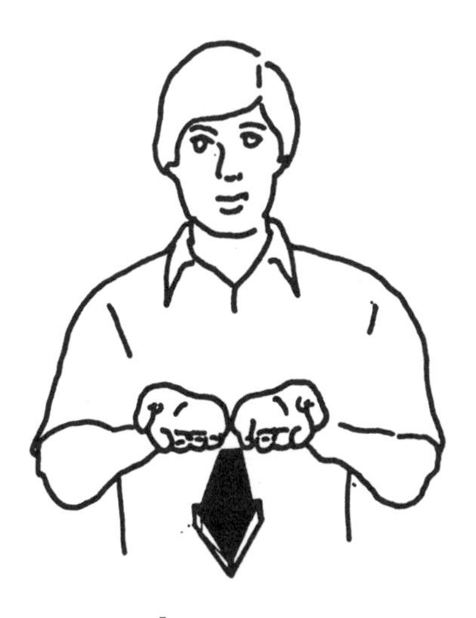

barge

bicycle

boat

bus

TRANSPORTATION

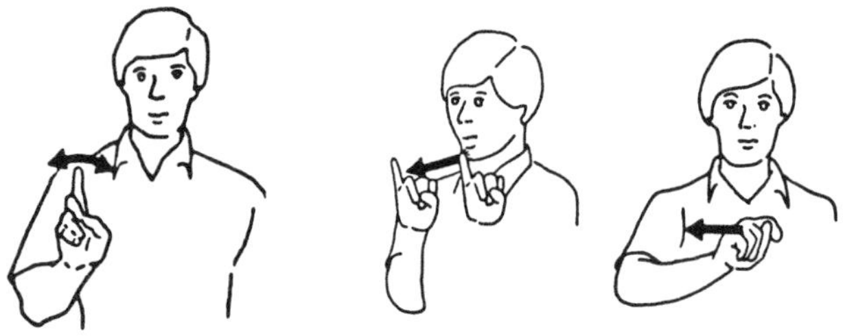

1. Where is the ______?

2. Is the ______ big or little?

3. Does a ___ go fast or slow?

4. Can a ____ go under water?

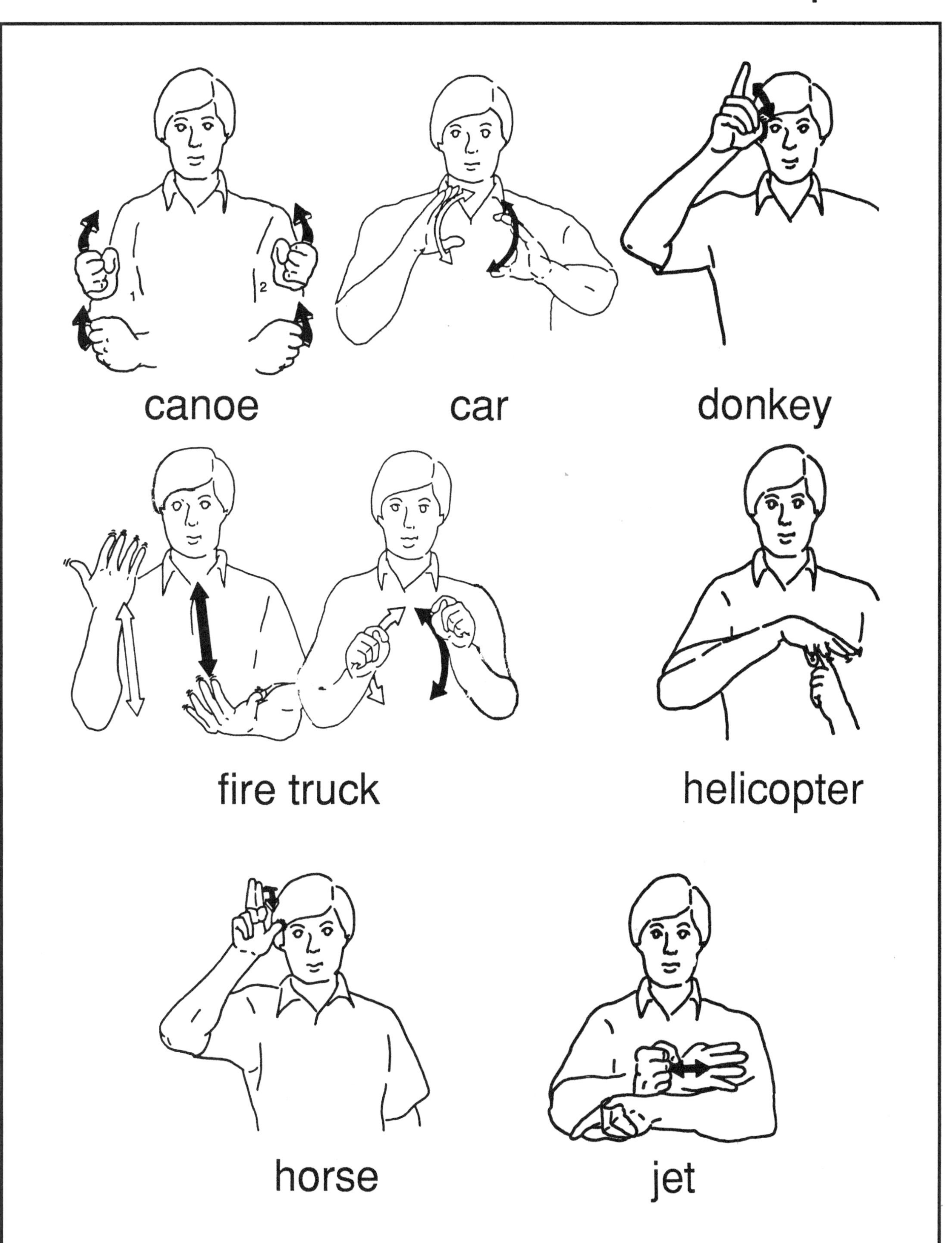

canoe

car

donkey

fire truck

helicopter

horse

jet

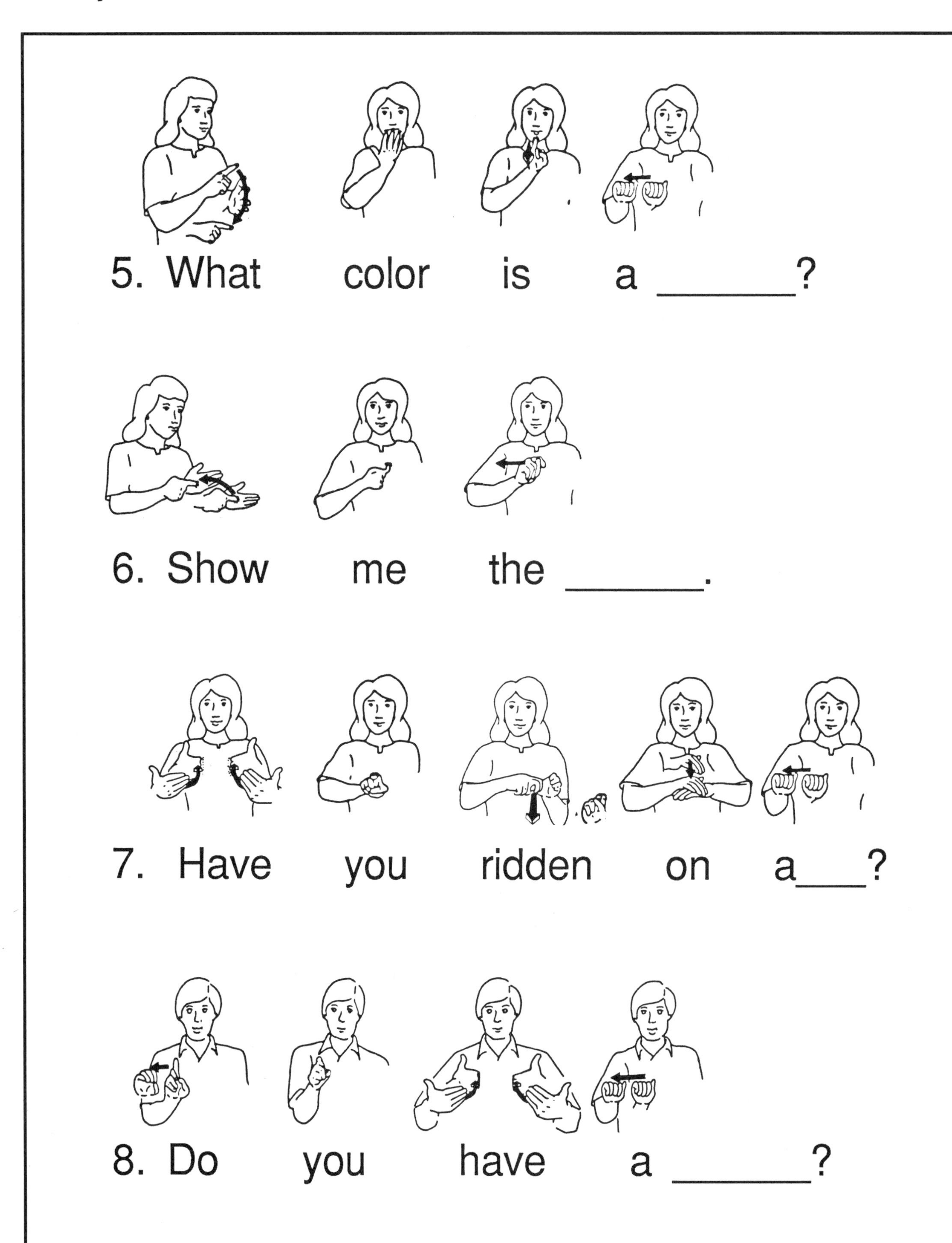
5. What color is a ______?
6. Show me the ______.
7. Have you ridden on a___?
8. Do you have a ______?

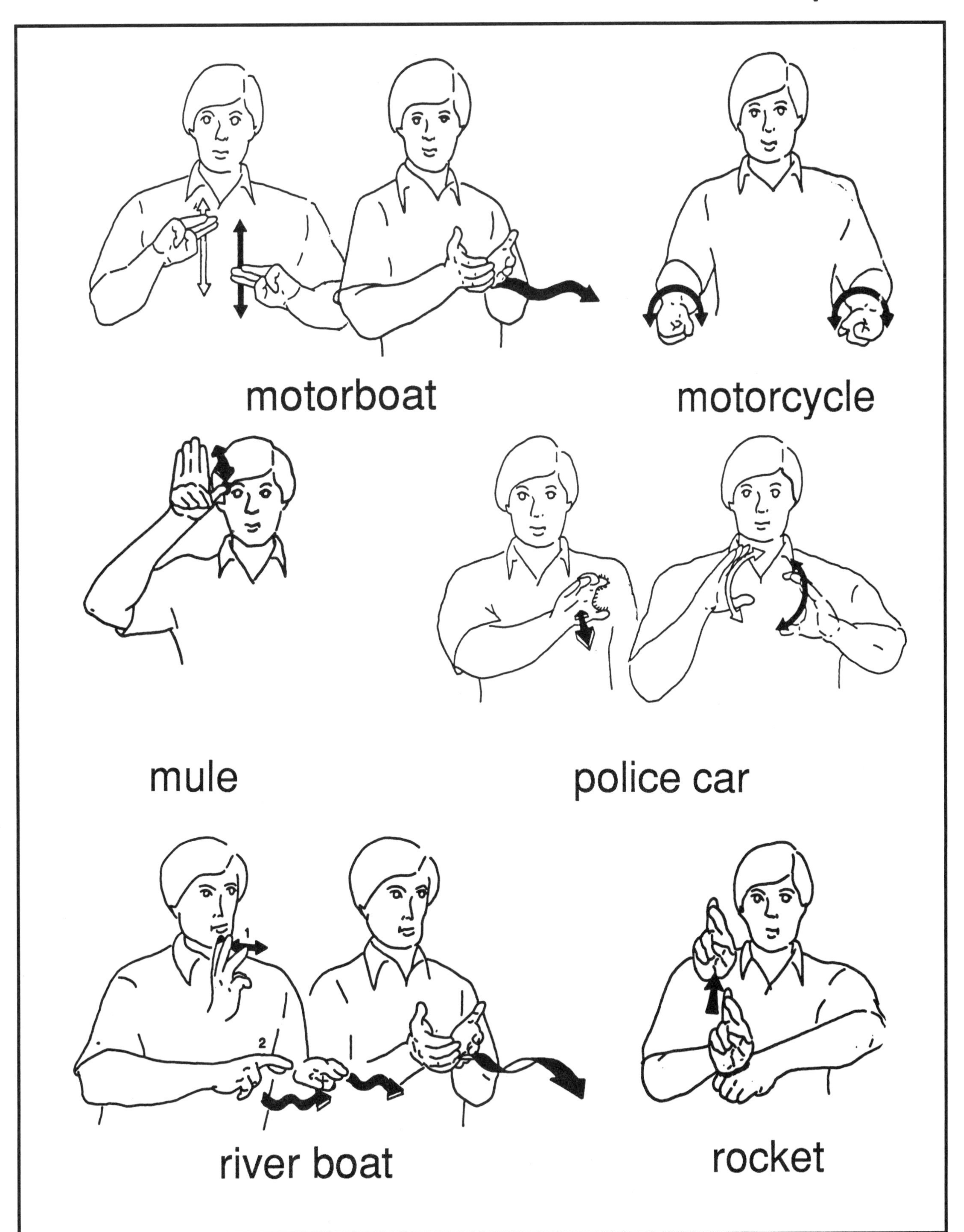

motorboat

motorcycle

mule

police car

river boat

rocket

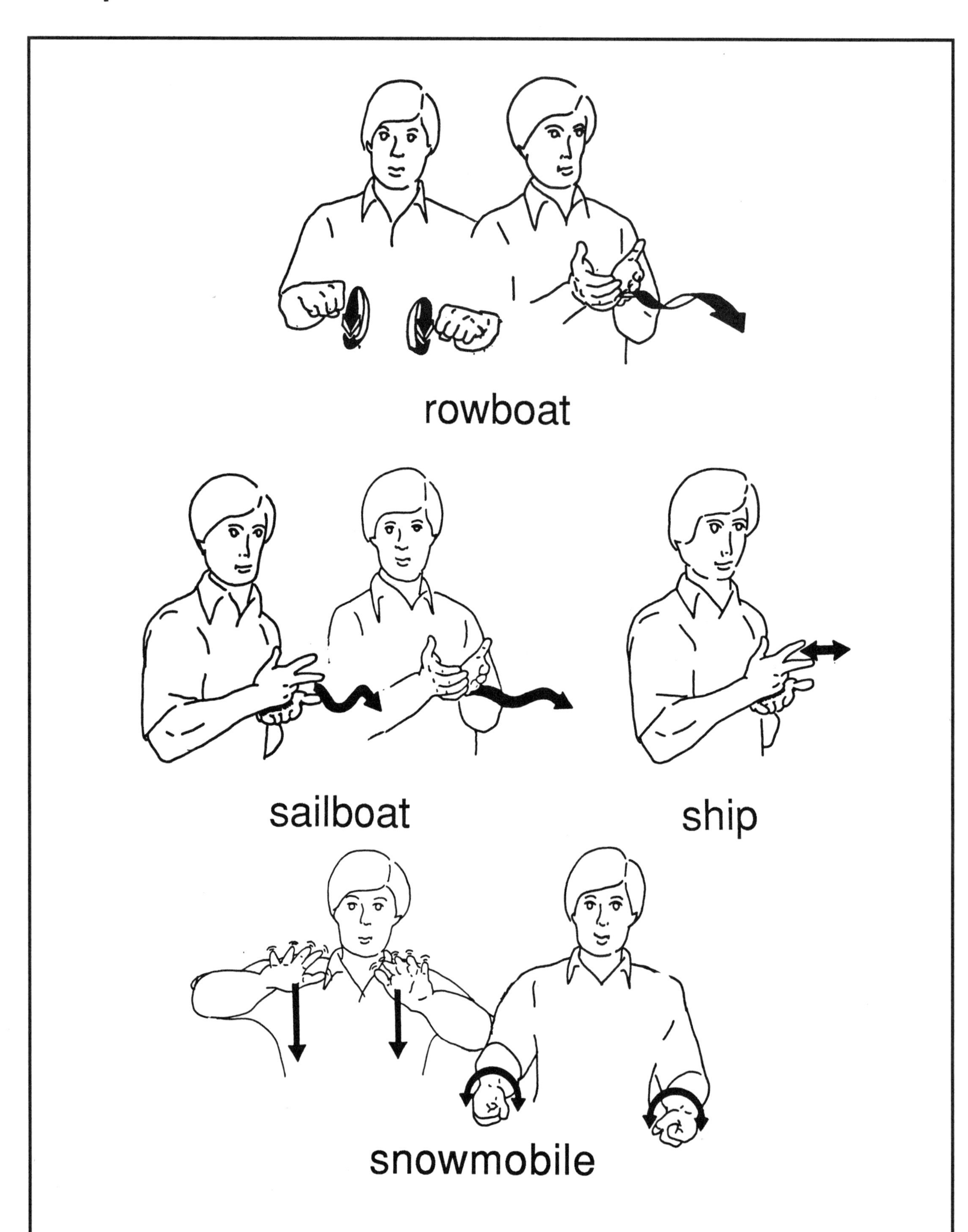
rowboat
sailboat
ship
snowmobile

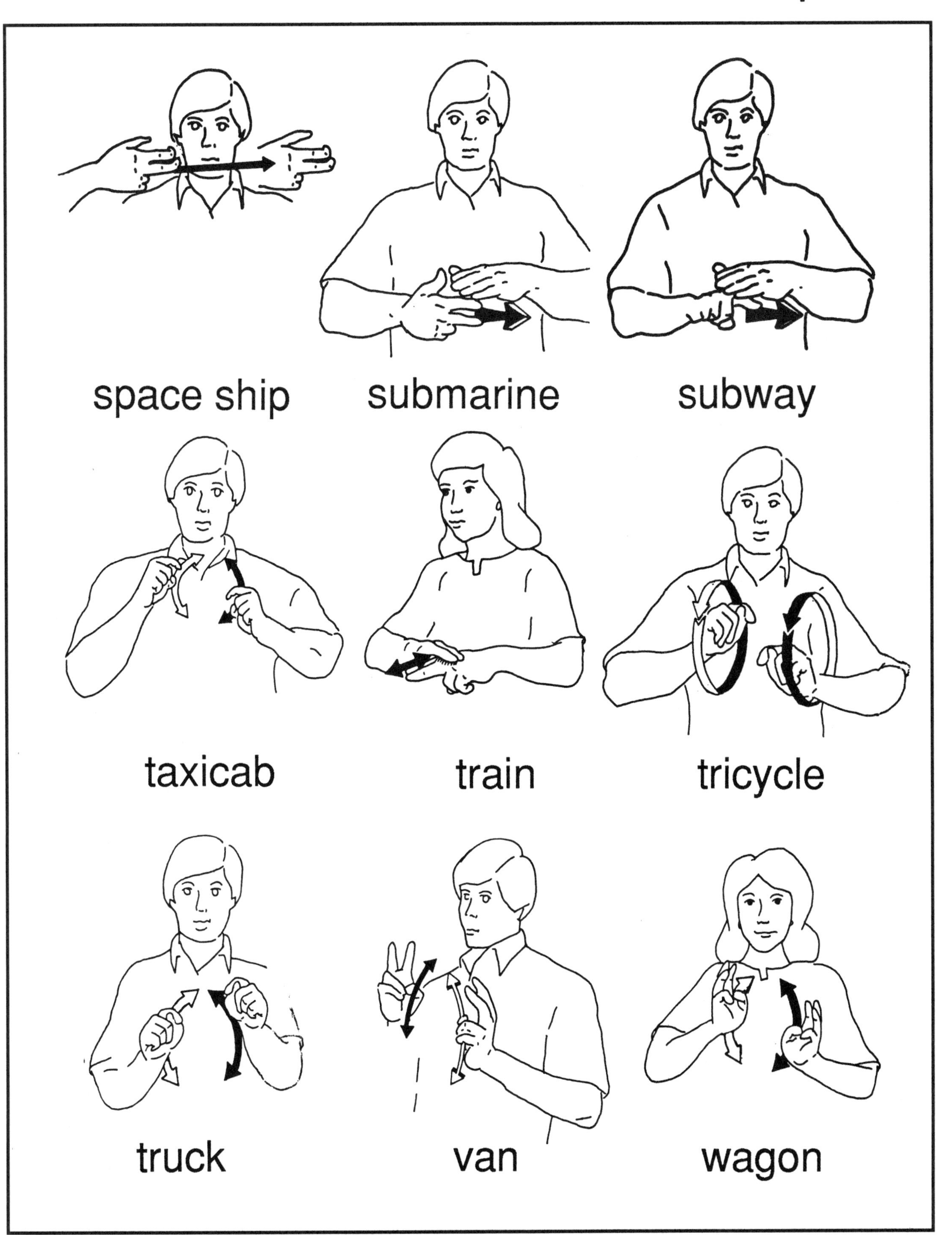
space ship
submarine
subway
taxicab
train
tricycle
truck
van
wagon

VEGETABLES

asparagus
bean
beet
broccoli
cabbage
carrot
cauliflower
celery
corn
corn on the cob
cucumber
greens
lettuce
onion
parsnip
pea
potato
pumpkin
radish
spinach
squash
tomato
turnip

ACTIVITY - VEGETABLES

Purpose: To identify vegetables which the child likes and to learn their names.

Materials: Drawing paper, crayons, pictures of vegetables.

Procedure:

1. Adult shows pictures of vegetables to child, signing/saying, "What do you like?"
2. Child points to vegetable.
3. Adult gives drawing paper to child, signing/saying, "Draw a picture of the _____." (veg. child pointed to)
4. Adult writes name of vegetable on child's drawing, signing/saying name of vegetable for child.
5. Adult points to original picture of vegetable asking child to sign/say name of vegetable.
6. Child again signs/says name of vegetable he drew.
7. Repeat procedures 1 through 6 with different vegetable.
8. Adult puts child's two drawings on table, signing/saying, "Where is the _____?" and "Where is the ____?"
9. Repeat procedures 1 through 8 with child's third drawing.

Variations: Child cuts pictures of vegetables from magazines, pasting them on file cards with name of vegetable written underneath for additional practice. Cut pictures from magazines or have child draw pictures to be pasted in scrapbook.

VEGETABLES

asparagus bean beet

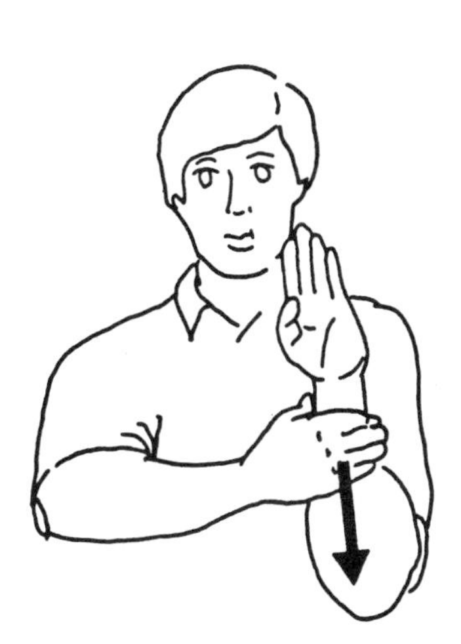

broccoli cabbage carrot

VEGETABLES

1. ______ is my favorite vegetable.
2. What will make us healthy?
3. Mom loves ______.
4. We made ______ for our party.

cauliflower
celery
corn
corn on the cob
cucumber
greens
lettuce
onion

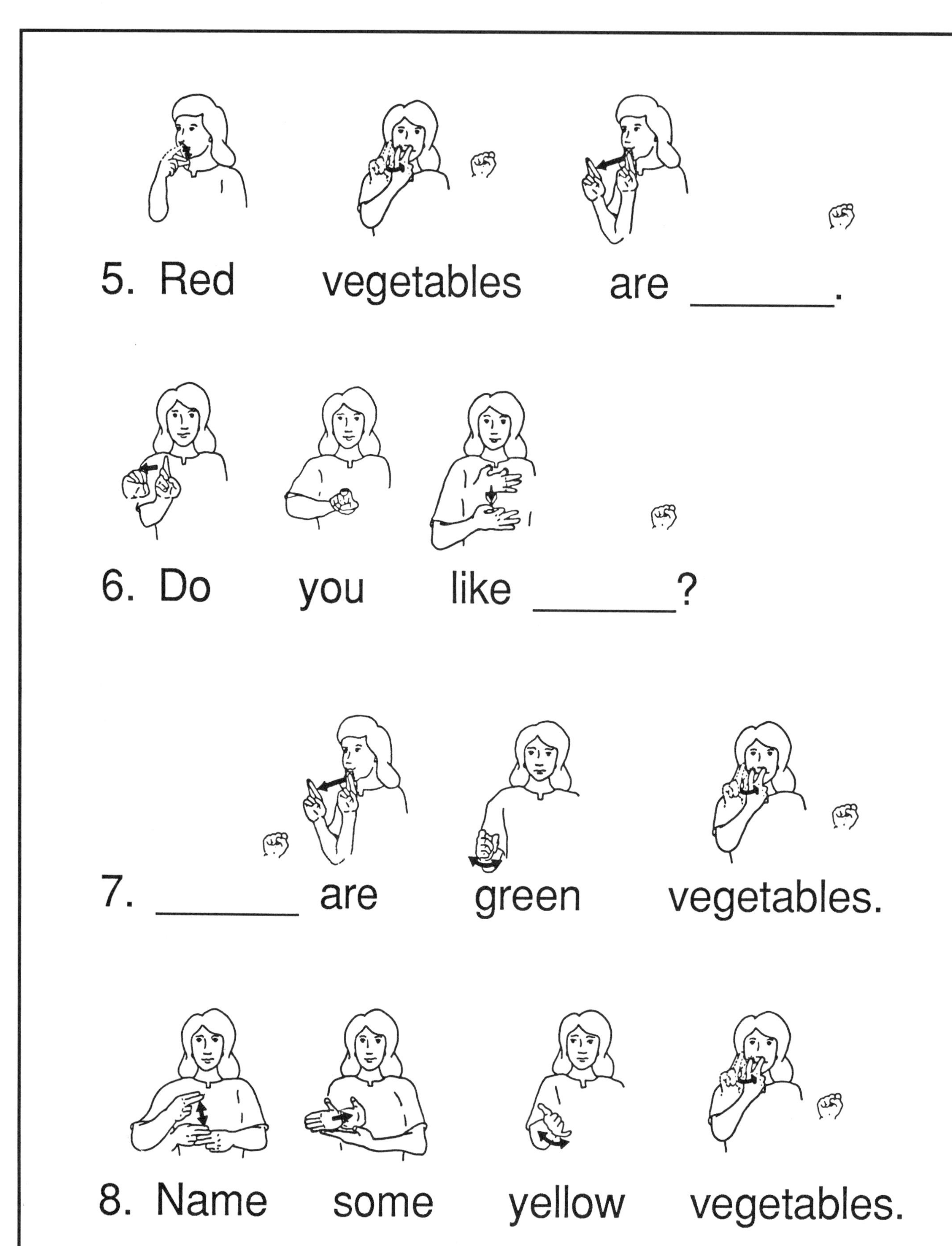
5. Red vegetables are ______.
6. Do you like ______?
7. ______ are green vegetables.
8. Name some yellow vegetables.

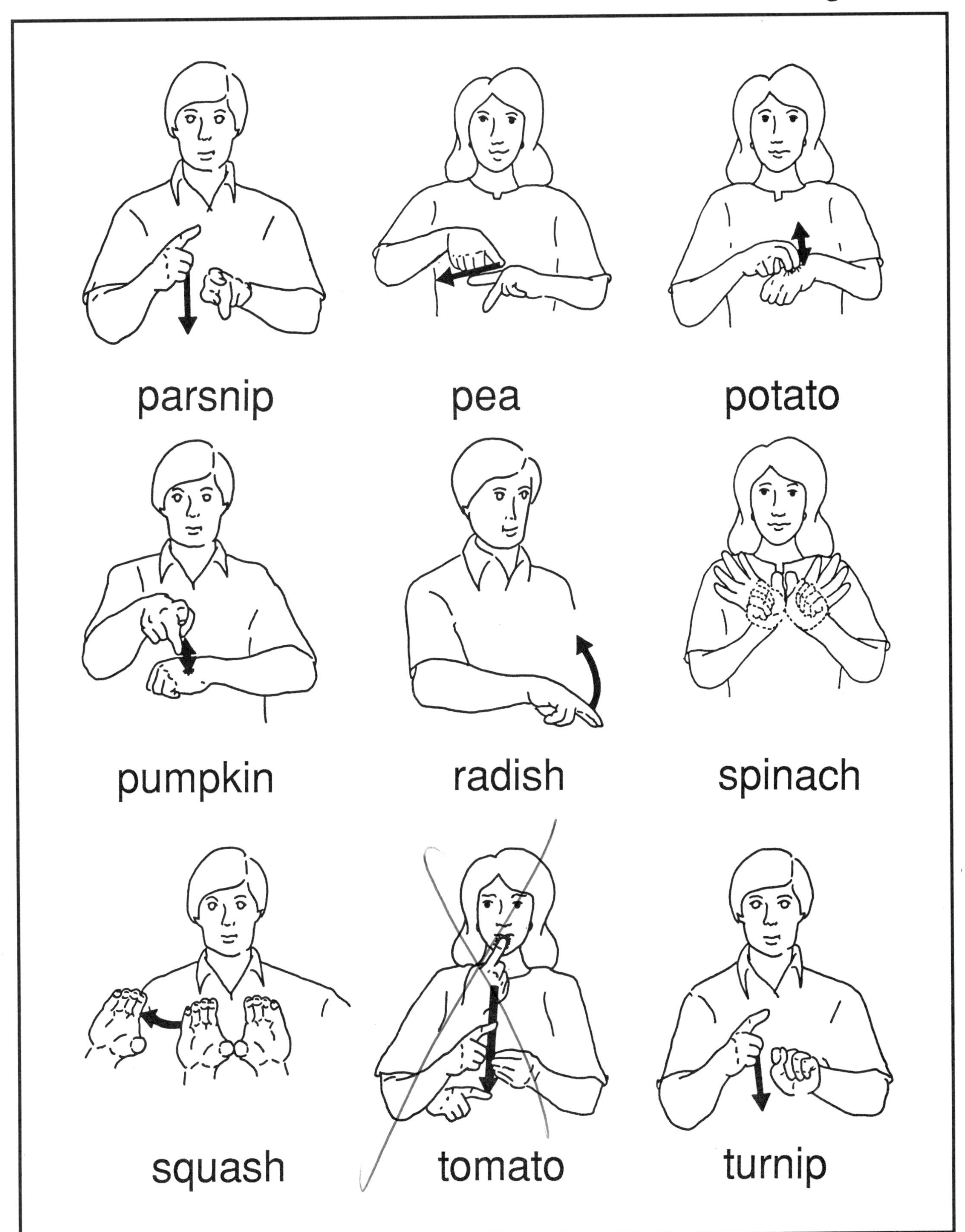
parsnip
pea
potato
pumpkin
radish
spinach
squash
tomato
turnip

WEATHER

centigrade
clear
cloud
cold
cool
damp
dark
degree
dew
dry
Fahrenheit
flood
fog
forecast

freeze
frost
hail
hot
humid
hurricane
icicle
lightning
minus
moist
plus
rain
rainbow
sleet

smog
snow
sprinkle
storm
sun
sunny
sunshine
temperature
thermometer
thunder
tornado
warm
wet
wind

WEATHER

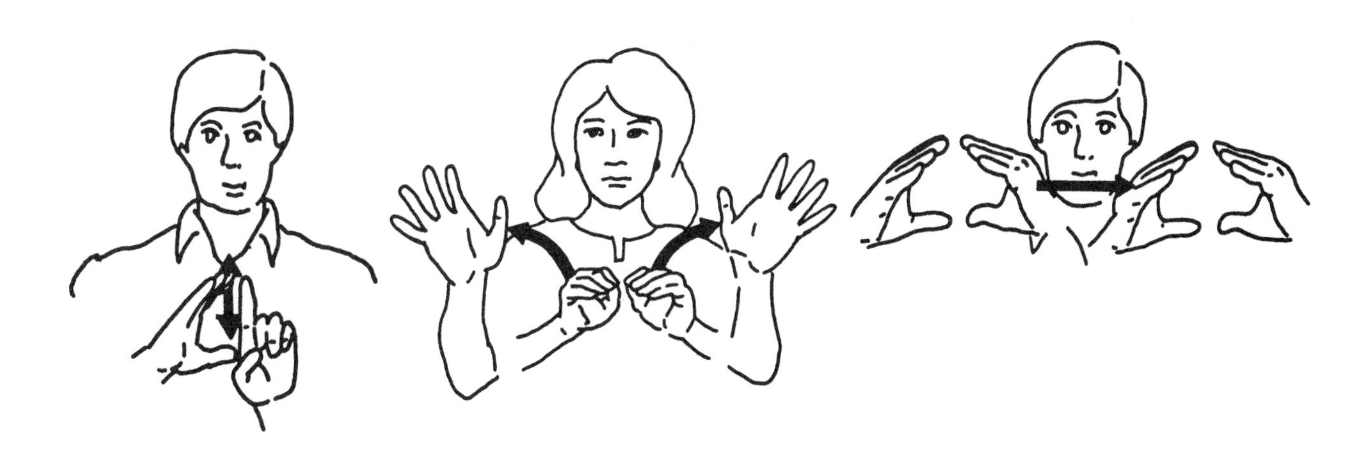

centigrade clear cloud

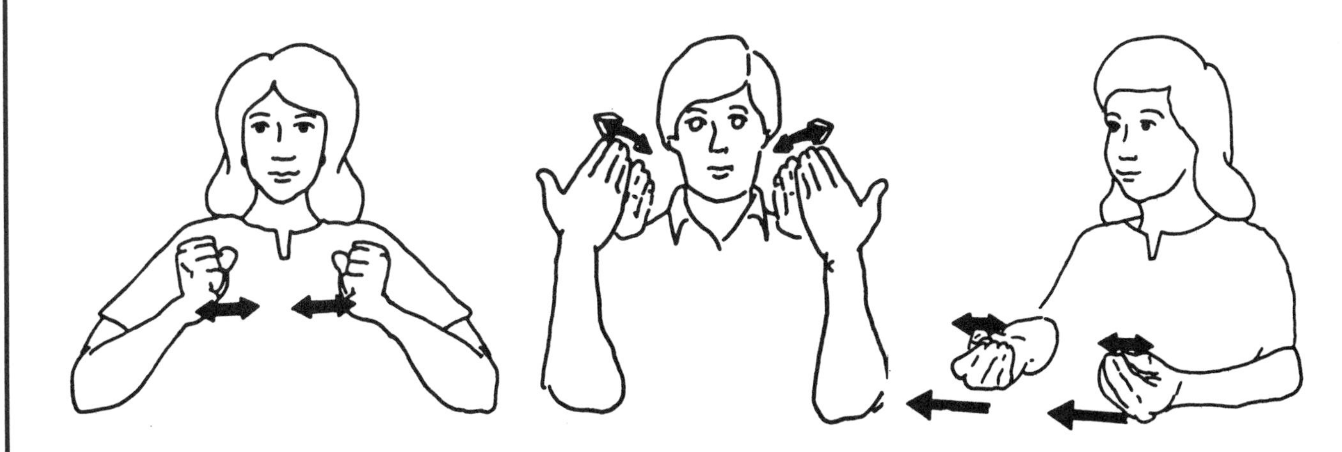

cold cool damp

WEATHER

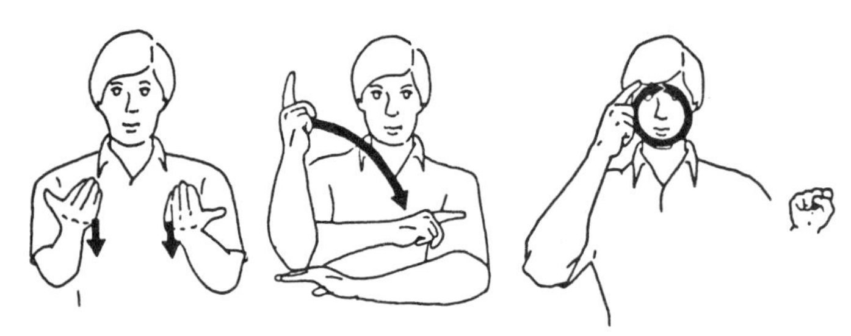

1. Today looks ______.

2. What is the weather today?

3. Do you like ______?

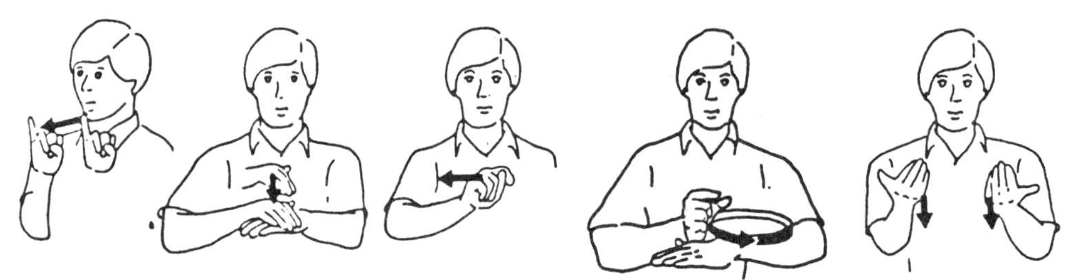

4. _____ is on the ground now.

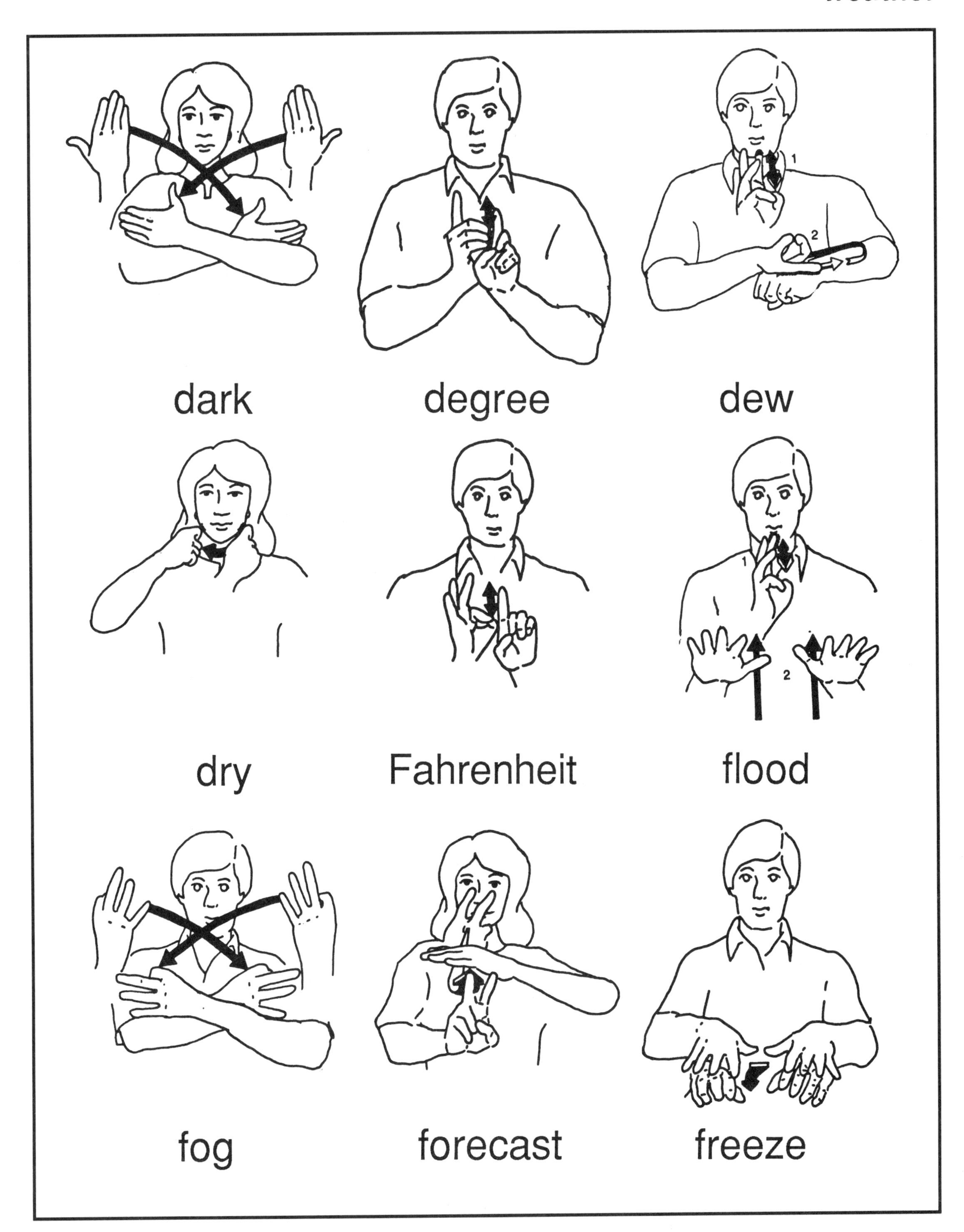
dark
degree
dew
1
2
dry
Fahrenheit
flood
1
2
fog
forecast
freeze

5. We don't like ______.

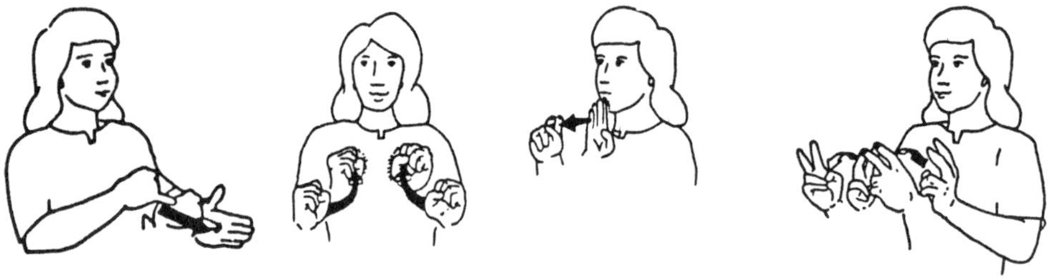

6. It has been very ______.

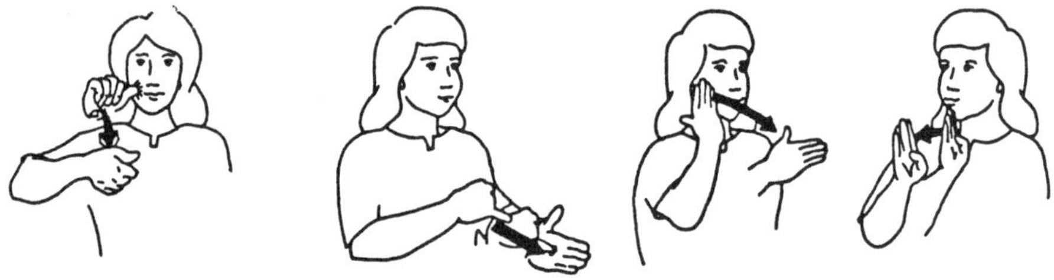

7. Tomorrow it will be _____.

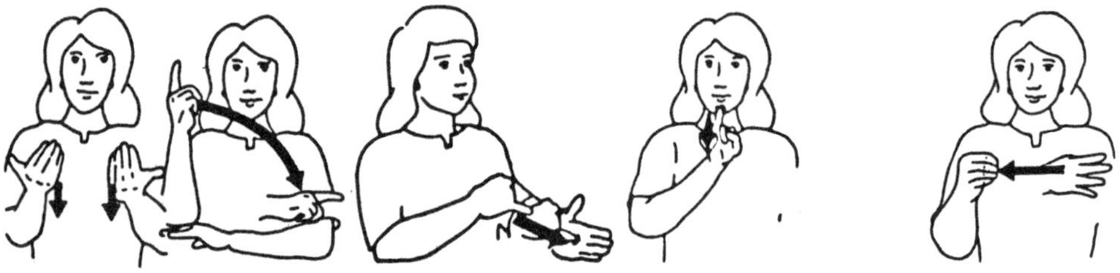

8. Today it is _____ and _____.

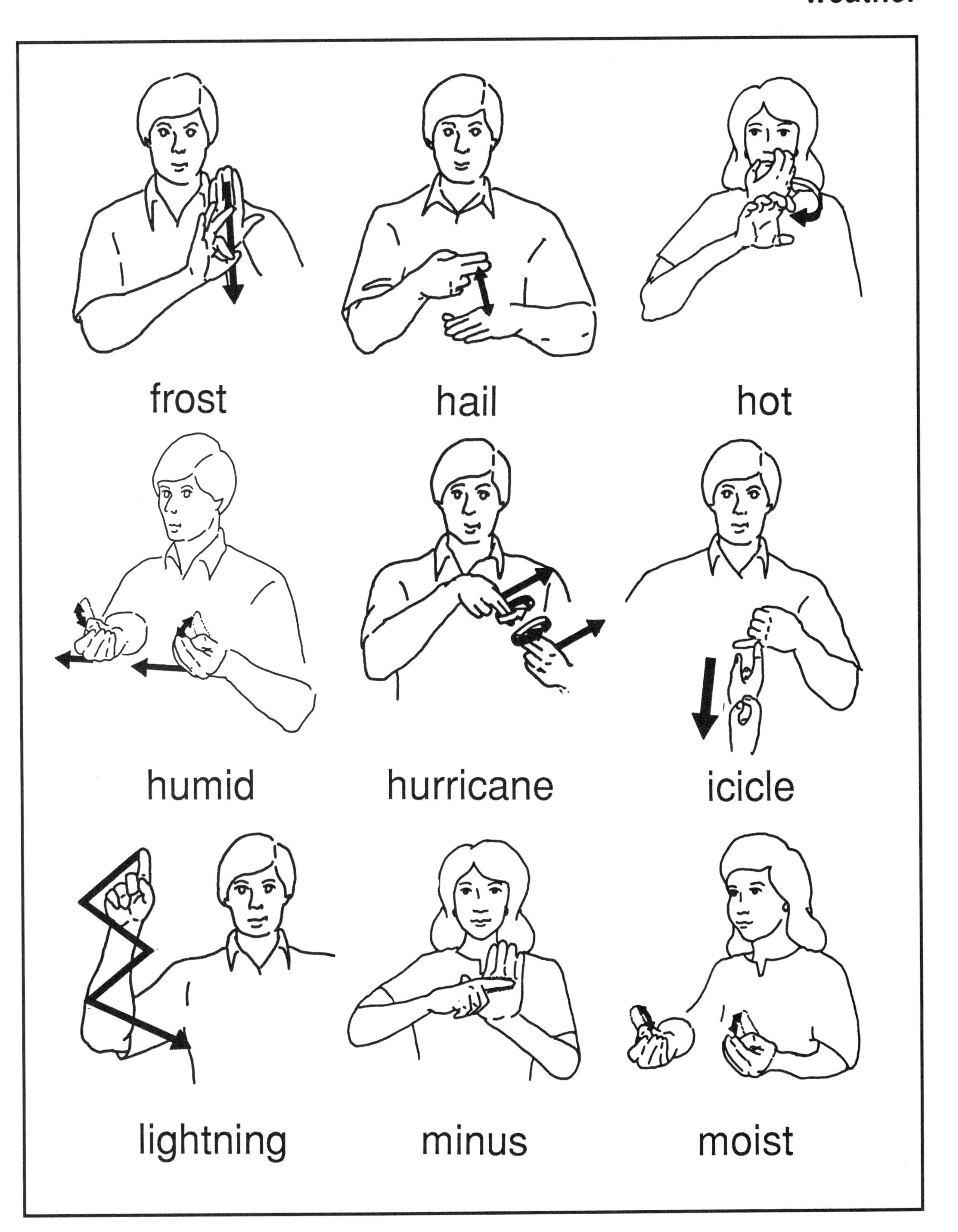
frost
hail
hot
humid
hurricane
icicle
lightning
minus
moist

plus
rain
rainbow
sleet
smog
snow
sprinkle
storm

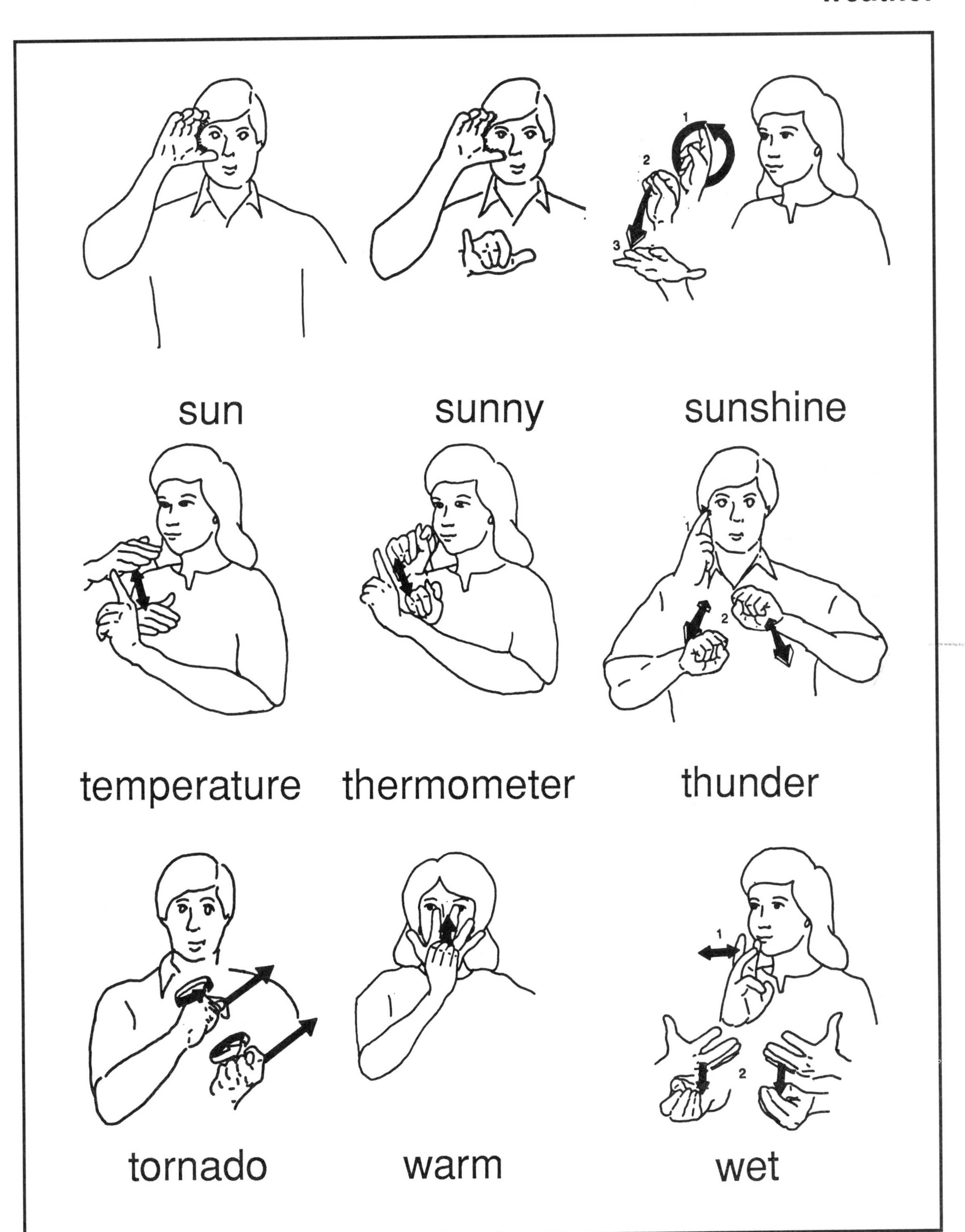
1
2
3
sun
sunny
sunshine
temperature
thermometer
1
2
thunder
tornado
warm
1
2
wet

wind

ACTIVITY - WEATHER

Purpose: To have child identify different kinds of weather.

Materials: Large calendar; crayons; pictures showing the different kinds of weather, e.g., sunny, raining,. snowing, etc.; flashcards with the different kinds of weather written on them.

Procedure:

1. Adult selects two weather pictures with one of them depicting weather for that day.
2. Adult takes child to window or outside with pictures.
3. Adult shows child pictures and has child identify picture similar to existing weather.
4. Child and adult go back into house to calendar.
5. Adult shows child flashcard describing the weather for that day.
6. Adult pins flashcard above calendar and child is allowed to draw, on calendar, weather for that day.
7. Repeat procedure everyday.

Variations: Take flashcards with weather's description outside for child to choose. In nice weather, do the activity outside.

INDEX

C

index

Q

R

S

T

U

V